Corresponding with Carlos

A Biography of Carlos Kleiber

Charles Barber

THE SCARECROW PRESS, INC.
Lanham • Toronto • Plymouth, UK
2011

Published by Scarecrow Press, Inc.
A wholly owned subsidary of The Rowman & Littlefield Publishing Group, Inc.
4501 Forbes Boulevard, Suite 200, Lanham, Maryland 20706
http://www.scarecrowpress.com

Estover Road, Plymouth PL6 7PY, United Kingdom

British Library Cataloguing in Publication Information Available

Library of Congress Cataloging-in-Publication Data

Barber, Charles.
  Corresponding with Carlos : a biography of Carlos Kleiber / Charles Barber.
      p. cm.
  Includes bibliographical references, discography, filmography, and index.
  ISBN 978-0-8108-8143-3 (cloth : alk. paper) — ISBN 978-0-8108-8144-0 (ebook)
  1. Kleiber, Carlos, 1930-2004. 2. Conductors (Music)—Biography. I. Title.
  ML422.K628B37 2011
  784.2092—dc23
  [B]   2011019943

Printed in the United States of America

For Jason

Un artiste se juge par la qualité de ses refus.

—Paul Valery

Contents

Acknowledgments

First thanks go to Carolyn Webber, who was, at the time, at Columbia Artists in New York City. Without her gracious willingness to take my phone calls and forward my earliest letters I would never have known Carlos Kleiber.

Thanks as well to friends and faculty at Stanford: Hilde Binford, Jock Friedly, Michael Jones, Chris Lanz, Paul Nghiem, John Planting, Mark Rubin, Andor Toth, and Arthur Woods. Further gratitude is owed the research staff at the Stanford Libraries, the Powell Library at UCLA, the music library at UC Berkeley, the National Library of Canada, the British Library, and the Library of Congress.

Over the years friends like Ann Assarsson, Kevin Bazzana, Douglas Berg, Edison Bewiahn, José Bowen, George Corwin, Tom Durrie, John Espley, Alan Farley, the always-supportive Jean Haber Green, Jaap Hamburger, Victoria Hart, Bruce Herman, the industrious Toru Hirasawa, Marshall Hollabaugh, Terry Humby, Jaroslav Karlovsky, John Kelly, Nora Kelly, Evgeny Kissin, Paul Kleiber, Lotte Klemperer, Marcos Klorman, Sharon Kravitz, Will Lacey, Sue Larsen, Judy and Charles Mackerras, Bob Milne, David Paich, the endlessly helpful Bob Reith, Valèry Ryvkin, Matt Schneider, Barry and Lee Shapiro, Rena Sharon, Grendel and Jason Sherbundy, Michael Steinberg, Jonathan Sternberg, Jon Tolansky, Evelyn Velleman, George Walker, and Norm Walker helped in countless and supportive ways.

I would also like to acknowledge kind replies to numerous questions, these from Bonnie Lynn Adelson, Alison Ames, Oscar Abril Ascaso, Rachid Bennamar, Rosamond Bernier, Elizabeth Bice, Sarah Billinghurst, Giuliana Bilotta, Barbara Bonney, Christian von Borries, Alfred Brendel, Anke Bryson, Donato Cabrera, Staffan Carlweitz, Kip Cranna, Mario Davidovsky, César Dillon, Helena Dobçnik, Plácido Domingo, Christina Drexel, Katherine Dunham, Tom Empson, Richard Evidon, Carrie Fischer, John Fisher, Sarah

Flanagan, Emmanuel Garcia, Ina Gayed, Michael Gielen, David Gilbert, Amy Giovannetti, Bernd Gradwohl, Helge Grünewald, Stefanie Hagen, Bernard Haitink, Judith Hirczy, Isao Hirowatari, Annelie Hopfenmüller, Marci Janas, Cathryn Johns, the always-helpful Sir Peter Jonas, Mauricio Kagel, Jason Edward Kaufman, Stewart Kershaw, Anne Kirchbach, Marko Kleiber, James Kreger, Alexander Lauterwasser, Christine Lemke-Matwey, Irena Lesjak, Ira Lieberman, Luis Lima, Felicity Lott, Mary Ludemann, Robert McGinn, Leila Manno, Lotfi Mansouri, Paul Meyer, Maria-Luisa Minio-Paluello, John Mordler, Alan Newcombe and Deutsche Grammophon, Barbara Nissman, James O'Callaghan, Richard Osborne, François Passard, Bohuslav Pavlas, Drago Peterlin, Felisa Pinto, Timothy Pfaff, the ever-generous Ulrich Plemper, Johan Ragnevad, Sylvia Reid, Richard Rosenberg, John Russell, Wolfgang Sawallisch, Andrea Schiermeier, Maria Stadlmann, John Stubbs, Irena Sylva, Georgia Taglietti, Augusto Danielo Techera, Sir John Tooley, Suzanne Verdan, Tomislav Vitchev, Giles Watson, Ron Wilford, Conrad Wilson, Bjørn Woll, and Jörg Zschenker.

I owe particular thanks to Bruce Phillips of Oxford for his wise advice about books and publishers. Special gratitude is also due Julia Roever, Mako Rova, and Paul Kling. Their work as translators made an immense contribution to this book. High thanks are also owed to journalist and researcher Matías Bradford Serra, and conductor-scholar Sebastiano De Filippi, both of Buenos Aires. Their superb sleuthing helped fill out the story of Carlos's early days in that great city.

Renee Camus, and my editor, Bennett Graff, both at Rowman and Littlefield, also deserve tremendous credit for whatever may be the worth of this book. In my hands alone it would have remained hagiography.

And finally, a most personal thanks to a woman who has put up with more foolish moments (years, really) than any friend should ever have to suffer. Her name is Michelle, she lives in my hometown, and I won't embarrass her any further.

Permissions

The author and publisher gratefully acknowledge permission granted to quote material from the following sources:

Adelson, Bonnie Lynn. Permission to quote from her correspondence with Carlos Kleiber.

BBC Radio 3, London. Paul Frankl, producer. *Who Was Carlos Kleiber?*

Fleming, Renée. *The Inner Voice: The Making of a Singer.* © 2004 by Renée Fleming. Used by permission of Viking Penguin, a division of Penguin Group (USA) Inc.

Jonas, Sir Peter. Permission to quote from his correspondence with Carlos Kleiber.

KD. Permission to cite musical examples and her conversations with Carlos Kleiber.

Lemke-Matwey, Christine. Permission to quote from notes and source materials.

Russell, John, the estate of. Permission kindly granted by Rosamond Bernier to cite text originally published in Russell, John. *Erich Kleiber—A Memoir.* London: André Deutsch, 1957.

Schäfer, Walter Erich. *Bühne eines Lebens—Erinnerungen.* © 1975, Deutsche Verlags-Anstalt, München, in der Verlagsgruppe Random House GmbH.

Stern, Isaac, and Chaim Potok. *My First 79 Years.* © 1999 by Isaac Stern and Chaim Potok. Used by permission of Alfred A. Knopf, a division of Random House, Inc.

University Press of New England, Lebanon, New Hampshire. Matheopoulos, Helena. *Diva.* Reprinted with permission, 64 words on page 7.

Weidenfeld & Nicolson, an imprint of The Orion Publishing Group, London. Matheopoulos, Helena. *Bravo: Today's Great Tenors, Baritones and Basses Discuss Their Roles.*

Preface

I got the news at 1:30 in the morning. Gottfried Kraus e-mailed from Austria to say that he just heard on the radio that Carlos had died, age seventy-four.

I e-mailed back immediately, telling him that there had been a false alarm along similar lines just eighteen months earlier. It turned out to be nothing, although it did annoy Carlos and his family no end. I spent the next couple of hours Googling online news sources, found nothing, and went to bed uncertainly.

I woke very early to another friend, Bob Reith of New York, telling me that there was an article in the German press. It came as a kick in the stomach.

As I write this, I am watching his performance of Beethoven Four, the first one I ever saw him give. There was in this man's art a force so truthful that it lived on the point of paradox. It was at the same moment both utterly correct—and something one had *never* witnessed before.

Reading the many obituaries, I find a troubling pattern. It is one that I hope this book may help to correct. Carlos is repeatedly described as aloof, contemptuous, dismissive. I concede that this may have been the experience of others. It was certainly not mine. As readers will see for themselves, he was also gifted with tremendous warmth, bizarre and quirky humor, and a genuine kindness toward someone who simply wrote him a letter, years ago.

Carlos Kleiber was a very private man who led, intermittently, a very public career. He found his own ways to balance such burdens and desires. Those of us who try to honor the same gods do not find him strange at all. And literature offers its own account. The poet he honored among all others was Emily Dickinson.

The ordinaries of life must have been difficult for him. To be able to see everything polarized and ironic, utterly clean and first-born, is a troubling gift.

So he is gone. Like thousands and tens of thousands I mourn his loss. And I grieve the fact that he never gave a *Ninth,* or a *B Minor Mass,* or a *German Requiem.*

But tonight I glory in the fact that he was able to make his miracles at all. Lucky him.

Lucky, lucky us.

Introduction

Confession: you are the only person that ever writes to me! I have successfully alieanated (spelling?) all other would-be correspondents. If they are American, I do it with Abe. With other countries . . . well, I find a way! My specialty (or, British, "speciality") is mocking serious young letter-writers à propos "MUSIC". They give up PDQ [pretty damn quick], *pouting.*

—*Carlos Kleiber, 3 May 1993*

This book is a biography, an examination of Carlos Kleiber's art and career. It is the voice of Carlos himself, in letters and faxes and postcards and cartoons. It is also personal, and claims no exacting academic objectivity. I knew him, and liked him very much, and admired him tremendously.

It all began in 1987. I was entering my third year in graduate school at Stanford University, there to study conducting with Andor Toth and to make a career in that absurdly difficult field. Prof. Toth was a generous and deeply musical mentor, one of the most graceful and elegant phrase-makers I had ever encountered. He encouraged me to look afar. He granted extraordinary opportunities for study, experiment, leadership, apprenticeship, and connection to the European tradition that so shaped his own art as violinist and conductor. He asked me to start planning ahead, post-school. I was to do so, but in a direction neither of us could have imagined.

In May of that year my friend Mark Rubin, a vocalist and physics major, came to the office and asked if I was interested in going on a bicycle trip. Sure, I said, thinking he meant pedaling four miles west to Woodside or thereabouts.

"Let's go to Los Angeles," Mark said, and spread out a map. I laughed.

Next month, we were on our way. We traveled like turtles along the five hundred miles and eleven days of our trip, but one night we camped out in a motel instead of the usual parks and ditches. Mark commandeered the shower and I sat on a bed, channel-surfing. I landed on the local public television station and heard Beethoven's Fourth Symphony. And then I saw the conductor.

Flashing energy and discipline, humor and release, this man was at the same moment doing everything and nothing. It was the most startling display of musical fireworks and singing eloquence I had ever seen on any podium. No other conductor worked like this, and within minutes I was shouting at Mark.

"Hey, get out here. You've got to see this conductor. He's incredible!"

"Who is he?" Mark asked. I didn't have a clue.

We watched until the end, utterly transfixed by a perfect Rolls-Royce of conducting power and beauty and comprehension. Only at the end did we learn his name. Weeks later I phoned Mr. Toth and described our summer's adventure, and told him about the Beethoven I had seen.

"So you've discovered Carlos Kleiber have you?" he asked. Yes, I said. "Well, you're absolutely right. There is no one else like him." He proceeded to tell me a bit about Kleiber's unusual career and reputation.

Over the next year, I listened to his CDs, read articles and reviews, and started collecting video and laser discs (we remember laser discs), marveling anew at each unexpected and inarguable turn he took—most particularly in opera, as I would discover.

In the fall of 1988 I met once more with Mr. Toth, this after our Stanford Symphony tour of Asia. I wanted to talk about postdoctorate planning. I was close to a decision and wanted his views.

"I'm going to study opera with Carlos Kleiber," I told him. "I'd like to be his assistant. What do you think?" Prof. Toth laughed with that unnerving smile of his, softened his voice and said, "I don't think you should count on it. I don't believe he's ever had a student. He hasn't had a regular job for years, and he hardly ever works. He's pretty eccentric. It would be wonderful, but don't get your hopes up."

I heard much the same from other teachers but wanted to give it a try. How could I get his address? He didn't seem to have an agent and wasn't listed in any of the professional reference books. Should I try CAMI?

"Well sure, try them. But just don't be too disappointed. Kleiber never talks to anyone."

I phoned Ron Wilford at Columbia Artists Management in New York, spoke to his secretary Carolyn Webber, told her who I was and what I was after.

"I don't believe that Maestro Kleiber has students," she declared, very politely.

"So I understand, but I'd like to try anyway. Would you have his address?"

"Yes," she said.

"I know you couldn't possibly give it to me."

"That's right."

"But could you forward a letter for me?"

"Yes, I can do that. But please don't expect a reply. Maestro Kleiber doesn't answer very many letters, and rarely sees people."

And so I spent some weeks fashioning a request intended to open his door, and early hit on the key: humor. He must receive letters from every ambitious young conductor in the world, I reasoned. If he answered none of them, they must share some common affliction. What might that be? Self-importance, no doubt, a reflux of self-interest. So I charted a path to demonstrate how I could be of service to him, and did so with self-deprecating jokes (it was self-evident he had a fantastic sense of humor) and a straightforward pitch. It went in the mail on 25 January 1989.

Two weeks later I came home one night, a long day of reading and rehearsal over. I lived in the back of a garage, and a friend was visiting. In the mailbox was a letter written in a hand I didn't recognize. It had no return address. I looked at the postmark: München. Absurdly, my hand started to shake.

"Artie, could you open this? It might be from. . . ."

"Oh no!" he laughed. "Carlos Kleiber?" He opened and read it aloud, three times.

Dear Mr. Barber!

Tho' honestly + immensely impressed by your qualifications and accomplishments (wish I could compete!) I am sorry to say: I hardly conduct at all; so that would mean you would be totally hors d'oeuvre (out of work) and horrified at my lack of interest, energy, initiative, and so forth [. . .] I'm a real mess, actually. Don't tell anyone, please.

Yours Sincerely

Carlos Kleiber

It went on like that, for two short pages. And so began my correspondence with Carlos.

His letters were in hand or typewritten, with occasional combinations of both. For the first five years they were sent by mail. Thereafter, except when one of us was traveling, they were usually sent by fax. He found someone in Grünwald (the suburb of Munich where he lived) who had a fax machine, and liked its speediness. My replies were always by mail, as Carlos said that the fax-owner didn't want to receive any on his behalf. He never owned a computer. E-mail was out of the question. Even typewriters troubled him.

The letters were as unusual as the man.

In this book efforts have been made to reproduce the layout of Carlos's originals, as their topography often spoke to his frame of mind and points of emphasis. He frequently drew pictographs, notated musical excerpts, wrapped afterthoughts around the edge of the page, and inserted visual interjections much as if, I imagined, he were speaking in person. I have made occasional changes in "paragraph" order so as to rationalize the actual thought-train we were pursuing at the time. No effort has been made to correct spelling or syntactical "error"—for the simple reason that it was often a joke or a crafty pun. It revealed his love of language and his remarkably idiomatic command of it.

We wrote almost entirely in English, Carlos's native tongue.[1] Because he had a deep awareness of American pop culture, there are numerous in-jokes sprinkled across his pages. For readers unfamiliar with that culture, with northern California, and with the trend-thought of the day (which he insulted hilariously), I have attempted to provide footnoted explications. Most of them are inadequate to the wry subtlety of his wit.

To protect the publisher, I have in a couple of instances substituted initials for a name. Wise readers will see through this scrim. I have also withheld a number of letters whose subject matter was wholly personal, unrelated to music in any way. These came along late in our relationship. Their content does not justify their publication.

Researching this book, I struck up a correspondence with London-born Sir Peter Jonas while he was staatsintendant at the Bavarian State Opera, a position he held from 1993 to 2006. Prior to that he had served in important posts at the Chicago Symphony Orchestra and as general director of the English National Opera. In 2000, he was knighted by HM Elizabeth II for his services to music. Sir Peter was also a friend of forty years' standing to Carlos Kleiber, and he persuaded Carlos to give his only symphonic performances in North America, among other *coups de takt*.

In the summer of 2009, at the invitation of producer Paul Frankl of BBC Radio 3, Sir Peter and I, together with Plácido Domingo and Christine Lemke-Matwey, participated in a long-form radio documentary, *Who Was Carlos Kleiber?* Paul and his colleagues did a terrific job on this project, having rounded up four people who actually knew its subject.[2]

During the course of preparation I received an e-mail from Frankl: "Incidentally, we interviewed Sir Peter Jonas this week. I asked him (pre interview) if he knew of you and he looked very surprised and said: 'It's very odd you should say that because the only other person who ever mentioned that name to me was Carlos. He said, "He understands more than most."' Rather a great compliment I would say. I hope you think so too."[3]

I certainly did; I was happy to know that the BBC engaged in due diligence, and I took the occasion to renew my connection with Sir Peter. Out of that came another dozen or so letters from Carlos to Sir Peter that now appear in this book, further illuminating his way of grasping and engraining music. My thanks to Sir Peter for his tremendous generosity. No wonder Carlos was so fond of him.

From the same radio broadcast came another surprise. I heard from KD, a professional bassoonist who had been for almost three decades a close friend of Carlos, seeing him privately and spending time with him discussing pretty much everything. I am indebted to KD for her recollections, her fascination with our mutual friend, and for her clear-eyed awareness of Carlos the man. As will be seen, her insights are both comic and telling. She recently came to visit when I was leading Britten's "Curlew River" at City Opera Vancouver, and her further analysis of him was sweet, modest, and wry. Invaluable.

And then, via my friend and colleague John Stubbs, I was put in contact with Bonnie Lynn Adelson. She is a gifted musician who trained in San Francisco, and with Saul Goodman in New York. Back on 12 April 1991, while playing principal timpani in the Symphonic Orchestra of Radio-Tele-Luxembourg, she received a fan letter. It was in French, and praised her playing "avec une alert et tension de tigre." Bonnie did not realize who had signed it and dutifully replied: "I can tell by your letter that you LOVE music, and that you attend many concerts. . . . I do hope that you will continue to enjoy our concerts on television." Bonnie laughingly declares that the shoe did not drop for some while. It is an extraordinary correspondence, and I am deeply grateful to her for allowing another avenue into his musical and very human personality.

Although I wanted to learn from Carlos, a conventional master-student relationship was not in the cards. Sending him videos of other conductors (including myself) and asking his views came to be the next-best thing. Over time I sent him fifty-three videos of leading (and "misleading," he would say) conductors. Asking his advice about them, and about upcoming concert and opera repertoire in my own career, provoked unmatched insights. We did, of course, eventually meet in person.

No one will want to read my own letters to Carlos. However, to make sense of his penetrating and occasionally caustic comments about scores and performance, other conductors, literature, politicians, Abraham Lincoln, Mohandas Gandhi, Danny Kaye, *nekulturny* and *kultur*, I have included excerpts from mine so to make context for the whole of his.

Similarly, I have footnoted the aural, visual, and printed sources to which he refers throughout our correspondence. Appendix C advises the insatiable reader how to obtain the source documents about which Kleiber comments. Concerning the videos that I sent him, and which he so usefully analyzed, several of them are commercially available. All of them are in the Conductors on Film Collection in the Archive of Recorded Sound at Stanford University. This is a collection that I created to aid in my own study and my own teaching; however, soon enough a significant motivation came to be that he liked to receive them, and he liked to talk about them. This ruse succeeded for years. I can't imagine he was deceived by my machinery.

During the period of our correspondence, I confided to a few close friends what I was up to. After expressing astonishment that such a dialogue even existed, to a person they declared the historic importance of these written materials.

While Carlos was alive he allowed release of one of them. He gave me a letter of recommendation in 1997, and I began to include it in my resumé. I soon came to learn that, among musicians and managers, it was widely viewed as a forgery or a joke. At first blush, no one believed that Kleiber had actually written such a letter, even though it was in his distinct handwriting, and he had helpfully stamped his home address on the bottom. At second, no one thought that anyone could "study" with such an utterly unique force in music and not end up a mere (and merely second-rate) puppet. For either reason, Carlos's letter did my early career no good at all. Rightly so, he would add.

A word about the "Hilde" referred to in our correspondence. Her name is "Hilde Binford"; she was my study partner in graduate school and did a brilliant PhD on tropes. When preparing for our doctoral qualifying exams, she got me through early music. I helped her with new music, and together we trundled up the heights of German. Contrary to Carlos's assumption—unchallenged by me because I was initially unsure of his attitudes, and afterward because it was too complicated to explain—she and I were never married. We did share an apartment, together with her now-former husband and her sons Trent and Alex, for some months. But it was no ménage, save in the most respectable sense. Hilde remains to this day one of my closest friends, and she gave me permission to disclose this much but no more.

As before, this book is not a biography in the conventional sense. Such a project will have to be undertaken by a scholar more objective than myself. I wish that author good luck. There will, I expect, be many such books over the coming years. As with any force of nature, Kleiber will be described from many angles. None of us will get it quite right.

This was the rarest of musicians, and most influential of conductors. He was a complex and self-doubting genius who never gave an interview, published virtually nothing under his own name, avoided the usual forums of public debate and scrutiny, for decades held no regular appointment, over time gave few and fewer concerts, and happily and sardonically contributed to the mystery-cult that surrounded him. For all of this, he had *such* an influence on our profession, and our audience.

The greatness of the art of Carlos Kleiber demands a bit of explanation.

I hope this book contributes to it.

NOTES

1. Letter to *Frankfurter Allgemeine Zeitung*, 20 May 1972.
2. At this writing, it may be heard at www.mediafire.com/?wn4lnykyqkk.
3. E-mail from Frankl to author, 21 August 2009.

Chapter One

Family

I'm nobody! Who are you?
Are you nobody, too?
Then there's a pair of us—don't tell!
They'd banish us, you know.

How dreary to be somebody!
How public, like a frog
To tell your name the livelong day
To an admiring bog!

—Emily Dickinson

Thanks a 10(6)¹ for the fabulous Kleiber-material and the snapshots etc! Very touching and amusing! Makes me thoughtful 'cause my father's mother came from a carriage-building family, her father (EK's grandf.) even made a carriage for the Emperor Franz Joseph who said to him: "Es fährt sich gut in dem Wagen"!² (Franz Joseph was notoriously ungarrulous so that's a lot of words, coming from him.)

—*Carlos Kleiber, 17 November 1989*

The first and cruelest commonplace about Carlos was that he stood in the shadow, and aped the conducting, of his father Erich. Subsidized by it is the claim that Carlos's reclusiveness was an attempt to escape that shadow by creating his own, and withdrawing into it.

On at least one occasion that shadow came to life, and Carlos was transfixed. As reported by Wolfgang Sandner, "During a rehearsal for the opera 'Elektra' an attentive observer described Erich Kleiber in a peculiar way: Toward the middle of the performance the conductor was apparently so much moved by the opus that his arms seemed to become longer and longer, and

1

the whole silhouette seemingly grew to enormous proportions. This was a strange, mysterious, unique gesture. Had that observation been expressed on the couch of Sigmund Freud, the analysis would not have been difficult for any psychiatrist. For this vivid description came from Carlos Kleiber."[3] The symbolic significance of Carlos's vision had an overwhelming portent. Erich was a monumental figure in his life, controlling and compelling, inescapable, and central to his whole way of perceiving music.

The second commonplace is that he suffered a fundamental antagonism toward his father, one of mysterious origin and implacable coldness. During our correspondence I was several times warned by others who knew Carlos that I should never—not once—raise the name or subject of his father, "or he'll cut you off forever."

In fact, Carlos was first to mention that name. It was in reply to photos I sent him of myself posing in a Santa suit on the running board of a 1925 Kleiber automobile. I had discovered that this massive vehicle was once manufactured in San Francisco.[4] Carlos was amused by my auto archaeology and by long-ago advertisements I dug up and mailed over.[5] It was one of these automobiles with which the founder's grandson, also named Paul, allowed me to pose.

Carlos used his father's name a number of times thereafter. I replied to the subject but never raised it myself, save on one occasion. I had been asked by producers at Warner Teldec to obtain Carlos's permission for them to restore and release a 1932 film of his father for use in Volume II of their Art of Conducting series, a project I had worked on for some while. I did, and he did. When I later asked him what he thought of the film, he never replied. I broached the subject once more, and his reply was again silence.

> *You know which pieces I'm good at and even with those, the singer, I feel, has to have everything in his/her genes because otherwise "working" with him/her is just showing off. NEVER ANY GOOD!*
>
> *That "WORKING" is never any good, is an axiom. One has to have an insight to understand it, tho'. Like it took me till the day before yesterday, practically, to understand what my father meant when he gave me this only piece of advice: "Versuch ja nicht zu musizieren!"[6] Hair-raising, isn't it!*
>
> —*Carlos Kleiber, to Peter Jonas, 19 February 1997*

There is good reason to accept that musical talent runs in families. Whole tribes of composers can be found: Bach, of course, and Stamitz, Andriessen, Strauss, Hassler, Gabrieli, Scarlatti, Tcherepnin, and Couperin come to mind. So too we find families of great performers: Casadesus, Goosens, Busch, Chung, Brain, Karr, Brubeck, Marsalis, Brendel, Romero, and Bjoerling are well-known. We find clans of instrument makers: Amati and Stradivari are two of many. And we find father-son relationships among performers: Kubelik, Brott, Oistrakh, Knussen, Schnabel, Harrell, Kuerti, Tortelier, and Kipnis are greatly respected. What about women? Brigitte Fassbaender as daughter of baritone Willi Domgraf-Fassbaender, the Boulanger sisters, and few others seem to be the canvass. It's hard enough for even one talented woman to succeed, much less two, male prejudice being what it remains.

But among conductors? It may have to do with the ego-driving aspects of the business, but it is unusual to find such pairs. Father-son connections do include Neeme, Kristjan, and Paavo Järvi, Arvid and Mariss Jansons, Edwin and Richard Goldman, Mikhail and Vladimir Jurowski, Armin and Philippe Jordan, Kurt and Stefan Sanderling, and Leopold and his sons Frank and Walter Damrosch. Most of those relationships have passed unremarked. They appear to be of no interest to the commentariat of the music business. Alas, not so with Carlos and his father.

For years, speculators have proffered imaginary insights into this father-son dynamic. Better-informed people largely kept quiet, save to note (discreetly) that the son did not appreciate invidious comparison to the father. (Who would?)

Carlos had to put up with a good deal of rubbish about the supposed meaning of his relationship with Erich. One of the more ridiculous claims was back in print after he died. In the *Telegraph* it was suggested that "the problem with Carlos is that once Erich was dead, he saw the entire musical world as a surrogate. When he cancels a concert, he is killing his father, when he conducts a great performance, he is identifying with him."[7]

Others insist that there were overt displays of embarrassing and insulting behavior from the father toward the son. Francesco Siciliani, one-time artistic administrator at Milan's La Scala, spoke of a moment when Erich "humiliated Carlos by saying he didn't think he would ever be able to conduct Viennese waltzes with the right rhythms."[8] However motivated, Carlos was soon to demonstrate in repertoire from *Rosenkavalier* to Viennese waltzes galore that such pulse was not foreign to him. I have been told privately of a number of similar incidents of cruel behavior. However, when pressed for times and dates and places, or any other kind of reliable documentation, these assertions generally fell apart.

Kleiber himself described, in a very painful way, one aspect of the relationship. In 1973, Carlos's recording of the Beethoven *Emperor* with Arturo Benedetti Michelangeli collapsed. The pianist, unable to reconcile his work with Kleiber's, had stopped talking to him altogether. The sessions rolled on, incommunicado, before the conductor finally walked out. Producer Cord Garben recalled Kleiber making a heartfelt admission. Michelangeli's constant silence reminded him of his father, Carlos said, and he just could not handle such coldness.[9]

> At one point very early on I passed up the opportunity of a lifetime. If I hadn't been trained as such a bloody WASP I would have followed up but I was and I didn't. Carlos and I were sitting at an outdoor cafe in Munich, sipping that delicious coffee and he said, "Kätchen, did you love your father?"
>
> Imagine an opening like that and I didn't know any of the background. I said, "No, not particularly", and he just sighed and took a sip of his coffee.
>
> —KD, e-mail to author, 9 November 2009

All of this created within Carlos a crippling ambiguity. How would he honor and love the father who did not want the son to follow him? The subject would never be vacated, in public or in private. This pain was a bedrock reason, I came to believe, why Carlos refused to talk to the press. He knew they would—always—compare him to Erich. The evidence of their intentions was everywhere. I have examined several dozens of newspaper and journal reviews covering the first twenty years of Carlos's professional life. Almost all were glowing, and many were near-manic in their praise. But there was, in so many of them, a ripping undercurrent of comparison. In 1959 he was "Karl Kleiber, des unvergeßlichen Erich Kleibers Jüngster."[10] In the same newspaper eleven months later he was "Karl Kleiber, der Sohn des großen, viel zu früh gestorbenen Erich Kleiber."[11] So too was he invariably named and described in such papers as *Die Welt*, *Hamburger Abendblatt*, *HörZu*, *Düsseldorfer Nachrichten*, and the *Westdeutsches Tagblatt* of Dortmund. It was many years before Carlos's name was judged on its own merits, without lineage or presumption. Much of a review of Carlos's 1964 *Der Rosenkavalier* was devoted to comparing it to his father's work in the same opera.[12] Four years later, a leading daily headlined its review of the same opera "In der Domäne des großen Vaters."[13] Another led with "Auf den Spuren des Vaters: Carlos Kleiber."[14] And so it went. However, a transition began in the late 1960s, when the general view arose that Carlos was perhaps, in fact, as talented as his father. Such stasis did not last long.

The dark side of that coin turned a few years later when some reviewers began asserting that the son was even greater than the father. Many players and singers felt the same way. Most were smart enough to say nothing. Headlines now began to describe "Carlos Kleiber's *Otello*" or *Carmen* or *Rosenkavalier* or *Elektra*. For Carlos, hypersensitive to any comparisons, good or ill, this was no progress. Those who knew him from the beginning understood why.

Erich Kleiber biographer and distinguished art critic John Russell kindly agreed to be interviewed for this book. He was able to add a number of details about the relationship between father and son that do not appear in his important biography, *Erich Kleiber: A Memoir*, published in November 1957. Russell knew the whole Kleiber family.

"I remember being with his father when Carlos came up, very excited to have gotten a job with an opera company," Russell declared. "Erich said, 'They have room for you?'"[15]

"Kleiber senior did not encourage his son, and did not help him to find work. His son made the best of it."[16] Russell finds a tragic dimension to the entire relationship.

"When his son dared to begin on his own, and to do well, there was a real mythological division between them. It was very bad luck for Carlos, except that he was so enormously engaging and straightforward and talented." Russell remembers the young Carlos very well.

"He had an extremely brilliant mentality—that freedom, spontaneity. He was an ideal youth, who was enormously gifted. Something extraordinary." Why did Erich not take pleasure in his son's exceptional talents?

"Kleiber senior was gigantically vain, and did not want his name to be used, even by his son. He felt that he never had the world-wide esteem he deserved. He was extremely sensitive about any comparisons with other conductors, or father and son, or anybody else. These vain people don't like successors or rivals," Russell said.

He remembers one poignant truth. Russell years ago was walking in Vienna with Bruno Walter. "Everywhere we went, Walter was recognized and hailed. Everyone knew who he was, and admired him. That never happened with Erich Kleiber. There was a tremendous edge to Carlos's success which his father never quite had."

Did the son admire the father?

Yes, Russell insisted, especially for what his father did in the Hitler era. "Those were terrible times. One false step would be doom. Carlos would admire him for it, undoubtedly. He admired his father's strength."

Was the son like the father?

"Not really. Carlos had no vanity at all. Just the opposite. We had lunch in Munich about 20 years ago. It was the most wonderful time, in a large restaurant. All of the waiters were praising him, and he would have none of it. He pulled their legs just awfully, and wouldn't stand for a word of their flattery. He was in a wonderful mood, and extremely funny. That would never have happened with Erich."

And what about his mother?

"She was a very strong woman. Very protective of her husband. Nothing could come between them, even the children. After Erich died there was no thought of abandoning the book I was writing. She would see that it was finished, to her liking. One didn't want to cross her."

Ruth Goodrich Kleiber would become an equally fierce protector of her son, but only after Erich could no longer be threatened in any regard. Many people in the profession found her very difficult to deal with.

Some saw the way she treated Carlos in public, and they were appalled. The first time Sir John Tooley, longtime intendant at the Royal Opera House, Covent Garden, met Carlos was in Munich. He had just seen him give a masterful performance of *Rosenkavalier*, and went backstage to congratulate him, and to introduce himself. "For some reason Kleiber was conducting with the score on his podium that night," Tooley remembered decades later. His mother was with him backstage too, and she commented on it. "I thought you knew this score!" she said, to Carlos's great embarrassment.[17]

It is widely reported that Kleiber almost always conducted with his score on the podium, unused. When I first saw him leading *Otello* at The Met, I looked at his score between every act. A house gofer opened it to the top of each succeeding act. The score was otherwise untouched by Carlos.

"In the 1960s when I knew him Carlos Kleiber was *so* insecure, *so* shy," remembers the distinguished stage director Lotfi Mansouri. "We did our first 'Fledermaus' together, in Geneva. He had a Lady Macbeth of a mother. We all felt sorry for him. Having a mother who was never satisfied, and living in the shadow of his father. No wonder he was so insecure."[18]

PARALLAX

Beyond contest, there were career and personal parallels between Erich and Carlos that moved past the ordinary. Each had one sibling, an older sister. Neither man was a child prodigy. Both came to serious musical study relatively late in life. Each began his career by volunteering at an opera house. Both had remarkably polyglot ears for languages, used to tremendous effect. Both relied on fastidiously marked parts, vivid verbal imagery, and high numbers of rehearsals to obtain their results. The father had predictably bad relations with most of the press. The son avoided the press altogether. Each began musical life as a composer and soon abandoned it for a career as conductor. Both were devoted to definition—aural and structural—and began that service by careful study of the manuscripts and by scrupulous faith in the composer's original intent. Each played timpani. Both demanded—and received—very high fees. Neither had perfect pitch.

And there were profound differences, too. Erich gave thousands of performances in concert and opera. He traveled the world to do so and built an enormous repertoire base. Carlos learned much of the same repertoire, but over time came to concentrate on rather few works and occasional appearances. Erich was uninterested in recording technologies, and his vinyl legacy is very uneven. Carlos was fascinated by every aspect of aural engineering, and fearsomely critical and controlling of the results. In fact, he ordered suppression and outright destruction of a number of would-be recordings. The father gave several important premieres. The son gave none. Erich adored the music of Mahler. Carlos thought it a neurotic mess. Erich longed for a permanent musical home, ideally in Vienna, and suffered for its want. Carlos loathed the idea and turned away countless delegations with alcohol and empathy. The father tried to keep the son from a musical career, and he gave advice to that end. The son took offense, and he ignored the advice.

And there were telling differences in temperament. Erich was notorious for outbursts of bad manners, but he would profess that he couldn't see how anyone would have been hurt by so *obviously correct* a criticism. Carlos might express disappointment, and sometimes acidly, but preferred to mount it in terms of his own alleged inadequacies. If frustrated sufficiently (it didn't take much) he would walk out. When convinced that his players—or singers—no longer shared his infinite devotion to the music, Erich would yell at them. Carlos would simply disappear.

And as anyone with eyes for semaphore will acknowledge, their baton styles were vastly different. Compare each of them on film conducting the *Blue Danube* waltz. Their styles are not remotely akin. Erich used a stick notable for its efficiency, clarity, and evidentiary purposes. His was a podium manner that drew little attention to itself. It served to illuminate the composer's purposes, and not much more. It could be exciting. It was always deeply practical.

Carlos? Generations to come will marvel that there ever was such an artist on the podium. He had the most eloquent baton of the modern era. Powerful and mesmerizing, supple and exacting, controlling and liberating, his was a style of conducting that had no apparent limitations. No one spoke more compellingly in *every* language of sound. In conducting's most visible aspect, no one even came close. Carlos was an Aurora Borealis of light and transparency, all electric and surprising, and perfect in beauty.

Regardless of expressive differences and personal conflict, there was none about this: Carlos's father was one of the greatest conductors of the twentieth century, standing in a pantheon of Furtwängler, Toscanini, Klemperer, and Bruno Walter. He gave the world premiere of Alban Berg's opera *Wozzeck,* and would long be remembered and admired for it. He refused Hitler. But in his sixty-five years he did much more: in a remarkable way, he created two great careers in conducting.

ORIGINS

A young musician and intellectual named Franz Otto Kleiber migrated to Prague from Saxonia in 1883. There he entered Catholic seminary, at fourteen, but found no heart in it. He then followed his father's path into mastery of Greek and Latin, and earned a doctorate in philosophy. This led to work as private tutor to Prince Karl Emil zu Fürstenberg. It proved a dead end. Meager income was then augmented by teaching piano on the side. Franz Kleiber was, in fact, a gifted pianist and organist. Over the years he would also work as a philosopher, writer, musician, and teacher of German, Greek, and Latin. Life became even harder when, at age twenty-one, he lost both his parents.

Vroni Schöppl's father, Johannes, was a highly skilled tradesman. In Prague, he served as carriage maker to the Imperial Court, and he was esteemed by the emperor himself. This fact was important in family history. Vroni was a trained and able singer, as committed to Austrian folk music as to Wagner and Mahler.

Franz Kleiber's teaching led to Vroni Schöppl's acquaintance, and to love, and finally to marriage at St. Nikolaus Church in Prague on 14 August 1888. They raised a highly cultured family. Their home was rich with music, and two children were raised in the power of it.

Erich Kleiber was born in Vienna on 5 August 1890, in the Kettenbrückengasse district, opposite the home in which Schubert had died. His older sister, Elisabeth, known as "Essi," was born in August 1889.[19]

Something in the family's genetic history conspired against long life. Erich's father died of heart disease on 5 October 1895, and he was buried in the Zentralfriedhof of Vienna.[20] Erich's mother lived less than a year more. In September of 1896, after yet another glorious day hiking with her children in the mountains, she fell ill. She soon contracted pleurisy and passed away. Erich was just six years old.

He and his sister Essi were taken to Prague to be raised by their Schöppl grandparents. Erich soon learned a good deal about the carriage trade from his grandfather. At the same time, he was introduced to the folk music of his own inheritance. John Russell reports that one of the earliest revelations in Erich's life occurred when the local "dudy" came to play.[21] This person was master of the "dudak," a bagpipe of passionate wails and whelps. Young Erich loved it. Old Erich remembered it.

Then Johannes Schöppl also died, and Erich was sent back to Vienna to live with an aunt. He entered the Wasa Gymnasium in 1900 and graduated eight years later. The future musicologist Hans Gál was in Kleiber's class throughout, and they formed a lifelong friendship. They were born on the same day in the same year and quickly found identical interests. Life in the gymnasium was less than perfect. Together they endured its multiple bruises.

In this period Erich first encountered opera and the major symphonic repertoire. He often recalled seeing *The Merry Widow* on its first night, 30 December 1905. Years later, he would coin the famous phrase describing its audience swaying to the great waltz "like hypnotized chickens."

In the same period, Erich first saw Gustav Mahler and was deeply impressed by his command and freedom—the idealizing combination he sought in his own career and that Carlos would find in his. At seventeen, he and Gál saw a troupe visiting from Breslau give Richard Strauss's new and dangerous opera *Salomé*. It was another revelation.

In late 1906 Kleiber attended a performance that would alter the course of his life. It was Mahler leading an early performance of his new Sixth Symphony at the Musikverein. At the end of the evening Kleiber told Gál that he had just seen his future. He wrote his sister that he had determined to pursue music whole-heartedly. He would do whatever it took to catch up with others who entered the regime much, much earlier. He signed his letter "Erich the Music-Donkey."[22]

Somehow he and Gál survived their eight years at the gymnasium, a borstal in which spirit and imagination were flogged as much as any back or limb. Said Gál, "Our school made us consummate stoics the rest of our lives."[23]

After graduation, Kleiber moved to the second music capital of the Austro-Hungarian Empire. In 1908 he entered the University of Prague and studied aesthetics, art history, and philosophy. Simultaneously he enrolled at the Prague Conservatory, where he continued work in violin and began study in Czech, timpani, composition, and conducting. Three years later, he wrote a symphonic poem and received The Dürer Society award (and 200 crowns) for it.

In the world of music there are many noble traditions. Students *always* sneak into rehearsals and concerts. (I once slithered into the Met carrying music and an empty viola case, and watched *Norma* from the third light loft.) Students copy music without permission. Students borrow great instruments from trusting teachers. And students cover the windows of their practice rooms for certain purposes. Erich Kleiber was no different.

He took to slipping into the Deutsches Theatre (German Theatre of Prague) to observe rehearsals, note inefficiencies, and learn the repertoire and the tradecraft of opera. He was soon caught, and by the intendant himself.[24] The famous Angelo Neumann (a graduate of the Richard Wagner school of diplomacy) confronted him, and demanded to know what he was up to. With trademark aplomb Kleiber replied that he had come to learn, but he would stay to help. He offered his services as volunteer and Neumann accepted. Kleiber had begun his career. In due course, he was appointed chorus master.

THE FIRST KLEIBER DEBUT

In the same year, 1911, he made his conducting debut at the Prague National Theatre. The work was Nestroy's inconsequential comedy *Einen Jux will er sich machen*, and the date was 1 October. The following year he accepted promotion to the Court Theatre at Darmstadt, and he would apprentice and work there as conductor for the next seven years. (Curiously, Carlos spent seven years at Düsseldorf, under identical circumstances.) Erich Kleiber met great success and was increasingly asked to take on more difficult and challenging projects.

It was in Darmstadt, while still third conductor, that Erich Kleiber met the next great influence of his life. Artur Nikisch had been invited to lead *Tristan und Isolde* and Kleiber had never seen such magic. "Our orchestra suddenly seemed transformed," Kleiber wrote. "We could none of us understand how Nikisch, with a single rehearsal, could draw from them such beauty of sound and such ecstatic depth of feeling."[25] Kleiber would recount that experience for the rest of his life.

He then worked for two years at Barmen-Elberfeld (modern Wuppertal), at Düsseldorf from 1921 to 1922, and in Mannheim from 1922 to 1923. At every house, he was acclaimed for a precision of purpose, a thoroughness of rehearsal, and a standard of personal preparation little seen in any of them. His first major appointment came the following season.

On 24 August 1923 he made his Berlin debut in an extraordinarily well-received production of *Fidelio*, with Frida Leider and Friedrich Schorr. Just seventy-two hours later he was named successor to Leo Blech as generalmusikdirektor of the Berlin Staatsoper. It was a five-year appointment and provoked Fritz Stiedry's resignation.[26] It also proved controversial to the conservative press of the German capital.

The Berlin Staatsoper was one of the most important companies in Europe. It still is.[27] Becoming generalmusikdirektor confirmed Kleiber's ascent into the leading ranks of European conductors. The appointment would ultimately last ten years, the longest and most important position of his career. And he was only thirty-three years old.

Erich Kleiber was unafraid of excellence. In his Berlin years Kleiber offered concerts and recitals, as well as a wide horizon of opera and operetta. He brought to his house some of the greatest conductors of the day, including

Busch, Furtwängler, Klemperer, Richard Strauss, Toscanini, and Mahler's protégé, Bruno Walter. In the same period, he engaged such assistants as Dmitri Mitropoulos and George Szell, and engineered the return of Leo Blech to the podium.

Kleiber used his authority as manager, and skills as conductor, to lead the Berlin Staatsoper into some of the most important new music of the period. In March 1924 he gave a production of Janacek's *Jenufa*, a masterpiece new to Berlin. Kleiber's success moved Janacek beyond a regional reputation and into standing among the leading composers of the day. (Thirty years later, Sir Charles Mackerras would amplify that tremendously.) Kleiber's personal mastery of the Czech language made an enormous difference. Its rhythms worked. Erich Kleiber did much the same for Krenek and his opera *Die Zwingburg*, giving its world premiere on 16 October 1924.[28]

But it was in 1925 that Kleiber gave the production with which his name would be identified and immortalized.

WOZZECK

He had been asked to lead the premiere of his friend Alban Berg's new opera *Wozzeck*. Reading the score, he instantly recognized its genius—and its problems. The work, based on a play by Büchner, is a remarkable fusion of disparate models and traditions. It contains such antique mechanisms as a passacaglia in twenty-one variations, a set of dances, interstitial symphonic sequences in Baroque dress, and passages of rhapsodic invention employing ultramodern techniques and shocking dissonance. Its narrative is, without question, nightmarish. Its final scene, a solitary little boy riding a toy horse, is heartbreaking.

Kleiber soon agreed to the project and did something for which his son would become equally famous. In this instance, Kleiber organized no fewer than 137 rehearsals.[29] He would honor the composer's every intention, or not do the work at all. His astonishing diligence and uncompromising discipline led to a famous opening night.

Wozzeck was premiered under Erich Kleiber's baton at the Berlin Staatsoper on 14 December 1925. Reminiscent of the first performance of *Le Sacre du Printemps* twelve years earlier, it provoked a near-riot.[30] Its reviews were often hostile, and Kleiber was widely attacked. (Berg and his friends gleefully printed a pamphlet incorporating the worst of these reviews, and they gave it out everywhere.) Kleiber was undeterred, of course. Today, *Wozzeck* is esteemed as one of the great works of the twentieth century. Its critics lie forgotten.[31]

SOUTH AMERICA

A year later Kleiber made the first of many visits to South America. He had been invited to conduct at the Teatro Colón in Buenos Aires, Argentina. Fascinated by such a distant land yet familiar culture, Kleiber agreed. It changed his life. He would conduct fourteen concerts, four more than originally planned. His singers and players quickly encountered the Kleiber method: many rehearsals (one hundred in fewer than sixty days), and ceaselessly demanding attention to detail. He offered mostly German repertoire but included Dvořák and Stravinsky. While there, Kleiber learned to dance the tango. (He was offered another eighteen concerts the following season, and accepted.)

It was in Buenos Aires on 12 September 1926 that he first met the American civil servant Ruth Goodrich. She had been born in Waterloo, Iowa, was in the employ of her country's embassy, and they were introduced by the German diplomat Dr. Günther Henle. Neither Goodrich nor Kleiber spoke the native language of the other. They arranged to have lunch the next day, and Kleiber's quiet attentions startled her. He drew pictures of his Berlin apartment. "If this seems acceptable, would you like to come and live in this apartment and be my wife?"

She politely declined but was utterly amazed by his directness and desire. A day later she learned that Kleiber had already booked her passage to Germany, chaperoned by the wife of the first German minister. Sail was scheduled for December. With characteristic thoroughness he also arranged warm clothing, a substantial allowance, and white roses every day. He returned to Berlin confident of her capture.

He was not disappointed. She arrived at Cuxhaven Harbor on 28 December 1926, and they were married in Berlin the next morning.[32] Two days later, the New York Times ran a brief story "sent by wireless" and headed, "Kleiber Wedding Surprise; Berlin Opera Director Mysteriously Marries Miss Ruth Goodrich." Never much surprised by anything, Erich Kleiber was an inveterate traveler and list keeper. He soon showed Ruth his master list of travel necessities. She was relieved to see that between the essentials "toothpaste" and "rehearsal jackets" he had penciled in "wife."[33] He also made time for other happy obligations. Their daughter Veronica was born on 28 March 1928, and a son two years later.

KLB KLEIBER

Karl Ludwig Bonifacius[34] Kleiber was born in Berlin on 3 July 1930. Following in the faith of his father, he was baptized Catholic at the principal church in Berlin, the St. Hedwigs-Kathedrale.[35] This famous building is located just behind the Staatsoper and appears as the Pantheon-like structure with dome seen in all the tourist photographs.[36] Although Ruth and Erich at that time lived in the small parish of St. Bernhard's Church, his fame may have required involvement at the great cathedral behind the Staatsoper itself.[37]

Intriguingly, St. Hedwig's was also a center of principled Catholic resistance to the Nazis. A number of its congregants and leaders opposed anti-Semitism and Hitler's policies generally. It is entirely likely that Kleiber knew about this and publicly associated himself with that institution for those reasons.[38]

His sister Veronica remembers a boy already like the man.

My mother confessed to me much later that when he was small she had truly thought that he wouldn't survive because he was so weak and skinny. As a little person he was very strong-willed. He gave orders. When we were going to go swimming in a nearby lake in Germany he went first, put his foot in the water, turned around and said, "Absolutely too cold! Don't anyone go in!" Ecco. Kein Mensch! [39]

He started to say that he wanted to compose something, then he wrote something. Since he was wonderful at learning, both languages and anything else, from my mother he learned musical notation. And he said, "Very well, now I'm going to try and see what I can produce."

When we were children our parents rented a house in Lugano. There was a piano in it. We played around with it, as all children do. Father took and locked it and threw the key into the lake. He was terrified by the idea that we. . . . Well, this was the encouragement we got to play music!

—Veronica Kleiber, RAI 3 broadcast, 18 February 2008[40]

During the Weimar Republic, Erich Kleiber at the Staatsoper was associated with the avant-garde in music and its allied arts. The brilliance of cabaret life became a nova. Kleiber was viewed as a daring and heroic figure by the young innovators of the day. Together with Otto Klemperer at the Kroll Oper (1927–1931) and Bruno Walter at the Städtische Oper (1925–1929), he was a leading advocate for new sound, radical production values, and fearless music making.

These traits were only emboldened by the criticism and applause rocketed his way. Kleiber gave the world premiere of Kurt Weill's one-act opera, *Royal Palace*, and his cantata "Der neue Orpheus" on 2 March 1927. He gave the first performance of Franz Schreker's expressionist and psychologically driven opera *Der singende Teufel* on 10 December 1928. Two years later, on 5 May, he gave the premiere of Darius Milhaud's historical opera *Christophe Colombe*, a work that has entered the standard repertoire in progressive houses and many a school of music.

During his career in Berlin, Erich Kleiber made two important films. In them he conducts Mozart and Johann Strauss Jr. The first of these offers one of Mozart's German Dances.[41] It exists today in little more than ninety seconds of grainy frames and fragmentary music. The film was made in 1931. It accounts for little of visual significance but is the earliest moving image we have of him.

The second is complete, and a delight. It was made in 1932 with the Berlin Staatskapelle Orchestra and across its ten minutes shows the elegant joy and impeccable phrase-making for which he was so renowned.[42] In Strauss's *Blue Danube Waltz* we see a conductor at the height of his expressive powers, never sentimental, never lingering falsely. This is the Erich Kleiber of surviving recordings and enduring legend. His work illuminates architecture, addresses phrase and cadence, and avoids egotism. Strauss is foremost, and the man on the podium much less so. It could be very favorably compared to his 1923 acoustic recording of the same work with the same orchestra. The earlier is a testament to willfulness, Sachertorte, and mere arbitrariness.[43] The film version is wholly superior.

Kleiber's social standing was of a high order in Berlin and in all of Germany. He knew everyone in the musical world and in literary and theatrical circles. He was welcome in every cultured home, and his attendance at a dinner, a party, a private event was considered a great prize. On 24 September 1932, for example, he and Ruth were invited by Albert Einstein and his wife to visit them at Einstein's summerhouse in Caputh, some six kilometers south of Potsdam. Kleiber left a wry inscription in Einstein's guest book: "gewonnen . . . genommen. . . . Wir haben sogar Briefe gelesen, die anderen Leuten verboten gewesen! Mit herzlichem Dank."[44]

However, come the onset of the Depression, the collapse of the republic, and the rise of Nazism, Kleiber's fortunes foundered. Social conservatism was on the march. Kleiber introduced Wagner's rarely performed comic opera *Das Liebesverbot* to the company's repertoire, and he began reintroducing any number of popular operettas. Even so, he continued to advocate for contemporary composers. Paul Hindemith was chief among his beneficiaries.

Hitler came to power on 30 January 1933, and was pleased to exploit the burning of the Reichstag twenty-eight days later. At every level, the Nazis, well aware of the power of art to influence opinion, began taking control. Josef Goebbels was given authority over all German musical and theatrical work in September of that year. Conductors Fritz Busch and Bruno Walter soon left Germany, and Klemperer prepared to do so. Composers Kurt Weill and Arnold Schoenberg would follow. Berg, Kleiber, and many others were required to prove their Aryan ancestry. Psychosis had captured public policy across all of Germany. Conservative clerics were delighted.

AGAINST THE SWASTIKA

Kleiber stood against Nazi meddling and prohibitions as long as he could. Nazi interference arose from the beginning and made Kleiber's life increasingly difficult. His progressive (but monarchist) political views were well-known, and his sympathy for the victims of Hitler's right-wing cultural policies was equally well understood. Although not Jewish himself, Kleiber often expressed sympathy for their plight. To this day, many believe that the grounds for Kleiber's escape from Nazi Germany lay in personal religion, rather than personal principle.[45] He never joined the Nazi Party, of course, and would have considered doing so absurd. The only time he ever gave the Nazi salute was in a sarcastic gesture from the pit during a performance of *Siegfried*. It went unnoticed by the brownshirts dozing in attendance.[46]

In May of 1934 occurred a bizarre encounter between Reichsminister Hermann Göring and Ruth Kleiber. Erich was conducting in Brussels at the time, and Göring summoned Ruth for a private meeting to discuss Berg's new opera *Lulu*. Kleiber and Berg had hoped to give its premiere at the Staatsoper. Göring began the meeting by asking if Berg was a Jew. No, she said, and neither was Erich. He then criticized her husband for never greeting him in person at the theatre. He was feeling snubbed and didn't like it. She offered no apology. Amazingly, Ruth then pressed him to support Berg. He actually consented, but nothing came of it—save to cement Kleiber's fear of Nazi meddling in the arts.

Kleiber's most heroic gesture of defiance against Nazi cultural policy came the evening of 30 November 1934. *Lulu* could not be produced, so he gave instead the first performance of a five-movement suite drawn from it. The audience reacted with wild enthusiasm, but this was the effective end of Kleiber's career in Berlin. Save for cleaning up loose ends, he would not conduct there for another twenty years.[47] Embarrassed by Kleiber's departure, Göring several months later actually invited him to return, at full salary payable to any bank in the world. Kleiber agreed, with one proviso—that his first concert be all-Mendelssohn.[48] Felix Mendelssohn was, of course, Jewish. Such a concert was beyond the pale to Nazis, and Kleiber knew it.

The Nazis were well aware of Kleiber's political views. Rather than exchange his Austrian passport for the document introduced by Hitler after Anschluss in 1938, Erich Kleiber renounced that citizenship altogether and became Argentine. Thereafter he lost his contract to lead Wagner in Amsterdam because he was "an avowed enemy of National Socialism." His protests were not restricted to Germania. In December 1938 he quit a production of *Fidelio* at La Scala, having learned that Jews were prohibited from attending. Standing for humanist principles cost him much work, much income, and many opportunities.

Fortunately, Erich Kleiber was wanted elsewhere. In the 1920s he began life as a touring guest conductor. He first worked in Soviet Russia in 1927, debuted with the New York Philharmonic-Symphony in 1930, and appeared regularly in Amsterdam and Brussels[49] from 1933 to 1938. He made his debut at La Scala in 1935 and in the same year first led the London Symphony Orchestra. In 1936 he served in Moscow as chief conductor for the Symphony Orchestra of the USSR. Kleiber first conducted at Covent Garden in 1938, leading a famous *Rosenkavalier* with Lotte Lehmann.[50]

Following his resignation from the Berlin Staatsoper in 1935, he was able to work in free Europe for four more seasons. Kleiber departed Europe for good in June 1939. He sailed for Montevideo and Buenos Aires, temporarily leaving his wife and two children behind. They would be apart for almost a year. On 4 July he instructed Ruth that, if war came, the children were to be sent to Switzerland. His foresight was paying off again. They moved to that neutral country after the invasion of Poland in September. Kleiber had already arranged an escape plan.

In South America, perhaps not so curiously, he and his family would thrive for a decade.

> I wonder if we shall ever have our two birthdays, and a 12th of September[51] and a wedding anniversary, with our children and grandchildren to celebrate them all quietly with us? Herr Stalin (who seems to have engaged Herr Hitler as his assistant) ought to make an alliance with the Vatican and declare a general peace at Xmas! Then I could become Generalmusikdirektor to the Eskimos.
>
> —Erich Kleiber, 29 September 1939[52]

SAFE IN THE SOUTH

That southern continent, especially in Argentina, Chile, and Brazil, has long enjoyed the presence of powerful German, Spanish, and Italian expatriate communities. They brought their love of opera with them, famously building one theatre in a jungle.[53] In 1926 they first invited Erich Kleiber to join their ranks, and he flourished. One engagement at the Teatro Colón in Buenos Aires led to many requests for return. It finally led to his appointment there, as director of German repertoire, from 1937 to 1949. Across the first four years, his work at the Colón was virtually uninterrupted. In the same two decades he guest-conducted in South and Central America, and he was well received in every quarter.

Contrary to Hollywood history, not every German in South America was a Nazi on vacation, secretly cloning boys in laboratories. A number were genuinely sympathetic to Jews and other victims of Nazism. The worst did not arrive until the collapse of Berlin. Kleiber came to the rescue of many others marooned as he was. The brilliantly irascible conductor Jascha Horenstein fled Hitler and landed in South America with little work and less prospect. He appealed to Kleiber for help. "Kleiber is extremely helpful and he behaves like a *real colleague,*" he wrote to Karol Rathaus, the Polish composer and teacher. Thanks to Kleiber's intercession, Horenstein was invited to lead concerts in Mexico City in January 1944, and two years later in Buenos Aires. Their success brought him work in several South American countries. Argentina, Brazil, and Uruguay gave him regular place for the next three years. Horenstein remained grateful to Kleiber the rest of his life.[54]

By October 1939 Kleiber was arranging documents to bring Ruth and the children to live with him in Buenos Aires and to assume Argentine citizenship. Switzerland was safe but very distant. (During this period Carlos attended school in Geneva, Lugano, and Monte Carlo.)[55] Erich continued conducting, but his daily letters to Ruth are full of love and anxiety. Visits to Chile, Uruguay, and Peru brightened the load a bit, but his letters suffer a forced humor that could not conceal his fears.[56]

It was on 1 December 1939, writing from the Miraflores Hotel in Lima, that Erich first committed to paper his interest in Carlos's musical ambitions. Much has been made of this letter. Much has been exaggerated. Those who quote only one line find it a Rosetta in revelation of father-son conflict. In fact, the whole letter is full of sardonic humor and wry observation. In tone and flippancy it is like almost all the others of the period. There are good reasons to accept the premise of a difficult relationship with an overbearing father. This letter is not one of them.

It is useful to quote more than Erich's notorious one-liner. Its whole spirit makes the comment a good deal more benevolent than it appears out of context.

The Bolívar Hotel turns out to be so noisy that I moved over to this one, which is called the Miraflores and is near the sea. It *ought* to be very quiet, but it isn't . . . three waiters in shirt-sleeves came and sat on the grass in front of my window and talked (*how* they talk here! You'd think it was a quarrel every time!).

And when I switched on the light in the evening three cucarachas[57] hopped on to my table in the friendliest way and sat on my passport. So, you see, I have all the modern comforts! I'm longing to see one of my son's compositions—what a pity he's "musical"![58]

A week later, still at the Miraflores, Erich replies to more news from his wife. It includes information about nine-year-old Carlos ("Pie" in their terms) continuing his first explorations in music. Again, quoting more of the father's letter gives a better picture of the context in which he expressed his sardonic concern.

> Today the new President is being sworn in so we can only rehearse in the afternoon. (Tchaikovsky 4 and Dvorák's: dog's work.) That Pie sings *and* composes is suspicious—he'll want to be a musician next!
>
> Christmas eve I shall be on the steamer with Schraml—direct to Antofagasta, a ghastly hole, with never a tree or a bit of green, just the Andes to look at, and ants and grasshoppers to nibble everything up, and then more and more clean-shaven Alps![59]

Further evidence suggests that Erich took the same teasing attitude with his daughter Veronica. She was Carlos's senior by two years. As a child she too expressed an interest in music, and particularly in conducting. Erich wrote her a revealing letter.

> My dear daughter, you seem to be getting dangerously musical in your old age! Now you even want to know how to start the Fifth Symphony? Well, you take a baton (not too long) in your right hand, and then you make a hole in the air, more or less as if you were trying to swat a fly after having missed it twice, and then the orchestra doesn't come in—well, it's not always the orchestra's fault![60]

Many more letters make clear Kleiber's devotion to his absent wife and children. He found Christmas particularly grim. He was invited to share it at the home of close friends, "but when I saw their Christmas tree all lit up I just couldn't bear it and crept off to the sea-front and ate by myself in the pensión. I didn't go to any of the people who'd invited me, for fear I might see another tree and start crying."[61]

Finally, after much duress and more finagling, Kleiber's family was able to join him. They reconnected in Santiago, Chile, in May 1940. The children were immediately placed at The Grange, an English-language private school. Fifty-eight years later, Carlos could still recall the words of its "School Hymn."

> *Petrovič! "Many lessons we've learnt, Midnight oil we have burnt, And results sound and true were the yield. . . ."*
>
> —*Carlos Kleiber, to Peter Jonas, 15 June 1998*[62]

It was at this point that Karl Kleiber first became "Carlos."[63] Soon thereafter, singer Alexander Kipnis arrived to sing with Erich at the Colón. He brought with him his son Igor, a boy the same age as Carlos. The two became fast friends. Igor went on to become a superb harpsichordist.

Within a year the Kleibers were living in Buenos Aires, where they stayed for the duration of the war. During those years, although the Teatro Colón remained his home base, Kleiber appeared in many South American countries, elevating standards with every appearance. When able, he took wife and children with him. Indeed, at various periods the family lived in several South American cities, in New York, and in Havana. Cuba offered special attractions.

From 1944 to 1947 Kleiber served as principal conductor of the Havana Philharmonic and raised the orchestra to levels no one had dreamed possible. That group was founded in 1924, but by the time of Kleiber's appointment, it had fallen well below expectations. He introduced those players, and their audience, to repertoire they had never heard. He created standards where none existed. He invested thousands of hours in coaching, sectional, and rehearsal sessions. He helped create a significant audience for European music. And he did all of this in a famously corrupt political culture, one dominated by bananas, sugar, and American gangsters. He also brought rising young artists to join him.

Conductor Antal Dorati was there in 1941 and remembered Kleiber's impact, describing it as "a sleepy, third-rate symphony orchestra improved beyond all sense and hope under the leadership of Erich Kleiber."[64]

Cuba also provided Carlos an opportunity to make an appearance, of sorts, on the timpani. It is almost certainly the case that only his father would invite him to do so, and only in an orchestra of such mixed capacity could Carlos get away with it. Forty-five years later he told timpanist Bonnie Lynn Adelson about his triumph.

> *I too "studied" with an erstwhile NY Phil. Tympanist, Saul Goodman. But since I can neither count nor tune the drums (in those days it was done by hand; and the smaller drums were on the right-hand side—where I think they belong, incidentally) my career climaxed and ended with the F-sharp roll in the Pathetique and the 9th Beethoven. I doubled this roll in both pieces in Havana wearing a borrow monkey-suit and making a tremendous noise when I was 16 in 1946.*
>
> —*Carlos Kleiber, to Bonnie Lynn Adelson, 17 April 1991*

Violinist Isaac Stern also knew Erich Kleiber in the Cuban capital. In his memoirs he marveled at Kleiber's gifts for teaching, inspiration, and effect. Though somewhat ahistorical, the book reveals Stern's astonishment at Kleiber's industry.

> It was in Havana that I first heard the great conductor Erich Kleiber, a legendary figure in Germany, which he left in the mid-thirties to travel from

one South American country to another, creating and training orchestras; he'd spend a few years in one place building an orchestra and then, satisfied with its quality, leave to do the same in another country.

Stern wrote that the Havana ensemble was essentially amateur. It included only two professionals in ranks otherwise dominated by white- and blue-collar workers of varying background. Kleiber held twenty or thirty rehearsals per concert in addition to a very heavy reliance on sectional rehearsals. These latter often took place in small groups meeting at his hotel. He was as interested in improving their individual skills as in their capacity for ensemble.

> He had a demonic passion for training, and was a superb musician. I remember with special pleasure hearing members of his orchestra play the Haydn Sinfonia Concertante, which is written with major solo parts for first violin, principal cello, oboe, and bassoon—a truly fine performance! He was a worker of musical miracles. And always, after building an orchestra, he would say, "I have done my job, and now I must go somewhere else and do the same thing."[65]

Unfortunately for Stern's fond recollection, Kleiber's work in Cuba actually ended rather abruptly—and very unhappily. He quit in March 1947. He had been asked to program *The Blue Danube*, and he refused. His message to the Cuban players compared the orchestra's management to Hitler.

In this period (some sources say 1940, others 1946) Erich bought a large country house, *La Fermata*,[66] at Alta Gracia in the Argentine province of Córdoba. The family spent many holidays there. Alta Gracia is a mountain town, popular among artists. Manuel De Falla spent his retirement and died there. *La Fermata* was built in two parts by a local artisan, Ángel Federico, who also served as caretaker. It consisted of a large family home and, at some distance, a music studio for Erich. This place would figure in a complicated effort to persuade Carlos to conduct at Vienna half a century later.

Following further guest work in other South American nations, his great 1949 season at the Teatro Colón, and a Beethoven cycle in Buenos Aires in 1951, Erich Kleiber was largely done in South America. For more than a decade it was home and safe haven. From 1926 to 1952 he had given forty-four productions in opera, two ballets, and more than eighty concerts at the Teatro Colón alone.[67] To this day he is revered in every musical arena he touched—including Cuba.

AFTER THE WAR

Once the war ended Kleiber was free to travel again, and he gradually resumed his international career. David Sarnoff and Toscanini appointed him principal guest conductor of the NBC Symphony in New York for the 1945–1946 season.[68] He returned to London in February 1948 and led concerts with the Philharmonic. He was given a generous contract at London's Covent Garden in 1950, and until 1953 he was heavily involved in revival of that war-depressed house.

His December 1950 production of *Der Rosenkavalier* was hailed as revelation, as was the *Queen of Spades*, which followed. *Tristan und Isolde* and *Figaro* were added to the lists of Kleiber's victories over routine and mediocrity. Covent Garden was becoming important again.

In 1952 he led Britain's first stage production of *Wozzeck* and once again demanded an extraordinary number of rehearsals. This time his work resulted in wild popular and critical acclaim, though not every seat was sold. In retrospect it was a Golden Age for British opera. Europe was in ruins. The presence in London of virtually every great singer was a given, Britten's masterwork *Peter Grimes* heralded a renaissance in English opera, and Walter Legge was overseeing an astonishing run of recordings that would influence the sound—and repertoire base—of orchestras and opera houses around the world. Unfortunately, in 1953 Kleiber had yet another dispute with management (a conflict over money), and he was not re-engaged.[69]

Kleiber did receive invitations from important German and Italian houses. He first joined with Maria Callas in 1951. At the Maggio Musicale in Florence they gave a thrilling production of Verdi's *Sicilian Vespers*. Under the same auspices they paired for a production of Haydn's *Orpheus and Euridice*, a work not seen there in over a century. He was also able to give concerts in Leipzig and Dresden.

At this time it was rumored that he would be offered appointment as music director of the Vienna Staatsoper. This came to nothing, save Kleiber's bitter disappointment. He was a native son of Vienna, but never allowed to assume that patrimony. It was widely believed that Kleiber's leftist views (and premature anti-Nazism) were unwelcome in the city that welcomed Anschluss. He would conduct that company once only, in 1951, in *Rosenkavalier*. Despite success he was not invited to return.

East Berlin called three years later. He was offered his old position as music director of the Staatsoper, and he accepted. The building had been destroyed, but the institution remained. Kleiber soon found that Nazi meddling was indistinct from Soviet meddling. The house was in the Russian sector, and he came to resent their political idiocies. Much to their embarrassment (and his relief) he quit the job on 16 March 1955, after some months of rehearsal for a reopening season that was several times postponed. Kleiber left Berlin forever. Carlos made a quick run into East Berlin, with the aid of an English journalist, to retrieve his father's effects. Less than a year later, on 27 January 1956, Erich Kleiber died of a heart attack, at age sixty-five, in the Grand Hotel Dolder in Zurich.[70]

Had he lived, Erich would have taken the Vienna Philharmonic on a North American tour in the fall of 1956. He was also negotiating for a *Parsifal* with Maria Callas and Ramón Vinay at La Scala the following season.

Had he lived, Erich would have continued an acclaimed series of recordings for Decca.[71] Had he lived, he would have returned to Buenos Aires in September 1956 for a series of concerts commemorating his first appearance there thirty years before.

In his early career Kleiber had also been a composer. He wrote concerti for piano and for violin, a set of variations for orchestra, and a capriccio for orchestra. He was also a good pianist who wrote numerous small works for that instrument, as well as music for chamber forces, and numerous songs. All of this music lives in the late-Romantic idiom of his early education.

In four decades of work, Erich Kleiber left behind a legacy of fanatical precision, unrelenting standards, ardent expression, and a willingness to cross swords with anyone who refused to see music in those terms. He also left a son who would follow in the trade and conjure it like no one else.

NOTES

1. Kleiber's mathematical shorthand for one million.
2. "Riding is good in those cars."
3. Wolfgang Sandner, *Frankfurter Allgemeine Zeitung*, 20 July 2004.
4. One day I attended a classic-car show in Sonoma County, California. A large white Kleiber truck was on display. I asked questions of its owner and was put in touch with the descendants.
5. The Kleiber corporation was founded by Paul Kleiber in 1913. In its several incarnations (Kleiber and Co., 1914–1919; Kleiber Motor Truck Co., 1919–1929; Kleiber Motor Co., 1929–1938) this company produced trucks and, from 1924 to 1929, passenger cars. It was an Arizona corporation until 1926, when it became a Nevada corporation. Its factory was in downtown San Francisco.
6. "Do not attempt to make music!"
7. The *Telegraph*, 21 July 2004, quoting a wisely unnamed "record producer."
8. Matheopoulos, *Vanity Fair*, February 1988.
9. Garben, 75.
10. *Süddeutsche Zeitung*, 11 February 1959.
11. *Süddeutsche Zeitung*, 26 December 1959.
12. *Die Welt*, 13 March 1964.
13. *Süddeutsche Zeitung*, 15 January 1968.
14. *Münchner Merkur*, 15 January 1968.
15. Author's interview, New York City, 31 October 2004.
16. Author's interview, New York City, 24 November 2004.
17. Tooley, author's interview, 3 June 2005.
18. Author's interview, San Francisco, 8 February 2005.
19. This chapter owes a great deal to the pioneering biographical work of John Russell, for which I thank him once again.
20. Essi too would later be buried in that vault, interred with the remarkable Czech personality and dancer Zdenka Podhajská.
21. Russell, 24.
22. Russell, 29.
23. Russell, 30.
24. In the German tradition, the intendant is the general director of an opera company or symphony orchestra.
25. Russell, 48.
26. Stiedry was a senior conductor in that house, and he expected the appointment that went to Kleiber.
27. Daniel Barenboim was appointed generalmusikdirektor in 1992, and at this writing retains that post.
28. Slonimsky, 523. *New Grove* asserts 21 October 1924.
29. Gerhard Brunner, *New Grove*, Volume 10, 100. Russell contests this. He declares that there were only thirty-four orchestra rehearsals plus an unstated number of coaching, blocking, and piano dress rehearsals. Russell, 94.
30. Slonimsky, 83.

31. John Russell takes a different view and posits that opening night reception was somewhat sympathetic. Conservative reaction took another week or so to set in. Russell, 98.

32. Russell, 188.

33. Russell, 116.

34. Often spelled "Bonifatius," but here named for the Catholic popes.

35. Russell, 215.

36. It was built by Frederick the Great, who also ordered construction of the Staatsoper. His architect was Wenceslaus von Knobelsdorff. This church became the seat of the Berlin Archdiocese in 1929. It was heavily damaged in WWII, rebuilt, and reopened in 1963.

37. The Deutsches Bühnenjahrbuch of 1931 gives Erich's address as Berlin-Dahlem, Rohlsstrasse 14, in that smaller parish.

38. One particular priest deserves memory. Fr. Bernhard Lichtenberg gained a powerful religious education and a searing social conscience. He served as a member of parliament for the German Catholics party, in 1931 was appointed canon of the Cathedral Chapter at St. Hedwig's, and in 1938 its provost. He bore special responsibility for care of the Jews of Berlin. After Kristallnacht on 10 November 1938 he led public prayers for its victims. Fr. Lichtenberger also organized demonstrations outside concentration camps. He was imprisoned in 1942, and on 5 November 1943 died in a cattle car en route to Dachau. Fifty-three years later he was beatified by John Paul II.

39. This is ambiguous, and it is not clear if Veronica is attributing or describing. "It seems probable to me that Carlos said in German something like this: 'Absolut zu kalt! Kein Mensch gehe hinein!' I think that her use of the Italian word 'Nessuno' is her translation into Italian of what Carlos had actually said in German: 'Kein Mensch (gehe hinein)!'" (Robert McGinn, 15 April 2010 and Ulrich Plemper, 2 August 2010, e-mail to author). Either way, this was a remarkable degree of assertion from a child.

40. Adapted from the work of Giuliana Bilotta and Robert McGinn.

41. K605, No. 3, "Schlittenfahrt" (The Sleigh Ride). It was a lifelong favorite and would be the last piece he ever conducted. Russell, 243.

42. This marvelous restoration was achieved by Marcos Klorman and his colleagues at Warner Teldec.

43. Sachertorte is a Viennese confection of stupefying sweetness.

44. "won't . . . taken away. . . . We even read letters, which others wouldn't have been allowed to read! With our best thanks." www.einstein-website.de/z_biography/guestbook.html, accessed 8 March 2010.

45. On 30 July 2004, Carlos's sister Veronica felt provoked to correct the record yet again. Replying to an article by Dino Villatico in the 20 July issue of *Repubblica*, she reminded the world that her father's reasons were ethical, not ethnic.

46. Russell, 147.

47. Russell, 149, writes that the Nazis required him to stay until the expiry of his contract at the beginning of January 1935, and reports three more performances after November's Berg event.

48. Russell, 149.

49. There, on 12 December 1936, he gave the premiere of Roussel's *Rapsodie flamande*, Op. 56. It was dedicated to him. Paris, 377.

50. Slonimsky, 505, says 1937.

51. The day of their first meeting, back in 1926.

52. Writing from Buenos Aires, to Ruth in Switzerland. Russell, 178.

53. The seven-hundred-seat Teatro Amazonas, built from 1885 to 1896 in Manaus. Today, that city is no longer in a jungle.

54. www.classical.net/music/performer/horenstein, accessed 6 September 2004.

55. Wolfram Schwinger, *Die Kleibers, Vater und Sohn-Eine Dirigentensaga des 20. Jahrhunderts*. SWR Radio feature, broadcast 29 October 2004.

56. Claims that he worked in Bolivia appear unfounded. Sebastiano De Filippi, e-mail to author, 11 March 2010.

57. Cockroaches.

58. Russell, 184.

59. Russell, 185.

60. Russell, 154. Veronica claimed to be a nonmusician, but spent much of her career assisting Claudio Abbado. The composer Salvatore Sciarrino dedicated his 1979 *Aspern Suite* for soprano and chamber ensemble to her.

61. Russell, 187. Here, "pension" describes a family home in which rooms are rented and meals provided.

62. From the "College Hymn," with words by P. B. Hobsbawn to music by W. C. Currie, Esq. The hymn's final stanza reads, "Then Sing For The School, 'Neath The Andean Range, And Play A Straight Game For The Sake Of The Grange." It is still sung at this school, founded by John A. S. Jackson in 1928.

63. It should be added that Carlos was also called "Carlitos" and retained that nickname for years. "Carlos" may have endured as a mark of respect for the violinist Carlos Pessina. This latter was a very close friend of Erich, and sat first violin in the Teatro Colón orchestra for over thirty years.

64. Dorati, 180.

65. Stern, 52–53.

66. The place of rest. Kleiber used the same musical term on his headstone.

67. Sebastiano De Filippi, e-mail to author, 4 March 2010.

68. Russell, 204, says it was 1947–1948. RCA sources declare the earlier date.

69. Haltrecht, 176–77.

70. He is buried at Friedhof Hönggerberg, near Zurich, in plot FG 81011. His wife was buried beside him a decade later. www.stadtzuerich.ch/content/dam/stzh/prd/Deutsch/Bevoelkerungsamt/Formulare%20und%20Merkblaetter/BFA_Formulare_Merkblaetter/PromiAlpha.pdf, accessed 2 February 2009.

71. As it was, that company did release his most important discs, including Beethoven 3, 5, 6, 7, and 9; Mozart 40 and "Marriage of Figaro"; Tchaikovsky 4 and 6; and a performance of *Rosenkavalier* unsurpassed until the achievement of his son. They are the finest examples we have of his sounds and strategies.

Chapter Two

Career

I've given up music, incidentally. But I'll still maybe conduct. That would make me . . . what? a professional?

—*Carlos Kleiber, 2 February 1996*

You are probably conducting all sorts of things, constantly, and giving lectures to your students and anyone prepared to listen. And all the while I am as idle as Oblomov. In fact I am Oblomov.

—*Carlos Kleiber, 6 July 1996*[1]

As ever with Carlos in such a context, it was never clear to me just how much he was kidding, or testing, or revealing. Looking back, I wish I had pursued the matter. What he could not directly confess about himself he could certainly allude to in the life of another—not entirely fictional—human being.

All Oblomov's anxiety resolved itself into a sigh and dissolved into apathy and drowsiness.

—I. A. Goncharov, 1859

After WWII ended the Kleiber family was free to return to Europe. They did not do so immediately. Carlos was only fifteen. The Kleibers kept their principal home in Buenos Aires to allow him to finish high school and to continue his sporadic studies in music. The family lived in the elegant and upscale Belgrano neighborhood. It was largely populated by European immigrants like themselves and was located about fifteen minutes from the heart of Buenos Aires.[2]

Argentinian soprano Nilda Hoffmann was an important member of the Teatro Colón's company of soloists and, for many years, a favorite of Erich. He often conducted for her in the German repertoire, giving her debut in 1947 under his baton in *Das Rheingold*, and a performance of Beethoven's *Missa Solemnis* a year later. It was recorded.[3] She became a friend to the entire Kleiber family.

As a young and very pretty lady, Nilda met Carlos in the Kleiber home at Belgrano. Erich was extremely fond of Nilda and often invited her to dinner. Erich himself cooked, and while doing so, he used to leave Carlos and Nilda alone, hoping that the two would become, if not "engaged," then at least good friends. But Carlos, according to Nilda, was far too shy. He hardly spoke a word to her.[4]

The family relationship was such that, after rehearsals at the Colón, Erich and Carlos escorted Nilda along 9 de Julio Avenue (the major street at the center of Buenos Aires, running in front of the Colón) to the bus stop at which she caught her transportation home.

Together with his mother and sister, Carlos regularly observed Erich's concert and opera performances. The father often discussed music and specific productions with his son. Erich several times wrote Carlos about scores and concerts. On one occasion he fantasized about repertoire he would like to conduct, and he shared those hopes with Carlos. In an undated letter from the period, he advised his son that "Act I of [Pfitzner's] 'Palestrina' is one of the greatest and most moving poems in all music. I should dearly love to do a concert performance of it."[5]

Carlos also traveled widely with his father, serving as amanuensis and valet. Together they visited and worked in numerous South and Central American cities. In 1947 Erich was engaged by the NBC Symphony. Father and son stayed in New York City, and Carlos was astonished by its drive and energy. He was enrolled at the private Riverdale Country School, graduating there in June 1948.[6] It was while in New York that he bought a typewriter he kept for many years, as he later told me. Almost all who corresponded with him saw that typewriter in action. It was a "Smith-Corona 'Silent.' (I bought it at Wanamakers, NY, in 1947 and it's loud as hell)."[7]

Margarita Wallmann returned to Buenos Aires in 1948, having served as principal choreographer at the Colón for much of the previous decade. The Austrian-born Wallmann would go on to become, it appears, the first woman ever to stage direct a professional opera and to work in such houses as La Scala and La Fenice with such artists as Callas, Bernstein, Raimondi, and Giulini. In her memoirs, Wallmann remembered a very young Carlitos attending rehearsals and coming to her in amazement, declaring, "Don't tell me Daddy gets paid just for handling that stick!"[8]

In late 1948 Carlos made his professional debut in the orchestra pit, but not as conductor. Erich was leading *Götterdämmerung* at the Teatro Colón, and Carlos may have played second timpani.[9] As Carlos matured in Buenos Aires he became more powerfully drawn to high culture and progressive thinking. Already able to read English and German, he now drew closer to the great world of Spanish literature. Throughout his teenage years, usually accompanied by his sister Veronica, he regularly visited bookshops and libraries and attended readings given by the leading writers and poets of the day. On several occasions in the late 1940s he attended the literary salon of María Rosa Oliver, for example. Hers was an important center of new writing. Oliver herself sat on the editorial board of *Sur*, a seminally influential literary magazine in Buenos Aires. It was founded in 1931 by her friend Victoria Ocampo. Its board also included Jorge Luis Borges, Adolfo Bioy Casares, Silvina Ocampo, and Alfonso Reyes. Such occasions also influenced Carlos politically. They were quite left-wing in outlook. Many of the writers who attended were desperate to see the world reborn along humanist and generous lines. Argentina was itself being rebuilt by General Juan Domingo Perón and his curious blend of socialist planning and capitalist reward. At the time, Perón (involved in the military coup of 1943 but freely elected in 1946) was a hero to the poor and impoverished underclass of Argentina. The left-wing circles in which Carlos found himself were excited by Perón's commitment to trade unions and industrial nationalization.

Veronica herself, now managing a travel agency, was often escorted to these meetings by her boyfriend Andrea, an Italian mathematician, physicist, and communist. (They later moved together to Milan.)[10] All of this ended at age nineteen when, with his father's permission, Carlos moved to Zurich.

"*Permission*," said Michael Gielen when I showed him the draft text of this passage, "is a euphemism."

Gielen, the distinguished German conductor, knew Carlos in this period. Gielen was the son of Berlin stage director Josef Gielen and a nephew of Eduard Steuermann. When the Nazis came to power, Josef Gielen knew what would happen next. His friend Erich Kleiber heard his plea and, through Erich Engel, in 1938 brought Gielen and family to Buenos Aires. To this day Michael Gielen credits Erich Kleiber for saving his family from the death camps.

He went on: "Erich *forced* Carlos to Zurich and chemistry."[11] There, for a semester and a half in the school year 1949–1950, Carlos studied at the Technische Hochschule.[12] It was an uneasy fit. He had a brilliant mind for learning but little heart in the process. Gielen told me that Kleiber was, in fact, little interested in chemistry, save between men and women. He spent most of his time pursuing *that* curriculum, and little else. If he recognized the name

Linus Pauling, it was probably by accident. Erich Kleiber was not pleased.[13] "Carlos did not study, but wasted his time. Erich finally said, 'An mis golles nicht liegen,'[14] and brought him home to Buenos Aires."[15] Increasingly, music was the allure.

At the end of the school year Carlos obeyed his father's instructions and returned home to Argentina. He might not be a Borodin after all.[16] Instead, he would study music. At his father's command he began work with Erwin Leuchter.

"Erich had heard that I had a good teacher for theory and harmony," Gielen recalled. This was understatement. Leuchter was one of the most important teachers on the southern continent.

From 1942 to 1949 Gielen had studied composition with Leuchter, a remarkable pedagogue, theorist, organizer, writer, conductor, and pianist. (Gielen also studied piano with Rita Kurzmann, Leuchter's wife, who died tragically young in 1942.) Leuchter's own classical education and early work was in Vienna, where he joined the Second School and befriended Schoenberg, Berg, and—most importantly—Anton Webern. Leuchter was particularly helpful to Webern in organizing the workers' symphony concerts in that city, and he served as Webern's assistant conductor. Like many Jews, and politically progressive people generally, Leuchter fled Vienna post-Anschluss. He landed in Buenos Aires, where he would make his home and build a large following the rest of his long life. Apart from teaching and conducting, Leuchter also served as principal music advisor to the publishing house of Ricordi Americana, today known as Melos.

Gielen, advised and mentored by Leuchter, took work as *repetiteur* at the Teatro Colón in 1947, and in 1949 he performed the complete piano works of Schoenberg. When later that year family friend Carlos Kleiber returned from Zurich, it was only natural that Gielen would send him to Leuchter. In fact, that is when Gielen and Carlos first met.

It turned out to be another poor fit. "Carlos went to Leuchter's lessons," Gielen said, "but his interest in piano and harmony was minimal. And he did not study anything else there either." He went on. "I don't believe that Carlos studied Analysis or Counterpoint. A little harmony. But he understood music very well, even without those studies."

A word about score study. Most people who love music but do not know its machinery are mystified by the phenomenon of reading score. In opera, the latter comes in three forms: piano-vocal, short score, and full score. Conductors acquire facility in all three, and there exists a fairly standardized way to gain it. Even conductors with perfect pitch are required to engage in this process. (Carlos did not have absolute pitch, but his relative pitch was speedy and reliable.) Here is the parallel: in the same way that one can read Barth's *Giles Goat-Boy* or Atwood's *The Year of the Flood* and hear the words without speaking them, so too can a conductor read Mozart Symphony No. 40, or *Peter Grimes*, or *Aux canyons des etoiles* and hear the notes without playing them. It is a learned discipline. Perhaps aided by Leuchter or his father, in his teens Carlos began learning how to read score. In time, he came to have a remarkable command. In the same way that he spent many, many hours reading poetry, novels, and histories, he spent thousands of solitary hours reading score. Never a great pianist, he nonetheless figured out how to read at an unusually high level. In this, he was essentially self-taught.

Carlos also began spending time at the Teatro Argentino de La Plata. In many ways this was a delightful place to learn. At least until the mid-1980s, La Plata was considered the quintessential Argentine college town. It still is, together with Córdoba and Rosario. As Carlos told me early in our correspondence, he never took a degree in music. Although many claims have been made that Carlos gained employment as co-repetiteur at La Plata (and later, Colón), no evidence from either opera house has ever been found to substantiate this. His older (by three years) friend Michael Gielen did work at the Colón, but Carlos did not. Gielen played the piano a good deal more ably than Carlos would ever manage. The best evidence is that Carlos was simply a frequent visitor, in the tradition of young musicians, listening and learning and watching. For this, there *is* evidence. It comes from two sources.

Mario Perusso, Argentina's second-oldest conductor still active, worked at the Colón for more than a half century, beginning in the children's chorus under Erich Kleiber, and eventually becoming its artistic director. He recalls seeing Carlos sitting in the Colón during his father's rehearsals, perched in the pit. Perusso never saw him conduct there.[17]

It was the same at the Teatro Argentino de La Plata.

Conductor and pianist Armando Di Giovambattista, director de estudios there, once had to ask Carlos to leave the house. The young Kleiber had sneaked in to watch rehearsals. Di Giovambattista told him, "You cannot be here, boy. Go away, or at least hide somewhere in the upper seats!" Decades later this maestro told Perusso: "That boy was the now famous Carlos Kleiber and I sent him away! Can you imagine that?"

Perusso, who was at one time also artistic director of Teatro Argentino, does not believe that Carlos conducted there either. "Maybe he managed to work as a repetiteur in one production or two, but that's it."[18]

In the 1995 DG liner notes for his compilation disc of Beethoven 5 and 7 with the Vienna Philharmonic,[19] it is said that "the young Carlos grew up in Argentina, studied music privately, and started work in the opera house in La Plata in 1952."[20] Given the degree of control and personal oversight exercised by Carlos in almost every endeavor, it is impossible that this text would have been published without his consent.

But what does it mean? The standard lore is that he made some sort of debut as conductor c. 1952 in South America. The theatre at La Plata burned down on 18 October 1977. Its archives were saved, but close study finds no reference to Carlos Kleiber *anywhere* in that house. It is possible he used a pseudonym, as he would later do in Potsdam. Examination of Argentina's main papers (*La Nación, Clarín, La Prensa*) finds no mention of Carlos until much later, when uncharitable reference is made to Carlos having "disowned" his Argentine citizenship in order to further his career in Europe.

In his exhaustive work, aided by Teatro Argentino de La Plata archivist Marcos Nápoli, examining every program, handbill, and press clipping, conductor-scholar Sebastiano De Filippi finds there is simply no evidence that Kleiber worked at La Plata *or* at the Colón. If he did—in any capacity—it may have been as repetiteur, something he would do upon his return to Europe.[21] He certainly did not conduct.

Similarly, no documentation is available to support the assertion that he conducted a radio orchestra in Montevideo. It should be noted that the dates don't work. When in 1949 Carlos was supposed to have been given "a few chances to work with the orchestra," at that time Erich continued to frown on his son's wish for a career in music. When in 1951 Carlos is said to have led "a little orchestra from the radio" in Montevideo, Erich was himself no longer working there in any capacity and, even if so inclined, would have few strings to pull.

It might also be added that, in 1951, Montevideo had a population of 1,114,000[22] and was a highly urbanized and "European" city. Back in 1935, Uruguay signed a radio treaty with Argentina, Bolivia, Brazil, Chile, and Paraguay. This ratified the founding in 1931 of their own radio orchestra, the Orquesta Sinfónica del SODRE, and arranged the orderly sharing of broadcast wavelengths.[23] This is the orchestra that Erich Kleiber often led, from c. 1941 to 1951. SODRE Archivist Augusto Techera confirms a complete lack of evidence that Carlos worked in any capacity with that radio orchestra, in any configuration.[24] The Orquesta Filarmónica de Montevideo (the city's symphony) was not founded until 1958.

It is impossible to prove a negative, of course, but his sister Veronica confirms that the story does not align.

> On the other hand, it was an interest that was not encouraged in the least by our father. Father said, "this one here evidently thinks that he has the road made, because he will walk on my path, but it will not be so." At a certain moment, father, in the final years of his life, helped him, accompanied him, gave him suggestions. At the end, yes, at the end he was

convinced and helped him. He told him about things and gave him "tips" about what could be done; but that was very, very close to the end.

—Veronica Kleiber, RAI 3 broadcast, 18 February 2008[25]

Carlos preferred murk. It may be the case that he volunteered in some capacity, that he "assisted" in some other, but none that he actually conducted *anywhere* in South America. His vagueness about his early days is likely insurmountable. When he moved to begin his career in Europe, he may have wished to suggest a greater depth of prior experience than he actually possessed. Padding one's resumé is not unknown in the world of conductors. And in that period, who would telephone La Plata for confirmation, or doubt the credentials of the son of Erich Kleiber? I myself conducted the Berlin Philharmonic when I was seven, but little evidence has survived.

Carlos left no trail that he ever chose to map or mark. In the citation that accompanied his 30 September 1990 appointment as a member of the German Order Pour le mérite for Arts and Sciences, it is declared that "Kleiber wuchs in Buenos Aires auf; er hatte in La Plata sein erstes Engagement."[26] The term "engagement" is certainly ambiguous and more likely to suggest activity as coach-pianist than as conductor.

Why is this important? *Because it is now clear that Carlos was almost wholly self-taught.*

As with his multiple languages and his vast command of literature and poetry, this was an auto-didact. As conductor he was his own creation.

But the city in which Carlos lived had a say in his musical development.

Buenos Aires[27] itself offered him an extraordinary cultural education within a city of teeming millions and rising global importance. It had been founded near the mouth of the Río de La Plata in 1536, as part of the Spanish Conquest. It was soon burned to the ground by natives unclear on the benefits of slavery and occupation. The city was permanently rebuilt in 1580 and in 1776 became the territorial capital. In 1816 Argentina seized independence from Spain, and the primacy of Buenos Aires as a center of commerce and politics was now well established. However, its residents felt alienated from the new nation and soon seceded from Argentina. Compromise followed, and nine years later Buenos Aires was formally declared the federal capital of the country, and the city of La Plata was built as the new provincial capital. Argentina was now the second-largest nation in Latin America.

Argentina in the nineteenth and early twentieth centuries pursued a policy of rapid expansion. Tremendous construction in its railway systems opened up the vast agricultural and ranching wealth of the pampas. An open-door immigration policy saw the arrival of millions of Europeans. By the time the Kleiber family moved to Argentina, 40 percent of that nation's population was of Italian descent and 32 percent was of Spanish descent. Basques and Irish flocked toward the sheep industry; Germans and Italians brought farming and opera; and large communities of French, British, East European, and Syrian peoples brought with them their own cultures and enterprise. The only Harrod's department store outside England opened at Buenos Aires in 1913. The only English-language daily newspaper in Latin America, the *Buenos Aires Herald*, has been published there for the last 130 years. And in many ways Buenos Aires became a kind of New York City. It welcomed many people and many cultures, and in consequence rose to a unique stature.

It has, for generations, been Argentina's principal port, its center of commerce, manufacturing, and industry—the financial and social heart of its many peoples. Roughly one-third of all Argentina's citizens live there. It has long enjoyed the presence of a strong and educated Jewish community. This is the largest such population in South America and dates from 1492 when its ancestors were, along with the Moors, expelled from Catholic Spain. By 1860 the first Jewish wedding was recorded in Buenos Aires. By 1920, there were more than 150,000 Jews in Argentina. The majority of them lived in the capital, where they also enjoyed a Yiddish press and theatre. (Oskar Schindler moved there after World War II. Jewish friends invited him to do so.) Other exiles included Polish chess grandmaster Miguel Najdorf, and writers Witold Gombrowicz and Ramón Gómez de la Serna. This truly international city was unlike any other on the southern continent.

Eugene O'Neill also knew its wonders. From 1910 he lived there in an inspired destitution. Fleeing Boston aboard a Norwegian bark, he landed in Buenos Aires and for the next two years took odd jobs at Swift Packing, Westinghouse, and the Singer Sewing Company. In between he also lived in drunken poverty on the beaches and in the deserted warehouses of its port area. Much great literature resulted. This city was also home to Jorge Luis Borges, Julio Cortázar, and Manuel Puig. Marcel Duchamp lived there for most of 1918. Antoine de Saint-Exupery lived there from 1928 to 1934, in the service of Compañía Aeropostal Argentina.

Buenos Aires also saw the birth of tango in the mid-nineteenth century and its export to the rest of the world within a generation. A unique and multinational music was being born. In Western terms, its roots dated from the first wave of postcolonial immigration.

The National Conservatory of Music was founded in 1880, and such composers as Alberto Williams flourished in every endeavor. In 1908, after eighteen years of troubled construction, the great Teatro Colón (named for Christopher Columbus) was opened in Buenos Aires. This seven-story Italianate opera house seats 2,487, enjoys miraculous acoustics, and from the beginning attracted such artists as Richard Strauss, Toscanini, Caruso, and Callas. It has long been one of the leading houses in the world.

Composers Mauricio Kagel, Juan Carlos Paz, and Mario Davidovsky were born in Buenos Aires and gained their early education there, particularly in the studio of Erwin Leuchter. The most important of all Argentine composers, Alberto Ginastera, was born and flourished in this environment, combining a love for nationalist impulse and framework with a European discipline and vocabulary. He was, for some time, head of the National Conservatory and designed much of its curriculum. In 1941 pianist Martha Argerich was born there, and a year later so was Daniel Barenboim. Some of Argentina's most important maestri have included Ettore (Héctor) Panizza, Carlos Félix Cillario, and Miguel Ángel Veltri, all first-class international opera conductors.

So too flourished the opera houses, orchestras, theatres, arenas, universities, conservatories, publishing houses, journals, and libraries of this great capital. And so flourished Carlos Kleiber.

In 1950 Buenos Aires was the eighth largest city in the world, with a metropolitan population of five million spread across an area of 1,408 square miles.[28] Its residents called themselves *porteños* in recognition of the "big harbor," but also to distinguish themselves from the people of the Province of Buenos Aires, who were pleased to be known as *bonaerenses*. Carlos was proudly porteño.

Only years later would it become clear just how much being raised in such a capital had influenced him. *Carlos Kleiber combined the rigors of German analysis, form, and discipline with the expressive vitality of Latin dance, pulse, and joy.* For nearly twenty years at the formative outset, a conductor baptized Karl gradually became Carlos. He never turned his back on that fascinating cultural biochemistry. It would shape everything he did.

One day a visitor arrived in town, and Carlos's conceptions of conducting were transformed forever.

In April and May of 1950 Wilhelm Furtwängler worked in Buenos Aires. He gave a set of nine concerts with the orchestra of the Teatro Colón. It was Carlos's first encounter with a conductor who operated in the same stratosphere as his father. Kleiber attended Furtwängler's rehearsals and avidly soaked up everything that maestro was doing.

Alas, the orchestra did not. Although fully professional and a very good orchestra under most batons, things did not go so well for Furtwängler. Rehearsals for Bach's *St. Matthew Passion*, for example, were held from 1:00 to 4:00 p.m., and 9:00 p.m. to midnight, day after day. Michael Gielen served as Furtwängler's assistant in the preparation of *St. Matthew*. It was exhausting for all concerned, and Furtwängler frequently got angry at their musical disabilities. "Furtwängler had problems because he treated them badly," Gielen said. "He was arrogant and certainly desperate about the destruction of Germany."[29]

Even so, Gielen and Kleiber were deeply impressed by the man from Berlin. Kleiber was in particular awe of Furtwängler's capacity to find and release the singing line. He saw and heard in Furtwängler one of the great exponents of unbroken *melos*, the underground river connecting every harmonic and melodic design above.

Kleiber was nineteen when Furtwängler appeared in Buenos Aires. He was open to everything that could be learned. During those weeks Carlos appears to have attended the rehearsals and performances of every work. He heard Furtwängler prepare and conduct Bach, Debussy and Haydn, Handel and Castro, Ugarte and Mahler, Brahms's Symphony No. 4, Richard Strauss's *Also Sprach Zarathustra* and *Till Eulenspiegel*, the Bartok Concerto for Orchestra, Beethoven, Schubert, Tchaikovsky, and, perhaps most impressively, Richard Wagner.[30] In particular, the Prelude and Liebestod from *Tristan und Isolde* was unlike anything he had ever encountered.

Gielen remembers Carlos, enchanted, describe a live recording of the *Ring* and "how the chords combine and melt into each other, and how Furtwängler achieves legato in the harmony." During his student days Kleiber was contoured as conductor by the formative experience of seeing Furtwängler at work for two months.[31] Thirty years later, Kleiber's own work would be reviewed in the same iridescent terms.

Buenos Aires also attracted the biggest names on the international circuit of solo artists. Carlos seems to have heard almost all of them. He once told me about seeing pianist Alfred Cortot in 1950 and marveling at his legato, wrong notes and all.

Such was Carlos's training and experience in South America. Once he returned to Europe, his name would rise to the first rank of conductors. This, however, took decades.

Carlos Kleiber stood slim and elegant, just over six feet tall.[32] He had blue and penetrating eyes, strong athletic skills, and was widely thought very handsome. He smoked cigarettes and drank whiskey. In the right mood he laughed a great deal. As earlier described he was baptized Catholic, although he was scarcely a conventional practitioner. He was fluent in English, French, German, Italian, Slovenian, and Spanish. He enjoyed wordplay in all of them.

Kleiber managed his career in very unusual ways. He traveled with no retinue, never hired a media agent or gave an interview, and generally recused himself from the politics of music. He may have known that Toscanini never gave an interview either. Carlos married the Slovenian ballet dancer Stanislava Brezovar, with whom he had two children, Marko and Lillian.

Although their marriage was tried by the usual difficulties, it lasted nearly forty-eight years.

In the last two decades of his life Kleiber worked rarely, and only when an exacting set of circumstances was met. He was likely the highest-paid guest conductor in the world and certainly the most sought after. At the height of his career he personally led all negotiations for concerts, films, recordings, and Audis.

His work requirements were considerable: for his first *Wozzeck* in Munich he took thirty-four rehearsals. For a Covent Garden *Bohème* he took seventeen, six of which were for orchestra alone. He was also known to appear, demanding virtually *no* rehearsal, if the repertoire interested and the ensemble pleased him. Kleiber was ambidextrous to a very high degree, able to show contrasting pulse at any moment. His rehearsal techniques relied on humor and intensity, matchless score knowledge and spontaneous inspiration, colorful verbal imagery, the use of "Kleibergrams" (little memos to players), closely marked parts, and an astoundingly clear baton. Wrote Harvey Sachs,

> He fights to realize every detail of a work and then fights still harder to obliterate all traces of constraint. . . . The intensely emotional elements in his music making usually function in perfect accord with his questioning intelligence and magnificent grasp of musical architecture.[33]

In later years all of his rehearsals were closed. In two 1989 letters to me, Kleiber made it jokingly but unequivocally clear how seriously he enforced this prohibition. Conductors gutsier than myself were known to sneak into them anyway, hiding behind railings and posts. The greatest of his colleagues saw that he worked at a level previously unknown in the trade. The esteemed conductor Bernard Haitink, surveilling Kleiber at Covent Garden during *Otello*, reportedly whispered to Simon Rattle, "I don't know about you, but I think my studies in this art have only just begun."[34]

Haitink and Kleiber were friends. Carlos's pal Isao Hirowatari remembered a particular gift. "He was on very good terms with Haitink. He must have loved the orange vinyl bag that Haitink presented him 20 years ago. Kleiber kept using it, even replacing its handle three times." Haitink, whom I interviewed in late 2004, recalled the bag as something he purchased at Harrod's, the London department store. When told that Kleiber still had it and kept replacing its handle, Haitink laughed out loud. "That's Carlos!"

This chapter provides an annotated chronology of his conducting career. It considers his profession's most important aspects and the vital artistic choices he made. It looks at the repertoire with which he was most famously associated and examines the signature flourished across it. It also describes some of his most important partnerships and the meaning they enjoyed in his professional life.

FABLES

Dealing with the work of Carlos Kleiber first requires disposing of mythology.

Common gossip has it that Carlos was the Howard Hughes of the music world, missing only the long hair, Mormons, and fingernails. This view is rubbish. He was intensely private, to be sure. He chose not to invest time in the serpentry of the business. He took pleasure in learning. He spent much of his career avoiding the egomania of celebrity. He served as music director of no opera house, nor of any symphony orchestra. When such offers came in, he declined or ignored them.

Some might imagine that, because Carlos did not waste time pursuing conventional success, he was cuckoo. But the same people marvel at the profundity of his score knowledge and deplore the superficiality of others in the same regard. Some even recognize that time he did not waste on self-promotion was largely spent on family, on a small but devoted circle of friends, and in mastering score.

Since his passing, a number of people have come forward to acknowledge that they enjoyed a friendship with Carlos, and over many years. While he was alive, respect for his privacy foreclosed virtually any public discussion of the fact. Stories arose that he had no contact with anyone. These rumors may now be discarded. It is certainly true that he went through periods of separation from some friends of long standing. Others better aware than I will have to explain all that.

Those who discovered Kleiber toward the end of his career may be surprised to learn how active was his baton and wide his public repertoire, early on. His ballet, concert, opera, and recordings include ninety-five separate works. (To be sure, other conductors have hundreds of works in their repertoires.)

Only toward the end did he restrict his activities as severely as legend now dictates. But rather like the stories of Fritz Reiner's imperceptible beat, their only truth applies to the last few years of his working life.[35] A comprehensive picture of Carlos's whole career will correct false and careless assertions and create framework to understand a career unlike that of any other conductor of his era.

There is another factor worth attention. Some guest conductors in opera don't arrive until the process is well along. (This may be more true in America than in Europe. Peter Jonas advises that most "arrive five or six weeks before first night" in any opera house worthy of the name.) An assistant will have prepared the orchestra, singers, and parts in advance. The conductor will meet with the directors, designers, and coaches, then the orchestra, the leads, and take the *Sitzprobe*[36] and dress rehearsal. This is a perfectly practical and ordinary way for star conductors (and singers) to work around the globe.

None of this applied to Carlos. He was known to arrive long ahead of time. According to Jonas, "Carlos sometimes would come even earlier than the first day of rehearsal."[37] He wanted to learn every aspect of the production, from costumes to seating in the pit to acoustics in the house. He would meet with every operating partner in the enterprise and look ceaselessly for ways to obtain a heightened unification of musical narrative and agenda across the whole production. Some directors found Carlos's involvement nightmarish. Until they got to know him, almost everyone found it surprising.

Those who wonder at the magnificent coherence of a Kleiber symphony or opera performance often ask how he did it. In reply, consider the exceptional detail and clarity of the marked parts he supplied to his players. Many of them had never seen anything like it and were astonished by the insight—and sheer industry—they revealed. Those who imagine that his repertoire base, seemingly sparse, implied laziness might ask how many other conductors worked as hard—and as thoroughly—as Carlos did in every angle of production. When these work habits and his unique investment of time in pre-production, scholarly research, and personal score study are made an element of the equation, it will be seen that for the first thirty years Carlos labored as hard as any member of his profession.

But Carlos sometimes found it difficult to collaborate with others operating on a similar plane of total immersion. Tenor Neil Shicoff is one of those people; he worked with Carlos on a *Traviata* at the Metropolitan Opera. It was a partnership never to be repeated. In an interview he gave in 2001, Shicoff accepted the proposition that "Carlos Kleiber once turned down doing an opera with you, giving the reason: 'One crazy person is enough.'" Shicoff replied genially enough: "Yes, but I wouldn't say Kleiber is crazy. He's the greatest conducting genius that I know. He's almost like an extraterrestrial who comes to earth and sees things in a completely new way. For me, he's Number One."[38]

There was an obsessive inquisitiveness about Kleiber. During phases of highest energy, *everything* was fascinating. This was certainly my experience with him, and several other friends have reported the same. One of them told of his remarkable new interest in harpsichords and clarinet reeds.

> . . . after every concert something had to happen to all that left over energy and emotion, besides drinking and smoking.
> My husband was a harpsichord builder. Carlos was fascinated. We spent almost 3 days discussing how to build a harpsichord (I worked in the shop). How do you do this? How do you do that? What kind of a tool was used? How do you plane soundboards, etc. . . . Drawing pictures, designing this and that. If he became interested in something it was a bit like dealing with some sort of intellectual sucking machine. No stone was left unturned and you couldn't get him off track.

On another occasion I happened to mention that before I learned the bassoon, I had been a clarinet player. The genius was so impressed. 'Really, so you play a single reed *and* a double reed'. Well, I explained that I didn't play the clarinet any longer. The embouchure was different and anyway I didn't care for the clarinet. This discussion went on for days. He wanted to know how much he could ask of a player, without killing them. I would have worded it a little differently but there you are.

I went on to explain that clarinets have what are called sub-tones which enable you to play *ppp* with little or no effort. Bassoons have to work very hard to play that softly and often one squeezes the reed and the pitch goes sharp. You would have thought that I'd given him the secret of life. Now he knew all of this from experience but he loved knowing it technically. I don't think he was putting me on. He seemed sincerely pleased. We went out and bought a clarinet reed and a cheap mouthpiece and I eventually made a bassoon reed and he spent a lot of time inspecting and trying and commenting.

—KD, e-mail to author, 10 November 2009

One more truth applies. It registers across a professional life lasting nearly half a century. Kleiber worked with an emotional intensity that would kill an ordinary man. In that precise regard, it killed any notion that he would pursue an ordinary career. No one who worked at his level of psychic involvement, or with his degree of musical intervention and facility, could possibly do so every day of the year. Over time, his efforts to conduct at those supra-human levels took a dread toll. Around the time he became world-famous he stopped working altogether.

In the last twenty years or so of his career Carlos wound things up in a typically mysterious way. Most conductors work to the end, perfectly happy to die on the podium. (*Pace* Sinopoli, Mitropoulos, Stoessel, Ermler, Merola, Kletzki, Konwitschny, Patanè, Keilberth, Viotti, Jordan, et al.) If ever they formally retire, conductors driven by ego seem to prefer commemorations and medals.

Carlos simply faded away. His life had become an atlas of compensations. People who learned his name only in that long sunset gained a misinformed awareness about the whole of his professional career. It was even more strange, tempered, troubled, and beautiful than legend holds.

HOW IT BEGAN

Ein Kleiber ist genug.

—Erich Kleiber, speaking to Carlos Kleiber, c. 1951[39]

We begin in 1952. As earlier described, in Buenos Aires and at La Plata, Carlos completed his "studies" in music. Later that year he immigrated to Germany, there to serve as volunteer repetiteur at the Theater am Gärtnerplatz in Munich.[40] He was twenty-two years old.

Remember dreadful times. The principal cities and industrial areas of Germany had been laid waste by Allied bombing and by the suicidal policies of the Third Reich. Returning to Germany just seven years after the end of World War II meant working in a nation ruined by Nazism, anti-Semitism, economic collapse, and widespread hunger. Carlos arrived just three years after the Soviet blockade of Berlin. And so it meant working in a nation split in two by the divisions of the communist and capitalist systems. Although Munich was safely within Western orbit, the city itself had seen the historical rise of the NSDAP (commonly known in English as the Nazi Party) and had been subject to special prosecution by occupying forces. Indeed, the whole of Bavaria was seen as bearing responsibility for Hitler. (That he was born in Austria and lived six years in Vienna is generally overlooked.)

From 1947 to 1952, in one of America's most astonishing acts of generosity—and political foresight—the Marshall Plan, was in full force. It gave $13.15 billion to the sixteen nations of the Organization for European Economic Cooperation.[41] Western Germany received $1.4 billion in grants and loans, France received $2.7 billion, and the United Kingdom $3.1 billion. This program (and the vision of Jean Monnet) helped lead over time to the 1951 Treaty of Paris, to the European Coal and Steel Community, and ultimately to the European Union we know today. The Marshall Plan was central to the rebuilding of whole nations and whole peoples. When Kleiber returned to live in Germany, having been away thirteen years since his family fled the Nazis, it was to a country struggling to rise from rubble. Culture was low on the agenda.

Munich itself was in desperate shape. Because of its tremendous industrial, publishing, transportation, and economic base, it too was flattened during the war. It is a large city, occupying about 120 square miles,[42] with a long history of art, music, commerce, and politics. Mostly Roman Catholic, the city began as a village market near a monastery founded c. 750. (The very name München suggests "House of the Monks.") In 1157, Henry the Lion, Duke of Bavaria, granted its first charter. For almost eight hundred years Munich had flourished. However, following World War II it was not to be wholly rebuilt until after 1960. While Carlos worked in Bavaria's capital, proofs of death and destruction were everywhere.

At Munich he chose a regional organization in which to learn his trade. The Gärtnerplatz was a house specializing in operetta. Originally founded in 1865, the theatre over time became a Bavarian center for light entertainment in music. By 1937 it bore the designation "Staatsoperette." It was reorganized after the war and gradually moved from operetta and ballet into a deeper involvement with opera. Its auditorium is a classical design, seating 893 in the orchestra, balcony, loges, and three further ranks of seats. While Kleiber worked at the Gärtnerplatz, that house gave the world premiere of Oscar Strauss's last operetta, *Bozena*, on 16 May 1952. The following year the Gärtnerplatz gave the first performance of Jean Cocteau's *La dame à la Licorne* on 9 May 1953. Kleiber was serving a rigorous apprenticeship in a system where heat was scarce, money was thin, costumes were tatters, but ambition was high. Much had to be made from little. Regardless of the fame of his father, Carlos was required to take on every menial job that came his way. The opportunity to watch rehearsals, study design, prepare choruses, and coach leads was his pay for the otherwise tireless work he donated as repetiteur to that company for two years. He survived on subsidies from his father.

On 12 February 1955 he made his conducting debut, posing as one "Karl Keller." In joking German, this suggests "Karl in the cellar." The initials are identical to Kleiber's birth name. He led Millöcker's *Gasparone* at Potsdam's Hans-Otto Theater. Erich sent him a telegram: "Good luck!" and signed it "The Old Keller." Local reviews noted, straight-faced, the presence at the podium of the "jugendlicher Gast Karl Keller," but otherwise said little about his work.[43]

Erich Kleiber died on 27 January 1956. For all the difficulty of their relationship, Carlos was devastated by the loss of his father. After briefly coaching (without fee) at the Vienna Volksoper, later that year he moved to the Deutsche Oper am Rhein in Düsseldorf. This would be his home and his graduate school in music for the next seven years. His work in Düsseldorf gave him a basic training in every aspect of opera coaching, production, score study, prompting, and leadership in the pit. It is the standard career path in Europe to move from pianist-repetiteur to assistant conductor, from there to staff and cover conductor, and finally to a solo career. It is a rigorous and practical training. Everyone starts at the bottom. So did Carlos.

The repetiteur is a member of the music staff of an opera house. It is the repetiteur's job to coach a singer in the repertoire being staged. This sounds easy. It is not. Several very well-known singers are functional illiterates who have to be taught every note. Others come with embalmed ideas that may run utterly contrary to those of the conductor. Great diplomacy is required. Repetiteurs generally have strong piano technique and superb language skills. Conductor Michael Gielen remembers that Carlos "was a very bad pianist. Every time we heard wrong notes coming out, it was Carlos. But he sang their parts, and he knew what to tell them, so it was all right in the end."[44]

Here, a word about Germany's unique system of hiring and promotion in its many opera houses. These artists are, effectively, employed by the state or the city. I am indebted to my friend and colleague William Lacey for advising, from experience, that the promotional track for staff conductors in Germany follows these rails: Solokorrepetitor (solo coach/accompanist); Korrepetitor mit Dirigierverpflichtung (coach with conducting duties); Dritter Kapellmeister (third conductor, today increasingly obsolete); Zweiter Kapellmeister (second conductor); Erster Kapellmeister (first conductor); Erster Kapellmeister und Stellvertretender Generalmusikdirektor (first conductor and deputy general music director); and, at the top of the system, the Generalmusikdirektor.[45]

Richard Trimborn was a colleague of Carlos in this period and remembered him very well. "He was not a good pianist, even though he had a good sense of rhythm, but quite a brilliant coach. His instinct for music was always sure and his imagination and intuition helped him to understand and interpret it accurately.

"He was very friendly, honest, direct and natural, already sharply sarcastic on occasion, but generally well liked and very hard working. He always studied not only the piano parts, but also the whole orchestral score very thoroughly . . . his perfectionism did sometimes cause friction. But never on a personal level. Any disagreements he had concerned factual, objective things which he considered an obstacle to the realization of a work."[46]

Carlos's gift for languages was deeply impressive. It permitted assignment to a much wider repertoire than most Italian-, French-, or German-only coaches would ever be granted. In Düsseldorf he learned and developed his basic rehearsal and coaching strategies. There, he mastered much of the canon, the core music in opera. And there he pursued a much wider repertoire than is today generally realized.

For example, in his seven years of apprenticeship, coaching and conducting at Düsseldorf he first led Verdi's *Traviata*, *Rigoletto*, *I Due Foscari*, and *Otello*. He conducted Puccini's *Madama Butterfly*, and *La Bohème*. He led Offenbach's *Les Contes d'Hoffmann*, *La Belle Hélène*, *Die Kleine Zauberflöte*, *Le Mariage aux Lanternes*, and *Lile de Tulipatan*. He first encountered the music of Richard Strauss, leading performances of *Daphne* and *Der Rosenkavalier*.

Such conventional works as Lehár's *Merry Widow*, Humperdinck's *Hansel und Gretel*, and Lorting's *Der Waffenschmied* were mixed with appearances in Stravinsky's *Oedipus Rex*, Werner Egk's *Der Revisor*, and Ravel's *L'Heure Espagnole*. Bringing up the rear was such lesser fare as Lorting's *Der Waffenschmied*, Leoncavallo's *Edipo re*, and *Der Bettelstudent* of Millöcker.

But during this formative period Kleiber's work was not restricted to opera. Ballet was a significant part of his training. These early experiences included Hans Werner Henze's *Ondine*, Delibes's rather more traditional *Coppélia'*, Egk's boldly rhythmic *Abraxas*, and three ballets by Ravel: *Boléro, Le Tombeau de Couperin*, and *Alborada del gracioso*. One particular dancer caught his eye. The well-regarded Slovenian artist Stanislava Brezovar danced the title role in *Tombeau*. She and Carlos often worked together and were finally married at Düsseldorf in December 1956.⁴⁷ She may be seen dancing at age eighteen in *Ples čarovnic* (Dance of the Witches). This was a 1955 Triglav Film production, presented in Slovenian as a ballet choreographed by Pia and Pino Mlakar to the tone poem *Ples čarovnic* of Blaž Arnič.⁴⁸

In the late 1950s, word about this young conductor was getting around. His father's name helped open doors. It never guaranteed a job. Only talent could do that. Wise managers were among the first to note his gifts. Among them was Walter Schäfer, intendant at Stuttgart. That house had become unusually important after the war. It was the *only* major opera house in Germany unscathed by bombing. Because of this it attracted singers, stage directors, designers, and conductors from across the nation, anxious for work. Schäfer heard about Kleiber through a letter from Walter Legge to Wieland Wagner. In consequence he invited Carlos to conduct a concert.

"It turned out to be complete failure because it never happened. A singer did not show up for rehearsal," Schäfer recalled in his 1975 memoirs. Kleiber sat at the piano, waited a while, and then said that he would now go back to Düsseldorf. Schäfer asked whether he needed money for the train ticket back. Carlos said no, he did not, and went home.

The Landestheater of Salzburg also invited Carlos to guest conduct and presented him in two productions in 1959. Both works were a personal debut. In February he gave his first *Bartered Bride*; in November, his first *La Bohème*.

In the same year he was approached by Decca, then a major recording company. Senior producer John Culshaw had an eye for exceptional talent. Across his distinguished career he worked with such artists as Monteux, Curzon, Britten, and Ashkenazy. Most famously, he recorded the first-ever *Ring* cycle, with Solti, Nilsson, and Windgassen. Culshaw's European colleagues were beginning to talk about a comet rising in the German-speaking world. In early 1959 he decided to approach Kleiber and ask him to sign with Decca. Culshaw may have been oblivious to Carlos's concern that Decca was, after all, Erich's label.

Culshaw arranged to meet him at the Frankfurt airport in March. They did so while changing planes. An offer was made. What twenty-nine-year-old conductor would turn down such an opportunity? Kleiber would.

Kleiber did. According to Culshaw,[49] Carlos "was vague." Nothing what-ever came of this initiative. Kleiber was profoundly unsure of his own talents and thought that such a contract would be hopelessly premature, unaccept-ably risky. He may have felt that no producer could do justice to the level of detail, insight, and rehearsal that he demanded. However, he would surely have loved Culshaw's own reputation for command of detail. In his *Ring* recordings, for example, Culshaw even commissioned building Stierhorns for Hagen. But none of that could overcome Carlos's self-doubt. He would not record for another fifteen years.

Kleiber took success in *La Bohème* to the Hamburg Staatsoper on 17 February 1960, but appears to have led it there on that date only. He first came to press attention on 7 December 1960 when he gave a concert under the auspices of "Podium der Jungen" in Hamburg. There, leading the NDR (Radio) Symphony Orchestra, he gave a studio concert that included Georg Philipp Telemann's *Suite aus der Tafelmusik*, three sets from de Falla's ballet *The Three-Cornered Hat*, Martinu's Concerto for Oboe and Small Orchestra, and the Cello Concerto in B Minor of C. P. E. Bach. He briefly shared the spotlight with cellist Irene Güdel and a twenty-one-year-old oboist, Heinz Holliger, but then stole it.

A review in the Hamburger *Abendblatte*[50] praised Carlos for a well-defined program of unusual content. "He made a sympathetic impression," the writer declared. "One could discern a loose and relaxed music-making, unobtru-sive, and manifestly pleasant leadership which achieves what it wants." The reviewer went on to speculate about what Kleiber could do with stronger orchestras and a stronger personal profile, but noted that "a radiant expres-siveness is already there." A pirate recording of the Telemann exists. The clarity of the Kleiber touch abounds, although it was in repertoire with which he was never again associated. The sound is not that of the early music ma-vens. It falls into the territory of standard pitch and luxuriant texture. But it works admirably.

The journalist must have been surprised that Carlos would not talk to him.

In 1964 he concluded his seven-year affiliation with Düsseldorf. It was time to move up and over to Zurich. The last time he worked in that city was fifteen years earlier, as a languishing student of chemistry and brilliant student of women. He now returned as an accomplished coach and rising con-ductor. He was thirty-four years old. In the two seasons that Carlos worked at the Zurich Opernhaus he moved into the role of staff conductor. In 1964 he gave twelve performances of Johann Strauss Jr.'s *Wiener Blut* (Vienna Blood), and six of Tchaikovsky's ballet *Dornroeschen* (Sleeping Beauty).

Much later Franz Willnauer recalled hearing Kleiber lead a performance of Tchaikovsky. It was an otherwise typical Saturday matinée. "I must be one of the very few people who has heard 'Swan Lake' conducted by Kleiber, and it was an experience I shall never forget! I walked out of the theatre in a state of total intoxication, wrapped in what seemed like the perfect Tchaikovsky perfume: soft, svelte, fragrant but not at all sentimental."[51]

In his second year at Zurich, Carlos gave another seven performances of *Vienna Blood*, and four more of *Sleeping Beauty*. On 4 March 1965 he made his debut in Verdi's masterpiece *Falstaff*. Willnauer heard *Falstaff* too. "To this day [it] remains the driest, wittiest, sharpest and juiciest Verdi I have ever heard!"[52] Kleiber was then assigned the company's first production of Hans Werner Henze's ballet *Ondine*, a work he had championed in Düsseldorf. He gave it eight times that year. Smetana's *Bartered Bride* followed on 3 September and would be conducted by him another seven times that season.

In between engagements at Zurich, Carlos was invited to lead his first *Die Fledermaus*. It was planned for seven performances at Geneva in 1965–1966. The invitation came from Dr. Herbert Graf. He served as director at the Zurich Opera from 1960 to 1962, and in 1965 he began an eight-year career in the same capacity at the Geneva Opera. This magnificent house was built in 1876, burned down eighty years later, and was restored in 1962. It seats fourteen hundred and enjoys a superb acoustic. Kleiber had been invited to a very good company.

Graf was another impresario who early spotted Kleiber's enormous talent. "Dr Graf was incredible," recalls stage director Lotfi Mansouri. "He found talent, and brought it out. Geneva was on the *stagione* system at the time, and Carlos and I were both hired on contract to do our first 'Fledermaus' together—in French. It was Dr Graf who really believed in him."[53] The newly acquainted pair of Mansouri and Kleiber spent little time actually discussing their production. When they met, it was in the canteen. Kleiber several times wrote me about *Fledermaus* and also remembered his debut in it.

PS: First time I did "The Bat" was in Geneva and in French. ("La Chauvre-Souris") Of course you know that the original play was a French one, "Le Reveillon". That's not important to know, however."

—*Carlos Kleiber, 8 December 1992*

Mansouri, who began life as a tenor and would go on to an important directing career in Europe, Canada, and the States, remembered the rehearsal process as very businesslike. "We had two and a half or three weeks rehearsal. I didn't know him at all at first. We never actually met to discuss the opera. We were so young. I was 35. We were all floundering, insecure, trying to make our reputations. Carlos and I never really discussed the opera. There was no meeting of the minds, but no arguments either."

The pit orchestra was superb: the Orchestre de la Suisse Romande, founded by no less than Ernest Ansermet in 1918. It was the finest orchestra Carlos had yet conducted, and he enjoyed it tremendously. His singers included Teresa Stich-Randall, Maurice Besançon, Jacques Doucet, Jules Bastin, and Eric Tappy.[54]

"It was harmonious, with a great sense of joy," Mansouri said. "I don't remember anything negative at all. I do remember that Carlos brought a love, an incredible sensitivity. He was *very* musical. There was one thing that will sound very strange. He was actually very shy, almost mousy. He would sit at the back and say nothing at all. I had no idea he would turn out to be such a star. No idea at all. The Carlos he became was not the Carlos I knew in Geneva."[55]

Carl Zeller's most popular operetta, *Der Vogelhändler* (The Bird Seller), was given to him in Zurich for November of 1965, and four performances resulted. From the beginning he had an affinity for operetta, never thinking it beneath him, but always determined to bring out the drama and power that so often lay within. A quarter century later I would discover for myself the power of his findings when he advised me on *Die Fledermaus*. He dug deeper than anyone else in this light repertoire and found riches there.

THE FIRST WALKOUT

In August 1966 Carlos left a production in the middle of its run, and while on tour overseas no less. It was the first time he had done such a thing. It was not the last. He ran a tremendous risk by making such a decision. No serious artist does so lightly. In time, unprofessional behavior and hostile attitudes have a way of catching up. (Phone The Met. Ask for Kathleen Battle.) Now in his mid-thirties, he was setting a standard for a whole career to come. Had he utterly mishandled the matter, that career might well have ended in Scotland. He survived because, as we shall see, his walkout was not without reason. The facts and implacable determination behind it would haunt and define his life.

But before this signal event, in his last season at the Zurich Opera, Carlos gave six more performances of *The Bird Seller*, another three each of *Vienna Blood* and *Bartered Bride*, and two of Verdi's *Don Carlos*. With the latter, on 19 May 1966, he closed out his staff career in Zurich.

He then moved up to the Stuttgart (Württemberg) Staatstheater where he took what may have been the greatest professional risk of his young career: Alban Berg's opera *Wozzeck*. Here came flooding in all the self-doubt, the living-in-the-shadow uncertainties. His father, who premiered the work, had died just ten years earlier. It was still very close to the moment. On 20 June 1966 the Stuttgart curtain opened on this bleak masterwork.

It was instantly clear that Kleiber was in total charge of the night. Not one note of this impossibly complex score escaped him, and his singers—and the critics—knew it. Further performances were given on 23 and 28 June, and again on 1 July. Six weeks later the company took the production on tour to the Edinburgh Festival. It was Kleiber's British debut, given at one of the world's most important musical events.

The first performance of *Wozzeck* attracted a tremendous amount of interest. Could Kleiber really be as good as rumor insisted? Presented at the King's Theatre on 27 August, this *Wozzeck* earned cloudcapping praise.[56] Carlos had let it be known that he was using his father's score, and everyone involved believed that they had heard Genesis.

The second Edinburgh performance was scheduled for 3 September. All 1,350 seats were sold out. The orchestra was in place, and tuned up at 8 p.m. Nothing happened. Twenty minutes later festival director Peter Diamand stepped before the curtain. The audience groaned. "I am very sorry to say that the conductor Carlos Kleiber has been taken ill. We have no alternative but to cancel this performance. We are very sorry indeed. This is indeed a tragedy. You will get your money back at the box office." No qualified substitute conductors were available. The festival reimbursed its audience, including Kleiber family members who had flown in from Switzerland and Austria, some £3,000.

Ferdinand Leitner, the company's principal conductor, said, "Never in 20 years of conducting operas have I known anything like this." He was decidedly unsympathetic to Carlos. "Even at my age, 54, with nine performances in 12 days, I would have been glad to take over, even on 40 minutes' notice, if only I had five or six hours to see how Mr Kleiber had rehearsed the opera."[57] The recriminations were just beginning. The audience included musicians from around the world and such British notables as Edward Heath, leader of Her Majesty's Loyal Opposition, a Californian who had traveled six thousand miles just for this performance, conductor Alexander Gibson, and every critic able to secure a ticket. It was the first such cancellation in the twenty-year history of the Edinburgh Festival. Its managers hinted to the press that Kleiber was hit by food poisoning.

Two days later, music critic Conrad Wilson received a letter. It was from Ruth Goodrich Kleiber, Carlos's mother. She declared that Carlos was in fact unhappy with Gunther Rennert's production, with the decision to cast a tenor, Gerhard Stolze, in the baritone title role, and with Stolze's insistence that the unsuitable Irmgard Seefried should be the soprano lead.[58] According to Wilson, the conductor had flown away that very afternoon, giving notice to no one. Whatever the cause, the consequence was irremediable. Carlos had lost faith in the integrity of the production. Regardless of overwhelming applause from the audience and splendid reviews from every critic, he would have no more to do with it.

It is now clear that production choices and pressures that Carlos could not resist in Stuttgart finally overwhelmed him in Edinburgh. It is correct that Franz Wozzeck is a baritone role. It was given to a tenor. His mistress Marie is written for a dramatic soprano but was given to a lyric soprano. Such choices redefined utterly the musical ambit of the opera. The production included such "gratuitous vulgarisms" as requiring Wozzeck to urinate for the doctor and such odd notions as portraying the doctor in a top hat. Menace became cartoon, and dramatic meaning was sacrificed to a visual joke. The era of "Regietheater," in which the stage director assumed supremacy, was dawning. For Carlos, this finally meant an intolerable revision of the musical content and dramatic significance of the work. At last he could go no further, and so he quit.

One first-night review, written by Wilson in *The Scotsman*, proved prescient. "The Stuttgart performance is a powerful emotional experience, for which much of the thanks must go to Carlos Kleiber, who draws sounds of eloquent, incisive, and wonderfully growing intensity from the Stuttgart orchestra, and who seems destined—if this performance is anything to go by—for a career as distinguished as his father's."[59]

Walking out set a pattern that would be repeated across his career. Public and critical approval meant almost nothing to him. If his own critical—and remorselessly self-critical—judgment was not satisfied, he simply would not proceed. He had no interest in building a career for the sake of celebrity and conventional success. And there was the issue of his health.

Feeling burned all-round, Carlos soon wrote a letter to declare his side. It did not make the same case made by his mother. Real illness was prompted by anxiety and dissatisfaction.

> I cancelled because I was ill. . . . Return to Stuttgart, followed by lengthy investigation of the 'affair'. The Theatre's solicitor was instructed by Schaefer and Co. to discredit me legally, so as to make my dismissal possible. But unexpectedly their lawyers' approximately 100-page 'opinion' hit the Württemberg [Stuttgart] Theatre between the eyes: the man stated that an artist who, even subjectively, does not consider himself fit enough to appear, had a right not to do so without fearing reprisals. When he cancels is irrelevant.
>
> This, for me golden, pamphlet had been hidden by the Theatre Mafia. For what would it lead to? So, as they couldn't dismiss me on legal grounds, grinding their teeth, they paid me further monthly salaries without giving me any work to do. This was supposed to soften me up and provoke me into resigning. It was the most beautiful time in my life: paid for doing

nothing and not giving a damn about the Theatre. This is the only truth of the matter. The behaviour of everybody, including Schäfer, Willnauer etc was indescribably horrid. The only Christians were the orchestral players and the children in the Wozzeck production, who stood by me. Those in charge were monstrous, as in all eternity, Amen.[60]

The Schaefer and Co. referred to Dr. Walter Erich Schäfer, intendant of the Württemburg State Theatre. It was he who first spotted Carlos's enormous talent and who lured him to Stuttgart. Kleiber had been offered a very high salary, the equivalent of that ordinarily paid to a music director. Schäfer and his assistant, Dr. Franz Willnauer, gave him the run of the house—a fact that annoyed and made envious other conductors in the organization. But regardless of their conflict over the Edinburgh *Wozzeck* and the embarrassment Carlos's cancellation caused the company, neither Schäfer nor Willnauer ever lost their respect for Kleiber's musical gifts. They never would.

Recalls Willnauer, "I don't think I have ever come across a conductor with a greater musical imagination. He represents the rebirth of the Mahlerian ideal, and has a composer's gift of visualising sound." Willnauer acknowledged the jealousy of others at the special treatment granted Kleiber. "I don't think that anybody had any idea of the thoroughness and time he devotes to his preparatory work. He always insisted on having the same orchestra from the first rehearsal to the last performance. . . . Kleiber's greatness, his genius, begins at the moment of performance, when all those carefully, analytically prepared results seem to happen spontaneously, as though improvised, and the music comes out alive and free."[61]

Walter Schäfer's memoirs, published nine years later, are instructive. Concerning the Edinburgh debacle, they take Carlos's side, regardless of the low opinion Kleiber had expressed of him. It turns out there was even more to the story. It favored Kleiber's cause.

Carlos Kleiber had not cancelled on such short notice as everybody believed. He had gone to the office in the morning, in order to tell them he was not feeling well and that they should start looking for a sub for the evening. On his way he ran into somebody (another member of our concert house) who was also on his way to the office and asked this person to tell them that. Kleiber felt a little dizzy. We never found out whether that person did not convey the message or whether people in the office did not take it seriously. Anyway, when the performance was supposed to start, Carlos Kleiber lay in bed and we had to cancel.

But there was more. Once again, it did not relate to the views on casting proffered by Carlos's mother in her letter nor to her son's unhappiness with that issue. It had to do with a traffic accident. Schäfer continued.

There is one more detail which we should take into consideration. It should give him credit. Right before the first performance of Wozzeck in Stuttgart, Kleiber had a car accident. One of the best Stuttgart surgeons had to sew the cut on his forehead with nine needles. Without saying a word Carlos conducted the opening night with those *nine needles* in his head. The surgeon later confirmed in writing that it was possible that his dizziness in Edinburgh was caused by this accident.[62]

Schäfer and Willnauer actually endured a good deal in this mess. They took Carlos's side much more strongly than he realized. It is why he didn't lose his job, even though two meetings in uproar were held by angry singers and members of the board. The foreign affairs ministry had to pay partial reimbursement to the Edinburgh Festival. On top of all this, Schäfer received some of the nastiest letters of his whole career. Evidently the worst of them was signed by twenty-two *Canadians*, and that is saying a good deal.

There is later film of Schäfer and Kleiber in conversation. Part of a 3sat (a public television network in Central Europe) documentary, in a 6:21 segment we also see Kleiber in three brief black-and-white clips conducting *Rosenkavalier*. While talking with Schäfer, Kleiber is well aware of the camera. They are getting along a good deal better than one might expect. The conducting clips are clearly taken from a kinescope and almost certainly from a pit camera monitoring his performances in Munich.[63]

Irrespective of bad feelings engendered by the problems at Edinburgh, there was no permanent breach. No one was in doubt about the rise of an exceptionally gifted young conductor. His assignments rose in the quality of artists assigned to him and in opportunity for extra rehearsal. He was soon appointed to the position of principal kapellmeister.[64] But for all of his success in Stuttgart, it was never a perfect union. There is a famous tale, one that comes from many sources. Many of the brass players in the Stuttgart pit had been there a long time, and in the late stage of their careers, "none of them had any lips left, and the story was that during a performance Kleiber suddenly shouted 'Scheiss Posaunen!' (shitty trombones!). The players committee then decided to demand an apology from him, except it had to be in the form of a telegram as Carlos had left town early the next day. He did indeed reply with his own telegram, which contained just two words—'Scheiss Posaunen!'"[65]

Kleiber led his first *Madama Butterfly* at the Stuttgart Staatstheater on 25 January 1967, and he would give another eight performances by the end of the year. Invitations to guest-conduct were now rolling in. But from the beginning, Carlos was choosy and cautious. He would only select repertoire in which he was supremely confident, to the extent his psyche ever allowed it. He would demand rehearsal time well beyond the norm. And, he would insist that the same singers and orchestra players be with him beginning to end, and no exceptions. This was to be an organizing principle across his entire career. With those conditions satisfied, he might guest conduct elsewhere. He soon accepted an engagement in Bavaria. Its capital city ultimately became his musical—and personal—home.

For his debut with the Munich Philharmonic Orchestra, made on 30 May 1967, he offered Haydn's Symphony No. 94, Schumann's Second Symphony, and (with pianist Richard Stein) Liszt's Piano Concerto No. 2. This was followed by his Viennese debut on 7 June 1967,[66] now with the Vienna Symphony Orchestra and under the sponsorship of the Vienna Festwochen. Here, he presented a program of Mozart's Symphony No. 33, and Mahler's *Das Lied von der Erde* with mezzo Christa Ludwig and tenor Waldemar Kmentt.

Although he learned most of Mahler's principal scores and often talked about them, this was the only occasion in his career Kleiber conducted any of his work. I once asked him about this, and he declared that "I don't love Mahler" and thought Mahler was surrounded by "daemonic ghosts."[67] Conductor Christian von Borries discussed the same with him and reached the same conclusion. So too did his friend KD, who reports that Carlos once compared the ghosts found in the music of *Der Freischütz* and Mahler.

"Carlos didn't like the desperation that he sensed in Mahler. The ghosts in Freischütz were healthy and open. Mahler's ghosts were bent and unnatural. There was an underlying darkness, even when Mahler thought he was being funny. Carlos made one exception. He thought Mahler's eighth symphony was about real love, and he liked it. It overrode his misgivings."[68]

An invaluable pirate recording of *Das Lied* has circulated for years and may be found on various ill-made CDs. I always thought that Kleiber found Mahler neurasthenic, a bit self-indulgent, overreliant on effect for its own magisterial or self-absorbed sake. If correct, this would account for Mahler's absence from Carlos's public repertoire. Those who imagine Carlos was incapable of stepping away from his father are confounded by the son's rejection of one of Erich's great heroes, personally and musically.

Even so, he took Mahler's obligations with the utmost seriousness. In late 1966, while preparing *Das Lied*, he paid a visit to conductor Otto Klemperer in Zurich. Klemperer knew Mahler personally and had conducted the offstage orchestra under his baton for the Second Symphony in 1905. He then studied score with Mahler, who honored him with the letter of recommendation that secured his first important appointment. (Kleiber would also have gone to Bruno Walter, who conducted the world premiere of *Das Lied* in 1911, but he had passed away five years earlier.)

Kleiber and Klemperer spent several hours together, investigating every corner of the score and its problems. In Peter Heyworth's splendid biography of Klemperer, he notes that "Klemperer was impressed by his visitor's musicianship, less sure of his character."[69] I recognize the latter comment. It comes from the late Lotte Klemperer, the conductor's daughter and faithful servant. We were friends. I enjoyed her California company as visitor for a week, and I know that she thought Kleiber a bit odd. The editorial opinion offered would have come from her twenty years after the fact and when she had fallen shy of total admiration for Kleiber. She thought him something of a slacker, although "very smart."

In fact, Lotte (a good friend of Veronica, Carlos's sister) once got into a small contretemps with him. It appears she took issue with something Carlos had done, now long forgotten. She almost certainly did not hold back, and it led to a typical reply. I don't know what she said, but here is how he answered. It is Carlos at his comic and semi-apologetic best, sent by him to her on a typed card, signed and dated 13 February 1985. Neither ever mentioned it to me.[70]

> Dear Lotte Klemperer! Excepting 'Material' and (perhaps) 'Wobble', you are quite right to dress me down for the irritable facetiousness and tactlessness I should keep (if at all) for people acquainted with my obnoxious sense of humour. Please accept my shame. Re 'Material' there is that saying about Jove and Bovi which explains everything quite clearly except to the musical fringe and to pretentious musicians. . . .[71] An old Klemperer-fan hereby wishes you all the best and stands abashed and rebuked as intended. Sincerely hoping you are well and happy, Yours, C. Kleiber.

On 23 July 1967, Carlos's mother Ruth died. According to biographer Alexander Werner, Kleiber told the conductor Matthias Aeschbacher that she died of a heart attack. The same book reports that Margarethe Schlee, a family friend associated with Universal Edition, felt that Carlos and Ruth had become deeply estranged and that she may have managed her own demise.[72] Carlos told his friends Lucia Popp and Peter Jonas, during an evening of some drink, that he had found the body at her home on Johannesgasse in Parsch, a suburb of Salzburg located on the side of the Gaisberg Mountain. He had not visited her for some while. Popp always believed that this alarming discovery did enduring psychic damage to Carlos.[73]

Kleiber spent most of the fall of 1967 perfecting his knowledge of a score that would years later lead to his first stunning success in recording. The work was Weber's cornerstone of German romantic opera, *Der Freischütz*. It is full of lyricism, dark foreboding, brilliant choral writing, and aural atmosphere, and it remains strange and rare to this day. Carlos poured every energy into the work. From this date, as the story is told, his artists first began to notice phenomenal gifts of verbal imagery. On 13 December 1967 the music world learned what Carlos could do with a score like that.

At the Stuttgart Staatstheater the ovations for *Freischütz* rang a long time. The experience would be repeated on Christmas Day and five more times in 1968, with uncertain thanks to stage director Walter Felsenstein. He and Kleiber quarreled throughout.

His relationship with the Bavarian State Opera began in early January 1968 with another masterpiece into which he had already vested many hundreds of hours of study, analysis, listening, and research.[74]

This was Richard Strauss's paean to Mozart, misplaced love, impossible triangles, and two notions of aging and departure. One in the person of Baron Ochs was absurd and selfish. The other, in the Marschallin, was all beauty and pain and touching withdrawal. There is much in *Rosenkavalier* that speaks about Carlos's own witness to rueful irony, unmanageable desire, and final remove when the contest can no longer be won. There would, of course, be nothing literal-minded about Carlos's identification with these events. But the process overall? He understood this particular kind of suffering, deeply. No less profoundly he understood the place of humor when covering retreat. In his hands the "Trio" sounded like "Holy Orders," rounded with a small smile. Across his career, Carlos would conduct *Der Rosenkavalier* 121 times. It was the last opera he ever conducted.

There exists a remarkable pirate DVD of *Rosenkavalier*. It is of the 23 March 1994 television broadcast with Felicity Lott (Marschallin), Anne Sofie von Otter (Octavian), Barbara Bonney (Sophie), and Kurt Moll (Ochs) with the Vienna State Opera and Chorus. It is unique for one reason: in Act III Kleiber is seen conducting throughout. His image occupies the bottom right quarter of the screen. In the prelude to this act he is also seen full-on. This film is a stunning revelation of the mechanics, the drive and inspiration, the podium leadership of Carlos in opera. He conducts entirely from memory. His eyes watch the singers 90 percent of the time. He rarely cues or mouths the text. His face is alert to every nuance, both in anticipation and reply. As we can now see, the tales of his magnetism, told over many years by many singers, appear to be true. Although not a prompter in the conventional sense, Carlos prepares, leads, and concludes every line at telling hand. Inevitably he makes little asides to his players, and their responses provoke quiet laughter from him. At one level, this is a document of the tradecraft and witchcraft of great conducting. As this pirate escapes into the public domain, it will become required study *ars maxima* at every conducting academy in the world.

You know, the "legendary" Rosenkavaliers of yore were the result of Rennert allowing a practically uninterrupted year-long series of the piece with a big rehearsal before each performance and with almost always the same blooming (they were *blooming, <u>then</u>!) cast. Thus we had "Roka"*[75] *the year over with longer or shorter pauses in between and the performances had a certain Selbstverständlichkeit.*[76]

Rennert let me do the same with Fledermaus, Wozzeck and Traviata. We were all very humble in them there days and no intent on making a splash or a smash.

—*Carlos Kleiber, to Peter Jonas, 12 January 1995*

Barbara Bonney tells a startling story of how Kleiber first hired her for the role of Sophie. She sang it with him in four different productions, at The Met, Vienna, Tokyo, and Munich. Bonney is a superlatively talented American lyric soprano who received her early training in Canada, and then with Walter Raninger at the Salzburg Mozarteum. She has sung at virtually every major house in the world, and under such conductors as Solti, Muti, Ozawa, Harnoncourt, and Abbado.

"The first time I met him was in Munich in 1984. The Staatsoper was looking for someone to replace Lucia Popp as 'Sophie' in Rosenkavalier for the Sommer Festspiele, and I guess they wanted a fresh face. I had never sung Sophie before, so I did my best to learn the 'Presentation of the Rose,' and went to Munich to audition. We ended up in the conductor's room on the souterrain, a tiny room with a rather brash piano," she recalled twenty-one years later.

> I sat there waiting for him. He came in alone, said hello, and promptly struck up a conversation with one of the cleaning ladies whose ankles were visible to us from the street. She was out having a cigarette on her break, and I guess she was one of his buddies. This was typical for Kleiber—he seemed to feel more comfortable with the average guy on the street. "Important" people always made him feel nervous. I was nervous, of course, so I took out a "Zuckerl," a bon-bon to combat the dry throat. I offered him one, and he was so pleased that he said, "Oh, you are a nice young lady. I think I'll give you the job." I hadn't sung a note! We did end up looking at the score a bit, and I sang a few phrases, and that was that.[77]

Bonney's first work with Kleiber was unorthodox in other regards.

> When it came to the summer Festival there were of course only two days of rehearsals, and my colleagues were Brigitte Fassbaender, Judith Beckmann, and Kurt Moll. Not bad company. I was the only one on stage who had never performed the opera before, so it was a bit of a leap of faith for me. And I must say, Kleiber carried me through as if I were on a silver tablet.
>
> I was pacing up and down in the wings before the beginning of Act II, and he came up to me and said, "Now, how fast do you think this should go?" His friendly little comment dispelled my nerves, and off we went.

(That was the night of a huge hail storm, which meant that we couldn't hear the orchestra, let alone each other nor ourselves for most of Act II, which was probably a good thing.) It all went by in a blur, literally—Kleiber conducted with such verve that one was swept along on his magic carpet of inspiration. One only saw those flashing teeth and his huge sweeping movements and we, the singers and orchestra, were thrown into his blender of musical genius, and came out of a performance not quite knowing how it all happened. It was always like that with him. It was glorious, and something I have never experienced with anyone else.

Three years after first appearing on the podium at the Munich opera, Kleiber gained a colleague worthy of his trust. This man, as much as any, is responsible for the fact that Carlos was able to work so often and so well in that house. In two decades Kleiber gave 260 concert and opera performances in Munich.[78] From 1971 to 1993 Wolfgang Sawallisch served as generalmusikdirektor of the Bavarian Staatsoper, and from 1982 to 1993 also served as its staatsoperndirektor. From this vantage he had unique knowledge of Carlos's work as guest conductor. And he had direct experience with Carlos's profound self-doubt.

Writing to me three months after Carlos's death, Sawallisch said,

In my eyes he was one of the most fascinating conductors of his time and I'm very proud that I was able, during my twenty years directorship of the great Bavarian State Opera in Munich, to convince him again and again to conduct much more opera and concert performances in Munich than anywhere else. These performances (Rosenkavalier, Otello, Traviata, Wozzeck, Fledermaus and and and) belong to the highest memories in my life.

The audience liked him immensely and gave him ovations over ovations before the beginning and even more before each new act. (I forgot Bohème with Pavarotti and Freni!)

You know, he was extremely shy, timid, and almost never convinced of himself. His feeling, not to be able to fulfill the expectations of the people outside was so extreme, that sometimes he was so hypersensible and nervous—he would not go on stage, although the light in the theatre was off.

Referring to a famous incident about which I had asked him, Sawallisch continued. "And it was not easy to convince him to go. And once (only once!) I gave him a little 'smack' on his shoulder to push him! I did it as a friend and colleague and after the brilliant performance—thanks to his conducting—he smiled and embraced me and was so happy due to the success. That's all I can say to this 'story'—no more. But certainly I did not 'save the performance.'"[79]

It was a busy new year at the first of 1968. On 6 January he gave another *Der Freischütz* in Stuttgart, a week later in Munich *Der Rosenkavalier*, and four days after that *La Bohème*—once again in Stuttgart. It was another success and would be on the boards seven more times that year.

He revived Stuttgart's *Madama Butterfly* in April, two days after making his personal debut in another score with which he would long be identified. It too would, in time, lead to a recording that earned tremendous acclaim and a permanent place in the catalogue. This was Verdi's *La Traviata*. He gave it in Munich's Nationaltheater on 25 April 1968.[80] By every account, every member of the company rose to the occasion, and Carlos's own star ascended in turn. Meantime, a historical hour and a gesture of solidarity now materialized.

The Prague Spring Festival had, in 1968, a powerful political connotation. The Velvet Revolution was well under way in Czechoslovakia. Under the extraordinary leadership of Alexander Dubček, old freedoms were being restored and new freedoms discovered. It was a deeply promising moment, and Carlos admired the possibilities. His own political sympathies were very much with Dubček and the reformers.[81] On 25 May 1968, together with the Prague Symphony Orchestra, he offered Dvořák's *Carnival Overture* and Beethoven's Symphony No. 7. Together with the rising young pianist Christoph Eschenbach he gave his only performance of the Schumann Piano Concerto.

He spent the summer preparing another signature work, Bizet's *Carmen*. In a personal debut at the Stuttgart Staatsoper, he offered it for the first time on 13 October 1968.[82]

As with many conductors his age (he was now thirty-eight), this was a period of rapid growth and highly disciplined study. Perhaps paradoxically, he mastered dozens of scores he would never conduct—but that was beside the point. He conducted *all* of them internally. Over decades, virtually every professional colleague observed that Carlos simply heard better than any of them—internally or externally made no difference. And besides, no audience and no critic could be tougher on Kleiber than Kleiber. Perhaps it was best to keep all of that indoors.

Yet another of his most famous works arose at this time: Verdi's *Otello*. He first gave it with the Bavarian State Opera on 30 November 1968 and would keep it with him the rest of his life.[83] Following a typical pattern it met a tremendous ovation, the warmest critical response, and a widening awareness that "young Kleiber" was becoming an old master. His success was repeated on 7 December and four more times the following season. (He would also conduct the same work three times in the same season at Stuttgart.)

In the summer he revived *Rosenkavalier* in Munich, giving it once each in June, July, and August. But his real work lay elsewhere, and in another masterwork new to him. Like *Wozzeck* before, the process left him riddled with self-doubt and artistic uncertainty.

He spent the first six months of 1969 in the most probing study of any score yet. He well knew the challenges and the risks. He had been offered Wagner's *Tristan und Isolde* in Stuttgart, and accepted. Kleiber's perfectionism moved to its highest levels, as did his devotion to the rehearsal process. He spent untold hours studying the manuscripts, coaching the singers, preparing the orchestral parts, and conjuring this music's mysteries. As with just a handful of other works first encountered in the previous three years, *Tristan* would become one of his few (and most important) recordings. It would become one of the ways we understand his genius.

At the Stuttgart Staatstheater on 13 September 1969 he strode into the pit and the curtain was raised on *Tristan and Isolde*.[84] Every resource had been offered, and every artistic insight argued. By the end of the evening Carlos had become a Wagnerian, and everyone in the audience knew it. This was a most moving departure from anything he had done before, and it provoked a great deal of attention. The opera would be given again on 4 October that year, with similar results. The rest of the year included two more performances of *Rosenkavalier* in Munich, and four more of *Otello* in the same house. *Otello* would be repeated, for Stuttgart, twice more.

As 1969 closed and the new decade began, Kleiber knew that he had moved into the ranks of conductors whose gifts could not be denied. In the next ten years would come virtually all of the repertoire with which he would be identified in his career and opportunities to perform it with some of the most important artists and orchestras of his time.

MOVING AHEAD

Carlos opened 1970 with *Tristan* on 18 January in Stuttgart, and a revival of *Bohème* in the same theatre on 12 April. But as with *Tristan* the year before, he was now spending the greatest part of his time mastering repertoire new to him. This meant examining in person the manuscripts and comparing them to the full scores. He was not only looking for mistakes. He was trying to find personality, those aspects of the score that—seen in the composer's original hand—represent struggle or ease, reconsideration or first bloom. For serious conductors this is vital, instructive information.

He was also looking for anomalies, those errors or inconsistencies between the manuscript and the full score, and between that score and the players' printed parts. There are many opportunities for error and misjudgment in such a complicated process, and he was determined to erase all of them. He followed such scholarly practices across his whole career.

Carlos now gave his first performance of a singular Beethoven. It would—above all others—make his international reputation on the concert stage: the mighty Fifth. He had been invited to conduct the Bavarian State (Opera) Orchestra in the sixth Academy Concert at the Deutsches Museum in Munich. On 13 April 1970 he offered his own first performances of Beethoven's Overture to Coriolanus and Symphony No. 5. He also worked with pianist Alfred Brendel. Together they played Beethoven Piano Concerto No. 4. To no one's surprise, this all-Beethoven concert was a dazzling success.

Years later, Brendel remembered Carlos with a fond curiosity. "What is astonishing for a man who does so little conducting is that every technical matter is in place. There is no problem with the beat, with adjusting every little matter of balance and detail. He's amazing, as if a pianist did not practise for months but was still able to play perfectly."

Brendel added a caveat that may account for the fact that Carlos gave very few performances in concerto across his whole career. It must have been very hard for the soloist. "We did Beethoven's Fourth concerto, and six months before he telephoned me with his phone on the piano and said, 'I've just listened to 24 records of the concerto and I think this detail should go like this,' and played the piano. He had very definite ideas . . . in the end the performance was good, I think, because we met halfway. But I wondered whether I should spend my life accompanying conductors."[85]

Among the recordings of Beethoven's Fourth highly recommended to Brendel was that of Walter Gieseking. "He asked me, 'What does dolce mean in Beethoven?' He was not joking. 'Innig, innig', I replied, 'an inward tenderness.' I never heard him conduct dolce. I think his question was in earnest. He really wanted to know."[86]

"Carlos was sometimes very difficult to work with, but could be enormously charming. The technical talent and technical perfection was so staggering that no one could get near it. He could suggest colors, character, everything. The moment was made by his conducting. Sometimes, though, the virtuosity enjoyed itself," Brendel added. "I saw his 'Otello' in Tokyo. It was very kitsch. I don't know why he worked with Zeffirelli so often."

Brendel went on to describe Kleiber's unique standing. "It was hard for mortals to understand his super-human facility, especially when he seemed to be doing so little. He could do virtually anything. He did not make use of his talents in the way that a great conductor should.

"He was a *most* extraordinary conductor, but not great in the ways of other great conductors. This was the price to be paid by someone who had complete awareness of detail—and who knew how to get every detail. He was the most gifted conductor of his generation. His ability was enormous, without limit." Brendel added that Kleiber had known his second wife Irena three decades earlier, in Buenos Aires, and attended their wedding in Munich.

Kleiber generally avoided performing concerti. He had a tremendous respect for the greatest solo artists, but kept his distance. When they were personal friends he would not perform with them at all. In conversation with Isao Hirowatari, he commented that he liked pianist Maurizio Pollini. "When I asked Kleiber, 'Why not perform with him?' he gently declined the idea saying, 'Hiro, as you know I do not have many friends. Regarding Pollini I want our friendship to take precedence over joint performance.'"[87]

Carlos alternated between *Otello* in Stuttgart, and *Rosenkavalier* in Munich, for the rest of the summer of 1970. Repeating a pattern that he was now adopting in all his work, Carlos again sequestered several months in order to relearn a work of exceptional demand. With a new team of artists[88] in a different house, the Bavarian Staatsoper, and with previous problems overcome, he revived Berg's *Wozzeck*. It went up on 27 November 1970 and would be repeated on the 7th and 28th of December. Critical and public response was extremely gratifying. This production was directed by Gunther Rennert. Carlos would conduct it fourteen times.

The German state has long maintained a superb system of radio orchestras. Many important artists have served there, including Scherchen, Schuricht, and Rosbaud, to say nothing of Schmidt-Isserstedt, Bour, Celibidache, Jochum, Fricsay, Rafael Kubelik, Dixon, Maazel, Wand, and Chailly. They provide apprenticeship for rising conductors and other young artists. Many European composers were first exposed to a European audience in that system. New music has always been a shining coin of the Rundfunk (a German public-broadcasting institution) realm.

Because of one such radio orchestra, the year 1970 is exceptionally important in Carlos's career. He led two rehearsals and two concerts with the Süddeutscher Rundfunk Orchester (Stuttgart Radio Symphony Orchestra) at the Villa Berg. In the first of them[89] he prepared and performed the Overture to Weber's *Der Freischütz*. In the second[90] he did the same with the Overture to Johann Strauss Jr.'s *Die Fledermaus*. What is supremely instructive about these events is that they were televised. They are the only known—and available—films of Kleiber in rehearsal.

In each of them we see how he leads, cajoles, sings the text and addresses its personality, adjusts balance, clarifies rhythm, illustrates everything with metaphor and apostrophe, makes jokes, attends to detail and structure, never yields, and transforms the work utterly. At the beginning, an orchestra of bored civil servants visibly resents Kleiber's demands. In the words of

Maurizio Pollini, "The orchestra looks at him completely stupefied . . . like a man who came from the moon."[91] At the end they play with total commitment, as if present at the work's creation. These most moving images are indispensable for anyone wishing to understand the Kleiber phenomenon.[92]

Carlos found working with them painful and exhausting. It is clear on his face. He later talked openly about their resentment and disdain of him. "I never worked so hard in my life to get players to understand me," he told his friend KD. Although he eventually succeeded, the energy he expended in order to do so helped drive him from the very idea of a permanent appointment. No one should have to work so hard to ask musicians to be musicians.[93]

In 1971 he gave *Wozzeck* another ten times. It was widely noted that he appeared to be conducting the score from memory, though it was physically in front of him the whole time. Such was the success of this revival that Alban Berg's widow presented Carlos with her husband's coat and ring.[94] Helene Berg was notoriously (or admirably) protective of her husband's work and reputation. Such a gesture meant a great deal to all concerned, and Carlos was moved by her kindness. Her gifts may have induced the rumor that Alban Berg was Carlos's biological father. This claim is based on a facial and phenotypical similarity between Carlos and Alban, and rather less between Carlos and Erich. It also derives from Berg's well-known womanizing—regardless of what that might imply about Ruth Goodrich Kleiber. Many distinguished musicians firmly believe it. On the day Carlos's death was announced, a principal Dutch cultural service blithely declared, "His real father was, reportedly, Alban Berg. His mother had an affair with the famous composer, as a result of which she became pregnant."[95] As usual, no facts were offered.

Similarly runs another story, endorsed by photographs. A different circle of musicians, including Sir Charles and Lady Judy Mackerras, believes that Zdenka Podhajská, the Czech dancer and another member of the Erich Kleiber circle, was Carlos's biological mother. I never discussed the matter with Carlos. Mlle Podhajská is buried in the Kleiber family tomb at Vienna's Zentralfriedhof. Her 1991 funeral and interment was attended by Charles and Judy Mackerras, and by Jessye Norman.

Kleiber would also give *Otello* and *Madama Butterfly* again that season, but his mind was already elsewhere.

Stuttgart invited him to lead a production of Richard Strauss's fiercely demanding one-act opera *Elektra*, drawn by Hofmannsthal from the Greek myths and tragic dramas of Aeschylus, Euripides, and Sophocles. Together with *Salome* it represented Strauss at his most revolutionary, most independent, and least overtly appealing. Matricide is not often considered a sweet subject for opera, but Carlos reveled in its hectic demands. As usual for him, he spent multiple hours inspecting the manuscript, correcting errors, and marking parts according to his own designs.

Joined by Steger, Möll, Lippert, Wildermann, Windgassen, Bertram, Unger, Kosso, and Merkl-Freivogel, he opened *Elektra* on 13 May 1971 and presented it three more times that season. Even though it was another critical success, Carlos returned to it only once in his career, six years later.[96]

Even Kleiber went to a teacher in order to master this difficult work.

> When he wanted to do "Elektra" by Richard Strauss, Carlos Kleiber wanted Herbert von Karajan to explain it to him. Herbert von Karajan told us that Carlos Kleiber arrived and remained for four hours. Karajan said that he had never learned so much in four hours as he did in those four hours with Carlos Kleiber, because he had taught him the entire score.
>
> —Dieter Flury, first flute, Vienna Philharmonic,
> RAI Radio 3, 20 February 2008[97]

Kleiber always had strong views about *Elektra*'s presentation, its core narrative, and its incompetent stage directors, framed as ever by a joke. Many years later, he saw a production he loathed.

> *To have ELEKTRA*
> *kill herself is*
> *as idiotic as*
> *having PENTHESILEA[98]*
> *(Kleist's) stab*
> *herself with a*
> *real dagger!*
> *For missing the*
> *point of the piece*
> *so precisely, Mr. W.[99]*
> *shall roast in hell.*
> *I hope!! (Hugo, hilf!)[100]*
> *Your old Charlie*
>
> ⟶ *(I left a margin for error!)*
>
> —*Carlos Kleiber, to Peter Jonas, 29 October 1997*

Back in 1971 Carlos wrote a letter to Wolfgang Wagner, grandson of Richard, and the intendant of the annual Bayreuth Festival. Carlos was looking ahead and thinking of *Tristan*. "I should esteem it an honour and a pleasure to kibitz during rehearsals at Bayreuth and also, perhaps, to sit in the orchestra pit (my father trained me to sit *still!*), thereby becoming somewhat more prepared for the possibility of an intimidating personal appearance some day."[101] Wagner sent a charming reply, one that would soon lead to Carlos's engagement there.

Asking to sit with the players was another sign of Kleiber's thoroughness of preparation. He was well aware that the Bayreuth pit, uniquely covered and projecting sound onto the stage, is a notoriously difficult place from which to hear. Wagner's famous "mystic abyss" is, for conductors, an acoustic sinkhole making it exceptionally difficult to hear the singers at all. It can also be impossibly hot, and Carlos was covering all his bases long in advance. He wanted to learn, and remedy, everything he might be up against.

The Bavarian State Opera now offered Carlos a new production of *Rosenkavalier*. He gladly accepted. It was directed by Otto Schenk. Carlos would lead it eighty-six times in Munich. This was the first time he worked with an artist who would, for the rest of her tragically abbreviated life, become a very important friend: Lucia Popp.

This luminous soprano (née Poppová) was a special force in Carlos's artistic and personal world. She was born in 1939 in Záhorská Ves, Czechoslovakia, and trained in Bratislava and Prague. Her remarkably pure voice, matchless intonation, and superb taste led to rapid promotion in the world of art music. She joined the Vienna Staatsoper in 1963 and was soon asked to perform at the Salzburg Festivals. Popp was heard by Klemperer, who immediately cast her as Queen of the Night in his famous recording of *Magic Flute* in 1964. Two years later she made her first appearance at Covent Garden. Her debut as Queen of the Night followed at The Met in 1967, and in the 1970s she became an integral part of Jean-Pierre Ponnelle's Mozart cycle in Cologne.

Meantime her voice was moving from the coloratura to lyric, and her career was being—quite deliberately—slowed. One of the things Carlos so admired about Lucia Popp was the decision she took in the 1970s to get off the escalator. She chose to work primarily in Cologne and to take time to probe and command a role. She would not be driven by mercantilism. Popp's integrity demanded focus on a role until it was a complete musical possession. Although her repertoire was, over the three decades of her career, very broad, her ambition was exquisitely focused—one role at a time, wholly absorbed. Once absorbed? Her faultless technique made anything possible. In 1983 she gave an all-Mozart recital. She sang the Countess, Susanna, *and* Cherubino![102] This was an astonishing feat, made possible by her years of devoted study and preparation. It can be no wonder that Carlos thought the world of her.[103]

Their first project together, in *Rosenkavalier*, debuted at Munich's Nationaltheater on 20 April 1972.[104] They would work together seven more times

that season. It is an open "secret" that Popp and Carlos were especially close
for some while, she leaving her first husband to be with him. This relationship
began in the early 1970s and at its peak lasted about six months. They were,
of course, never married. Their mutual intensity led to extraordinary music
but a somewhat less successful friendship. Even so, when she died at fifty-
four, of brain cancer, Carlos was broken by the news.

Mezzo Brigitte Fassbaender often sang for Carlos and had a very direct appreciation of the man and his methods. "He is almost in a trance, so absorbed
in recreating the work that it's as if he were performing it himself and we're
just there to help make the noises for him."[105]

Around this period Kleiber was first approached to give a concerto with
the extraordinary Italian pianist Arturo Benedetti Michelangeli. Details of
that event, which took place in April of 1973, follow below. However, prior
to that time Kleiber did something amazing. He wrote a letter to the editor of
Germany's most important daily newspaper. He did so to defend Michelangeli.

In early May of 1972 Michelangeli had been scheduled to give recitals in
Hamburg, Munich, and Frankfurt. He played the first two but canceled the
third. In Frankfurt, he was evidently dissatisfied with the quality of the pianos
offered him. (He usually traveled with his own.) As reported in the *Frankfurter Allgemeine Zeitung*, Germany's leading daily,[106] Michelangeli had said
"I don't feel like it" when asked to account for the cancellation. His blunt
language made no friends.

The FAZ published an opinion piece on 15 May 1972, signed "HL" and
headed "Irritating." It was highly critical of Michelangeli's decision to cancel. It highlighted the annoyance of the concert promoter. On the 20th, Carlos
came to the defense of his colleague. His arguments are similar to those he
used in 1966 to justify his own withdrawal from *Wozzeck* at the Edinburgh
Festival. They are, at heart, the credo of Miles Davis: "An artist's first duty
is to himself."

Dear Editor:

*According to your column, "Irritating" (in 'Feuilleton' May 15, 1972), the enraged
promoter of three Michelangeli concerts did end up getting two of them. Fair play
(English is my native tongue) cannot be the end of the question. Mister or Mistress
"HL" is of necessity a daylight-ghost (like every newspaper) and understands colloquial speech.*

*What does "the purpose of contracts" mean (were there any at all?), and what
does "at the cost of other people's reputations" mean? Did the promoter by any
chance have his reputation fractured?*

*Would "HL" perform a piano recital, even if he/she was in bad shape, just in
order not to damage some kind of reputation, even if it was his/her own? Please:*

briefly close your eyes and think this through. And? Basically, all of these things (says Doderer) are just mean things to say. Now that is irritating.[107]

—*Carlos Kleiber, Conductor, Musberg*[108]

This letter was startling because Kleiber maintained a lifelong distance from the press, much to the dismay of writers, editors, and publishers everywhere. I know of one exception only: Christine Lemke-Matwey, a music journalist and critic based in Berlin.

P.S.: I ADORE Christine Lemke-Matwey (spelling?) for puncturing so many balloons especially the hot-air ones of YL-the-ape and Everding-the-emetic! If called upon, I will defend with my life her right not to be a bore like WS or an idiot like the TZ and AZ-"girls"! (And boy don't tell her I love her or she'll savage me very likely if I ever creep onto a Pult[109] again. That's the way . . .)

—*Carlos Kleiber, to Peter Jonas, 19 February 1997*

P.S. How careless of the SZ to let perennially unindoctrinated Christine L-M cover dear Gunga Din's "Traviata"!! Must we really know that (apart from musical stuff) ". . . for all 'is dirty' ide / 'E was white, clear white, OUTside . . ."[110] at the end? "INside" will do very nicely, thank you!

—*Carlos Kleiber, to Peter Jonas, 13 July 1998*

There are four instances when he chose to communicate not with but through the media. Three more would follow his letter defending Michelangeli. If the subject was the right of an artist to control final choice, Carlos would find a way to speak.

The Radio Symphony Orchestra of Cologne invited Carlos to appear with them on 27 May 1972. He gave Haydn Symphony No. 94, Beethoven 7, and "Three Pieces for Voice and Orchestra" from Berg's *Wozzeck*. It is instructive to listen to these performances, so to judge their further evolution as his career proceeded.[111] He was beginning to perfect a genius for total technical command married to spontaneous departure from it.

He performed in Switzerland that summer with the Berne Symphony Orchestra. Together with Windgassen, Crass, and Bjoner he presented Act II of Wagner's *Tristan und Isolde*.[112] There is some reason to believe it was not a wholly happy occasion. (It was never repeated.) The rest of the year would be taken up by further performances of *Otello*, *Rosenkavalier*, and *Wozzeck*.

Kleiber now made a semiofficial recording of Borodin Symphony No. 2 with the Stuttgart Radio Symphony Orchestra, broadcast on 12 December 1972. (It exists in audio only. He no longer permitted filming of his rehearsals there, or anywhere.) It is an unexpectedly dramatic reading of the work, invested with a raw and inexorable power rarely heard outside Russia itself. It is not believed that he had access to the manuscript, but you'd never know it.

The following year, 1973, would be marked by a significant expansion of his artistic prospects. He was offered the musical directorship of an important German opera house. He would make his first commercial recording. And Vienna would call, from its highest plateau.

New Year's Day opened in Munich with a revival of the *Rosenkavalier* he had so enjoyed with Lucia Popp, and was repeated on the first of March.

Overcoming a deep-seated inhibition, Carlos now entered a commercial studio. It was in order to record Weber's *Der Freischütz*. His singers included Bernd Weikl, Siegfried Vogel, Gundula Janowitz, Edith Mathis, Theo Adam, Peter Schreier, and Franz Crass. He was joined by the Staatskapelle Dresden and the chorus of the Leipzig Radio organization. Recording sessions were held at Dresden's Lukaskirche from 22 January to 6 February 1973. Many critics were—and remain—of the opinion that this is the most vital recording ever made of the work that, at ground, foreshadowed the whole of nineteenth-century German opera. Kleiber always considered himself a kind of authenticist, going back in every instance to the manuscript and first sources.[113] His *Freischütz* was no exception.

As usual, he declined to participate in marketing. His first recording would have to succeed on its own merits or not at all. But in a note to Dorothee Koehler in the PR department at Deutsche Grammophon (DG), dated 5 September 1973, he enjoined her to tell anyone interested that "It would of course be good if people know re Freischütz that my use of legato and staccato (and non legato) AS WELL AS PIZZICATO (plucked) AND ARCO (bowed)!—strictly follows the score, and that also goes for the text, phrasing and dynamics."[114] He continued with a caveat.

"The only exception: I've had the 'UHUI's[115] in the Wolf's Glen (don't tell) sliding upward [from the single notated pitch] because Weber himself once (very vaguely) indicated that, and because the spirits are <u>so</u> looking forward to Agathe's blood! (Should be!)"[116]

Carlos might have mentioned other special touches applied throughout the whole of this recording. Soprano Gundula Janowitz took the role of Agathe and sang its Cavatine with a matchless purity. Examine a score and see what Carlos asked her to do at its measure 25 and its *subito pianissimo*. The effect does not appear in the vocal score but on the downbeat is made to appear in the vocal line at the tied dotted-quarter, on the A-flat. Astonishing. No less fervent, but driven by the usual high-voltage wiring that so compelled him, was Carlos's treatment of the French horns and the hyper-articulate men's chorus in the brilliant "Jägerchor" of Act II, Scene VI. I have not yet had the opportunity to conduct *Freischütz*, but if ever granted, I would steal this reading without a second's hesitation.

> *Dear Peter and Lucy!*
> *I was told that one or both of you listened to "my" Freischütz. I hope you noticed the HORNS? They were super (in those days of GR.[117] and I bought them lots of whiskey after the sessions. Only for the horns!) ***
> *Yours ever,*
> *Charlie*
>
> *** *FREISCHÜTZ is one of the horniest operas!*
>
> —*Carlos Kleiber, to Peter Jonas, 8 July 1997*

In the meantime, it was the moment of first encounter with an artist widely viewed as even more particular (and eccentric) than Kleiber himself.

The pianist Arturo Benedetti Michelangeli was a child prodigy who earned his diploma from the Milan Conservatory of Music at age thirteen. At nineteen, he won first place in Geneva's Concours International de Piano. During this period he also commenced study of medicine but, contrary to legend, never actually earned his MD. During World War II, he served as a lieutenant in the Italian Air Force. Following Mussolini's capture and the Nazi occupation he joined the anti-Fascist underground, in which he distinguished himself until war's end. (He was held prisoner by the Germans for some months.) Postwar touring gave him a reputation as an impeccable technician able to control every register and voice every color with unparalleled poetry and exactness. He developed a small but breathtaking repertoire and in the 1950s became widely esteemed as a unique artist. That reputation held for years. As with Carlos, the repertoire base diminished over time, and cancellations abounded. In private study, both were men of enormous intellectual curiosity. In public, each chose to focus on music that spoke in special ways.

So it was that they were paired. Although Michelangeli was ten years Carlos's senior, they worked with complete mutual respect. With the Hamburg State Opera Orchestra, Carlos led performances of Beethoven's *Coriolanus* Overture, his first essay of Strauss's moving *Death and Transfiguration*, and his first Beethoven Piano Concerto No. 5, *The Emperor*.[118] It must have seemed like a bizarre pairing.[119] For all of that, it was later proposed that the two record the Beethoven *Emperor*. Their live performances had gone surprisingly well, and it seemed like a good idea at the time. In 1975 they gave it a strange try, more of which later.

The distinguished reviewer Klaus Wagner attended the Hamburg concerts and understood the tension between conductor and pianist. "This concert really seemed to bring together fire and water: the ecstatic expressionist musician Carlos Kleiber, and the Hypersensitive among the great pianists of our time.

"But in reality this was not an example of the laws of attraction between two contrasting elements; no, this was two soul mates coming together, two very similar personalities guided by the quest for the utmost perfection." Wagner hinted at difficulties to come. "It drew its unity from the tension between the interpreters. This tension also refers to the character and the structure of the work. To put it simply: Carlos Kleiber insists on the traditional 'Emperor' style for the E-flat major concerto. Arturo Benedetti Michelangeli constantly appeals against this interpretation through the early romantic style and vivid classicism of his playing."[120]

Hamburg then made the only serious managerial offer that Kleiber ever considered. Unanimously their orchestra, music staff, and administration had been overwhelmed by his artistry on their platform. His performances with Michelangeli had startled everybody by their newness of line and rightness of pace. Discussions were held, and gossip disseminated, at every level. Enquiries were made into Carlos's work in Zurich, Düsseldorf, and Stuttgart. Wolfgang Sawallisch was stepping down as general music director in Hamburg, and a first-rate replacement was required. This shooting star was a real force, and they wanted him. After some weeks of consideration, Carlos decided he didn't want them. Thanks and regrets were extended all round. He realized—correctly—that the administrative and social obligations of a music director were, after all, anathema.[121] He would never again consider any such offer, even when the Berlin Philharmonic came calling.

The collapse of that negotiation led to the rise of another. In late April, a kind of summit meeting was held to consider the possibility of bringing together Kleiber and Michelangeli to record the *Emperor* for Deutsche Grammophon. It would take two years to accomplish and would ultimately fail. In the process of the collapse of this project, we learn much about Kleiber's own ways of working and his standards of assertion and artistic impulse.

Meantime, Kleiber granted a rare insight into his own personality that September. Seven months earlier he had recorded *Der Freischütz*. Apparently not knowing what she was getting into, Dorothee Koehler at Deutsche Grammophon's Press and Artist Promotion agency asked him to participate in various promotional activities. Every other conductor in the world would have said yes, naturally. Not Carlos. In the 5 September postcard cited earlier, he also wrote about his relationship with the media.

Dear Frau Köhler:
Many thanks for your friendly letter and the magazines. I can't choose the interviews that I'd enjoy (Stern would be one) and refuse the others (which I'm always

*doing). And so I can't do <u>any</u> at all. Otherwise I won't be able to say no any more
(even in Vienna). So that's how it will remain: that I don't give interviews or present myself to the press "talking" (press conference). So Sorry!
Best regards
your old C. Kleiber*

PS It's better that way: When I talk, it's rubbish.[122]

Carlos returned to ground in Stuttgart with *Tristan* and *Otello* that summer.
The Wagner was, in useful ways, an out-of-town tryout.

Some months before, he had been contacted by management at the Vienna
State Opera. Would he like to conduct *Tristan* in their house? Many would
argue that Vienna, Covent Garden, La Scala, and The Met are the top houses
in the world. Vienna would be an exceptional opportunity for Kleiber. If he
accepted, it would signal a step to the very top of his profession.

Carlos well knew what that organization meant to his father, how Erich
had been disappointed by them, and how bitterly that fact figured in his life.
The son might accomplish what the father could not. He could build a connection at his pleasure, with no fear of disappointment—as there was no hunt
for permanence. If that was his strategy, it certainly worked, as both the opera
house (and its pit band, the Vienna Philharmonic) would call on Carlos for
years to come.[123]

Carlos held out for very good terms in Vienna. He demanded and got *fourteen* orchestra rehearsals for *Tristan*. He demanded the authority to cancel
as required. (He used it at the second performance. Tenor Hans Hopf fell ill,
and Carlos would not permit a substitute with whom he had not coached. The
evening was cancelled.)

Such were the conditions under which Kleiber made his famous debut
at the Vienna Staatsoper, on 7 October 1973. He led the superb company
of Hopf, Sotin, Ligendza, Neidlinger, Helm, Baldani, Nitsche, Tichy, and
Dermota in one of the great experiences of their lives.[124] As was increasingly
common, the critics were simply stunned and quite unanimous.

"Carlos Kleiber has done the almost impossible: with a single performance
he has established himself as one of the few great conductors in the house
since the days of Mahler," wrote Joseph Wechsberg. "He did this without
magic, by sheer hard work and dedication to the music. . . . He produced
miracles of dynamic shading, articulation of chamber-music care, and clear
phrasing, and abundant excitement and climax. The orchestra played as happily for him as it has not played for months."[125] The astounding success of this
Tristan would pave the way to Bayreuth the following season.

It also reached ears in New York. Members of the Board of the New York
Philharmonic read reviews and evidently heard from people who attended.

According to Dr. Walter Schäfer, two of these trustees more or less forced Pierre Boulez (their music director at the time) to invite Carlos to conduct in New York. "Of course Boulez never got an answer," Schäfer said.

There was little time to savor Viennese success, however. Carlos roared back to Munich for *Rosenkavalier* on 12 October and four more performances of it later that year.

MOVING ABROAD

Come the mid-1970s, Carlos's career began to move internationally. He had long received invitations from beyond Europe, but he never believed that he was wholly ready (or willing) to enter that working environment. His exceptional demands for rehearsal time, for the closest consultation in every element of production, and for a family life unknown during his own childhood militated against such offers. He knew that companies abroad wanted him. He was not sure he wanted them.

Even so, 1974 marked a sea change in attitude and confidence. Encouraged by his friend Helga Schmidt, he would make his debut at Britain's Royal Opera House, Covent Garden. He would enter Wagner's cathedral in Bayreuth. He would take the Bavarian Staatsoper's production of *Rosenkavalier* to Tokyo and Osaka. He would make the Beethoven recording that allowed him to escape the gravitational pull of his father. And he would be entrusted with a Vienna Philharmonic tour. The year 1974 was Kleiber's breakthrough year.

It opened slowly in Hamburg, where once again at the Musik Halle, he led the Hamburg State Opera Orchestra in concert.[126] In March he was back at the National Theatre in Munich leading *Rosenkavalier*.[127] The performances went well, but he was already concerned about his debut at England's most important opera house. This was the company that had brought in Erich Kleiber to help revive its fortunes after the war. Having used him, they let him go. It was a painful family memory. It would be complicated later that month.

In March and April 1974, he made the one recording through which he would forever be compared with his father: Beethoven 5.[128] Erich had made his famous version for Decca more than twenty years earlier. For many critics it was a definitive realization of the work, and of the conductor. Taut, powerful, driven, and inspired—it was all that, and more. When preparing for his own sessions, now with the Vienna Philharmonic, Carlos felt a terrible burden and a singular opportunity. For all those who imagined him merely a pale approximation of his father, he would now escape that solecism forever.

Escape he did. The reviews were ecstatic. First commentary declared that every powerful and expressive aspect of the father's performance was now doubled in the son's. By virtually every measure, this was a kind of eclipse—intentional or otherwise. The album became legend, regularly mentioned in the pantheon of the greatest Fifths ever recorded. I am always amazed by how many reference and anthology books list it as their "First Choice." It has appeared as such on National Public Radio, Classical CD Guide, Amazon, CBC Radio, The Gramophone, and elsewhere. Perhaps most famously, Michael Walsh in *Time Magazine* a decade later declared that Kleiber "fashioned a performance that unfolded with the clarity of a Euclidian proposition, yet had the intensity of a hammer blow. . . . It was as if Homer had come back to recite the Iliad."[129] By any standard, such a public and critical reception should have erased all doubts. It did not.

In June 1974 Carlos traveled to London to work for the first time at Covent Garden.[130] He had been asked to replace an ailing James Levine, who was originally to have made his own debut on that occasion.[131] From Kleiber they were expecting something truly exceptional, and they were not disappointed. A good many people still remember the event as if it occurred yesterday. Britons were treated to a *Rosenkavalier* of unimaginable beauty, tenderness, and remorse, and an orchestra drilled to the point of complete technical mastery and emotional expressivity. Only with Carlos would this not be a contradiction.

According to Norman Lebrecht, for his Covent Garden debut Carlos "spent three hours rehearsing eighty seconds of the Prelude to *Der Rosenkavalier*."[132] Exaggerated or not, such a claim hints at the ongoing truth of Carlos's rehearsal strategies. He found an element of musical speech that would serve as template for many others. He worked slavishly to master it. Then, once in hand, the orchestra would see how it might be applied elsewhere to create a consciousness of unification rarely—if ever—revealed by anyone. He worked this way for years. It was very time-consuming. It was part of his secret.

Kleiber was also an oracle of unequalled imagery. Early on at a Covent Garden rehearsal he was having problems conveying—even with *that* baton—the subtlety of his intentions. During the Act I monologue with the Marschallin, he finally found a way to get the special sound and entrance he sought, telling his players, "Only those people with psychic tendencies please play this chord."[133]

He did run into some difficulty dealing with players who had *no* psychic tendencies. Sir John Tooley[134] recalls Kleiber's first rehearsal with the orchestra as being troubled. "He was well aware of his father's standing and popularity with the musicians, which made him ultra-sensitive to players' reaction on his first appearance. At the end he said that the players spent most of the rehearsal staring at him and wondering if he was the son of his father."[135]

Things got worse when he attempted to perfect a rhythm in the trombones. "He went on remorselessly, humiliating them and causing them to say that they never wanted to play for him again." But the performance changed all that, once the orchestra realized what he was up to with everybody else. Tooley noted that the orchestra ended up "clamouring for his return." So did management. So did everyone.

The distinguished conductor Sir Charles Mackerras remembered it the same way and understood Carlos's insecurities. "His first appearance in The Rosenkavalier engendered a lot of praise and comment from the Orchestra," he said, "many of whose members at that time still remembered Erich Kleiber's performances of the same opera at Covent Garden.

"I know that Carlos was very modest in the presence of those players who had played The Rosenkavalier under his father, and was always saying 'Do you think that's how my father did it / would have done it?' In those days at Covent Garden, the Orchestra was quite used to very eminent conductors working with them and they all said that really Carlos was the best of all the interpreters of the four operas which he did at Covent Garden."[136]

Carlos did not always reciprocate. Although relations improved with the orchestra, "He was very critical of the cast. He wanted me to get rid of some of them," recalled John Tooley. Tooley refused. "I haven't hired you to fire the cast. I hired you to conduct them." Carlos was soon abashed and backed down. "My wife phoned me and told me to be more Christian," he told Sir John.[137] In public, however, the response to this *Rosenkavalier* was unexceeded admiration.

The great conductor Bernard Haitink, after being appointed music director at Covent Garden, offered praise. "What can I say? He is an extraordinary man, above all the others. One of his secrets, I think, is that he knows the pieces he works on better than anyone else. He goes back to the original scores, the autographs, and he will only do an opera about which he feels he has something special to say. He is enormously self-critical. Don't be fooled by the small repertoire. His knowledge of music is immense."[138] He added, "I admire that man so much. He did an Otello here which was so fantastic that I just can't do it any more."[139] Kleiber left London thinking he might return one day.

AT BAYREUTH

After two July performances of *Rosenkavalier* in Munich at the Opernfestspiele (one with Lucia Popp), he was off to make his debut at Bayreuth. Beginning on 24 July 1974 he would lead six performances of the only Wagner opera he ever gave: *Tristan und Isolde*. This was a new production and his first collaboration with director August Everding and designer Josef Svoboda.[140]

After first writing Wolfgang Wagner a year earlier, in August of 1972 he received the coveted invitation. A *Tristan und Isolde* scheduled for the summer of 1974 had originally been offered to Georg Solti. He canceled, and Wagner immediately got in touch with Kleiber, who just as readily accepted—in principle. "A long series of conversations" ensued, and a contract was eventually signed.

For Wagner, it was a happy collaboration. "Although Kleiber was reputed to be a most difficult conductor, he differed from Leonard Bernstein and Georg Solti in being able to reconcile his wishes with the requirements of the Bayreuth management. His three years with us, 1974–6, were almost completely devoid of friction."[141]

It was not so easy for Carlos's onstage colleagues. Everding found him more demanding than any other conductor. "He dried me up completely. I just couldn't think anymore. He interbred with my instructions to the singers, and I got the impression he would like to be his own stage director and just get someone to design the sets and costumes for him."[142]

It is hard to see what Carlos would have been troubled by. According to Frederic Spotts, the stage "was pure *son et lumiere*."[143] It was cleansed of anything extraneous to the music. The enchantments of lighting, the clever use of transparencies and scrims, a subtle use of visual symbol and abstraction—all of this put the music and its singers first. "Colour and light seemed liquid," said Spotts. "The effects ravished the eye with visual magic." And it was overwhelmingly human, a value Carlos always sought in his productions. Everding "introduced any number of small touches—such as Tristan's enraptured look as he caught sight of Isolde a moment before he died—that many critics found deeply affecting."

The notices I have read[144] were uniformly glowing. Whatever tensions existed between Everding and Kleiber were not manifest onstage. Writing in *Musical America*, critic James H. Sutcliffe found that "in an admirable effort to avoid repeating his Met 'Tristan,' Everding devised unusually vigorous movement which appropriately underlined the score's white-hot passions. . . . (Kleiber's) malleable approach to the score—only occasionally spoiled by an overdriven tempo—the hushed string tone, the mellow woodwinds, the perfect ensemble even of the big brass, all audibly reflected the light and shadow on stage, a remarkable achievement and like no other Tristan in my experience."

Readers of the *Times of London* found in William Mann's essay similar praise for Kleiber's comprehensive realization of the score. "Mr Kleiber's reading was nobly and dramatically shaped, by the clock quite fast but impassioned, full of detail and ideal in pace for the singers as well as for the action. He does not mistake juicy moments for climaxes: the summit of the first prelude was intense but not ear-shattering because the music must (and did) sound even more tremendous when Tristan and Isolde drink the cup of atonement . . . then, Mr Kleiber and the superb orchestra, and the unique Bayreuth acoustic, thundered forth and we were all duly shattered."

One more notice may suffice. Jean Mistler in *L'Aurore* found that "the debut of Carlos Kleiber at the head of the Bayreuth orchestra will leave a great memory. His direction was nervous and fast (it cut a good ten minutes from the traditional time) and displayed the orchestra marvelously. The polyphony of the second act found with him all its profundity and variety (and) an astonishing lightness."[145] Kleiber would conduct *Tristan* at Bayreuth for the next two summers.

DONKEYS IN JAPAN

He was then away to a land with which he always felt a charmed affinity. Something about their quest for acceptance in the world of classical art music touched him, as did the Japanese reverence for history, ancestry—and privacy. Even by Japanese standards of good manners, he was treated exceptionally well, as were his colleagues. Audiences in Japan are not given to the explosions of applause heard in America or to the partisanship of the Italians or to the head-nodding sobriety of the British. But when Carlos arrived those rules changed, at least for the time he was there. They adored him, openly.

For Carlos's Japanese debut, the Bavarian State Opera gave *Rosenkavalier* at Tokyo's Bunka Kaikan Theatre on 24 and 28 September 1974, and again on 9 October. Audience response was tidal and overwhelming.[146] But it could have gone very badly. Isao Hirowatari was the technical supervisor at the theatre on opening night.

"In the middle of the performance we got a phone call from the police," he recalled years later.

> We were ordered to bring down the curtain right away because a phone message claimed that a bomb was placed inside the concert hall. We did not have time to report it to him [Kleiber] but in the middle of the First Act the curtain was closed.
>
> He was struck dumb with astonishment. He had cancelled performances for his own reasons, but never the other way around! I reached him, almost crawling through the orchestra pit, and explained the situation. The players overheard me and started to run away—it was a simply unbelievable happening. Later on it became clear that a man who could not buy a ticket made that phone call.[147]

Strange incidents connected Carlos to Japan. Prof. Hirowatari told a tale of donkeys. Together with Claudio Abbado and the whole staff of La Scala, Carlos arrived on tour seven years later, in the fall of 1981. Over six hundred people, and some one hundred trucks of costumes, props, and scenery came in from Italy, and Hirowatari was serving as superintendant of the stage production itself. In that capacity he was assigned to deal with Kleiber, "who did not have any manager who normally takes care of schedule for rehearsals and performances as well," he said.

"Kleiber is the artist known not to give his signature on any contract until all performances are done with; he might be the only one in the world in this respect. All seven performances in Tokyo, as stated in the contract, went without a hitch." Not so in Osaka. Carlos was conducting *Bohème* on 25 September and had reached the fourth act. Mimi was on her deathbed, and the whole audience was in tears. It is the most delicate and time-suspending moment in the entire opera.

"All over a sudden, heaven forbid, a loud scream was heard from stage right, in the wings. It did not take long to realize the scream did not belong to a human being but to an animal. The owner of that scream, which lasted for a good five minutes, was the donkey which had appeared onstage during the Second Act," Hirowatari recounted. (This was, no surprise, a Zeffirelli production.)

Inclement weather, almost typhoon-like, on that day brought down very heavy rain. The soft-hearted Italian staff took pity on the donkey. Rather than let him stand in the storm they kept the animal indoors. It was thoughtfulness in the Italian style. But it was also "la rapida condotta di molto Italiano."[148] They were so afraid to face the wrath of Kleiber that they all disappeared, not waiting for the end of performance!

I could not very well run away with them. . . . I stood waiting for him at the exit of orchestra pit, his favourite beer in hand. Several minutes seemed like several hours. There were another two extra performances scheduled. This incident ought not to be the reason why he would cancel them.

Hirowatari put on his bravest face.

Kleiber, who was soaked with perspiration, came out of the pit, almost bending his tall figure from the waist. I started saying my apology immediately with insensible English. "I am really sincerely sorry . . . if you knew how difficult to control animal behaviour . . . no matter what we tried it kept screaming . . ." I kept on and on. Perhaps my desperate and sincere thoughts reached his heart. He smiled kindly, took a swig of beer and said, "Well, we had an extra performance of two tenors competing with each other."[149]

Japanese audiences seemed to grasp that Carlos took a very special pleasure in their reception of him. The unique beauty of the Japanese landscape touched him no less, and the thousand-year achievement of palaces, temples, and pagodas in ancient Kyoto moved him even more. It was reverie. He repaid all in kind. Well past his numerous public activities in Japan, he later made two private visits there. In 1996, for example, he toured Kyoto and Okinawa with his friend Hirowatari. In a recent memoir, Hirowatari recalled, "He loved to eat Japanese food. He could not handle *ama-ebi* (small shrimp) and *ayu* (sweetfish), but he appreciated and understood subtle delicacy that usually only Japanese could enjoy. His sense was very delicate and able to detect when 'something is missing,' which made me realize a feature common to his music."

Hirowatari also remembered a couple of un-Japanese mannerisms on Carlos's part. "His emotional ups and downs were a frequent occurrence. When he flared up while dining it happened many times that he threw *o-shibori* (a small Japanese hot/cold towel offered before the meal) at me. When this happened other people left him there, but I stayed with him and tried to cool him down."[150] Prof. Hirowatari also revealed that people in Japan's music industry had a nickname for him, of which Carlos was never made aware. "*Kyanseru ma*," it went.[151]

Returning from Japan after that first visit in 1974 Kleiber went back on tour in Europe, and for a brief journey to two obscure towns with a pronounced love of music. As much a favor to his wife as for any other reason, he took the Vienna Philharmonic to Bratislava, in then-Czechoslovakia, on 19 October 1974, and to the Konserthuset in Gotheborg, Sweden on the 27th. The program[152] was identical in both halls. He closed the year with two more performances of *Rosenkavalier* in Munich,[153] and then it was on to a work with which he will be forever identified.

FLEDERMAUS

Carlos had a deft hand, a very light touch with the sweetly comic. His ear caught the ironic underline of any score that found ways to poke fun, with affection. He always responded to absurdity. He found humane truth in laughter. When all of this might be graced by music with those verities in aim, it was a near-perfect marriage. (All of this enjoyed a parallel frame in his private life, I came to learn.)

So it was with Carlos's famous production of *Die Fledermaus*, the finest of Johann Strauss Jr.'s operas.[154] It would bring out the silliness, cantabile, and intuitive hunt for secret longing at the heart of things that so qualified his work. He had first done *The Bat* as an apprentice, years before in Geneva—

and in French. He was now ready to restore all of its fussy and exacting glory. And he had given it tremendous thought, as ever. He later shared some of those ideas with me.

In 1992 I was preparing my own first performance of the opera. I wrote to ask his advice about preferred editions and parts, singer issues, tempi, and the like. Over four letters he answered my questions, and in one of them he made a very unexpected offer. In sequence, here is what he had to say about conducting *Fledermaus*.

Take care approaching "The Bat". Listen to Clemens Krauss and fix your orch. material + or - by what you hear there. Take out a lot of the "fortes" and reduce them to "pianos". Don't do the ballet which is in the score. Never beat the "3" in a Waltz. Rosalinde's Csardás is difficult 'till you know it well. Krauss is great there. Take it seriously, it's a HOMESICK piece, the Csardás. Hey, look at me, giving advice to a Maestro! What nerve!

About the 'after the beat playing', I know of no literature. It's a subject in-delicate and universally avoided. (Maybe because it makes 50% of the rehearsals unnecessary?) Maybe you do it anyway and don't know it. That's best. The thing is to keep the boys in the band listening to each other and to the singers.

However good your reflexes are, theirs are better. You can sense the places where it's WISE to let them take charge. They have to know you <u>want</u> them to, though! Aw, shut up Carlos!

—Carlos Kleiber, 19 October 1992

I did as instructed, returned to study, and a week or so later wrote Carlos again, asking which particular score he would recommend. It was time to choose. He replied in detail.

FLEDERMAUS
Score: Johann Strauss (Sohn) Gesamtausgabe
Herausgegeben von der Joe Strousses (sorry) Gesellschaft, Wien
Serie 2: Buehnen- und Vokalwerke. Band 3: Die Fledermaus.
Wien, Im Gemeinschaftsverlag Doblinger/Universal Edition.

What I don't know is whether or not they have also printed orchestral Mate-rial and vocal scores. I used the material by the [expletive deleted] *Kalmus, which I had already prepared with lots of Eintragungen[155] (by me) before the above-mentioned score was on the market. The score (see above: score) is big, thick, heavy, well-printed, etc, but uninspiring in lay-out, somehow. However, I believe it is the only full-score extant. Look carefully at the Kalmus parts. They are seething with mistakes.*

I had my own private parts (OK, OK) fotocopied once and they are lying around somewhere, weighing a ton or more, dusty and completely loose (unbound, I mean).

Now listen. If you are a real artist (whatever THAT is) then 1/2 the fun will be marking the parts (bowings, dynamics, etc) yourself according to what you think you want to hear. Saves a lot of rehearsal time, if you don't happen to be a Stokey or a Karajan.

If you take someone else's material, the flight of your genius will be hampered. You will be confessing to laziness disguised as willingness to learn.

Furthermore, you will have to look at the orch. parts ANYHOW, if only to figure out what the guy who arranged them wanted. Then you will have to "want" it too or rehearse like wild to get all the work the other guy did OUT.

BUT, BUT, BUT!

IF you want two tons of flying leaves containing Fledermaus, arranged to death, here's what, out of extatic gratitude, I might just offer. If you send someone over to Aurikelstrasse 1a, W-8022 Gruenwald (outskirts of Munich) who will collect the unwieldy carton with his grubby little paws and get it over to you, somehow, undamaged (if possible) and then (you) take over my markings (I won't tell) or those of them you think are any good, that's OK,

But my gratitude (unending gratitude) is not such that I can go to the post-office lugging this stuff after packaging it properly (a thing I just can't do, even to save my life), doing the Customs-ritual, etc.

Do you understand what I mean? Whatever you decide, be aware of the fact that I have never made an indecent proposition of this kind to anyone in my life before. So I want you to make a big show of being very moved, OK? Let's see some abject gratitude. (Just kidding) I COULD send you my score (very heavy, as I mentioned above) but there is almost nothing in it except what Joe S. composed (or what has been relayed to us as such).

You will want to mark your own score according to your intentions (like the young girl's father said to the boy who was courting her "what are your intentions?" The boy: "do you mean I have a choice?") if you are able to focus on any intentions you will later be capable of remembering, which is the great difficulty in this business, I feel.

—*Carlos Kleiber, 17 November 1992*

He followed this with a quick postcard about the condition of the parts he had offered, and then another letter about questions of marking parts and score.

About the Bat: you didn't get me about my score. There's nothing in my score, so no point in comparing. I have always, maybe mistakenly, had the notion that, since the PARTS are what the players play from, the parts have to be perfectly in order. Scores, I believe, are irrelevant. UNLESS you mark the score and give it to a copyist with instructions to transfer the markings to the parts. This is not my method, though. With "bat", if the players are Viennese it's less important to mark and/or bow everything. But with a Senegalese orchestra it might be a good idea. (No offence meant!)

Where the REAL difficulty arises is when the dear, talented conductor, armed with his precious, marked score hasn't grasped the style. If he has, OK, It takes a few seconds to mark a cresc. or a p or a gliss or a spicc. in a part; but it takes minutes to ask for such things in rehearsal. The conductor has to talk and (at least hereabouts) every word is a nail in his coffin.

Regarding ORIGINALITY: the warm glow one gets from growing things from scratch on one's own dungheap IS gratifying, though I'd hate to have to re-invent the telephone, for instance. Remembering that the BAT is a supremely persnickety piece, I'd therefore suggest that the best bet would be to listen to Krauss (now on CD, even) and consider "marking" well-nigh accordingly.

—*Carlos Kleiber, 20 December 1992*

It was, of course, typical of Carlos *not* to recommend his own recording of *Fledermaus*. It wasn't just modesty. He had a bone-deep appreciation of the old masters, and we talked about them a great deal. I ended up declining his offer of marked parts and did them myself. He said that was good.

Better, far better, was his own legendary essay of this opera. At the Bavarian Staatsoper in Munich, the team of Schenk, Schneider-Siemssen, and Strahammer mounted a new production. According to many of those who saw the performance that season, it may never gain an equal. It opened New Year's Eve 1974, as right and canny a decision as all the others this team took.[156] The Bavarian State Opera chorus was in magnificent form, and the orchestra rose to every occasion. The reviews got lost in a tsunami of superlatives.

Those who imagine Carlos avoided work don't know the whole story. After celebrating New Year's with *The Bat* he spent the next night, 1 January 1975, leading *Rosenkavalier*, and would do the same again on the 4th. Thereafter it was back to *Fledermaus*. With a cast that alternated slightly, Carlos would roar into making *Fledermaus* wholly his own. He gave it eleven times in thirty-three days, alternating with performances of *Rosenkavalier*.[157]

Consider the astonishing energy that Kleiber invested in every performance. Consider the complete psychic shift required to offer two such "comedies" in quick succession and how profoundly they must be given separate life. Nothing he would ever do was more virtuosic than this. Superficial jet setters pull such stunts all the time, of course. For Carlos this was, in its way, deeply wrenching. In time, it would drive him from the art altogether.

Meantime, and with little moment to recharge, Kleiber was assigned *Traviata* and gave it nine times in the summer of 1975.[158] Throughout, this was basically the Cotrubas, Linser, Jungwirth, and Aragall cast. After less than a month off, he came back to *Rosenkavalier* with the Jones, Fassbaender, and Popp cast leading the way.[159] Then Bayreuth beckoned and he once again appeared in *Tristan*, giving the first of six performances on 26 July 1975.[160]

After a few weeks spent in further score study, Carlos recorded *Fledermaus*—and in only seven sessions. His chosen cast included Lucia Popp, Hermann Prey, Julia Varady, René Kollo, and (rather controversially) Ivan Rebroff as Orlovsky. Otto Schenk served as Dialog-Regie. The recording was made with the Bavarian Staatsoper orchestra and chorus in October, an event that further strengthened his reputation as master of this frivolous but touching repertoire.[161]

This exhausting season continued with six more performances of *Traviata*[162] in Munich, followed by another of *Rosenkavalier*[163] and four more of *Fledermaus*,[164] all concluding on New Year's Eve one year and nineteen performances after it began.

In between his *Fledermaus* performances, he worked with typically fevered energy on another studio recording project. With the Vienna Philharmonic, and once again at the Musikvereinsaal, he now recorded Beethoven 7.[165] It is a technically superlative accomplishment. To my ear it lacks—slightly—the incandescence of his film of the same piece made with the Concertgebouw Orchestra eight years later.

TWO EMPERORS, NO KINGDOM

In April and May 1975, one of the worst might-have-beens in Carlos's career began to unfold. Two years earlier he had enjoyed immense success performing Beethoven's Piano Concerto No. 5, the *Emperor*, with the equally perfectionist Arturo Benedetti Michelangeli. And now, two years later, Michelangeli was getting ready to leave EMI and join Carlos's own label, Deutsche Grammophon. A team assembled by producer Cord Garben had been working for months to reconnect these giants of music and record the Beethoven. Hans Hirsch at Deutsche Grammophon had already decided that Garben would be an ideal artistic supervisor for the recording. Garben knew the pianist, the conductor, and the Radiosinfonieorchester Berlin[166] very well, and he could as ably as anyone negotiate the diplomacies of such a mating. Organizational meetings had already taken place when Michelangeli and Kleiber agreed to meet with Garben in a Munich beer garden.

"The comet was in charge," Garben recalled. Kleiber was very talkative and funny, and tremendously interested in Garben's stories about von Karajan and other great personalities of the day. "There was a whiff of Schadenfreude not quite concealed" by Kleiber's jokes, Garben added. The three discussed every aspect of the project, with Kleiber doing most of the talking, and Michelangeli nodding silent assent.

The recording sessions took place at Sender Fries Berlin, in the Haus des Rundfunks, Masurenallee. The first ran with orchestra only from 10:00 a.m. to 1:00 p.m., and 2:00 p.m. to 5:00 p.m., on 14 December 1975. On 16 December, from 2:00 p.m. to 5:00 p.m., they were joined by Michelangeli. The final session ran from 2:00 p.m. to 5:00 p.m. on 17 December, with Garben conducting. All rehearsals were recorded, as was the piano test and (twice) the first movement with piano.[167]

The team stayed at Berlin's Hotel Schweizer Hof, located near the center of the city.[168] Late on the night before recording was to begin, Kleiber summoned Garben. He gave the producer his study score of the concerto by the "Dutch composer," and pointed out its special contents.

The book was filled to capacity with "little red marks," Garben remembered.[169] It was replete with dynamic indications and shadings, all enriching the sonic facts of the work. Garben thought that Kleiber had turned the piece "nearly upside down," especially in its phrase-making. Other changes were equally profound. The same pocket score was full of very unusual "and very adventuresome bowings creating a very refreshing interpretation." He and Kleiber talked about a recording directed toward the "Nachwelt," the generations to come. Carlos then made an astonishing demand. He wanted all of his markings entered in the players' parts overnight, before the first session started next morning at 10:00 a.m.

Garben was appalled. Where would he find a dozen music librarians at midnight? Somehow he did. Within an hour, Garben's new army was on a forced march. They finished their work by morning. Kleiber was notoriously fussy about getting perfectly marked parts to his players. However, such a last-minute demand was out of character for him and unheard of in the industry. Garben and Deutsche Grammophon were desperate for the project to succeed. They would do whatever their unique artists wished.

They might have succeeded but for one wretched coincidence. While waiting for the sound engineers to finish their setup, Michelangeli strolled into the engineering booth. There, on the desk, lay Kleiber's much-marked score. He picked it up. He read it through. His face darkened. This was nothing like the musical statement that he and Kleiber had made two years earlier. Kleiber had rethought *everything*—but not told Michelangeli. He saw that Kleiber had gone well beyond what they had agreed to long before.

From that point, everything ran downhill. Michelangeli, who loathed conflict as much as did Kleiber, avoided eye contact altogether. Very quickly there was no communication at all between the two. However, the pianist needed contact with the orchestra. He began consulting directly with its leaders—particularly the concertmasters, Koji Toyoda and Hans Maile, and the principal cello, Georg Donderer.[170] This went on all day. At one point, the principal flute observed that the pianist was making deals behind the back of the "Clueless Leader."

None of this passed unnoticed by Kleiber. It did, however, throw him off-balance. He had worked with Michelangeli before, once written a letter to the editor to defend him, and now felt betrayed and insulted by a man he considered a friend. Conductor Ettore Gracis, a pal of Michelangeli's, defended his friend's practice of consulting players. There was nothing conspiratorial, he insisted. Michelangeli always worked this way. Only a hypersensitive personality like Kleiber would have taken it ill, he said. "It was simply typical of Arturo."[171] The second day finished miserably, and everyone headed back to the hotel.

At breakfast next morning, Garben learned that Carlos had checked out overnight. Before the producer could tell Michelangeli, the pianist asked, "Did he disappear?" Garben, himself an accomplished conductor, assumed the podium at ten. The session was finished. The recording has never been released.[172]

Afterward, Kleiber explained that "Michelangeli's communication with the other musicians had completely de-motivated me." But there was more. "Two decades later," Garben wrote, "Kleiber admitted to me that his best efforts on this score did bear a reasonable amount of responsibility for the failure of the production."[173] Tacitly, Kleiber seemed to acknowledge that his complete rethinking of the concerto, without consulting Michelangeli, might have added to the debacle. But it all turned on that wretched coincidence.

"Had Michelangeli never seen Kleiber's 'work of art' in the booth, the world would have known a great performance," Garben acknowledged. Worse yet, there might have been more. In the early euphoria about the Kleiber-Michelangeli partnership, talks were seriously pursued about recording a complete Beethoven cycle. It would have been Carlos's only exploration of such a set. Those talks went so far that Kleiber asked Garben to locate all extant cadenzas and recordings for the second piano concerto. He had heard that Michelangeli did not have it in his repertoire. (He didn't.) It is indicative of how seriously Carlos was examining the possibility.

With the collapse of the *Emperor* project, nothing would come of it—at least for Kleiber. Six years later, with Carlo Maria Giulini and the Vienna

Symphony at the Musikvereinsaal, the pianist recorded and filmed the first, third, and fifth concerti in the cycle. His performances were quite wonderful.

PAYING A PRICE

By 1976 Kleiber had entered the hectic and unyielding world of the star conductor. For a while he managed it reasonably well. In time, he paid a terrible cost. There is no surprise in the fact that opera was the first to be shed from his career. His last years were restricted to the concert stage and, even then, in a very small repertoire. But in the mid-1970s, that was not so. He worked hard at whatever assignment he accepted.

Carlos's obligations were particularly heavy in 1976. He gave numerous performances of *Fledermaus*, *Rosenkavalier*, *Traviata*, and *Otello*. His last of the year was becoming a new tradition, giving *Fledermaus* on New Year's Eve. In 1976 he also returned to Bayreuth for what would be his last appearances there, made the first-ever television broadcast from La Scala, and recorded a concerto with Sviatoslav Richter.

For two years in a row Carlos was moving toward the edge of his energies. It is no secret in the profession that conducting a symphony is, relatively speaking, an easy job. Three or four rehearsals, three or four concerts, and it's done. Not so with opera. It is a vastly more difficult proposition. Planning the production, identifying dramatic line and personality, choosing and coaching the singers, preparing the chorus, negotiating a thousand matters with directors and designers, moving through multiple orchestra, blocking, and dress rehearsals (and Carlos always required many more than anyone else), and putting up with the usual collisions of ego and vision (Carlos had plenty of both)—all of this makes opera the most demanding of all the performing arts. And Carlos was the most demanding of conductors. This is a principal reason why a number of symphony conductors considered "stars" in the States and Canada are barely taken seriously in Europe. They lack the gravitas of an opera career. Perhaps they lack the humility to submerge themselves in a large collegial enterprise. Perhaps they know the audience will never see them prancing in the pit. A few conductors, considered poodleheads in early life, are now in their later careers deeply invested in opera. Success there is creating a new, and much higher, reputation for these musicians.

A good orchestra, fully trained, will be able to play most symphonic works of the classical period without any conductor at all . . . an opera cannot even *begin* to be performed without a proper conductor directing the whole proceedings.

There is a feeling among orchestras that, although they do not really admire symphony conductors so much, they have a grudging respect for opera conductors, because they realize that opera conducting is so much more difficult and complicated. The general suspicion that orchestra players have of conductors is a great deal more prevalent in the concert hall than in the opera house, where the smallest mistake can show up the conductor.

—Sir Charles Mackerras[174]

Those who believe that Carlos was a charismatic lazybones, so disabled by perfectionism that he could barely function, might consider the following.

For the Bavarian State Opera, he led eleven more performances of *Fledermaus*[175] that spring of 1976, seven of *La Traviata*,[176] and two of *Rosenkavalier*.[177] He then headed south to set up shop at La Scala. There, with a new cast he gave seven more performances of *Rosenkavalier*.[178] Then it was back to Munich for another two performances of *La Traviata*,[179] and later that summer, three more of *Rosenkavalier*.[180]

It was one particular performance of *Rosenkavalier* in Milan that added so much to Carlos's reputation for single-mindedness. In early May 1976, twenty-three temblors were recorded on seismographs across northern Italy. The strongest of them hit 4.7 on the Richter scale. Something dangerous was happening about six miles underground. On the evening of 6 May, the Friuli earthquake struck at thirteen seconds after 8:00 p.m. Its epicenter was placed in northeast Italy, near the border with Austria and modern Slovenia. It registered Richter 6.5 and was felt across Europe. More than one thousand people were killed, 1,750 were injured, 105,000 people lost their homes, and some $2.6 billion in damage was suffered. And two hundred miles distant, an opera was under way.

At La Scala, the earthquake was felt by almost everyone. The building was old, and barely able to withstand the shock.[181] Chandeliers swayed, walls rocked, and people in the upper galleries abandoned their seats. Singers hesitated, and players in the pit wondered why the performance had not been stopped. Only one person didn't realize what was going on. Afterward, Kleiber asked why so many people seemed "distracted" during the performance. Only then was he told about the earthquake. He had noticed nothing. (Eighteen years later he was in the center of another major earthquake, the 8.2 Richter event in Japan. The Hokkaido/South Kurils temblor shook violently at 10:22 p.m. on 4 October 1994, while he was on tour with the Vienna Staatsoper. Once more he noticed nothing.)

Carlos spent June in the studio, laying down what would be his lone recorded concerto. The pianist was the extraordinary Sviatoslav Richter, and the work was Dvořák's only piano concerto, Op. 33. It had been composed one hundred years before, and this EMI project was intended to commemorate that centenary.[182]

At Carlos's insistence and with Richter's full consent, they played from the original version. Over time the Czech pianist and teacher Vilém Kurz had induced stylistic and other changes to the solo part, and these had become the standard—especially among Czech pianists. Kleiber and Richter determined to go back to its first voice.

The album's liner notes are somewhat odd. They don't even mention Carlos by name: "The conductor is an artist whose father, Erich Kleiber, was unforgettably linked to Prague and to Czech music and who thus understands Dvořák as few people do, on the basis of a natural family feeling." Indeed.

The recording itself was not an unqualified success. Richter had a tremendous regard for Carlos, describing him as "the greatest conductor I've ever been privileged to meet."[183] But he felt the recording caught neither of them at their best. "It's not a good recording, I'm afraid, because the atmosphere wasn't good. One of the players, idle as always . . . had said to him, 'If you continue to make remarks like that I'm leaving.' To speak like that to Kleiber, the greatest living conductor! I was furious. Besides, I wasn't on form, and neither was Kleiber."[184]

Producer John Mordler, responsible for these sessions, adds another dimension to them and a remarkable fact. "My impression was that at the beginning, despite their obvious mutual respect, they were both a bit wary of each other. In fact they got on famously, probably because Carlos's extraordinary sensitivity responded in total harmony with Richter's seemingly childlike innocence and enthusiasm and total commitment.

"They were both totally uninterested in listening back to the takes, so they rarely came to the control room, leaving the decisions to the producer."[185]

NIGHT AND PERFECT LOVE

Carlos worked for only three summers at the Bayreuth Festival. In 1974, 1975, and 1976 he conducted sixteen times altogether but in just one opera: Wagner's *Tristan und Isolde*. He was to have continued this production in 1977, according to his contract. Unnamed "personal reasons" prevented this, and he never appeared there again. He did write Wolfgang Wagner on 16 and 17 May 1977, "each time in a most original charming vein," according to Wagner.[186] Carlos was expressing regret for having left the production, and he rejected entirely the "improper and absurd" gossip about the matter. Kleiber and Wagner continued to keep in touch.

In fact, Carlos was invited back on many occasions, and to conduct any opera he wished. He was offered any cast he chose. Given that he had carte blanche, his choice of *Tristan* is significant. Kleiber could have given a splendid *Meistersinger*, for example. Imagine what he would have done with Beckmesser! Or consider how he would have treated the torment and eternal search of *The Flying Dutchman*. But none of it ever came to pass.

"Tristan and Isolde" speaks to Carlos's fascination with the originating legend and the very notion of love-death conveyed in its final text. It derives from his deep knowledge of Schopenhauer, whom Wagner cited as his first inspiration. It rises from his searching commitment to the German romantic chains that link ideas of night and mystery and perfect love. Think of his spellbinding realization of *Der Freischütz* ten years earlier and you have something of the moody enchantment he sought. Above all, remember the opera's obsession with bliss transcending itself "in unbounded space" and we gain an awareness of why he chose *Tristan* as his only transport into the world of Wagner. That choice encompassed one more curious dimension. Think Oblomov.

> The heartfelt and intense longing for death: total unconsciousness, complete non-being, the vanishing of all dreams—the only, final release!
>
> —Richard Wagner, to Franz Liszt, 16 December 1854

Tristan offers particular challenges to its conductor. It is in three acts. Its music runs about four hours.[187] Perhaps more than any other Wagner opera it conjures atmospheres of desire, despair, serenity, and rapture through its entire design. These mysterious forces shimmer and detonate in the air. The conductor must judge climax in all its forms and find proportions in phrase and tempo and dynamic that are, essentially, incalculable. The unique chemistry of *Tristan* offers no table, no grid to point the way. It must be induced, considered, suggested, implied, inferred. As every music major knows, *Tristan* runs for page after page without any apparent reference to key and that ordinary set of traceable aural journeys. In its famous "dissolution of tonality," corresponding to the dissolution of life itself, this work was a generation ahead of its time. Conductors must find ways to resolve those questions of tonal identity and their representation within human identity.

I believe that Carlos chose *Tristan* precisely because its multiple demands are unanswerable. He did not avoid these mysteries. He turned them in his hands, looking for all of their secret sides, over and over. For Carlos, *Tristan* was a verb.

Sviatoslav Richter attended one of Carlos's last performances at Bayreuth. Years later he declared, "I fear that as long as I live I shall never hear another

'Tristan' like this one. This was the *real* thing. Carlos Kleiber brought the music to a boiling point, and kept it there throughout the whole evening, unleashing an interminable ovation at the end. There's no doubt he's the greatest conductor of our day." After the performance Richter sought him out backstage.

"He seemed rather depressed and displeased with himself," Richter continued. "I told him what I thought and he suddenly leapt into the air with joy, like a child. 'Also wirklich gut?' he asked. (So it was really good?) Such a *titan*, and so unsure of himself."[188] Unquestionably, everyone in the house itself was aware of Kleiber's magic. Because he would not allow anyone to watch his rehearsals, even Boulez would conceal himself backstage just to watch the black-and-white monitor feed of Carlos working in the pit. Kleiber never found out.[189] Recently, some forty-two minutes of Carlos's conductor-cam video at Bayreuth has surfaced. Although the sound is adequate, and the lighting less so, it is a revelation to see how he actually worked in *Tristan*. He conducts in a dark, short-sleeved shirt, uses a baton, makes little reference to the score but does turn its pages, sits most of the time, has the orchestra playing "on the beat," frequently but not always mouths the words, is clearly obsessed with balance and audible text, subdivides more often than in other filmed opera of his, occasionally smiles at the orchestra, often smiles at his singers, directs countervailing lines in the oboe and bass clarinet, conveys much joy and little apprehension, often lunges forward and to the floor to extinguish overbearing orchestral sound, drives and propels and articulates pulse, points to himself when accepting blame for a brief rhythmic impairment, mouths and smiles the text in the Liebestod more often than in any other element, and provides in these forty-two minutes essential information for all who have been enchanted by his CD of the same work. He does not speak a word.

No date is certain, although July 1976 seems most likely. Several have argued that this *Tristan* is Spas Wenkoff (1976), and not Helge Brillioth (1974, 1975). Three sequences exist: 10:37 from the orchestral Prelude to Act I; 25:08 from Act II, Scene II, the duet "O sink hernieder, Nacht der Liebe" of Tristan and Isolde ("Descend, O night of love, grant oblivion that I may live"); and, 6:46 from the Liebestod concluding Act III.[190] There is also a pirate recording, audio only, of Kleiber rehearsing the Prelude and Liebestod. It was recorded (illicitly) with the Stuttgart Radio Symphony Orchestra on 24 and 25 July 1972, and may be found on two CDs at Golden Melodram, GM 4.0081, among other enterprises. Kleiber speaks a good deal in these rehearsals. Their sound is rather poor.

After four last performances in the summer of 1976,[191] Carlos never conducted at Bayreuth again. However, within four years he was persuaded by

Deutsche Grammophon to record his definitive version of the opera. Expectations were high. Consequences were disastrous.

This project ended, for him, in a deeply unsatisfactory way. It led to a lengthy breach with his recording company and to his insistence that the final product did not represent his final wishes.

In the trade, this luminous recording has become known as "The Dresden Tristan."[192] Deutsche Grammophon had originally proposed recording a live performance at Bayreuth or in some comparable setting. Carlos was adamantly opposed, although he did not care much for the recording studio either. A live performance would lead to false compromise, inept balance, and the dangers of audible vocal fatigue by the end of a long evening. He wanted something better.[193]

It was finally agreed to record the work in Dresden's Lukaskirche. Dresden was in the former East Germany. During WWII that unique city was almost entirely undefended, and it was destroyed by Allied bombing over 13 to 15 February 1945. The British sent 796 Lancaster bombers and the Americans 311 B17s. Some forty-five thousand civilians lost their lives in the firestorms. (In some ways this was revenge for the Nazis' comparable destruction of Coventry, beginning on 14 November 1940. That city was also a marvel of medieval architecture.) The Lukaskirche barely survived. During the GDR (German Democratic Republic) era it became a recording facility. The Staatskapelle Dresden would provide the orchestra and Leipzig Radio the chorus. Kleiber's demands for rehearsal were unprecedented. In August 1980 he had *ten* orchestra-only rehearsals. In October, he began a series of *twenty* recording sessions with the whole company. In between he worked with his stellar leads in the usual intense manner. He did the same with the chorus.

According to Richard Evidon, writing for Deutsche Grammophon many years later,[194] Carlos seated the orchestra in an unorthodox manner. (It was the same plan he so often recommended to me.) Violins sat in stereo, firsts on audience left and seconds on the right. Violas filled an arc behind the firsts, cellos behind the seconds, and basses between them both. He was deeply convinced that this seating allowed for the best of blend and the highest of articulate speech, among the string sections of the orchestra.

The recording was made seriatim, although as is customary in Europe the preludes to the first and third acts were to be taken at the very end of the process.[195] His casting was remarkable. René Kollo had long been a distinguished Tristan, Kurt Moll a similarly respected King Marke, his old friend Brigitte Fassbaender a perfect Brangäne, and the esteemed Dietrich Fischer-Dieskau a Kurwenal for the ages. It was in his choice of Isolde that Carlos went well beyond the norm.

He chose Margaret Price. This Welsh soprano had never sung the role on stage and never would. Everything she brought to the recording came in pure form, unfiltered by stage experience or theatrical tradition, unmediated by any other hand than his. Price was almost eleven years younger than Carlos and wholly open to his point of view. Her attitude, the startling purity and ardent passion of her voice, her superb diction and collegiality made an ideal partner in this enterprise.

So too was bass Kurt Moll, singing the conflicted role of a king agonized by betrayal and doubt. Kleiber understood these things. "I was greatly helped by the insights and sensitivity of Carlos Kleiber during our collaboration at Bayreuth and during the preparation of our recording," Moll said years later.

"It was wonderful to sing this role with Kleiber, who feels and experiences the work very deeply. Although he knows a great deal about it—and about a great many other things—and rehearses minutely and analytically, the end result emerges not out of 'intellect' but from his heart and feelings. That's what I love about him."[196] One prominent critic praised Moll's work with Kleiber at Bayreuth as "a performance in a thousand."

Things did not go so well with all the others.

For the celebrated Dietrich Fischer-Dieskau, singing the role of Kurwenal, rehearsals began at a very high level. Interviewed in 1995, he remembered the project clearly. "That recording was the last experience in my life with someone who *really* knew how to rehearse. We worked through the role of Kurwenal alone. Only a coach was present. And while it was going on I had the feeling: Every second of this rehearsal, everything that is being said here, is important. I can really use this." That mood soon ended, at least for the baritone.

"The next day at the second piano rehearsal he didn't correct me any more, which made me uneasy again. Because if from one day to the next I had put into practice everything he wanted, that could be a bad thing. And then during the recording he paid very little attention to the soloists, unfortunately."[197] It proved even more difficult for others.

Kleiber nearly came to blows with René Kollo during the session recording Tristan's crazed delusions in Act III. The two artists were now in open conflict. Diplomacy would not prevail. Quarrels led to disaster. Carlos walked out, deeply angered by what he thought to be insubordination and a want of support from the producers. When he left the recording was incomplete, or so he believed.

In fact senior producer Werner Mayer had left all the microphones open and all the recorders running, during the rehearsal sessions. Clever editing, inaudible to any listener, finally permitted a "whole" version to be released two years later. Carlos never forgave the betrayal and quit Deutsche Grammophon.

Every recording he made thereafter was "live." He could control those events. He had enough of the studio and never returned to it.

But this was all in the future. After that one last *Tristan* in Bayreuth, Kleiber spent much of the fall of 1976 as a commuter, hopping back and forth between Munich and Milan for performances of *Rosenkavalier*,[198] *Otello*,[199] and *Fledermaus* again in Munich on New Year's Eve.

Carlos made history when he opened La Scala's new production of *Otello* on 7 December 1976. This was the first time that great house had ever televised a live performance. It was conceived by Paolo Grassi and directed by Franco Zeffirelli, with an obvious eye toward the camera. Its staging was as opulent and rich as everything Zeffirelli ever did but was blocked in close consultation with Kleiber. Domingo starred, with Freni, Cappuccilli, Ciannella, Jori, Raffanti, Roni, Mori, and Morresi. All Milan, and most of the opera world, knew what was coming.

So did the demonstrators. They had gathered outside the theatre in order to protest the costs and subsidies of opera in the face of other social needs. Some of them had purchased tickets and were in the house when Carlos entered the pit. The television broadcast recorded audible disturbance in the house and the remarkably patient look on Carlos's face as he waited for the noise to subside.

The broadcast would be seen by some twenty-four million people across Europe that night. Although not as celebrated an international event as his New Year's performances at Vienna in 1989 and 1992, it nonetheless had a major impact on Kleiber's public profile. It also led to a happy relationship with a stage director. "It was awesome to work with Kleiber for the first time," Zeffirelli wrote. "Here was a man who exacts from musicians the very highest standards and who brought the La Scala orchestra and chorus along with Domingo to a pitch of perfection."[200] Kleiber was equally responsive to Zeffirelli's view of the Moor.

The director saw Otello as "a truly cultured man of the Renaissance whose goodness makes him blind to the sheer force of evil that is brought to bear on him. Mine was a Catholic view of the opera—a religious struggle with Otello finally surrendering the western faith he has adopted and returning to his African roots, to the faith of his own people and the religion he possessed before being taken into slavery. Iago represents the cancer that eats away within Christianity, his evil is all our failures to live up to the very standards it purports to represent." Kleiber could work with a man of such convictions and of such views about Catholicism, the unclaimed faith of his own childhood.

Zeffirelli also saw Kleiber on a larger horizon. They did four productions together: *La Bohème, Carmen, Otello,* and *Traviata.* "Kleiber provoked in my soul a particular reading through extraordinary stimulus that only a man gifted with supernatural powers can suggest to you. Working side by side, strong, completely new ideas arose inside me," he said, modestly adding that, "He had the power to broaden my musical horizons well beyond the limits, however vast they already were."[201] There is film of Kleiber and Zeffirelli working, side by side, in a piano staging rehearsal for *La Bohème*, evidently taken at La Scala. They clearly get along very well.[202]

It was at this point that Plácido Domingo first began to take a view that has prevailed: "His gifts—musical and dramatic insights, analytical abilities, technique, methods of explaining himself—make him the greatest conductor of our day."[203] In his autobiography *My First Forty Years*, the great Spanish tenor writes for many pages of his admiration for Carlos's artistry but with a smart awareness of the problems.

> His extraordinary seriousness toward his work makes Kleiber's career a difficult one . . . there are singers—those whose musicianship is weak—who are either frightened to death or simply put off by him. When he does not achieve something that at least approaches what he is seeking, he becomes very frustrated. . . . He does not realize just how extraordinarily gifted he is. . . . The outward results of his complex makeup are his rough relations with certain artists, his walking out of rehearsals, his cancellation of contracts—not out of capriciousness, but as a manifestation of his overall dissatisfaction. If he were to become the permanent conductor of a major orchestra, he could turn it into the greatest ensemble in history. He would probably drive the musicians crazy in the process.[204]

Kleiber's rehearsal technique for the La Scala *Otello* differed greatly from that which he employed in other houses, in other repertoire. It has been many times remarked that his principal tools were imagery, metaphor, the development and embodiment of character, and an adamant refusal to conduct by the bar. One concertmaster had a very different experience.

> I remember that with "Otello" he never rehearsed more than two or three consecutive bars without stopping, and he told everyone what they had to do note by note, something that came from his incredible research. And therefore, at a certain moment, I remember that those close to top management became nervous because effectively we had never played things through from start to finish.
>
> Well, after a *month* of rehearsals, at the end, he started to do something without interruption. There was an explosion and everyone jumped outside themselves. Everyone knew what he had to do, note by note. One thing that I remember, for example, in the entry of Otello, that Kleiber conducted all the beats, one, two, three, four! I swear: the baton hissed!
>
> —Giulio Franzetti, concertmaster, Orchestra of La Scala, RAI Radio 3, 21 February 2008[205]

In short order, Zeffirelli made plans to direct a theatrical film of the production. He desperately wanted Carlos to work on it, and they held a number of conversations. Zeffirelli arranged for the services of Plácido Domingo, Katia Ricciarelli, and Justino Díaz in the lead roles. But Carlos soon got cold feet and pulled out. The final film, now with Lorin Maazel on the podium, was released in 1986.[206]

He gave *Otello* four more times [207] at La Scala and bounced back to Munich for two more *Traviata,*[208] seven more *Bats*[209] and a wind-up *Rosenkavalier* on 27 February.

Carlos then turned to the other voice of Richard Strauss. This was a special oratory of ferocious power, unalloyed edginess, and fearless dissonance. In a word, *Elektra*. After an exhausting rehearsal period and incessant demands on every member of the company, Carlos was finally ready to return to the subject. Joined by Birgitt Nilsson, whom he had specifically requested for the title role, they opened at London's Covent Garden on 6 May 1977.[210] In Kleiber's career, this was rare and distinctly important literature.

Veteran operagoer Tom Durrie attended the last performance. Years later he remembers the pairing of Nilsson and Kleiber.

"I saw her many times in other operas, and in recitals," Durrie said in a 2010 interview.

> I listened to her recordings, and thought I knew her voice very well. I was not prepared for that night. Formidable as Nilsson was in every other role, when she sang *Elektra* for Kleiber she was suddenly a tigress onstage. I had never seen anything like it. It was only later that I realized how much of Nilsson's power came from her conductor.
>
> At the time I had no idea who Carlos was, other than being Erich's son. He got a unique performance out of her. I remember it being tremendously exciting, beginning to end. Of the many productions I have seen since, none has come close to the sheer energy of that one. Its success was wholly due to the partnership of the fabulous Nilsson and the unknown Kleiber.

Two pirates exist to confirm the audacity of Carlos's work in this repertoire.[211] Part of that audacity lies in his adherence to Strauss's own view that this music has, lying in wait, a Mendelssohnian transparency. Get that right and everything else falls into place. In his 1977 performance, Kleiber never backs away from the shattering orchestral power and structures of the work. Contra-tonalities do not bother him. He gives them their weight and friction. But he never does so at the cost of distending the narrative line or of demanding vocal self-immolation from his singers—Nilsson in particular. She makes wonders. Regardless of the tape hiss endemic to this bootleg, it remains one of the most important documents we have of Carlos's overwhelming command of this music.

It was a summer of Strauss. He returned to the bittersweets of *Rosenkavalier* in Munich on 19 June with his favorite cast, headed by Jones, Fassbaender, and Popp.[212] Kleiber always appreciated Gwyneth Jones's work as the Marschallin. From 1972 to 1984 she sang that role for him fifty-three times. Years after their last performance together, for a book celebrating her life and roles, Carlos wrote a public remembrance.

In 210 well-crafted, deftly presented, and admiring words, Carlos talked about Jones's capacity. She was a woman of endless good humor, an originality, a vivacity that he felt central to the core of three women and the tremendous success of *Der Rosenkavalier* they enjoyed for many seasons. He praised her technical and vocal skills, of course, but went far beyond to convey his appreciation of her spirit and her generosity. Although effusive, his paean included a few digs at himself. He implied that there were times when he had been "impatient" with her, all to no avail. Such a tactic never worked with Gwyneth Jones. She would leave him hanging, clumsily, with no retreat. This must have embarrassed Carlos a good deal—when she would not run away or fight back. It seems she just stood there, smiling and impervious. Not without cause did he refer to his hero of forbearance, Lao-Tse, as he had often done with me and others. All considered, this special letter, written for publication in 1991, sports tremendous admiration and no small degree of rue. Above it reigned his gratitude for her company over many years. This was a near-unique document.[213]

Then it was back to the recording studio, this time to make his definitive version of Verdi's *La Traviata*, with the Rumanian Ileana Cotrubas in the title role. He had already given thirteen performances with her in this role in the 1975–1976 season, and a refresher on 11 January of 1977, all with the Bavarian State Opera Orchestra and Chorus. Now she would be joined for the first time by Plácido Domingo and Sherill Milnes. Together, they made a recording still unequalled in excitement.

This Deutsche Grammophon *Traviata* had actually begun back in the spring of 1976. Cotrubas, Milnes, and Domingo started their work with Kleiber in a Munich beer hall, from 14 to 21 May. It was not a good choice. Domingo reports that Kleiber was unhappy with the seating of the orchestra and other acoustical problems. Time fled, and so did Carlos. The whole event had to be put off to the following year. Carlos wanted to get out altogether "and we had to talk him into continuing."[214] These sessions resumed on 26 January, and 25 to 26 June 1977. Producer Hans Hirsch did an amazing job in the editing booth, and Carlos was ultimately very happy with the results.

That fall, Kleiber had planned to make his first appearance in America.

It is widely reported that Kleiber made his U.S. debut leading *Otello* on 8 September 1977 at the San Francisco Opera.[215] Although announced by Kurt Herbert Adler, longtime general director of that great house, this engagement never actually took place. (The error has been picked up and repeated by writers of liner notes, program books, and obituaries all over the world. Carlos's first appearance in America was actually in Chicago the following season.)

The reason he didn't appear at the Golden Gate involves dentists. In Adler's oral history, a weird story unfolds. He knew Carlos from Munich and had been trying for years to get him to work in San Francisco. Over lunch at the Savoy Grill in London, and joined by Eva Wagner, they "discussed everything and signed the contract."[216] It was agreed and announced that Carlos would lead *Otello* in Jean-Pierre Ponnelle's production, and with Katia Ricciarelli as Desdemona.

However, in February 1978 Adler received a letter from Carlos. It turns out that he had to take his son Marko to the dentist and would therefore be unable to fulfill his contract. Adler was enraged.

"That was an absolutely unique case, and only Kleiber can do such things. One is so taken aback—you are furious, of course—but you cannot be mad at him. What can you do if someone says, in February, that on September seventeenth I have to take my son to the dentist?" Later that year, Kurt Herbert Adler and Carlos bumped into one another in Munich. Carlos looked abashed and, without even saying hello, asked Adler, "Are you going to sue me?"

Adler replied, "Mr Kleiber, I have *time* to sue you. Just wait a year." Adler never did.

After Carlos's nonexistent work in California he gave three more performances of *Rosenkavalier*,[217] and later *Otello*, both with the Bavarian State Opera. The latter cast was headed by Varady, Wewezow, and Cossutta.[218]

Kleiber spent the first two months of 1978 in Munich, treading familiar turf: *Rosenkavalier*, *Otello*, and *La Bohème*. He was now more comfortable with this core repertoire than he had ever imagined possible. Such confidence showed in an exquisitely expressive baton and in rehearsal procedures that began to rely on good humor more than ever. Never relinquishing the drive, he began (sometimes) to ease up on the reins a bit. The Kleiber the world came to know was now in full flight.

A performance of *Rosenkavalier* on 22 January with Jones, Popp, and Fassbaender was followed by *Otello* on the 25th. It was a rare excursion into this work without the much-wanted Plácido Domingo in the title role. *Bohème* was revived a day later, with Freni and Pavarotti.[219] This *Bohème* was supervised by Otto Schenk. It would be conducted by Carlos another five times between 1978 and 1984.

Kleiber worked with Freni on dozens of occasions, considered her a personal friend, and admired her artistry and voice in equal measure. She was "Mirellina," a treasured colleague, and dazzled in *Bohème* and *Otello* as did few others. In 1990 he was asked to contribute a public statement to Giuseppe Gherpelli's new book about her. He said yes, immediately.

"Mirella Freni is a miracle of voice, character, and sweetness," he wrote. "When she sings and acts everything amalgamates itself and her art appears like a simple thing, natural. She was born a singer, and on the stage it is her voice, her technique, and her heart that sing. A true primadonna, without artificiality."[220]

At La Scala his only work in 1978 was a production of Wagner's *Tristan und Isolde*. He had in the past conducted the opera in Stuttgart, Vienna, and Bayreuth, all houses imbued with the Germanic tradition. He accepted the Milan engagement, in part, out of curiosity to see how that house—with its unique apprenticeship and sensibility—would handle it. He was especially interested to see if that sometimes chaotic orchestra would respond to his conception of melodic design. With some difficulty, it did. Together with Wenkoff, Ligendza, Moll, Nimsgern, Corradi, Baldani, De Palma, Foiani, and Gullino he gave six performances that summer.[221] He was not happy with resistance he found in the orchestra, but blamed it on his own shoddy technique.

The American critic Harvey Sachs remembers how it happened.

Kleiber's demand for 1 / full rehearsals had been met. But instead of allowing the orchestra to read through substantial stretches of the score at the first sessions and going over the details later, he pounced on the inevitable errors from the first minutes of the first rehearsal. The Scala musicians adored him, having performed other operas with him during the two previous seasons, but in "Tristan" players and conductor seemed at cross-purposes. During a break, I was stretching my legs in a corridor when I saw Kleiber walking toward me. (Through the intercession of a shared friend, I was one of the lucky few he allowed to observe his rehearsals.) Although I knew him only slightly, he asked, "Why do I keep trying to conduct?" My jaw must have dropped, because he continued: "I can't get them to understand what I want. I shouldn't be conducting at all."

I began to make a tactful comment about the orchestra's unfamiliarity with Tristan; he saw where I was heading and stopped me short. "I know, I know," he said. "That's just the point. I can't bear to let the errors go uncorrected. It's bigger than I am."[222]

Wolfgang Wagner, who had maintained very good personal relations with Kleiber, was the producer and designer of this production. He remembers it well. In his memoirs he writes that, "Losing his temper with the solo cellist, a celebrated '*professore*' from the Milan Academy of Music, [Carlos] told him to change places with the tutti cellist at the furthest desk who had, he said, been playing with admirable intensity."[223] Kleiber was also audibly unhappy with Spas Wenkoff's diction as Tristan. Wenkoff evidently "cherished a tenacious belief that he was singing a special Wagnerian brand of German," and Carlos was not amused.

Once again returning north, Carlos entered the Munich pit on 12 and 20 June for a revival of *Traviata*. This was followed on 16 and 30 July by another revival of *Rosenkavalier* with Jones, Fassbaender, and Popp in that summer's Munich Opernfestspiele.

From 11 to 15 September 1978, on an exceptionally economical schedule, Carlos recorded Schubert's third and eighth symphonies for Deutsche Grammophon. This was done with the Vienna Philharmonic at the Musikvereinsaal and the services of executive producer Hans Hirsch, line producer Hans Weber, and engineer Klaus Scheibe. It proved to be one of his most successful recordings, both critically and commercially.

HAND ACROSS THE SEA

Later that fall Carlos was finally off to conduct in America. It did not set much of a pattern.

The Los Angeles Philharmonic, for example, twice had him on the hook. As reported by Mark Swed,

> In the mid-'70s, after agreeing in principle to make his American debut in Los Angeles, Kleiber decided he didn't want to make the trip from Munich after all. The next time, in the '80s, Kleiber told then-Philharmonic music director Carlo Maria Giulini that he would conduct in Los Angeles for two weeks if he were given a house here for three months and a school was found for his children. Kleiber said that [managing director] Ernest Fleischmann should call if that could be managed, and he gave Giulini the phone number. "I made all the arrangements he asked for," Fleischmann said, "and I called him at the number he had given to Giulini. 'Mr. Fleischmann, where did you get this number?' he answered. 'It's private.' And that was the end of the conversation."[224]

And sometimes players took matters into their own hands. In the mid-1980s, members of the San Francisco Symphony held a meeting. They had been begging management to invite Kleiber. Nothing had come of it, so they tried it themselves. The players wrote him a letter, and all of them signed it. Amazingly, he replied. He sent them a postcard, declining the opportunity in amusing and self-deprecatory language. The card went up in the players' area backstage at Davies Symphony Hall but was eventually stolen.

The Chicago Symphony Orchestra (CSO) was the only American ensemble that ever succeeded in luring him to its podium. They got Kleiber there in October 1978 and again in June 1983. Many other managers tried to do the same, on behalf of orchestras across the United States and Canada.

Pirate recordings of Kleiber's Chicago concerts are prized as platinum among collectors. He was happy to work there, and his concerts were tremendously successful. But why Chicago? As so often with Kleiber, the reasons were largely personal. Beyond the fact of his deep respect for that orchestra, Carlos had an affection for Chicago's conductor Georg Solti.[225] He also struck a real friendship with its artistic director, Peter Jonas.[226] According to Jonas, these concerts were long in coming, "and took two years of planning."[227] The first set was given on 12, 13, and 14 October 1978. Kleiber performed on familiar territory: Weber's Overture to *Freischütz*, Schubert's Symphony No. 3, and Beethoven's Symphony No. 5. But Kleiber was spooked.

"When Carlos arrived, about a week before the first rehearsal, unlike most conductors, he was so nervous, so frightened, as he always was, jittery really. He spent the last two or three days of spare time going into the library with his own material, which he had sent ahead of time, checking that the librarians had marked every single bowing exactly as he wanted it, from his master part," said Jonas.

"He was always absolutely in panic before a concert. This happened throughout his career—whether it was an orchestra concert, or an opera performance, he was in panic. He was scrupulously prepared, scrupulously rehearsed, he demanded rehearsal conditions that nobody else had. He was so prepared, over-prepared if you like, but in panic. He would be in the dressing room before a rehearsal, three hours before, before a performance three or four hours before, and would live in the opera house or the orchestra hall and soak up the atmosphere, working himself up into a frenzy of fear."[228]

The Chicago audience didn't seem to notice. After those concerts, the clamor for his return never stopped—nor was it ever answered, not that the CSO didn't keep trying. It had nothing to do with Carlos feeling that Chicago was inadequate or unresponsive; to the contrary, he admired them. After I sent him a film of Tennstedt conducting them in Mahler's Symphony No. 1, he praised the Chicago players mightily. He deeply enjoyed both of his concert sets in that city.

Beyond the music, there was something very personal about that first concert in Chicago—an unexpected visitor, backstage. He had fallen in love with her when he was very young. Argentine pianist, composer, and teacher Pía Sebastiani traveled to Chicago from Muncie, Indiana, where she taught for many years at Ball State University. She was admitted to Carlos's dressing room, and greeted him in a porteño-accented Spanish. "My name is Pía Sebastiani. Many years ago your father conducted a piece of mine at the Colón." She couldn't get another word out before Carlos interrupted.

"Pía, dear, how could I not remember you!" he replied, in Spanish. "I was madly in love with you when I was fifteen!" She smiled. Back in 1946, Sebastiani had received a phone call. "This is Erich Kleiber. I saw the score of your composition 'Estampas' and would like to include it in one of my upcoming concerts." The then twenty-one-year-old musician couldn't believe it. A few weeks later, at the Teatro Colón, Erich Kleiber conducted "Nocturno" and "Carnaval" from her suite *Estampas*. It was an extraordinary career breakout. She stayed in touch with the Kleibers until she moved to France, two years later, to study with Messiaen, Milhaud, and Marguerite Long, among others.

Pía Sebastiani, now eighty-six years old and revered in South America, remembers the young Carlos as a peculiar German boy with fat legs, in short pants and long socks, "the ones called three-quarters, as they go almost to the knee." She also recalls how Carlos used to call her by phone rather too often, and she tried to avoid him. Today Pía recollects how, sixty-five years before, she broke the heart of a boy who was to be an outstanding artist, but whose appearance at that time "was not precisely that of Leonardo DiCaprio."[229]

One of Jonas's successors, the widely admired Henry Fogel, kept trying to get him back to Chicago.[230] In 1996 he went online, answering a plaintive query in a well-known classical music discussion group: "President Fogel, Why can't we get Carlos Kleiber to guest conduct the Chicago Symphony again? He has done it before and I know he's a hard fish to catch but wouldn't it be wonderful?"

Fogel replied with a rueful truth known to concert managers and opera intendants the world over.

"Kidnapping is illegal. Bringing him at gunpoint would probably result in a less-than-ideal concert. Everything else, we keep trying. We are regularly in touch with him, and we ask him every single season. You must recognize the reality—Carlos Kleiber is actually conducting less and less now than he ever has (and he never conducted all that much). I understand that he has given exactly one concert in the past year! Believe me—the CSO invites him consistently, and not just *pro forma* either. We have flown to visit him, and tried everything else known to man."[231]

Kleiber was certainly received and treated very well in Chicago. The whole city seems to have recognized what a great prize he was. Many people walked on cat paws, afraid of upsetting him. Not so Alison Ames, head of North American operations for Deutsche Grammophon. This is the company with which Carlos had bitterly quarreled about release of his iconic recording of *Tristan und Isolde*. According to David Patrick Stearns, Ms. Ames approached Kleiber backstage after one of the Chicago concerts. "Standing in a sweaty T-shirt (that he promptly pulled off), he smiled radiantly while holding both her hands. But upon being told she was from Deutsche Grammophon, he said in German, still smiling, 'Scheiss Firma' (comparing the company to excrement). And when she returned the following concert he said, 'You're back for more!'"[232]

There was to have been a third Chicago engagement. To national acclaim, the CSO announced that Kleiber would appear again on 21, 22, 23, and 25 March 1985.[233] Circumstances changed. Eleven months later they advised that Carlos had canceled his third appearance "for personal reasons."[234] His concert career in America had come to a halt.

Carmen called at Christmas 1978, postmarked Vienna. In a new production designed for him, the Staatsoper presented a realistic and un-gilded portrayal of the woman who makes men suffer. Kleiber loved it.[235] The first of these performances was televised live and is available in various bootleg versions and under various titles on the Internet. With barely time for the holidays, he was once again required at the Bavarian State Opera. There, on 4, 7, and 11 January 1979 he revived *Rosenkavalier*, with a happy and largely familiar cast.[236] This had become a signature work.

In what would be a harbinger of a very strange concert two years later, Carlos was suddenly asked to substitute for an ailing Karl Böhm, the distinguished German conductor. With little rehearsal time, he jumped in and led, on 4 and 5 February, Rome's Orchestra of the Accademia di Santa Cecilia. They gave a comfortable program of Weber's Overture to *Der Freischütz*, Beethoven's Symphony No. 5, and Schubert's Symphony No. 3. The orchestra may have been unfamiliar to him, but the territory certainly was not.

In Milan, the spring of 1979 has been immortalized as a season of unmatched vocal beauty. Carlos contributed eight performances of Puccini's *La Bohème*.[237] His casts included Pavarotti, Cotrubas, and Popp in the first seven, with Dvorsky singing Rodolfo in the last of them. It was an astonishing array of singing talent, with each of these leads in their absolute prime. With tremendous foresight, it was agreed to film and televise this production, and it is thus possible to recreate its enchantment. It was originally broadcast by NHK (Japan Broadcasting Corporation) on 22 December 1979.

Pavarotti had a special appreciation for Kleiber's capacity to convey personality from the pit. He found it tremendously reassuring. "Maestro Kleiber experiences the emotions of every character so vividly and intensely that if you look at his face you cannot make a big mistake."[238] "These geniuses can make you hear things in the music you never heard before, and they make you alert to new possibilities in the drama. Kleiber inspired me to try different approaches.

. . . I found myself singing without effort." He went on to say that Kleiber was particularly demanding about the original key. "Che Gelida Manina" is often transposed down a half-step, to make it easier for tenors. "But Kleiber made me sing the aria in the original key. Somehow I soared up to the high C with no strain. It may sound like superstition, but I am sure that was due to the inspiration of working with him and the way he conducted."[239]

Carlos appreciated his artists in turn. On 23 March 1979 he sent a note to Romano Gandolfi, the chorusmaster at La Scala. "Dear Roman!" he wrote. "I beg you to tell the chorus that I am very grateful for the 'La Boheme' last night. And you too, dear friend! Hello, with love Your Carlos Kleiber."[240]

Another of Carlos's famous might-have-beens now ghosted forward. Arrangements were made to record *Bohème* at La Scala in June 1979, with Plácido Domingo in the role of Rodolfo. These sessions actually started, but "Carlos became upset in the middle of the first act and refused to go on," said Domingo. He could not be persuaded to return. Those who remained ended up recording the Verdi *Requiem* instead, now led by Claudio Abbado. "I understand that he later listened to what had been done, found it wonderful, and could not imagine what had angered him," added Domingo. "But that's Carlos."[241]

It was soon up to Munich again, and for another five performances of *Rosenkavalier* with the Bavarian State Opera.[242] His cast gave him much pleasure, and working with Lucia Popp was more than reward. He remained unstinting in his admiration for her. It was in this period that his first film of *Rosenkavalier* was made by Deutsche Grammophon, from the end of May through the beginning of June.

Then Big Ben called once more, and Kleiber spent November at Covent Garden in seven performances of Puccini's *La Bohème*.[243] A quarter-century later, it was still remembered by his colleagues. "His Bohème at Covent Garden made a huge impression because it was such an original interpretation," recalled Sir Charles Mackerras, "with far more detail and logic to the timing and tempo of the various episodes than we had ever experienced here in London."[244] Mackerras was onto something.

"When we first discussed his doing a Bohème for us, we treated it as something special from the very beginning," said John Tooley. "We talked at great length about taking it apart, going back to the basics, and creating it absolutely new. And so we took it apart. Carlos responded wonderfully. There was poetry and magic in every performance he conducted. He took us to another level of achievement altogether."[245]

The calendar closed with appearances at the Vienna Philharmonic, and in familiar repertoire: Brahms's Symphony No. 4, Mozart's Symphony No. 33, and Weber's Overture to *Freischütz*. The audience and its orchestra seemed never to tire of these works, and neither did Carlos.[246]

Carlos became an Austrian citizen in January 1980. On the 7th of that month he was issued an Austrian passport and thereafter traveled on that document.[247] It was more a matter of practicality than anything else. Tooley remembers Carlos realizing that his Argentine passport was about to expire and that his personal appearance in Buenos Aires was required in order to renew it. Kleiber simply didn't have time for such a long trip.[248] Someone told him that he could get an Austrian passport much more easily, and so he did. He thus became "Austrian."

His fourth decade as conductor began in Vienna. On 17 January 1980 he conducted at the fortieth Philharmonie Ball, a rare "social" outing for him—and a brief appearance in the newsreels. The following month he was back to London, leading another series of Verdi's *Otello* at Covent Garden.[249] Plácido Domingo was once again his lead, and their partnership continued to flourish. Critic Peter Heyworth offered, "The house was ablaze. The Covent Garden chorus sang as if terrified out of its wits by the conductor."[250]

Well, it was. "We had a problem with Carlos, and it came to a head during his first *Otello* with us," said Sir John Tooley.

> The first performance was simply brilliant. *Brilliant.* I missed the second, but when I got back Carlos was jumping up and down, furious. He told me "Your chorus was terrible!" It seems the basses missed an entrance because their leader got lost that night. Carlos would have none of it. "I won't cue the chorus any more!" he insisted.
>
> He was very angry. He went so far as to tell me that "I won't conduct any opera with choruses any more!" It took me a while, but he finally backed down and it was all OK in the end. I actually couldn't imagine a better conductor to work with. He was wonderful, demanding, inspired.[251]

From 12 to 15 March, Kleiber recorded his wondrous Brahms 4 with the Vienna Philharmonic, and once more in their home at the Musikverein. This too was achieved on a remarkably tight schedule. Just as speedily, on 1 December 1980 he approved its release by Deutsche Grammophon.[252]

Carlos's work on this Brahms was changed, at least briefly, by a curious intervention. He enjoyed, for many years, the company of a professional bassoonist, an American known here as KD. She was married to someone else in this period. Her husband, a harpsichord maker, died in 2002, and she has recently been a bit more forthcoming about her relationship with Kleiber. She is also an acquaintance of Gunther Schuller and friends with members of the Slovenian orchestra with whom Carlos performed twice, late in life.

She introduced herself to me in an e-mail and talked about how they met and what it meant to her. They first encountered one another in Bavaria when she was twenty-nine. The depth of her affection cannot be mistaken.

I find it very difficult to talk about Carlos even though I could go on for hours talking about him and I'll tell you why. We knew each other for over 30 years. I met him in Munich, in 1972, while I was teaching in Switzerland and visiting a friend. I was being a tourist and wandered into the hall, because I heard an orchestra rehearsing. I was sitting on a bench in the outer hall and I fell asleep. He came along and woke me up. It was all very embarrassing. I didn't know who he was except that he was ravishingly handsome. We had lunch and talked until he had to go back to work. That's how it began. I was young, somewhat pretty, American and a bassoonist. He couldn't seem to resist that combination.

At our second meeting, he told me he was married and had 2 children and I told him that on my return to the States I was getting married. He didn't suggest separating, his plan was that we would never talk about our respective families with each other or share our friendship with anyone else. I know it will seem ridiculous but I blurted all of this out to a friend of mine just a year ago. I never mentioned Carlos to anyone for all of those years. When I left Europe (after 3 years) we became phone buddies. We would have marathon conversations about everything about twice a year. He often chewed gum while we were talking on the phone. He would pop it and ask, "How's my breath?" He could be very silly.

In a nutshell, Carlos Kleiber was the kindest, gentlest, most intelligent and the funniest man I have ever had the pleasure to know. And, for me, he was the ultimate musician. He was a strange and often times unreadable man, but just being able to peer into the world where he lived every once in a while was magic for me. I always used to laugh when he made a tremendous effort to try to act like everyone else and his shyness was a complete mystery to me.

My husband died (2002) a year before Stanka and even though Carlos was very ill, he spent a lot of time helping me through the hard parts. Then Stanka died and then Carlos left too. It all just disappeared in a puff of smoke. In the end I guess that's what magic is all about.

—KD, e-mail to author 21 October 2009,
and author's interview of 23 June 2010

And we did work on some of Brahms 4 when he was preparing it for the Vienna recording. There are 6 small chords in a transition situation preceding a huge chord. . . . You're never going to get this, but it's the best I can do right now. I've listened to every recording possible and everyone does these 6 short chords as connected (slurred) triplets: quarter, eighth - quarter, eighth - quarter, eighth.[253] What happens when you slur them is that they lose all sense of rhythm. I suggested that he separate them and "bounce" them to the final chord. He loved it and did it on the recording. But only on the recording so maybe he changed his mind. I don't know. That's my claim to fame; 6 short chords in Brahms 4th. This was discussed and done on a hotel floor,[254] with music scattered everywhere.

—KD, e-mail to author, 10 November 2009

We were discussing the bassoon part(s) and he was saying that they were incredibly difficult because almost everything happened in octaves. Keeping everything in tune was paramount. I then happened to say that playing in octaves wasn't that difficult (example Sibelius) but counting Brahms was a real trial for me. He then went off on the fact that conductors conducted notes and measures, not phrases. Conducting lines and phrases solved all those problems. Evidently Brahms (Carlos thought) had a thing about bar lines. Carlos said that Brahms was constricted by bar lines and wandered over them at every opportunity. Now you have to imagine this as it happened. In the middle of what I considered a somewhat serious discussion, Carlos suddenly stuffed a pillow under his shirt and started imitating Brahms (with a very thick German accent) and talking about the hated bar line. That discussion then dissolved into laughter and silliness.

However, at one point after this and having removed the pillow, he got very serious and asked me what I would do with the 3 figures that I've been talking about. . . . Well, I happened to notice that the dreaded bar lines were interrupting everything and I suggested that perhaps the whole thing needed a little bounce, to get over the "slipperiness" of the passage. I don't know what inspired me to say this and I have no idea why he thought it was a good idea. My reward was a kiss, a hug and of course, the recording which I think was done not too long after. As I've said before, he apparently only conducted this this way once and having rethought it, he probably didn't like it after all. I have no idea.

—KD, e-mail to author, 1 January 2010

Score in hand, he flew to Milan for another four performances of *Otello* at La Scala.[255] This opera was now becoming central to Carlos's musical identity. He had first performed it in 1968. Across his career he gave it eighty-one times. His preferred tenor was Plácido Domingo. Together, they gave the work thirty-three times. And everyone understood how trenchant it was in Carlos's hands, and how there was always something new to be said. In fact, *Otello* is a vivid example of his methods.

Kleiber went to the sources. He studied the Shakespeare, the Verdi-Boito libretto, and the standard performing editions struck by his predecessors. There is nothing unusual in this. Conductors of conscience do it all the time. What was unique about his work was the unyielding intensity of these applied insights, and the kinetic—and spiritual—manifestations of its compass. These strengths were passed to every member of the company. His questing mind, his boldness of design, and his compulsion to tell the story—all of this was fused to the working apparatus of every colleague in the house. Declared Bram Gay, a one-time orchestra manager at Covent Garden,

> I have never encountered such an intellect at work. How many conductors have told us what is in the Shakespeare which the librettist Boito omits and where exactly we must remember this because it is important to Verdi?
>
> Working with him is an electric experience. The orchestra is never relaxed. The better the work goes, the greater the tension because the more fragile the creation. An evening with him is one of the great lifetime opportunities for self-realisation.[256]

His greatest Otello saw it much the same way, and from a position of even greater intimacy with the conductor. Said Domingo,

> He has assimilated the score to such a degree that he can read through the notes to uncover all the drama and feeling of the music, everything the composer imagined. It seems so natural and simple, yet even with all the preparation it sounds spontaneous.
>
> Every night is a different experience. He never repeats. With one hand he can give the idea of a big long line beaten in four, while with the other he is beating in twelve with total independence. With him in charge, I just feel that the music and I are absolutely as one.[257]

Years later, Domingo's memory remained as vivid as ever. In a BBC3 radio documentary, he was once again asked about his now-legendary *Otello* with Kleiber.

> One of the unbelievable things that I remember is to see the public at the beginning of Otello. He was conducting and I was about to come to sing the "Esultate," I was going from the side of the boxes in Covent Garden and I could see that nobody was paying any attention to the stage. Everybody was looking at Carlos, what he was doing. And that's really unbelievable. And that was really so special that the people they were captivated, they were really, absolutely hypnotized by what Carlos was doing, and that I will never forget as long as I live, you know."[258]

Carlos's summer of 1980 was occupied by two more performances of *Rosen-kavalier* in Munich at that summer's Opernfestspiele.[259] He closed out the year in appearances at the Musikvereinsaal on 11 and 12 September, with the Vienna Philharmonic. They played Schubert, Symphony No. 8 and three bon-bons by Johann Strauss Jr.: the Overture to *Fledermaus*, "Accelerationen," and "Unter Donner und Blitz," a work he often interpolated in *Fledermaus* itself. Its original ballet is fairly tedious, and it appears that Kleiber never used it. "Donner und Blitz" was his substitute. (He told me to do the same when I was preparing the work some years later. I did. It worked.)

Giuseppe Verdi's romantic tragedy *La Traviata* spoke directly to Carlos. And like Verdi's *Otello* it was another key to his career and to understanding the man. The story is a convergence of sympathy and desire, love found impossible and inevitable.

Kleiber was moved by the suffering of Violetta and by the dread course of her disease. He was fascinated by the dynamics of the three people at the center of a hurricane. He read with an absurdist's eye the meaning of partied wealth disguising intractable pain. He understood the many layers of loyalty being implied, demanded, and expected. (How he was always torn by multiple loyalties, personal and aesthetic.) And he understood intimately the moral dyslexia at the center of the demands made by father and son Germont. In 1959, it was one of the first operas he conducted in Düsseldorf. He went on to conduct it forty-eight times in his career.[260] When he gave the work in January 1981, it was once again in Munich, a place where he felt comfortable experimenting night after night with altered tempo and weight and nuance. He was not, and constitutionally never could be, satisfied with a single performance. With him, there never was a "Final Edition."[261] After this masterwork it was time for brief consideration of another kind of opera altogether.

Jacques Offenbach's *Tales of Hoffmann* is, among conductors, an infamous score. It exists in multiple versions. None of them was completed by Offenbach. He died four months before its premiere, and his practiced hand would have made changes and cuts that his musical executor Ernest Guiraud never managed. The entire work is far too long and tedious to be practical. Carlos knew all this when he was approached by Sir John Tooley and asked to do it at Covent Garden, with the well-regarded stage and film director John Schlesinger. Carlos considered the matter, doing his usual research into the work's troubled manuscript and production history. The project died one night, however, when he went to see Schlesinger's 1971 film *Sunday Bloody Sunday*. He hated it. The project was dead.[262]

It was soon time to travel to an alien and fascinating culture, and a memory of his youth.

Carlos's only working tour of Mexico took place in April 1981. The Vienna Philharmonic had again asked him to serve as musical shepherd, and he happily consented. There were five concerts in all,[263] and two repertoire sets: Beethoven Symphonies 5 and 7, and *Coriolanus*; Schubert No. 3; Mozart No. 33; Strauss, "Acceleration" Waltz and Overture to *Fledermaus*, and Weber's Overture to *Freischütz*. The encore was the raucous "Unter Donner und Blitz."

The most important thing about this tour is that the concert of 27 April was televised. His appearance in the ancient colonial city of Guanajuato[264] was broadcast, with a charming hostess chattering away during the opening measures of *Coriolanus*, *Fledermaus* and the *Fifth*. It is the only known film of him conducting Beethoven 5. I sent it to Carlos. He liked it as a souvenir, but insisted, "I'm terrible on it!"

With blithe self-deprecation, writing to an American correspondent eighteen years later he purported,

> *My 'Mexico Coriolan' was a) a mess and b) I hadn't learned Stoki's version yet. (I'm a little better now, but still not good.)*
>
> *—Carlos Kleiber, to John Kelly, 10 January 1998*[265]

On return from Mexico he also returned to *La Bohème*, and gave it four more performances at La Scala that summer.[266] Less than a week later he got an urgent phone call. He was once again asked to cover for an ailing Karl Böhm. This event, the only symphony concert Carlos ever gave in the British capital, was a critical disaster. It led to emotional fallout that lasted a lifetime.

Böhm had been scheduled to lead the London Symphony Orchestra on 9 June 1981 but was now critically ill.[267] On very short notice he canceled. On shorter notice yet, Carlos agreed to take his place. No extra rehearsals would be required, as the LSO and Kleiber had given the same performance in Milan just days earlier.[268] There, the audience response had bordered on the absurd. A bootleg recording made on that occasion immortalizes the "inhuman screams" that followed the finale of the Beethoven 7. Things would be different in the British capital.

The repertoire was, for Carlos, now standard: Schubert 3, Beethoven 7, and the Overture to Weber's *Der Freischütz*. There was not a warning cloud on the horizon. The Milan performance had enjoyed tremendous success. In London, at the three-thousand-seat Royal Festival Hall, every ticket had been sold. Every distinguished musician, visiting or otherwise, was in place when Carlos walked to the podium. The air rattled with electricity.

At concert's end—by every account I have read—the response was overwhelming. Carlos's first symphony concert in London took wave after wave of applause. It went on for many minutes, and everyone present knew they had witnessed "An Event."

Except the critics.

In *The Daily Telegraph*, Robert Henderson described it as a "disastrously unhappy affair," and "bewildering in its coarseness and insensitivity." Over at *The Guardian*[269] Edward Greenfield was even more hostile. "At no point, with such aggressive exaggerations and idiosyncracies, was it quite possible to dismiss the suspicion that here was a conductor determined at all costs to do things differently, to attract to himself rather than to the music." Only Peter Heyworth, writing in *The Observer*, took a different angle, pronouncing the night as "one of the most marvellous concerts I ever heard." Much other commentary was bleak and ungrateful.

Kleiber took it very hard. So did his players. One of them commented, "It was desperately unfair and terribly stupid of the critics," and many of them expressed their apologies to Kleiber. He was unforgiving. The concert had been recorded by the BBC and was to have been transmitted by them shortly thereafter. Following the reviews Carlos forbade broadcast and ordered the tapes destroyed. They were. He vowed never again to perform on London's concert stage. He never did. To the day of his death, management of the LSO kept trying to get him back.

After the London fiasco, home looked good. The Munich Summer Opera Festival had requested two appearances, and Carlos threw himself into *Der Rosenkavalier* with more than customary intensity. The results, given on 12 and 28 July 1981, were magnificent.[270]

He was back to Japan that fall. Earlier appearances, and wide distribution of his films and recordings, had turned Carlos into a cult figure there. Tickets sold out almost immediately. This time he brought with him two operas, Zeffirelli's La Scala productions of *Otello* and *Bohème*, and two stellar casts.[271] *Otello* was given three times[272] and *Bohème* seven times.[273] They played in Tokyo, Osaka, and Yokohama. The *Otello* of 2 September and the *Bohème* of 15 September were televised by NHK.

A young John Fisher worked on both *Bohème* and *Otello* at La Scala with Kleiber, and on tour in Japan. He was then head of music administration and an assistant to Claudio Abbado. Across eleven years, Fisher saw Kleiber at work many times.

"Abbado worshipped him," he said.

We all did. I was one of his assistants, and learned so much from Carlos. People tended to pussyfoot around him, afraid to be the one that caused a blow-up. We were all in awe of him. I think he was actually quite lonely, because people thought of him as a god—but that never came from him. He didn't believe a word of it.

In fact he was inordinately sensitive, all music, incredibly astute and intelligent. It is true that when he was frustrated he could be very demanding, and appear vindictive. If his sensibility was disturbed, he could react very aggressively. I sat behind him in rehearsals for "Bohème" and saw this myself. But he also had a child-like quality, and hated the idea of having hurt someone.

I was once playing a rehearsal for him in Japan and he became very impatient. It was extremely unpleasant. To my surprise he then took me to a steakhouse, saying, "I'm getting you lunch. It's the least I could do."

Fisher continued.

He would become very frustrated if he couldn't get what he wanted. I was also surprised to realize that he never used solfège in his rehearsals.[274] He would sometimes get a bee in his bonnet, and wouldn't let it go. He could be slightly capricious too, but he was never nasty or mean. I spent a lot of time with him in his dressing room, and all we did was discuss notes from rehearsals. He never bad-mouthed people.

I remember a fragility, an unpredictability. He was afraid of being in anything sub-standard. And there was always a *geist*, a fantasy about him, living in parallel with logic. He could be in a state of delight and enchantment, but still very rational. He was a truly multi-cultural man, and bore the traits of all of them.

John Fisher is today the chief executive and artistic director of the Welsh National Opera. "Carlos Kleiber was one of the greatest conductors, one of the greatest musical minds who ever lived. Today, all I feel is great affection and gratitude. Gratitude."[275]

November 1981 brought Carlos's sad participation in a special concert. It memorialized his friend Karl Böhm, for whom Carlos had twice deputized. Böhm passed away on 14 August, having been gravely ill for months. In the days prior to his passing Carlos went to Salzburg to see him and to say goodbye. Böhm took the occasion to say how much he appreciated Carlos's work. Kleiber was surprised and touched.[276] At Munich's National Theatre on 1 November, with the Bavarian State Orchestra, Carlos gave the second movement of Schubert's "Unfinished" Symphony.

He paid a visit to Ljubljana later that month and conducted the RTV Ljubljana Symphony Orchestra in his now-standard menu of Schubert 3, Beethoven 5, and Weber's *Freischütz* Overture.[277] His Slovenian-born wife Stanka may have had something to do with this, as did a longtime member of the orchestra who is, even to this day, hesitant to talk about its problems. The concert did not go well, although some of its members were convinced that Carlos could hypnotize players and make them play better than they could.

The story goes that Carlos was a bastard from start to finish, beginning by throwing out the first horn and another principal. Everyone who had anything to play that was important had severe diarrhea during the rehearsals and concert. People were positively terrified of him. No one was allowed to observe the rehearsals and only one photo was allowed after the concert, during the bows.

—KD, e-mail to author, 26 November 2009

Soon thereafter he was back to Munich for two performances of *Traviata* with Cotrubas, on 28 November and 1 December, and one of *Bohème* on 6 December, also with Cotrubas. After three weeks off Carlos once again took the New Year's Eve performance of *Fledermaus* at the Bavarian State Opera.[278]

A VERY BAD YEAR

The year 1982 was the lowest point in Carlos's career. It was wrought with cancellations, hard feelings, and crushing disappointment for all concerned. If there was a purely personal or internalized cause, I have never found it. All his manifestations of doubt, dissatisfaction, and relentless self-demand aligned to produce one disaster after another. He was to have made his debut with the Berlin Philharmonic, to have recorded *Wozzeck* and Dvořák's *New World Symphony* for EMI,[279] to have stage directed his first opera, and to have led an important concert set with the Vienna Philharmonic. None of this happened. He canceled all of them.

Indeed, it has been widely reported that Carlos first conducted the Berlin Philharmonic in 1982. Like Kleiber's alleged appearance in San Francisco it was announced—but never occurred.[280] He would not conduct in Berlin for another seven years, although he had been invited many times over many years.

However, two appearances with the Vienna Philharmonic did take place on 27 and 28 February 1982. The Beethoven 7 was by now a glorious chestnut and Haydn 94 a happy memorial to a long-ago favorite son. The real surprise of the evening was the performance of "Three Pieces for Voice and Orchestra" from Alban Berg's *Wozzeck*, with soprano Dunja Vejzovic. His father had, of course, given this opera's world premiere half a century prior. Whenever his son performed *Wozzeck*, or any element drawn from it, every audience knew that they were as close to the fountainhead as they might ever approach.

The Berg was followed in Munich with two performances of *Rosenkavalier*, on 12 and 21 March 1982, and at La Scala in three more performances of *Otello* on 15, 19 and 21 April, with Domingo, Freni, Carroli, De Palma, Manganotti, Foiani, Turtura, Morresi, and Banditelli. Once again he sent a lovely note of appreciation to the chorusmaster at La Scala, thanking him for his work on the *Otello*. "Dear Romano Gandolfi," Carlos wrote. "You know how good is your chorus, so kind and full of soul. Tell them this from me, please, Roman, my friend. Thank you for your kindness to me, and give me more courage. If ever you need anything, I'll do my best, you know. . . . Always faithful, Your Carlos."[281]

Kleiber returned to the Bavarian Staatsoper and one of his favorite orchestras on 2 and 3 May 1982, playing in Munich's National Theatre. He had been asked to conduct a fund-raising concert for a good cause and agreed. The event was recorded, but there were no immediate plans for release. Two years later, it was agreed that it could be published by the Orfeo label. That release saw Carlos breaking one of his own rules.

He once told me that he *never* wrote anything for publication. I was trying to tease out of him the truth behind the story that he had concocted a letter, "from Heaven," attacking Celibidache in the pages of *Der Spiegel*. He didn't bite. However in the liner notes of this unusual recording of Beethoven 4,[282] he did write the following:

For me, okaying a recording is normally a horror. But the Bavarian State Orchestra's playing made the approval of this live recording my very own pleasure. We neither could nor wanted to use any cosmetics or make even the most minute corrections in this aural 'snapshot' of a performance. For any petty critics we have an alibi: A benefit performance for the Prinzregentheater and a live performance. But for those who have an ear for vitality there are things here that no orchestra can play for you as eagerly and pertly or as inspired and delightfully as this orchestra on that day. Many thanks!

—*Carlos Kleiber*

Not straying far from home, Carlos returned to the National Theatre in Munich for performances of *Der Rosenkavalier* on 9, 26, and 29 July 1982, and another New Year's Eve *Fledermaus* on 31 December.

He was to have led a new production of Alban Berg's *Wozzeck* in Munich late that summer, but something went wrong. He had been granted what he wanted, including being personally responsible for stage direction, and seemed satisfied. Everything looked promising. But at the end of July, citing personal reasons, Carlos withdrew. On 31 July the story made it into the papers. It was Wolfgang Sawallisch's first full season in his capacity as music director for the Bavarian Staatsoper, and cancellation on such short notice was difficult. One newspaper story appeared over a large photo of Kleiber in rehearsal, and the caption "Will Not Conduct: Carlos Kleiber."

Interviewed by Karl-Robert Danler, Sawallisch spoke diplomatically. Who will now lead *Wozzeck*? he was asked. "We are still in the middle of negotiations. In about a week we will be able to go public with a name. It is self-evident that the conductor who was originally scheduled for the performance first has to be released from the contract. When this has happened, the new conductor, the director Dieter Dorn, the designer Jürgen Rose and myself will have a meeting."

Sawallisch was asked why Kleiber quit the production. "Personal reasons cannot be interpreted," he said. "I have to respect them whatever they are. But I know that he means neither the Bayerische Staatsoper nor its opera director. There are absolutely no bad feelings between myself and Carlos Kleiber." Danler then got to the heart of his concern.

"Will there be any future projects with Carlos Kleiber?" he asked.

Yes, said Sawallisch. "We are talking about concerts and opera productions for the next four seasons. We haven't got anything final yet, but we have very specific plans."[283]

It was at this time that Carlos's reputation moved, in some circles, from genius to madness. (For the Greeks, of course, this was distinction without difference.) No one accustomed to the standard mechanism of success—press conferences, glam photos, ceaseless upward mobility, fake camaraderie, and air kisses—could readily adapt to Carlos's indifference. To them he made no sense at all. Even some of his most esteemed colleagues began to see it that way. Film producer Brian Large was one of them.

"There are really only a few top conductors today," he said. "Carlos Kleiber is one. Valery [Gergiev] is another. Both are crazy, both are geniuses. But to me Kleiber's craziness is pure craziness. Valery's craziness is with a purpose."[284] This view, in the 1980s, became received wisdom for many. The events of 1982 added momentum to it.

Indeed, that year ended even worse than it began. It ruptured his relationship with the Vienna Philharmonic. Kleiber agreed to conduct a subscription set and had nearly finished rehearsals. According to the Philharmonic's Clemens Hellsberg, things fell apart completely. It led to "the complete breakdown of the relationship in December 1982, shortly before the end of the final rehearsal for a Philharmonic subscription concert, when Kleiber stormed out of the hall, leaving behind a bewildered orchestra which, in his mind, had failed to realize his concept of the opening rhythmic figure of the second movement of Beethoven's Fourth Symphony—a figure which to him should reflect the name of Beethoven's 'immortal beloved.'"[285]

"You're not playing *Therese*, you're just playing *Marie*," he cried. This refers to a well-known mnemomic musicians use to articulate a tricky passage involving 16th notes and 64th rests.[286] "In this outburst was manifested the complete desperation of an artist who reaches for infinity, and shatters in the attempt."[287] His concert was canceled.

All was eventually forgiven and he worked for the Vienna Philharmonic, and its Staatsoper, many times thereafter. After Kleiber's death, and evidently writing on behalf of every member of that extraordinary orchestra, Hellsberg added the rest of the tale.

"His artistic demands were limitless, yet when he sensed anxiety or ill health on the part of a musician he was full of generous understanding. His attacks of rage were boundless and spared no one, but his manner with children was one of such affection, understanding and tenderness, so as to transform such encounters into most precious examples of ideal human relationships."

Hellsberg added one more touch. It rings true.

"Extreme inconsistency characterized Kleiber's entire being. On the one hand, there was constant concern about whether a rehearsal would proceed smoothly or suffer a breakdown, yet on the other hand, aside from an occasional moment of despair, he was available to each musician for private consultation, and displayed a shy and genuine sympathy. He had a huge repertoire and was familiar with practically the entire world literature, yet he limited himself to conducting just a few selected works."

Few people claimed to understand this truth, then or now. It was Carlos Kleiber's way of moving in the world.

SURVIVING FAME

The new year rolled on in Munich with four more "Bats," this in the longest personal tradition of Carlos's professional life, here given on 3 and 7 January, and 12 and 14 February. Altogether, he would conduct *Fledermaus* on New Year's Eve in Munich on nine occasions in the period 1974 to 1987.[288] Those who imagine that Carlos's life consisted of early retirement and hiding from the public never saw him on those New Year's evenings. His laughter, bubbling energies, and obvious joy were as real as the music that sparkled within.

Earlier recounted was the history of Carlos's own 1978 work in Chicago. While his friend Peter Jonas still served as artistic administrator, Kleiber agreed to one more set. He appeared at Orchestra Hall on 2, 3, and 4 June 1983 in Mozart 33, Brahms 2, and a rare piece of lapidary musicianship, George Butterworth's English Idyll No. 1.[289] Yet another pirate has long circulated of this event. The blazing virtuosity of the orchestra more than compensates for the second-rate sound of the recording.

The Butterworth itself has long surprised Carlos watchers. It is not well known, especially in America. How did it come about? Once again, it was friendship with Peter Jonas. "This derived from lazy afternoons in Chicago and Munich when Carlos and I would listen to records together," Jonas said.

"He knew I loved Elgar, Vaughn Williams and Butterworth and he liked the two Butterworth English Idylls as well (Elgar was not his 'beer') and surprised me by offering to programme them to open the 1983 concerts as my birthday present for that year."[290] He surprised Jonas again by telling him that he would also like to conduct *The Mikado* of Gilbert and Sullivan.

Jonas recalled these 1983 performances in Chicago and compared them to his 1978 work there. They were "if anything, much more important in that by that time Carlos's reputation had caught up with him, even in America." The Butterworth got off to a strange start. "It was an idiom so completely unfamiliar to the orchestra that at the first rehearsal our great first oboist, Ray Still, started the melody at double speed. Fortunately, Carlos was amused."[291] Jonas talked about the "difficulty" of working with Kleiber.

"Carlos has this great kind of inhibition, combined with a desire to scrupulously seek some kind of perfection. The hassles, the demands, the nonsigning of contracts, these are all part of an effort to create a framework in which he can make truly sincere artistic statements—on his terms. He is not concerned with amassing great wealth or a power base—his ego doesn't function that way. In fact, he has very little ego to speak of."

Ego or not, Kleiber never relented on issues of technical perfection and original intent. Jonas has kept a letter in which Carlos expressed his exacting demands as to the marking of players' parts. Kleiber was always fanatical on the subject. "You know how diffident, apprehensive, shy, kind and peaceful I am, but I assure you I will leave the Windy City on the spot if the librarians do a bad job with the material.—C.K."[292] They did a very good job, and Carlos was well pleased.

As always, he offered a poetic way of communicating how passages should be played. Many players offered memories of a surprising phrase, a turn of an image, truth concealed as joke presented as painting. Preparing Mozart's Symphony No. 33 in Chicago, he said that a slow section should sound "like a parent tugging a child away from a toy-store window as they walk along the street."

Returning to Germany after his success in Chicago, Carlos gave rather few performances that summer: four of *Rosenkavalier*, on 18 and 26 June, and 10 and 24 July and, with Pavarotti and Freni, two exceptionally well-received performances of *Bohème* on 14 and 16 July.

THE SEVENTH

A good deal of Carlos's contemporary reputation derives from a film made with the renowned Concertgebouw Orchestra of Amsterdam in the fall of

1983. He was fifty-three years old at the time. These are the first films in which I ever saw him work. His presentations of Beethoven Symphony No. 4 and No. 7 changed my musical life. I suspect many others—especially conductors—would declare the same. On 19 and 20 October the Concertgebouw was jammed with people sitting (and standing) in every square millimeter of space available, including the terraces behind the orchestra.[293] The film was released by Unitel/Philips later that year. Over the decades that have followed, it has never been out of print. It declares almost everything that could be said about Kleiber's interpretive and mesmerizing powers.

Here, an aside. Earlier was mentioned the only known films of Carlos in rehearsal, at Stuttgart in 1970. Today, they are widely available. There is also another rehearsal film of Carlos, preparing the Concertgebouw in this all-Beethoven set. Rumored for years, it exists. I have seen clips. They first came to light during the Unitel film showing given at the Bayerische Staatstheater Matinée in Munich's Nationaltheater, on 12 December 2004. This was directed by Götz Schulz-Temmel and later broadcast by Classica as "In Memoriam Carlos Kleiber" on 16 July 2006 and again on 7 August 2010. The rehearsal films were, presumably, tests for the recordings of the public concert performances released on video and DVD by Philips.[294]

I find the Seventh particularly compelling. Beyond the element of arresting charisma that prevails from first to last, it incorporates elements of sustained musical line rarely encountered in the work of any other conductor I know, save Furtwängler. Examples? Consider these.

In the first movement, at measure (M) 63, Beethoven marks a sudden change from Poco Sostenuto to Vivace. Kleiber prepares this by dictating four bars prior the absolute value of the quarter notes. Then, at Vivace he makes no sudden jolt at all. Rather, he presents a four bar *accelerando*. In its fifth bar he suddenly pulls back the dynamic (watch how he does it) and thus re-starts the whole energizing process. The *sforzati* which follow are conveyed by a wholly unorthodox gesture. Then, he makes a *fortissimo* with a wind-up of astonishing power, and the breathtaking race has begun.

The second movement, Allegretto, is all eyes. Kleiber takes the tempo marking seriously, and rejects the morbid funeral march it can so easily become. He takes the ornament on the downbeat (he sternly corrected me for doing otherwise) and asserts a perfect unification of the dactylic rhythm that governs the whole movement. Humphrey Burton directed this film and here made a very wise and revelatory choice. The camera stays off Carlos for the first fifty bars. The viewer imagines that in the past movement he has learned what Kleiber looks like. At this point he suddenly sees a face—and eyes!— that have changed utterly. There is such pain, such entreaty, such communication of inner meaning in those eyes that no player could resist them. And no witness could be unmoved. It is the finest frame of Carlos as storyteller we will ever know.

When the movement transits from A-minor to A-major, Kleiber moves the tempo ahead, very slightly, but with such ease and grace as can scarcely be imagined. When he makes a gesture apparently sniffing flowers, one can only laugh and smile in his garden. It is a uniquely enchanting moment. The dark colors of that paradise soon restate themselves, an exacting fugato follows, and at the end Carlos makes a choice that few other conductors do. He omits the conventional *arco*[295] in the last four bars and continues with an austere and unsettling *pizzicato*,[296] thus reinforcing the essentially severe and unstable quality of the 6/4 chord by which the movement is concluded. He once told me that Richard Strauss, Otto Klemperer, and his father did this. He also advised that the original manuscript declares it. At his instruction, I obtained a copy from Bonn. It is nearly unreadable.

The third movement, Presto, is a charging relay race. The thematic baton is speedily passed—with many good jokes along the way—among the choirs of the orchestra. *Assai Meno Presto*[297] in the middle is given an almost come-hither allure, all very seductive and insistent. A time-suspending *ritard* sets up the return to *Presto* that follows in M 236, its mirrors recur, and the whole movement burns to the end.

Carlos does something very important at the top of the fourth movement, Allegro Con Brio.[298] He moves into it *attacca*,[299] leaving almost no time between the third and fourth. Why? Surely to replicate the sense of shock and astonishment Beethoven's own first audiences must have felt. Why so? The third movement ends *fortissimo*[300] in F Major. The fourth opens *fortissimo* in *E* Major (functioning as the fifth of A). This half-step drop was in its day as revolutionary and shocking a refusal to follow rules of modulation as could be imagined. Historically informed conductors abut the F to the E so that no one will miss the startle of it. This is a glorious idea and a dramatic choice that Carlos would not overlook.

This final movement opens like a sky-burst, pent-up thunderclouds released and flashing. Carlos is clearly delighted by its impulsive spirit, save at one moment. Look closely at M 153[301] and watch his face. The trumpets have (briefly) lost cohesion in their rhythmic replies,[302] and Kleiber lasers a very displeased look, a two-hand gesture of clarification and correction, and a shrug that does not suggest total satisfaction.[303] This too was part of Carlos's hearing and drive toward "The Perfect." The symphony ends in a hail of stupendous applause. There is no finer film with which to introduce people to Kleiber, or to Beethoven.

Nearly ten years later, and well into my correspondence with Carlos, I used it in a senior conducting class I was teaching. None of the students had seen him before. A while later I told him about it. His reply was a very good vintage.

> *I'm tickled to death to hear that your class liked the Beethoven 7 with Concertgebouw. At the time, I felt very frustrated because they were so stolid and uninterested and because my hair was flying every which way (I had forgotten the hairspray, the most important thing for a conductor right after knowing how to tie your own bow-tie, having shirts the right size and wearing braces[304] that don't shrink when they get humid) and the clarinet was taking deep breaths where I told him not to, etc. But who cares, eh?*

> —*Carlos Kleiber, 8 July 1992*

It was while in Holland that Kleiber first spent time with the conductor Bernard Haitink, who had been asked by management of the Concertgebouw to entertain Carlos in-between concerts. On 21 October 1983 the two of them drove to the famed Mauritshuis Museum at The Hague. This seventeenth-century mansion houses splendid art from the Golden Age of Dutch painting, including work of Hals, Steen, Vermeer's *The View of Delft*, and Rembrandt's *The Anatomy Lesson*.

"Carlos liked the idea very much," Haitink recalled twenty years later. "He was very knowledgeable and enthusiastic about art. Half-way there he pulled out a flask, and for the rest of the trip all we talked about was tempo. It was very amusing. But I didn't dare try to get close to him. I was shy and insecure myself."[305]

Haitink added detail. "We spoke in English. He was a very nice and charming man, but difficult to get to know. Carlos was an enigma, but also *not* an enigma. I saw his insecurities and could understand them. He wanted to be better and more unique than any other conductor. But when he got there he doubted himself, and never thought he was good enough. Ever. His tremendous charisma covered up his deep self-doubt. Also his humor."

Soon after his return from Holland, he appeared in another concert that only added to his reputation for exceptional work.

With the Bavarian State Orchestra on 7 November 1983, at Munich's National Theatre, Carlos gave his *only* performance of Beethoven's Sixth Symphony, the *Pastorale*. (There was to have been an earlier *Pastorale* with the Vienna Philharmonic, on 18 December 1982, but he canceled.) As word got out that this would be the repertoire, every seat was sold. The event also included his Haydn 94 and Weber *Freischütz* Overture chestnuts, but they were of less interest. His *Pastorale* was destined to become the property of legend. Because he did the work only once, stories abounded that Kleiber hated it, that the tempi were impossibly fast, that the orchestra couldn't handle his demands, that its phrasing was wildly eccentric, and that the audience was stunned—or confused—into silence at the end.

So it would remain for twenty years until a private recording was discovered. The house archival recording had badly deteriorated and was in any case never planned for release. The private version, a cassette dub made at the time for Kleiber's son Marko, had miraculously survived. Restored by engineer Christoph Stickel, it was released on the Orfeo label in 2003. In her liner notes, Carlos's daughter Lillian wrote that "it is an astonishingly lively interpretation precisely because it is so unpretentious."

It is Kleiber's only recording by which I remain unconvinced. I've listened to it eyes closed half a dozen times, and with score at least as many. It's clear that he was searching for the original voice, a sense of first discovery. He labored to erase all traces of cheap sentiment and fake tradition. He followed Beethoven's own retrospective metronome markings, although not exclusively. (Who could?) Even so, in this recording those markings provide a kind of arbitration that never wholly succeeds. It passes from *allegro* to *hectic* in a steady state of exhaustion.

There is one exception to this pattern: the storm scene. It may be the most frightening, and the most startling, ever recorded. If it was the point toward which Carlos drove all other forces, then in that regard he surely succeeded.

However, he was sufficiently unconvinced of his own reading that he never returned to it. The audience seems to have been nonplussed. They knew perfectly well when it was over, but the recording preserves several seconds of hesitant silence, a spackling of uncertain applause, more silence, and finally the slow beginning of an ovation at its end. This was a strange reply to an unorthodox and perplexing performance.

His friend Peter Jonas discussed the Sixth with him once only. Carlos declared his devotion to the piece, that he was going to give it a try even though it was "immensely difficult," but that everybody else had failed to do it justice.

The issue "was not to do with anything pastoral but more to do with the clash in us all between the longing for Arcadia and the turmoil of our real lives (my words not his)."[306]

His sister Veronica was in attendance. "It was incredibly amusing because at the end of the piece there was a silence and my brother turned around as if to say, 'Well, it's finished, I can't do anything more,' and the audience, widely moved, that hadn't . . . and then 'uaaahhh' great applause! But the idea of . . . in short, 'You still want . . .? I have nothing more.' Well, it was amusing."[307]

It was soon back to "Batland." Again appearing on New Year's Eve 1983 and repeated on 2 January and 3 and 5 March this time with Lucia Popp and a similarly stellar cast, Kleiber gave another sparkling set of *Die Fledermaus*. This was followed by three performances of *Rosenkavalier* on 11 May and 12 and 22 July and two of *Bohème* with Freni, Popp, and Dvorsky on 13 and 15 July 1984, all of these at the Bavarian State Opera. He did rather little that summer but in the fall returned to the orchestra of the Bavarian State Opera to give three symphony concerts.[308] These were exceptionally well received.

Another appearance followed, this at the Teatro Communale of Florence, in four performances of *Traviata* on 7, 9, 16, and 20 December 1984, with Gasdia, Dvorsky, and Zancanaro. By now traditionally, Carlos gave a New Year's Eve performance of *Fledermaus* in Munich, and with his preferred cast of Popp, Fassbaender, and Perry. Further performances, without Popp, followed on 2 and 4 January 1985.

The new year opened in treasured repertoire. After *Fledermaus* he traveled to Vienna to give three performances of *La Bohème* on 18, 21, and 24 January 1985 with Pavarotti and Freni. It was then back to Munich for two more "Bats" in February, and five more *Traviata* on 26 and 29 May, 2 June, and 18 and 21 July.

His summer performances of *Traviata* seem to have been a joy for all concerned and gave rise to one of the great Kleiber stories. The American conductor Richard Rosenberg, now artistic director of the Hot Springs Music Festival in Arkansas, was that summer a young conducting assistant at the Bavarian Staatsoper. "Maestro Kleiber was leading a morning rehearsal of *Traviata* with the soloists and piano at which the Violetta, Edita Gruberova, could not be present," Rosenberg recalls. "In his usual fashion, Maestro Kleiber conducted the rehearsal from memory, and saw fit to sing Violetta's part himself.

"Early in the rehearsal he made a glaring error in his rendition of Violetta, whereupon he stopped the rehearsal, animatedly pointed at me and declared, 'HE will go back to America and RUIN my reputation as a LIVING LEGEND!' After the general laughter subsided, he conducted the rehearsal without further incident."[309]

Rosenberg adds another detail. "My usual seat at the National Theatre was in the forward box seat, which had no view of the stage. I spent the performances watching Carlos Kleiber, in whose face it was clearly possible to read the entire opera."

Kleiber was now perceptibly reducing his appearances in opera and concert. Perhaps more importantly, he had not given a "new" work in years. Although he remained a voracious reader of score and in private had a massive repertoire, it was in public that critics were noticing a growing constraint in performance materials.

The year ended as it began, with *Fledermaus* in Munich on 31 December and four more of the same soon thereafter, on 2 and 5 January and 10 and 11 February 1986.

The spring of 1986 was wholly occupied by concert music and in taking the Bavarian State Opera Orchestra on tour. His first two concerts were given at home on 9 and 10 March. The tour proceeded to Nuremburg, Augsburg, and Regensburg. Its repertoire consisted of Beethoven, Symphony No. 4 and No. 7; Brahms, Symphony No. 4; Butterworth, English Idyll No. 1; Schubert, Symphony No. 3; and Weber, *Der Freischütz* Overture. At the end of April the whole group flew to Japan. They gave the same programs, slightly re-ordered, in Tokyo (five times), and in Yokohama, Nagoya, and Osaka. On 19 May, at Hitomi Memorial Hall, he was so moved by the response of the audience that he actually addressed them, something he almost never did. He spoke one word, "Koumori," Japanese for "The Bat," and so launched into the first of two encores.[310] Carlos and his orchestra toured Japan from 9 to 19 May that year, the only such tour they would undertake together.

Carlos's rest periods after such extended work were beginning to lengthen. This was especially so after the Japan tour. He did not conduct again until his traditional News Year's Eve performance of *Die Fledermaus* in Munich, followed by the same on 2 and 4 January 1987. The performances of 30 and 31 December formed the basis of the Deutsche Grammophon live video released the following year. It only reinforced his reputation for brilliance and surprise, one well known to his colleagues.

Sir John Tooley of Covent Garden enjoyed a rewarding relationship with Carlos, based on a careful perception. "He is very demanding, but in the sense that he galvanises the entire house when he is here. He is, of course, a conductor and musician of the very first rank, one of the very few who fires the imagination to get more and more out of the players. There's nothing he cannot do with a baton. I don't think it's an exaggeration to call him a genius."[311]

The legendary English conductor Sir Reginald Goodall agreed. He led the world premiere of *Peter Grimes* in 1945 and rose to a curious set of assignments at the Royal Opera House, Covent Garden. He was a tremendously self-effacing maestro whose 1973 *Ring* cycle at Sadler's Wells became the stuff and sum of legend. Carlos once wrote him a letter, praising his Coliseum recording of it. In turn, Goodall thought Kleiber as someone with "Geist."[312]

In 1996 I sent Carlos a BBC documentary film, *The Quest for Reginald Goodall*. It moved him tremendously. The man was obviously a kind of hero, and a gentle soul with whose reticence, reclusiveness, and modesty Carlos identified. His too was a life for music.

Goodall Video (THANKS A 1000000) made me happy and thoughtful. The sweetest man and a great conductor! Perhaps he could only achieve if venerated; and had luck in finding the right ensembles and orchestras for that. He was 100% pure. This quality he shared with nobody.

—Carlos Kleiber, 4 May 1996

Goodall told a friend about a typically odd encounter with Carlos. "Kleiber came rushing up with his arms open. 'Ahhh, Herr Goodall,' he said, 'Your Ring is so . . .' And I said, 'No, no I don't think so . . .' But he seemed to think it was."[313]

At the beginning of 1987 Carlos led Covent Garden performances of *Otello* on 13, 17, 20, 23, and 26 January. This was a new production, directed by the esteemed Elijah Moshinsky. He then traveled to Italy for four more performances of the same work.

Otello was presented at La Scala on 5, 8, 11, and 14 February 1987 with Domingo, Freni, Bruson, Gavazzi, Manganotti, Roni, Nosotti, Sammaritano, and Banditelli. Opening night was a commemoration of its premiere, given exactly one hundred years earlier. This rebirth led to the usual stunning reviews and public acclaim. This is the well-known event that led to the dismissal of Renato Bruson after a near fistfight with Kleiber. Bruson was replaced by Piero Cappuccilli. On its heels came another *Fledermaus* in Munich, on 1 and 3 March 1987. His company included Coburn, Fassbaender, Perry, Streinbeißer, Wåchter, Kuhn, Hopferwieser, Weber, Gruber, and Muliar.

In the fall of 1987 he played guide on another tour, leading his home band in a series of seven concerts[314] in what was entirely standard repertoire for him: Beethoven 4 and 7, Mozart 36, and Brahms 2. The Bavarian State Orchestra opened the tour with a warm-up concert in Munich's Philharmonie am Gasteig on 18 September 1987. Audiences were satisfied with the results, and their tour lasted five weeks. On his return to Munich, in the now-standard pattern he gave *Die Fledermaus* on New Year's Eve and again on 2 January 1988.

When the Metropolitan Opera finally managed to lure Kleiber to its house, it was considered an extraordinary coup for all concerned. But before he first appeared there, that New York house had been trying for twelve years to get him. Their energies were poured into the attempt, even at the risk of offending some very great and longtime colleagues. Conductor Erich Leinsdorf was one of them. He took umbrage at their efforts.

Leinsdorf wrote to managing director Anthony Bliss. He had been trying for months to get a firm commitment toward a production of *Rosenkavalier* he wanted to lead in the 1976–1977 season. And he had been given the runaround. As he wrote with some bitterness, he was required to cool his heels while "four months were spent on a fishing trip for Carlos Kleiber."[315] Such were the risks that The Met was willing to take.

Everyone was pleased to take credit when Kleiber finally did appear, but that seems to have been earned by one man more than any other. General Manager Bruce Crawford traveled to Europe to secure talent ordinarily overlooked by The Met's machinery. He went looking for small game and returned with Kleiber. His company had been trying for years, but all prior efforts had failed.

Like John Tooley at Covent Garden, Crawford had a good reading of Carlos. He recognized the genius, understood the insecurities, and got the jokes. He created a working environment where Carlos felt able to obtain everything he wanted. Their first project was Zeffirelli's production of *La Bohème*, with Freni and Pavarotti as Mimi and Rodolfo. Kleiber found the orchestra exceptionally responsive. They reciprocated with unmatched awe and wonder. Everything was going extremely well, save for this: Crawford's abundance of caution.

As reported by Joanna Fiedler, "The atmosphere at the Met outside rehearsals seemed peculiar to Kleiber. Everyone in the opera house had been instructed not to speak to him unless spoken to first, because Crawford and Levine were so worried that he would take offense at an offhand remark and bolt. The conductor wandered the halls, smiling cheerfully at everyone he encountered, all of whom nodded silently in return. 'I can't understand it,' he finally said to one of the stage managers. 'Everyone in New York is so friendly except in the opera house.'"[316] His Met debut took place on 22 January 1988.[317] His arrival was much remarked upon. One review spoke for virtually all reviewers.

In *The Village Voice* Leighton Kerner simply declared, "Yes, it was worth the wait. . . . [He] sparked a box office furore not equalled since the 1965 return of Maria Callas."[318] Members of the Metropolitan Opera Orchestra felt the same way. Numerous memoirs were written by those artists. All carried the same message. One spoke for many, offering an image of his own that Carlos would have enjoyed.

Said tubaist Herbert Wekselblatt, "We did La Bohème with Kleiber—there's very little for tuba—but what a pleasure. It was like—my God, you opened up a book of poetry that you've been reading all your life, and suddenly, I was ready to cry."[319]

His activity at The Met did not include demand for a new production. Kleiber often preferred one that was well established in the systems of the house. Said James Levine, their artistic director, "Carlos Kleiber was not interested in new productions per se, because he wanted to work on the opera and not on the problems of costumes and scenery. He conducted with singular success works in the current repertory that he particularly felt like doing."[320] The same practice applied across much of Carlos's operatic career. After his buoyant success in New York, Carlos tentatively agreed to appear there again and then returned to Europe.

Continuing in his happy addiction to *Fledermaus*, of which neither he nor his Munich audience seemed to tire, two more performances were given on

15 and 16 February 1988. His cast included Coburn, Fassbaender, Perry, Streinbeißer, Wåchter, and Kuhn.

He would conduct the Vienna Philharmonic twice more that spring, in Mozart 36 and Brahms 2. On 18 March they appeared at the Bruckner-Halle in Linz, and then back in Vienna's Musikvereinsaal on the 19th and 20th. After the summer was over, Carlos led his colleagues at La Scala over to Japan. There, the Kleiber-cult was seen everywhere he went, a source of bemused consternation to him. Their performances of *La Bohème* were rapturously received.[321]

APOGEE

For all his success in Europe, New York, Chicago, and Japan, Kleiber's name was by no means common currency in the music world at large. There were rumors of a meteoric talent and stories about the son of a famous conductor, a musician of sometimes caustic intensity, and a recluse who refused to talk to the press. There were a few recordings. But relatively few people had actually seen him work. That all changed with a concert in Vienna, broadcast around the planet.

When he appeared in the Vienna Philharmonic's all-Strauss concert on New Year's Day 1989, it was televised live and globally. Viewers were astonished, and old-timers more so than anyone. Such natural command of the repertoire had not been heard since the days of Willi Boskovsky. Such a grasp of Viennese pulse took the audience back to the era of Clemens Krauss. And such sound was thought to be the exclusive property of Karajan. In 1989, Carlos showed an audience of millions what those gifts might accomplish, unified. No one had ever witnessed anything like it.[322]

Like his films of Beethoven 4 and 7, his New Year's Concerts in Vienna have—rightly—become essential property for anyone hoping to understand Carlos's means and purposes. No conductor in the modern era could show more in a wider, or more intimate, horizon. These films offer undying testimony to the fact of it.

Look closely at his account of *Die Libelle* (The Dragonfly). It is an astonishment of good humor and wry entomology. It is also a seminar in Kleiber conducting technique. His flightful and darting wrist, his abandonment of control in order to find it on higher ground, the quick technical repair of unexpectedly dragging violas at the very end—it is all there. Whenever I have wanted to give a class a *very* short course in the art of Carlos Kleiber, this is my only illustration. It speaks to his greatness, his innovations, his natural and charmed inspiration.

Later that year he made his first visit to Berlin as conductor. That engagement had been a long time coming.

Carlos appeared twice with the mighty Berlin Philharmonic, in 1989 and 1994.[323] It wasn't for want of opportunity. Berlin had been trying for years to get him, but he always declined on the basis of one evasion or another. For what every other conductor on the planet would have done anything, Carlos simply waved aside.

Wolfgang Stresemann was longtime intendant of the Berlin orchestra, and, in April 1978, he recalled his many efforts to get Carlos into the auditorium.

> I've invited him myself, and even persuaded him to conduct an all-Beethoven programme. It consisted—if memory serves—of the Egmont Overture, after which Maurizio Pollini, whom Kleiber knows well, would have played the Fifth Piano Concerto, and the concert would have ended with the Seventh Symphony.
>
> I said, "Listen, there's no point in having more than three rehearsals. You know the score, the orchestra knows the pieces and you have to give your own interpretation. The more you rehearse, the worse it could get." He saw the point of what I was saying. But then he demanded DM (Deutsche Mark) 15,000 per concert—and that was four or five years ago.[324] I had to tell him that, with the best will in the world, I couldn't accept that, though I'd gladly offer him the highest possible fee simply so that he would come. But it had, of course, to be less than Karajan gets.
>
> I suggested a princely sum, which I'd never offered anybody else. He replied that he'd have to ask his wife. Needless to say, I never heard from him again.[325]

Kleiber held off for decades, asserting incompetence and admitting insecurity.

Curiously, his friend Herbert von Karajan never *formally* asked him to conduct in Berlin, appearances notwithstanding. They knew one another well. In fact, they were frequently compared to one another by the best in the business. Reginald Goodall insisted that the only conductor whose name could be uttered in the same breath as von Karajan was Kleiber. No one else need apply.[326]

Carlos deeply respected Karajan. He was often heard asking other conductors how he got the sounds that he did. Jeffrey Tate reports such a conversation,[327] and so does Bernard Haitink. According to him, Kleiber once said of von Karajan that it was strange and mysterious, as if there were no interpretation at all. By simply playing the notes before him, he conjured magical forces.[328] Kleiber also found in Karajan a man of uncommon personal power.

Von Karajan was "the only shark in a pond of carp," he said to Michael Gielen.[329] He once used a dolphin metaphor in a letter to me. Something about von Karajan seems to have inspired Carlos to think like an aquarium director.

Their admiration was mutual, as was their friendship. According to KD, in private he referred to von Karajan as "Heribert," an evident play on his birth name.[330] On slightly more-formal occasions, he became "The Karajan." KD believes that Kleiber always felt "very subservient" to the older man and greatly admired Karajan's sporting and athletic attributes. According to Richard Osborne, author of two distinguished books about (and with) von Karajan, there was a regular exchange of postcards and letters between the two. According to Joachim Kaiser, Carlos sat for fourteen days watching Karajan rehearse Wagner's *Siegfried* in Salzburg.[331] Carlos was once approached to do a *Freischütz* at Salzburg. (Von Karajan was music director there at the time.) Kleiber replied that it was almost impossible to stage, and that—after giving it some thought—there was really only one director who could do justice to such a strange and beautiful work. So it happened that, on behalf of Carlos, Karajan telephoned Ingmar Bergman. The great Swedish director was vaguely interested but did not commit, and nothing ever came of it.[332]

Von Karajan is the source of a famous remark that has been round the block so often that the original text has been forgotten. Here's the whole of it.

> I like him enormously, but he was also very much under the thumb of his father. He has come to discuss things with me on many occasions and I am always asking him to come and do just one concert with the orchestra. He has a genius for conducting, but he doesn't enjoy doing it. He tells me, "I conduct only when I'm hungry." And it is true. He has a deep-freeze. He fills it up and cooks for himself and when it gets down to a certain level, then he thinks "Now I might do a concert." He is like a wolf! But he is someone I have the greatest admiration for.
>
> —Herbert von Karajan[333]

Some doubt whether or not Kleiber ever said such a thing. Others say that if he used those words it was as a joke. One element rings quite false: he "cooks for himself." Carlos may have done so on tour, alone, but there was no "deep-freeze" in his retinue. At home, his wife Stanka always cooked for him and their children. Many mutual friends have reported this. It's a widely circulated story, to be sure, but may well be no more than a typical Kleiber jest about his domestic life.

Carlos finally appeared in Berlin just five months before von Karajan died. The last several seasons of Karajan's life with his orchestra were not easy. Many bitter remarks were exchanged between Karajan and the faction that wanted to get rid of him. Kleiber was well aware of these politics and would not participate—save to tell Karajan that he would have no part in trying to ease him out. When Kleiber learned that the Berlin invitation he finally accepted had been proffered without von Karajan's knowledge, he was mortified.[334] The way some members of the orchestra treated von Karajan disturbed him deeply. Provoked by that embarrassment and tied to his own first appearance with that ensemble, Carlos wrote him a letter.

Whenever I feel that people might perhaps be causing you trouble, I'd like to strangle them with my own hands. I have no ambitions as a conductor. I prefer to listen to you. So if you tell those bandits, 'It's not on', the matter will be closed and everything will be fine again.

I am—perhaps this sounds very conceited—one of those few people who have the pleasure of knowing what endless miracles of conducting you have achieved. I remain your unworthy pupil and, if I may say, your friend.

—Carlos Kleiber, to Herbert von Karajan, 1988[335]

As an aside, it should be noted that Carlos was extremely sensitive about the appearances of his relationship with von Karajan. The music director of the Berlin Philharmonic was twenty-two years older and deeply venerated by the younger man. The numerous references to him in our correspondence, all tremendously respectful, demonstrate the fact of it. When Richard Osborne's *A Life in Music* came out in 1988, Kleiber read it immediately. It led him to write an angry letter, the only one Osborne received from anybody. Carlos did not dispute the letter quoted above, but wanted to set a proper context for it.

He was dismayed to read that it was *Der Rosenkavalier* Karajan had invited him to conduct (this is what Karajan had told Osborne) when it was in fact *Der Freischütz*.

Carlos's letter itself was vintage, and in format identical to dozens I received: "It was typed (fairly badly) on unheaded paper and was heavily annotated in pen with underlinings, afterthoughts etc.," Osborne said. "He didn't ask for the book to be corrected (he ended 'Oh, well. Forget it'). He signed himself, memorably, 'Carlos Kleiber (out for lunch).'"[336] The text was revised for the second edition and a copy sent to Carlos but nothing more was heard from him.

Both times Kleiber appeared at the Philharmonie it was in a benefit concert hosted by the president of the (West) German Republic. The first was for UNICEF and the second for the victims of the civil war in Bosnia. This first concert, given at the Philharmonie in Berlin on 9 March 1989, presented Brahms Symphony No. 2, Mozart Symphony No. 36, and Weber's *Der Freischütz* Overture. There were more than a dozen curtain calls for Kleiber alone.

Herbert von Karajan died 16 July 1989. Kleiber was deeply depressed by the loss of his friend and by the world's loss of his talent.

He spent several days that summer with Zeffirelli, at his villa in Positano on the Amalfi Coast. He often visited Zeffirelli there, usually in the company of a different "little angel," as the director put it. "He changed young female companions with the seasons." He was not there for business, avoided shop talk, and with Zeffirelli spoke only of "flowers, Pompeii, art and people." Even when Leonard Bernstein came calling at the same time, Carlos would not bend. Bernstein tried to engage him in conversation about Brahms Symphony No. 2, and Kleiber deflected him with jokes, cigarettes, and whiskey—his standard stratagem.

He would employ the identical device of polite evasion when members of the Berlin Philharmonic approached him after the death of its music director. According to Helge Grünewald, dramaturgie of the Berlin Philharmoniker, that well-known story is entirely true. Following the tremendous success of the 1989 concert and the death of von Karajan, "The orchestra was indeed interested in Kleiber. And he was in the discussion as a possible music director." So, after a short while, "There was a visit of a delegation from the orchestra to Munich which talked to Kleiber. It is not difficult to imagine his reaction: he was very polite and friendly (maybe he really felt very much honoured) but he never said 'yes.'"[337]

In the fall he was back to The Met in New York, and gave two performances of *La Traviata*, on 16 and 20 October 1989, with Gruberova, Shicoff, Brendel, White, Capecchi, and Kelly. There were to have been five performances, but in quick succession, two of the leads fell ill and had to leave the production. Thus, so did Carlos.[338] This may seem odd to non-conductors. For Carlos, however, leaving after two of his most important singers had departed was inevitable. Why? Everything Kleiber had done, planned, rehearsed, and—above all—heard within was based on the *actual sound* of those *actual singers*. All of the nuance, the small entreaties, the creation of personality, the cueing, the phrasing, the choices of timbre and timing, the interpersonal relations onstage and off—all of this changes profoundly when even one singer departs.

Carlos would have kept his commitment to the remaining three shows. However, to do so meant starting all over again with the "new" cast, working in the special ways that he had to work, with the time he had to take, in order to obtain the results that only he could achieve. Everyone knew this is how he labored. From that perspective, of course he had to leave. With Kleiber, even the most talented substitute in the world started from ground zero.

The conductor Paavo Järvi was one of the lucky ones. Twenty years later he remembers this production of *Traviata*, and its conductor, in blazing detail.

> When I was living in New York, a friend of mine who had subscriptions to the Metropolitan Opera called me up and said, Paavo, would you like to come? I have a ticket for Traviata. Carlos Kleiber is conducting. And what

was interesting was that Carlos Kleiber showed up and, as he was walking in, he got a standing ovation from the audience. The ovation was longer than most performances got after the opera is over.

Just as the house went dark, somebody came down the aisle and was speaking quite loudly and everybody looked back and there was a seat right behind me that was empty—it was Bernstein. And Bernstein, of course, liked to make an entrance. There was a really high note when Violetta was singing, one of those amazing diminuendos on a high note, and you could hear a pin drop, literally. It was the quietest moment I can remember. Then Lenny behind me said, "Wow, man." I will never forget that and it was quite loud.

In conversation with Gilbert Kaplan, Järvi recalled his discernment of Carlos's work.

He's not conducting in an academic sense. He is conveying characters and only characters. And it's so difficult to really put your finger on why is it so different from the others. But he has a technical vocabulary that is so individual and yet so expressive. He is able to show certain things with his eyes and with his hands and with his physical movements that leave no doubt of what has to happen. *He is the piece* and one cannot possibly do it any other way than what he shows."[339]

Kleiber occasionally broke his own prohibition. In the right mood, he would enter at the last minute to cover for a colleague or allow a singer to do so, and with no rehearsal at all.

In the October 1989 *Traviata* cited above, he allowed tenor Walter Mac-Neil (son of baritone Cornell) to substitute for Neil Shicoff on only a four-hour notice. In 1990, while doing *Otello* in London, Kleiber found that its star, Plácido Domingo, had contracted influenza. He could not possibly sing. Carlos was asked to accept a substitute, Jeffrey Lawton, a former mail-order salesman with a splendid voice. He agreed. Said Lawton, "I am not exactly sylph-like but they rushed around to throw a costume together. Mr Kleiber was marvellous. He told me not to bother following him. He would follow me."[340] They rehearsed briefly on a Sunday, again Monday morning, and went on that night.

When he first conducted *Rosenkavalier* at Covent Garden it was to cover for an indisposed James Levine. Kleiber was pleased with the experience and afterward told senior management, "If you get stuck for a conductor, do ring me. Either I have to have stacks of rehearsals, or none at all."[341]

He was usually adamant about working only with those in cast and orchestra who had been with him throughout the rehearsal process. He always sought continuity, institutional and production memory, coherence at the deepest levels. However, this norm has led to many distortions of fact.

> We were returning to Japan. After having prepared the first time with I don't know how many hours of rehearsal, this time he wanted just three hours of rehearsal and that's it, for all of *La Bohème*. The only thing that happened is that he asked La Scala: "I want all the persons that were in the orchestra the first time, no one excluded." They said to him that four people weren't in the orchestra any more. Nor was there one particular principal.
>
> "Very well, I'm not coming."
>
> Management said, "Listen, Franzetti, you're always in contact with him because as principal violinist you have a tie with him. Try to do something. Explain to him that we are able to do absolutely nothing. These people have retired. Aside from the fact that now they no longer play, it isn't possible, we can't make them return."
>
> I went and said to him, "Look, Maestro, they can't be brought back. What I can assure you is that they have been replaced by worthy substitutes." And he looked at me and said, "Do you guarantee me that?" "Maestro, look, in my opinion they are very worthy people, they are only these four. All the others are the same. They have done all the hours of rehearsal, all the performances."
>
> "Very well, thank you." He accepted.
>
> He had this capacity for taking people and transporting them to another world, with visions that are beyond those of others. Who knows what was inside of him, in his soul, what it meant, this acuteness, his way of feeling? At one special moment he stopped himself and made a gesture, with a smile, like this . . . he made a gesture to me—there was the oboe too, because we were playing in octaves—and I said to him, "Yes, but it is difficult this way."
>
> He said, "Even so, between you, perhaps you succeed." I was dumbfounded.
>
> —Giulio Franzetti, concertmaster, Orchestra of La Scala, RAI Radio 3,
> 21 February 2008[342]

Kleiber's 1992 New Year's Day performance with the Vienna Philharmonic was originally intended for Leonard Bernstein. After Bernstein died on 14 October 1990, Carlos stepped in. As much as for any reason, it was to provide backstop to his late friend. He had liked and respected Bernstein very much. Their worlds were far apart but orbited the same sun. Even so, Kleiber was often embarrassed by him.

Zeffirelli recounts how La Scala management once sent over a tape of *La Bohème*, hoping for release approval from director and conductor. Zeffirelli knew that was always a troubling obligation for Kleiber. Nothing ever met his standards. Doubt would easily be compounded by any outside factor. On that day the factor was Bernstein himself, eager to see the new film. Zeffirelli, not wanting anything to go wrong, asked Bernstein to withdraw from the screening. He sneaked in anyway, at the back of the room, on tiptoes, hoping not to be noticed. Bernstein then took a seat with a glass of whiskey in his hand, mesmerized.

During the screening of the last act, Kleiber and Zeffirelli heard a hopelessly sobbing Bernstein overcome by beauty and fear. He burst out to Kleiber: "You are a god. You are a god!" Kleiber was deeply embarrassed and asked him to calm down.[343]

This wasn't the only time that Bernstein's over-the-top effusiveness would mortify Carlos. The tale is told by Alison Ames, one-time head of Deutsche Gramophone's operations in North America and the person whom Carlos had genially confronted in Chicago.

> My only other near-contact with Mr. Kleiber was after one of his Met performances of, I think, La Traviata.[344]
>
> I was to meet Leonard Bernstein immediately after the performance to rush him backstage—he wanted to say hello, and Kleiber was known to be whisked out of the building within minutes of any performance's end. We got backstage, but CK (who used the last dressing room at the women's end of the corridor) was taking his time.
>
> LB was schmoozing with singers and friends and others, and when I saw CK at the end of the hall I grabbed LB's hand, took away his cigarette [!] and pushed him toward his prey. CK, accompanied by an attractive woman, looked dazed as a deer in headlights as Bernstein threw himself down on one knee and kissed CK's hand.[345]

It is almost impossible to think of a single gesture that could have horrified Carlos more than bent knees and hand kissing. Had it not been Bernstein, Kleiber would have run back into his dressing room and called the men with nets.

CARLOS THE CRITIC

Maybe I should become a critic (my father said I should) and set things "right". But then I'd have to go to performances; and if I savaged my colleagues, people would say I was jealous. And my pieces of reviewing would be so short (z.B. "Scheisse" or "Schweine" or "Völliger Mist" or "Keine blasse Ahnung")[346] that paid by the line as I would be, I'd starve.

—*Carlos Kleiber, to Peter Jonas, 12 January 1995*

Kleiber frequently said that he never wrote for publication. He certainly wrote long and fascinating letters to his friends, but his public voice spoke through his baton. With the exception of liner notes composed for the live recording of Beethoven 4 described earlier, occasional endorsements of colleagues, and his practical little "Kleibergrams," he maintained lifelong public silence as a public figure.[347] To date, there is no evidence that he ever gave a single interview to the press, in writing or in person. Alexander Werner, in his biography of Kleiber, holds that in December 1960, during the interval in a radio broadcast of the Hamburg Symphony Orchestra, Kleiber gave his only recorded interview. This is borne out by the 2011 DVD *I Am Lost to the World*.

He certainly considered most journalists lazy, ill-informed gossips who make whole careers out of personal peevishness. His friend, the music journalist Christina Lemke-Matwey, now writing for *Der Tagesspiegel* in Berlin, was a remarkable exception. Carlos had been following her reviews, once sent her an anonymous fax praising a caustic review she had written, and eventually they met.

> When we met he was very hysterical and nervous. This was a morning in Gran Canaria in his hotel suite, actually. He changed the location several times before, and in the end we ended up in his suite. And this was a date of maybe one and a half or two hours. And during all this time he was looking for his credit card. And this was really shaking him. He was, well, of course we were talking to each other and about music, and about critics, and about other conductors, and about Beethoven and so on, but mainly he was dealing with his credit card.
>
> This was Carlos: not being there but also being there. He was a very ambiguous and very ambivalent personality. And on the third hand, he was the most, really most intelligent person I've ever met in my life. There was something in his eyes which said "I know everything, but I don't talk about everything." And this was something which I really adored and loved.
>
> —Christine Lemke-Matwey, BBC Radio 3, 26 September 2009[348]

Regardless of his general opinion of critics, he did read their reviews. There was usually no reply from him, even in private. But he was provoked once. His rejoinder was hilarious. His subject? Joachim Kaiser, author of a review of a concert that Carlos had given in Munich.[349] Kaiser closed his review by comparing Carlos to his father:

"If Kleiber, then Erich."

In private, Carlos answered.

"If Kaiser, then Schmarren."[350]

There are four documented exceptions to Kleiber's "rule" of never dealing with the media. The first (earlier described) defended Michelangeli, the second was fascinatingly facetious, the third just plain friendly, and the fourth was a formal and cosigned letter to the editor.

In April 1989 the magazine *Der Spiegel*[351] published a letter by "Toscanini" concerning a distinguished—and controversial—Rumanian conductor. Sergiu Celibidache had managed a peculiar career since winning postwar appointment as successor to Furtwängler at the Berlin Philharmonic. Five decades later he was conductor-for-life at the Munich Philharmonic. Carlos lived in Grünwald, a suburb of Munich, and was directly aware of Celibidache's reputation and musical procedures.

Superficially, the two had much in common. Each was perceived as eccentric, charismatic, a genius, and very difficult. Both demanded many rehearsals, and if unhappy simply walked out. Both had legions of admirers. I wrote the essay on Celibidache for New Grove 2000 and was astounded to find how many—and severe—were the personal and critical judgments of the man. For months after that volume was published I received vitriolic mail from his fans and from his critics. Such are the contradictions. I have a film of Celibidache, from May 1994, in which he torments the Munich Philharmonic in Ravel's *Boléro*. It runs seventeen minutes! (The average is thirteen.) It is nearly ridiculous in its glaciation, and Celibidache's face flashes the hostility for which he was not loved.

I also have a film of Celibidache rehearsing the London Symphony Orchestra and Chorus in Fauré's *Requiem*. Dating from 1983, it is a cameo of grace and beauty, patience (mostly) and warmth, and the man absolutely at his best. Taking the rehearsal without score, everything rises from his passionate declamation of its text. It is one of the most wondrous rehearsals I have ever seen. I never discussed it with Carlos.

He thought Celibidache a charlatan, a poseur, a laughable phony. His opinion may have been enlarged by typically injudicious comments that Celibidache made back in March 1988, at an evening of "The Friends of the Munich Philharmonic." Celibidache spent much of the time comparing himself to other conductors.

Der Spiegel recounted the worst of his comments in April 1989. The article, "The Flying Dutchman in LA," cited many charming observations. According to Celibidache, von Karajan was "horrible. Either he's a good businessman, or he is deaf." Toscanini was "a note factory," Riccardo Muti "talented, but a great ignoramus," and Karl Böhm "a sack of potatoes who never conducted a note of music in his life." Even the brilliant writer Theodor Adorno was "the biggest chatterbox in world history."

Celibidache raised the stakes by describing Claudio Abbado, soon to be conductor of the Berlin Philharmonic, as "a wound; totally bereft of any talent. I could survive for three weeks without food; but three hours of listening to him would guarantee a heart attack." He said nothing about Kleiber, nor did he attack Jesus.[352]

In *Der Spiegel's* sixteenth issue of 1989 was printed a bizarre letter. Evidently, Celibidache's remarks had been read by conductors in the "Great Beyond." They held a little meeting. One of them was delegated to answer on their behalf.

> Telex from Toscanini (Heaven) to Celibidache (Munich):
> Dear Sergiu!
> We have read you in the Spiegel. You get on our nerves, but we forgive you. We have no choice anyway: forgiveness is in style Up Here. Potato-sack Karli[353] made some objection, but after Kna[354] and I had a heart-to-heart with him, he stopped whining.
> Wilhelm[355] now all of a sudden insists that he has never even heard of you.[356] Papa Josef,[357] Wolfgang Amadeus, Ludwig,[358] Johannes,[359] and Anton[360] all prefer the second violins on the right and claim that your tempi are all wrong. But actually, they don't really give a damn about it.[361] Up here, we are not supposed to care a damn about anything. The Boss does not allow it.
> An old Zen master who lives next door says you got it all wrong about Zen Buddhism.[362] Bruno[363] is totally cracked up by your comments. I have the suspicion that he secretly shares your views about me and Karli. Maybe you could say something mean about him for a change; otherwise, he feels so left out.
> I hate to break it to you, but everybody up here is totally crazy about Herbert. In fact, the other conductors are a little jealous of him. We can't wait to welcome him up here in fifteen or twenty years. Too bad you can't be with us then.
> But people say that where you will go the cuisine is much better, and the orchestras down there never stop rehearsing. They even make little mistakes on purpose, so that you have a chance to correct them for all eternity.
> I'm sure you will like that, Sergiu. Up here, the angels read the composers' minds. We conductors only have to listen. Only God knows why I'm here.
> Have lots of fun,
> In old friendship,
> Arturo[364]

Soon after it was published, those familiar with the rhythms of his speech and the content of his views deduced that it was in fact written by Kleiber. He never owned up to it. According to Klaus Umbach, Kleiber did let it be known that he "might" be the author. When Celibidache himself was asked about the "Telex," he affected a reply: "I don't know them. I have no idea what you are talking about."[365]

Kleiber and Celibidache did have a relationship, of sorts. Carlos attended a number of his concerts with the Munich Philharmonic. In 1992 Celibidache suffered a heart attack, and Kleiber's was the second get-well card to arrive. (Michelangeli's was the first.)

On 18 October that year, Carlos returned from a private trip to Japan aboard a Lufthansa Boeing 747-400. He sat in first class. So did Celibidache, returning with the Munich Philharmonic from their tour of Japan. Each conductor saw the other and pretended otherwise. They passed in the aisle and avoided eye contact. Finally, Carlos got up and walked to the back of the plane to smoke a cigarette.

Several members of the Philharmonic approached Celibidache. "Go talk to him," they said. "Make the first overture." After two hours the old man heaved himself up from his seat and walked toward Kleiber.

"Why do you conduct everything so terribly fast?" he asked Carlos.

Carlos's reply was drowned by engine noise. Players hovering nearby, hoping to overhear, caught nothing. However, Celibidache did amplify his opinion of Kleiber elsewhere. "For me he is an impossible conductor," he said. "Nobody can experience anything at the crazy tempi he takes. Kleiber misses the Holy sound. That I find tragic. He has never experienced what music really is."[366] Carlos never said anything about the encounter.

Carlos's third "public" statement concerned a friend whose work and voice he admired very much. The tenor Luciano Pavarotti was to be the subject of a major profile in the monthly journal *Le Monde*. Its writers knew full well that Kleiber would never talk to them, but Pavarotti knew Carlos even better. They soon received by courier, in French and in hand, a note from Carlos:

Cher monsieur, Quand Luciano Pavarotti chante, le soleil se lève sur le monde.

—Carlos Kleiber[367]

Carlos's fourth public statement was a cosigned, legitimate, and decidedly unfunny letter to the editor of *The Times of London*. It was an open missive to the Board of the Royal Opera House (Covent Garden) and the government minister co-responsible for same. The letter protested the closing of the house (it was being retrofitted), and the concomitant shuttering of its orchestra and chorus. All eight signatories were conductors who had enjoyed tremendous success in that famed company. They were defending the interests of the employees who would be put out of work: "It is not they who have brought disrepute to the place." Their letter was printed in *The Times* edition of 27 October 1998.[368]

Kleiber had not actually worked at Covent Garden for eight years, nor would he again. But such was his reputation that it was considered a very great coup to get his name on the document. It was to be Carlos's last public utterance.

CARLOS THE TEACHER

With the exception of his own children, Carlos never established a conventional master-student relationship with anyone. He seemed genuinely to believe that he had nothing to teach and everything to learn. His first letter to me in 1989 made that much clear. I have heard that numerous others made various appeals to him, asking that he serve as their teacher or mentor. He generally ignored such requests. Those to whom he did reply were, almost invariably, turned down. The young student Christina Drexel was able to engage in a three-letter correspondence, but it did not go far.

> Four years ago—when I studied conducting—I wrote him (like you) because of a few things about conducting. And he answered 3 times. But it seemed to me a little bit, that he finally liked to have his peace, although he wrote so pleasant.

> —Christina Drexel, e-mail to author, 25 November 2006

Another student also feared to disturb Kleiber, but spent an hour in front of his house hoping to be noticed.

Fernando Álvarez is today a distinguished Spanish-Argentine conductor, has worked with such artists as Sherrill Milnes, José Cura, Marcelo Álvarez (no relation), and with Plácido Domingo on an international zarzuela tour. He has served as music director for numerous houses and orchestras in South America and as guest conductor in Europe. But in 1993, on scholarship from the Teatro Colón Foundation, he was a young student en route to Bavaria. There, he would study with Sergiu Celibidache, music director of the Munich Philharmonic.

He took with him on his visit to Carlos a letter of introduction from soprano Nilda Hoffmann, the Kleiber family friend from Buenos Aires days. Álvarez hoped for permission to attend a Kleiber rehearsal. "Asking for lessons was too much to think about—almost science fiction."[369] He added to Hoffmann's a letter of his own and took the tram to Grünwald. Wisely, he forgot to mention that he would be studying with Celibidache.

When he arrived at Aurikelstrasse, he hoped to find courage enough to knock at the door and present his letters. Once there he saw Carlos's car and, inside it, a red scarf and an audio cassette of a recording with the Vienna Philharmonic.

"I was overcome by sudden shyness and deep respect paralyzed by contradictory feelings," Álvarez remembers. He remained there, simply standing, for almost an hour. He hoped that he would be noticed, that someone would come out of the house and mediate an introduction. No one noticed. No one came. After an hour of this contemplation Álvarez gave up and returned to

Munich, taking with him "mate" and "bombilla," the Argentine folk artifacts he had brought as gifts for Carlos.

He did leave behind the two letters, adding *post scriptum* that he would return in hope of meeting Kleiber. "My extreme devotion, respect and fear of disturbing his peace prevented it," Álvarez added. They never met.

Only four people seem to have penetrated his barriers. In my case, humor and distance provided the portal. In two others, simply appearing at his doorstep did the trick. Conductors (and composers) Bernd Gradwohl and Christian von Borries were granted entry, and their lives changed because of it.

Problems associated with Beethoven's Seventh Symphony were what first took Gradwohl to Kleiber. He was beginning a career conducting chamber orchestras and had met good success in Korea, Hungary, Germany, and his native Austria. He was constantly seeking performance solutions in the music of Mozart, Haydn, Bach, Handel, and Schubert. He had been overwhelmed by Carlos's work in Beethoven. Like most conductors, Gradwohl believes that these solutions are to be found in the scores—and not the biographies—of their composers. "I prefer the art of artists," as he told me. He also wanted to know about the differences, if any, between leading symphony and chamber orchestras. Gradwohl decided to visit Carlos Kleiber.

"I had no connections, no phone number, and no address," he said.

All I knew was that he lived in Munich and somewhere in South-America. So I took my father's car and went to Salzburg. On the way I called a friend (Jaqueline Altenburger) and asked for her help because I knew that she is very talented to find out anything, also the address from Carlos Kleiber.

I stayed in Salzburg for a night, listening to a (terrible) contemporary concert and went with some members and former members of the Camerata Salzburg for having some beers. They asked me what I'm doing here and I told them that I went to visit Kleiber for asking him about music. None of the musicians wondered about my intention just to "go there"! Next day I went to Munich and I visited a friend who is a singer in the opera, Johannes Beck. In the evening we went together to the operetta where his wife (Ruth Beck) was singing the solo-part. Reactivating my mobile phone I got a SMS from Mrs Altenburger with the address for Kleiber: "Aurikelstrasse 1A. Good luck."

Gradwohl continues.

It was a beautiful Sunday afternoon and I just went to that address, not being sure if he really lives there, is at home, has time . . . but all the time since I was on the way I had the feeling that everything is programmed (which of course is stupid). I watched out for some name-card on the house, and on the garden-door there was a funny little kind of cheap paper with a handwritten notice "KLEIBER" fixed with a Tixo (the most unspectacular name-card I've ever seen).

I stood at that door, "unarmed" (no scores, nothing) and rang the bell, not knowing if dangerous dogs will come out.

Then a woman asked me "Bitte?" and I only said, "I come from Austria and I want to learn something." The woman (later I found out that she was Kleiber's wife) said to me, "I will ask." I was waiting till she came back and told me, "He comes." When Kleiber came I told him the same, "I come from Austria and I want to learn something." His first question was to ask if I know Sandor Végh.

I told him that I have been studying violin with Ola Rudner who had been the concert master of the Camerata Salzburg and who is now the chief-conductor of the Haydnorchestra Bolzano (Italy). I also told him that Ola introduced me to Végh and that I attended many many rehearsals with Végh. Kleiber asked me about the rehearsals and I told him about Sandor Végh's work. (I have learned in one Végh-rehearsal more than in one lifetime at the University so I always went there). Kleiber told me that I am very lucky to play the violin because what we violin players do with the bowing is very helpful for conducting. The beginning of the conversation was very warmhearted and I felt very comfortable and I think we had a good connection—maybe because he felt that I did not come BECAUSE OF KLEIBER, he must have known that I came BECAUSE OF MUSIC.

Gradwohl continued, and with an insight that clearly reached Carlos.

I think that the work of composers is so much more important than conducting, so I was not afraid of Kleiber and could talk to him in a very natural way. I told you that I was "unarmed" with scores but I had a lot of questions for him. First I asked him about the difference between conducting big and small orchestras and he told me that in general there is no difference (later I also found that he was right!).

Then we had a discussion about listening—acting—proacting and reacting. I got the chance to know him as a friendly, sensible and of course humorous person—he also cracked a lot of jokes about himself. During our acting-reacting talk he told me that sometimes he falls in love with his beat(ing) and then he forgets to listen.

I asked him about some conducting problems, how to do this and that. It is not possible to write about that because you can only "see" it. In the context of conducting specific pieces we also talked about other famous conductors. In general he always found good words about his colleagues—except when I asked him about his way to start with the 2nd Brahms Symphonie. He said: "I just wanted to show Abbado that it also works that way."

At the end of the "session" Carlos Kleiber told me that the real conductors are only the score. Before I left he said: "Sie haben ihr Gesicht und ich habe meines."[370] These words have been a kind of Sanctus to continue what I always did, to go on my own way and never go back.[371]

And there is Maurizio Pollini. Extraordinarily well known as a pianist, Pollini has also pursued a career as a conductor in both operatic and symphonic repertoire. Most often, he has conducted from the keyboard. In September 1981, he made his podium debut leading Rossini's *La Donna Del Lago* at the Pesaro Festival in Bologna.[372] A year earlier, he had been to see his friend Carlos Kleiber.

In 2008, Veronica Kleiber remembered how it came about.

One person whom he loved a lot was Maurizio Pollini. They were true friends. I have a letter that I must find because it is so witty. It says . . . "Maurizio is here with an enormous cake [torta]. He sits there and asks me . . . 'For example, Carlos, when you have an entrances . . . something quite brief, how do you do it?'"

And Carlos writes to me and says: "I don't have the foggiest idea what I do, I must first think . . . what is it that I do?" In short, technical details which Carlos had never worried about, but Maurizio wanted to know precisely how it was.

—Veronica Kleiber, RAI 3 broadcast, 25 February 2008

Pollini remembered it the same way.

I remember the trip that I made because I had agreed to direct *The Lady of the Lake*. It was a completely new experience for me and the most natural thing was to seek Carlos's counsel on the score. So I brought the score, put it in front of his eyes and he started to turn the pages.

For me one thing was extremely significant. This man had the capacity to understand instanteously a work or a score. He immediately had an espressive or interpretive idea in his head, and all this resolved itself immediately, instantly, into a gesture appropriate for orchestra directing. He was a person with an absolutely astonishing rapidity of learning and immediate comprehension of music.

I went several times to Munich for concerts and found him in his house. He was there many days and was continuing to study the classical repertoire every day. And to think of possible solutions [that were overarching] always more convincing, always more adapted to express the musical moment. He had a talent beyond any imagination. He was able, at every moment of his life, to go into rehearsal with an orchestra and direct any piece of the repertory because he knew perfectly every classical score. He didn't do it in his life because he was incredibly anxious about perfection, because of a kind of extreme self-criticism, absolutely exaggerated, that certainly tormented him, not a little, in his life.

—Maurizio Pollini, RAI 3 broadcast, 25 February 2008[373]

Christian von Borries also found a way to reach Carlos, to spend time with him and, perhaps surprisingly, to discuss politics as much as music. Von Borries is today a well-known composer and conductor, producer of art events, the originator of *Masse und Macht* (his response to the G8 summit that drew so much negative attention), a participant in the Berliner Festspiele's Maerzmusik Festival, Lucerne Festival, Kunstfest Weimar (among others), and a leader in a rigorous avant garde in music and political theatre. When he first met Carlos, in 1988, he had served as principal flute at the Zurich Opera, followed by conducting studies with Gerhard Samuel and Nikolaus Harnoncourt. He also worked with Vladimir Fedoseyev and the Moscow Radio Symphony Orchestra.

"Classical culture was my own kind of Neverland. I met Carlos several times in 1988 and early 1989, at his home in Grünwald. I first wrote him a letter, and he replied saying that he was not sure that he could help me with more than a few Chinese truisms; however, I was welcome to stop by," von Borries told me in a lengthy note.

> We sat on the terrace, he in his pyjamas and a light coat. He was a friendly, calm old man. He asked me a lot of questions before answering any himself. It was a very comfortable situation, and eventually I could even criticize his interpretations and not worry about his reaction.
>
> He told me again and again to use the score to learn the music, but also insisted that I listen to recordings. He felt they were equally important. He also emphasized that one can only be a good artist if you feel and act in favour of the suppressed people of the world. In fact, Kleiber asked me if I was left-wing "as well." We talked a lot about politics. He eventually defended his big car in front of his garage by stating it was leased, and that he would only conduct when he needed money, asking the highest fees possible. He had a great deal of cynicism about the capitalist system.

Von Borries continued.

> Carlos suggested that I contact the German conductor Peter Gülke as a possible teacher. He had met him during the Freischütz production in Dresden.[374]
>
> In the time I spent with Carlos I saw how difficult it was to have the same profession as a famous father. I believe that's the reason for his rather small and conservative repertoire. We talked about the Mahler symphonies, and about Charles Ives, which music he knew very well. But, he said he could not do them—there was too much sampling and ripping and free form in them.[375] He would rather stick to the classical 19th century repertoire *sonatenhauptsatzform*[376] in a cultural system that he detested. I later sent him Günther Anders' "Die Antiquiertheit des Menschen," which he didn't know. He was glad to read this book.[377]

My impression was that Kleiber suffered from his fame, from the stardom he endured within a bourgeois system he could not endure, and that he was not well. Anomie? Maybe. Classical culture as *his* Neverland? For sure.[378]

Von Borries added that, in March 1989, "in Berlin, I tried to sneak into the rehearsal, but they actually checked all the rows and threw me out." Many people got thrown out of Kleiber rehearsals.

THE LONG GOODBYE

The decade of the nineties was the last in which Carlos stood as conductor. It was his fifth decade of work in the profession. His appearances were few and his repertoire—with one famous exception—a recollection of all that had gone before. A case can be made that the work he achieved was as close to his ambition as anything he ever managed.

Many who collaborated with him in these last ten years aver that he was more relaxed, more serenely certain, and closer to artistic contentment than he had ever come. In one remarkable year he even appeared in Vienna to accept a public honor. In retrospect it seems to have been a signal and a small valedictory.

The new decade opened with a return visit to the Royal Opera House in London. For Carlos, working with that company's orchestra and chorus, it was the beginning of a year devoted to two masterpieces. In Verdi's *Otello* his colleagues Domingo, Ricciarelli, and Díaz were in the lead roles, joined by Leggate, Mason, Moses, and Caproni, and onstage 6, 9, 12, and 15 January. Two months later, the same cadre headed across the Atlantic.

At the Metropolitan Opera on 5, 9, 12, 16, and 19 March 1990, Carlos and his three leads gave *Otello* once more, now joined by Kelly, Plishka, McCauley, Anthony, Hartman, and Parce in secondary roles. These were the performances in which I first saw him work, live.

So did Donal Henahan and every serious American critic. They were all there. Writing in the *New York Times*, Henahan held that "there is nothing quite like hearing one of opera's greatest scores led by a master musician like Mr Kleiber. Good singers sound better, production flaws fade into the background, and the entire work seems to flow naturally and unimpeded. . . . From the sheer polish of the orchestral sound, one might have guessed the conductor to be the ghost of Herbert von Karajan; from the headlong impetus of the drama, Toscanini."[379]

One rumor has endured and metastasized for over a decade, and it may now be put to sleep: there is no rehearsal film of Carlos preparing this *Otello*. It doesn't exist, gossip on the Internet notwithstanding. I am indebted to Dr. Ira Lieberman, a first violinist at The Met and a member of the orchestra when Carlos did *Otello*. At my request Ira kindly made enquiry and confirmed the disappointing truth. It didn't happen. Carlos would never have permitted such a thing. "I took your question regarding a possible tape of Otello rehearsal tape to Bob Sutherland, Chief Librarian of the Met. He said that there was absolutely no tape made of Kleiber rehearsals. However, the Met does operate a stationary camera to tape its productions as an aide to directors. That camera, focused on the stage would not contain any Kleiber except perhaps as a blur. . . . I'm certain no one could have surreptitiously taped anything."[380]

Perhaps unexpectedly and almost certainly in consequence of his first guest appearance at the Berlin Philharmonic, Kleiber now accepted an important honor. On 30 September 1990, he was inducted into the Order Pour le mérite for Arts and Sciences. Founded in 1740 by King Frederick of Prussia, this was originally a military decoration. In 1842, Frederick William IV of Prussia created a civilian order and over time it has been awarded to von Humboldt, Gauss, Mendelssohn, Faraday, Darwin, Brahms, Verdi, Einstein, Planck, Furtwängler, Ionesco, and Eco.

The citation, accompanied by Kleiber's photograph and signature, read,

Carlos KLEIBER. Dirigent. Geboren am 3. Juli 1930 in Berlin. Kleiber wuchs in Buenos Aires auf; er hatte in La Plata sein erstes Engagement. 1954 kam er als Kapellmeister nach Potsdam. Es folgten Düsseldorf, Zürich und Stuttgart, Gastkonzerte in Wien und beim Prager Frühling, später München und Wien. Seit 1975 hat Carlos Kleiber feste Bindungen gemieden. Er arbeitet als Gast an den berühmtesten Opernhäusern und mit den groben Orchestern der Welt. "Seine Opern—und Konzertaufführungen sind selten, wenn sie aber stattfinden, bedeuten sie ein grobes Erlebnis" (Ligeti, 1975), so Beethovensymphonien, Rosenkavalier, Tristan (auch in Bayreuth), Wozzeck, Elektra oder 1989 das Neujahrskonzert der Wiener Philharmoniker und—erstmals mit den Berliner Philharmoniker—im März 1989 das Benefizkonzert der UNICEF. Kleiber lebt in München, ist österreichischer Staatsbürger. Aufnahme in den Orden am 30.9.1990.[381]

In English, the citation reads,

Carlos Kleiber. Conductor. Born on 3 July 1930 in Berlin. Kleiber was raised in Buenos Aires, and at La Plata had his first engagement. In 1954 he was Kapellmeister to Potsdam. This was followed by Düsseldorf, Zurich and Stuttgart, guest concerts in Vienna and the Prague Spring, and later in Munich and Vienna. Since 1975, Carlos Kleiber has avoided permanent appointment. He works as a guest at the most famous opera houses and with the greatest orchestras in the world. "His opera and concert performances are rare, if they take place at all; however, they signify a major adventure" (Ligeti, 1975), and include the Beethoven symphonies, Rosenkavalier, Tristan (in Bayreuth), Wozzeck, Elektra, the 1989 New Year's Concert of the Vienna Philharmonic, and—at his first appearance with the Berlin Philharmonic—in March 1989 a benefit concert for UNICEF. Kleiber lives in Munich, and is an Austrian citizen. Admission into the Order on 30.9.1990.

In the fall Carlos returned to New York to give seven performances of *Rosenkavalier*, on 25 and 29 September, and 4, 9, 13, 17, and 20 October 1990. He was replacing James Levine, who had originally been scheduled to lead all seven days. Players in the pit, though by now familiar with Kleiber's methods, remained in awe of them. Over the years, many players in many pits had received, and preserved like holy relics, Carlos's little "Kleibergrams," as they came to be called. He deployed them for very particular reasons.

He often cautioned me against talking too much in rehearsal and the price conductors pay for doing so: "Every word is a nail in his coffin," he once wrote.[382] And so, at least by his standards, he spoke rather little from the podium. Instead, he wrote out by hand his exact instructions and left them on his players' music stands. One example speaks for many. It was given to the French horns in this production of *Rosenkavalier*, and written on the same stave-lined note paper he first used with me.

Rosenkavalier
TAKE NOTE
HORNS (I, II and III)
Act III, 4 before 22
 Please do not hurry the 12/8 [XXX musical example here] *etc but place them very exactly toward "2" and "D.C.". (There is a lot of difficult* [XXX musical example] *stuff going on the while!) Bassoons and violas are with you.*
—With best wishes and regards
Your C. Kleiber

He closed it with his rubber-stamped "THANK YOU," and his usual imprint of a happy face.[383]

The 1990 Met *Rosenkavalier* was for him a dream cast. Lott, von Otter, and Bonney were joined by Olsen, Hornik, Haugland, Gondek, Walker, Laciura, Best, Anthony, and Wells. Reviews were of the predictably laudatory type with no exceptions that I have been able to locate. Many expressed gratitude (or surprise) that he had shown up at all.

It amused and appalled Carlos no end that sightings of him were reported as if a yeti had been netted or an alien spacecraft found parked on Fifty-Seventh Street. He was, of course, a very private man, and would never imagine trespassing on the solitary facts of a stranger's life. But as is now known, he would make exceptions. Robert Cardinalli was one of them.

Around 1990 I was on a flight from Tokyo to Zurich, and found that for most of the flight I sat in the seat next to Maestro Kleiber. During the first part of the flight I worked on an anthropological paper for a conference I was scheduled to attend in Vienna. I saw that he often looked over to see what I was doing.

Having been intrigued by words like "Tibet, Nepal and caravans" he struck up a conversation that lasted on and off for about 3 hours. Normally, I do not engage in conversations with seat neighbors on long flights (not to be aloof, just to be respectful of privacy). I thought he had a somewhat familiar face but did not make the connection for at least an hour, and only after I asked what kept him out of trouble. He was very funny, a little shy to speak about himself as musician, and we ended up talking a lot about Asian food—he was a big fan of Asian street food, as am I.

For the flight he had pre-ordered a special high-protein non-dairy meal and he proceeded to tell me how it prevented flatulence on flights. It would have been nice to listen to him parse his conducting approach of Traviata or Tristan but that's not what he was interested in discussing, or gossip about various singers, conductors and directors, but it never went in that direction.

I noticed during the flight, when not reading or napping, he listened to CDs of Sondheim musicals, including Sweeney Todd and A Little Night Music, usually tapping his fingers on the arm in beat with the score. I mentioned that I had seen the original cast of Todd, and he said Sondheim is a genius, "the closest thing we have today to a real theatrical opera composer." I gave him some names & contacts of friends in India and Nepal, and on a subsequent visit to India he had lunch with one journalist friend who ended up doing a feature article on Kleiber for the Hindustan Times.[384]

The year 1990 was the final year Carlos conducted at Covent Garden. According to Sir John Tooley, their relationship ended in dispute over house policy and a remarkable woman.

"Carlos and I were in close touch for several years, but he broke off regular contact with me because I had to part company with Eva Wagner from Covent Garden on the insistence of Bernard Haitink. I explained this to Carlos, but he was offended on Eva's behalf and never replied to any further communication. This was huge sadness for me."[385]

Eva Wagner-Pasquier had been appointed director of the Royal Opera House, but it was not an easy fit, culturally or personally. Descended from the composer, she would also serve as director of the Bastille Opera and, on 29 March 2001, was appointed to succeed her grandfather Wolfgang as intendant at the Bayreuth Festival. That didn't last. Much later, on 1 September 2008, she and her sister Katherina were appointed by Bavarian Culture Minister Thomas Goppel to co-manage the festival. This arrangement appears to be stable, but one never knows—Wagner family quarrels being what they are. She is a powerful and talented woman who managed to deter universal admiration. At the Royal Opera House, Haitink and Claus Moser found themselves unable to collaborate with her as they would have wished.[386]

Because Carlos sided with Eva Wagner in this dispute, he chose not to work in London again, although Covent Garden had treated him very well. It was one of only three companies in Carlos's regular orbit. When asked how he managed to keep Kleiber coming back over all those years, Tooley initially said, "I don't know. Certainly we became personally very friendly. I think that conditions at Covent Garden were very good for him. He had an orchestra that never changed, beginning to end. Because of our policy of *stagione*, we saw to it that he not only had the same orchestra but also the same singers, all the time, throughout the entire process. This was essential to the way he made music, and we gave it to him. This is hard to do in London."[387]

Tooley's successor, Sir Jeremy Isaacs, kept trying to get him back. He made repeated overtures, but Carlos waved him off in a typically rueful way: "You offer me the two things I most value," he said, "money and flattery. But I shall say no."[388]

In early 1991 Kleiber initiated a pen-pal relationship with a timpanist he had seen on television. On 12 April he wrote a fan letter, in French and carefully typed (with none of the usual decorative afterthoughts I saw so often), to Bonnie Lynn Adelson of the Radio-Television-Luxembourg Orchestra. As earlier described, she had no clue who he was but was charmed by his letter nonetheless, and by the several that followed.

Dear Madam,
In sometimes following the concerts of the RTF television orchestra, I have found absolutely remarkable the way you play the timpani. I would like to be a timpanist able to play like you do. Generally, in the orchestras that I know, your colleagues are like ventriloquists, pretending to have nothing to do with the sounds they produce and affecting a poker face even in the most fulminating passages. They apparently do not realize that one must perform with the body, the face, the sticks and that all of themselves should be brought into play. (My French is very bad, sorry.)

But you are different. You know that this instrument can be a harp, can create pizzicato, a surprise, pure wild rhythm, etc. You send the sound to the listener's understanding with comprehension of the <u>moment</u>, with the alertness and tension of a tiger. (And you are very beautiful, if I may say.)

Having always been at war with percussion (usually they have missed their calling—or they do not care, I do not know what it is) I wanted to express, even if awkwardly, my admiration for your performance.

—With best wishes, yours
Carlos Kleiber [author's translation]

Carlos also provided his home address, something he virtually never granted to anyone. Adelson replied three days later with a gracious pro forma, declaring, "I'm always so happy when I can bring such happiness to anyone who listens to music. That's what it's all about. . . . Music comes from God, and we simply are His 'instruments' who are *privileged* to 'transmit' His music. . . . Thank you again for taking the time to write me."

Carlos must have answered the same day he received hers. He did so in English, and again quite carefully typed.

Thank you for answering what was just an appreciation in pidgeon-french [*sic*]. English is easier: my mother was from Waterloo, Iowa . . .

At a moment when apprehension, doubt and what a friend of mine calls 'end-life crisis' seems to be taking the chirpiness out of things, your enthusiasm and conviction is enviable and, I hope, a little contagious. Yes, I do like and admire your orchestra, its discipline and versatility; and some of the soloists are first-class, I think. And that principal conductor (?) with the French name (about my age) is not to be sneezed at either. But the rare thing in the band, maybe the last of the great drum-dinosaurs, disguised as a beautiful young lady, ç'est vous, sans aucune doute. When you speak of 'what it's all about' and 'His instruments', it confirmed my intuition that there was more to it than met the ear. Or eye. Absolutely wonderful.

I cherish your photograph which makes me happy just looking at it.

Wishing you a joyful life, Yours very sincerely, Carlos Kleiber

PS. Am enclosing, bashfully, a sample of what happens when a frustrated would-be timpanist dabbles in the arm-waving business, which he <u>very</u> seldom does. If you have time to listen to it: centering it on your CD player might take a lot of patience.

—Carlos Kleiber to Bonnie Lynn Adelson, 17 April 1991

Carlos enclosed a special radio edition CD of highlights from his 1989 New Year's Concert with the Vienna Philharmonic, "Promotional Only. Not for Sale."

Adelson now realized who had been sending her fan mail. She replied on 19 April, across three pages: "Dear Maestro Kleiber! I've never known such **MODESTY** before in my life from a **conductor**! Your first letter surprised me by all your knowledge of orchestras, musicians, etc. . . . very different from most 'fan' letters that I receive . . . but your second letter really 'takes the cake' as far as surprises go!" She told him about working in Yugoslavia, the possibility that they might have met before, synching to playback, her conductor Louis de Froment, studies with Saul Goodman and Roland Kohloff, and Carlos's idea of "doubling the rolls" at the end of the Tchaikovsky and Beethoven. It was an altogether playful reply.

Once again unaware of Kleiber's ordinary rules, she then got to the point: "Now I'd like to ask a big favor of you . . ." and requested that he give her a letter of reference for an upcoming position with the Indianapolis Symphony Orchestra. She provided names and the address, and said, "Excuse me for being so bold, and asking a favor of you . . . but I have a feeling that you'd love to do this for me!" Thanking him once again, she closed by asking, "By the way . . . why in the world are you feeling an 'end-of-life crisis'??? You are not too old for anything, and as a conductor you're probably just the 'right' age. Why are you feeling so depressed? I thank you from my heart. . . . If you do write the Indianapolis Symphony for me; please feel free to write whatever you want. I'm sure that it'll be lovely! Sincerely Yours, Bonnie."

Carlos now replied in hand, on 24 April 1991.

Dear Ms Adelson,

Thanks for your charming letter.

1) No, it wasn't I who 'conducted you' 20 years ago: I would have remembered a lady-timpanist.

2) Yes, I'll write to the ISO, Indiana.

3) When I mentioned the conductor 'not to be sneezed at', I meant Froment, not Hager. Froment may be deaf, but he's not incompetent, by any means.

4) Searcy is a great drummer, too!

5) The Germans say that the little drum on the left originated in the horseback (military) timp-use and made it less difficult to mount (from the left side of the horse). You get the picture?

6) I saw Saul in NY in '90. Looked chipper and had his new lady-friend with him.

7) Kind of in a hurry today; but wishing you all the very best,

Yours Sincerely

Carlos Kleiber

Kleiber conducted twice in 1991. Both times were with the Vienna Phil-harmonic. He had an open invitation to work there, and hard feelings had mended. When he did, the Viennese showed him all the love, respect, and demand for his presence they withheld from his father forty years earlier. Car-los led their extraordinary orchestra in Mozart 36 and Brahms 2 in October.[389] These were released as a Unitel video the following year. When Carlos sent me a copy of it, he drew graffiti on his face.

Carlos often expressed self-doubt as self-mock. John Mordler was asked to supervise the audio track for this film recording. Years later he retains the memory of Carlos's insecurity in the face of a tremendous success. "During the filming of the two symphonies, he at times fell into deep depression when he was unable to obtain the results he wanted. He was forever telling me that he wanted to stop conducting. On the other hand he would say jokingly that when he went to his safe and saw the pile of banknotes begin to go down, he would accept another concert!"[390]

Kleiber also appeared twice in a treasury of Viennese waltzes, polkas, and operetta at year's end. These latter concerts were given in identical reper-toire[391] on 31 December 1991 and at the famous New Year's Day concert the afternoon of 1 January 1992. This latter event was filmed, broadcast world-wide, and made available commercially. As with the earlier concert in 1989, this Viennese celebration reinforced Carlos's international celebrity. No one else conducted like that. Together these two films and CDs sold in the tens of thousands and made Carlos a household name to music lovers everywhere.

And just as his name reached its greatest heights, he took steps to bring it back to earth. Celebrity was never his best friend.

Carlos was now rapidly winding down his career. He was sixty-two years old. It was two years since he had conducted in an opera house. He was also restricting his choice of orchestras: from 1991 to 1993 he conducted only the Vienna Philharmonic. After the New Year's Day concert noted above there was one other concert in 1992. It was given to advance the cause of a new book about the Vienna Philharmonic itself.

According to conductor and violinist Clemens Hellsberg,

> Professors Werner Resel and Walter Blovsky, at the time chairman and busi-ness manager of our orchestra, asked Carlos Kleiber if he would take over the musical embellishment for the presentation of my book "Demokratie der Könige," written at the behest of the Philharmonic on the occasion of the orchestra's 150th anniversary. Kleiber accepted instantly ("I'll do it—if I get a book!"), and came to the Golden Hall in Vienna on November 14, 1992 and conducted Otto Nicolai's Overture "Die lustigen Weiber von Windsor" and the fast polka "Unter Donner und Blitz" by Johann Strauss. This was certainly a unique demonstration of his affinity for our orchestra, his interest in our work together, and our personal friendship.[392]

There was to have been a concert tour of Japan, given in March 1992, but Carlos canceled. According to Blovsky, Carlos was hospitalized with pneumonia contracted while visiting his wife Stanka's family in Zagorje, Yugoslavia.[393] This tour also marked the celebration of the 150th anniversary of the founding of the Vienna Philharmonic. Carlos was to have appeared with them in Paris, Osaka, Nagoya, and Tokyo.[394] Tickets to these concerts sold out almost immediately they were put on sale, and very high prices were charged. Tremendous disappointment followed. (Carlos did manage a private visit to Japan in October of that year.)

Early in 1992 he briefly resumed his correspondence with the American timpanist Bonnie Lynn Adelson. She was still working in Luxembourg. He sent her a postcard in reply to a holiday greeting, dated simply "January '92."

> *. . . And a Happy New Year to you, too! Thanks for sweet note! I wrote to the orchestra you were interested in when you asked me to. Wonder if it did any good? Keep up the good drumming. Saw L. Hager in Vienna and he is also a fan of yours, he says. You see!*
> *All the Best!*
> *Yours, C. Kleiber*

Adelson wrote again a few weeks later, prompting a handwritten reply on 5 March 1992. He talked about auditions, conducting, and what "noble" orchestras should do when dealing with difficult *dirigenten*. Vienna must have been on his mind.

> *Hi there!*
> *Many thanks for your very nice letter!*
> *A timpanist behind a screen (!) is unjudgeable, sez I! The backwoodsier the place is, the fuddy duddier the orchestra managers get. S_ _ _w Indianapolis!*
> *I have no manager & have practically stopped conducting. But (tell no one, OK?) it's not ethics; it's laziness! It was illness, tho', made me have to cancel the WPH-Tour (Japan) which thank God, Sinopoli took over.* [At this point in the letter Carlos drew a cartoon of Sinopoli, resembling nothing so much as an Hasidic rabbi. See the following.]

I'll give RTL an affectionate thought (good!! band!!) but don't let anyone write or call me. (Wish that the RTL orchestra were on TV oftener.) Spring is here, too, with a gala performance by birds and flowers. No 'conductor's grim baton' (Emily Dickinson) needed for this supreme show, eh?

Sorry L. Hager is waxing tetchy. Hardly know him, just met him that once I told you 'bout. The main thing for all of us, conductors and semi- or non-conductors is to stay true to our lousy characters. All other ploys never fool the players who everywhere are, I maintain, quick and smart!

Anyway LH purported to be a fan of yours when I sang a little panegyric about your pantherlike Pauken-approach. The best reaction a noble orchestra can show when a conductor goes into a fit is silence and patient, poker-faced meditation on something else. (The Vienna Phil. are past masters at that!) Then it's like it never happened.

Best regards, take care, keep your buoyant and outgoing charm! And your health and happiness!

Vôtre trés vieux
Carlos Kleiber

He then taped to the bottom of the letter some helpful information found on a printed card he had acquired, and headed it "A Conducting Lesson."

+ To start the music
Open the upper cover to start the music. The second hand starts moving to the music.
* The music plays for about 30–50 seconds.
* The movement of the second hand differs depending on the music played.

"We hope!," Carlos added.

+ To stop the music
Close the upper cover to stop the music.
(The music will stop automatically in about 30–50 seconds even if the upper cover is left open.)
* When the music stops, the second hand will return to the accurate time

In hand below, he added, "As easy as that, is it?"

Carlos seems to have come across a watch capable of leading orchestras, the Lorus V621 model. It came with a good tune built in: the Mickey Mouse March, © 1955 Walt Disney Music Company.

Later in 1992 Carlos and Stanka finally created a vacation home in the tiny Slovenian village of Konjsica.[395] They would visit there often. Unrecognized in her homeland they would hike, listen to music, and slowly ease away from the world. They also spent time in the village church nearby. There was something about St. Jernej's simplicity they liked very much.

As Sir Peter Jonas reported, "About twenty years before he died, at Stanka's insistence, he bought a little cottage in Slovenia and used to go there in the summers . . . a very modest little cottage near to the village where she was from. They sort of renovated it and made it quite comfortable and they would go there. That was their real, real hiding place."[396]

Although considered an outsider by most of the residents of Konjsica, Carlos managed to make friends with a few. One of them traded in Slibovitz.

> When in the village, Carlos was extremely funny (another impression). This will make you weep. He used to spend a lot of time with a brandy maker, in the village, named Dolanc. Carlos talked his head off and bared his soul to this man. Unfortunately this man died last year—heart attack at someone else's funeral.
>
> —KD, e-mail to author, 26 November 2009

The year 1993 was another of those what-if years. He appeared with the Vienna Philharmonic on 15 and 16 May and gave his only performances of Richard Strauss's epic and autobiographical tone poem *Ein Heldenleben*,[397] and his much more familiar statement of Mozart's Symphony No. 33. Some months earlier he had asked me to enquire into the availability of an *Heldenleben* part-set in the States. He didn't want anyone in Europe to know what he was up to. I was sworn to secrecy and kept it. The concert was a tremendous success. Its recording was suppressed by Carlos. Pirates have circulated for years.[398]

At the beginning of 1994 Carlos accepted a medal at a public event. The occasion was the fifty-fourth Annual Ball of the Vienna Philharmonie, held at the Musikvereinsaal on 20 January. Singing for his supper, Carlos conducted the Overture to *Gypsy Baron*. He had given it twice before with that orchestra, in 1975 and 1980. There is a film, held in the Conductors on Film Collection at Stanford, of Carlos leading the Vienna Philharmonic at the balls of 1975 and 1994. He seems to have had a very good time.

He wrote to tell me about the latter event a couple of weeks later. By that time, some awkward regret had already set in. He wanted to talk about it but could only do so in a frame of self-negation and mockery. There were many people present when he was honored. The only person in the room who doubted his genius was Carlos. Quoting from his letter makes clear, yet again, what a difficult time he had accepting the praise and affection of strangers.

> *Wanna hear bout me? I actually conducted something! The Gypsy Baron Ouverture. It was for the opening of the Vienna Philharmonic Ball. It is a great piece*

and I love it and people seemed to like our rending rendering. (About 4 minutes)
(Rent-a-Rendering?) The Ouvert. is kinda like a TV spot, every couple seconds it
jumps to another picture. First, in come the Gitanos, crashbang. Then: careful!
Don't sing that tune too loud: it's a forbidden tune. Then, something jolly, then
something brutally ethnic; then a blind seer, age 99 1/2, telling (monotonously) the
gruesome future; then a cry of "what the hell, who cares", then a lilty walzer, und
so weiter. What a genius, old Johann Jr!

   I got a decoration, quite a nice one, too. I am now exteriorly decorated. But my
interior decoration leaves everything to be wished. I am a silly, empty old coot;
but I do still enjoy my food and, yeah!, <u>drink</u>! you betcha! (Evviva C2H5OH!)[399]

—*Carlos Kleiber, 1 February 1994*

He soon returned to work, driving to it in fast cars whenever possible. Back
to Vienna, in March he gave three more performances of *Der Rosenkavalier*,
with Lott, Moll, von Otter, Bonney, and Hornik in the lead roles at the Staatsoper on 18, 21, and 23 March 1994. Another letter followed. He was having
a good time.

   I answered your missives so late, on account of I was in Vienna until yesterday, do-
ing 3 Rosenkavaliers at the Grand Old Opera. A fun thing we will re-do in Japan
in Sept-Oct 1994, 6 times, to the elation of the natives

—*Carlos Kleiber, 31 March 1994*

Soprano Barbara Bonney remembers that, during its rehearsal and performances, "He was always nice, very sweet to me, and the only criticism he
ever had was that we all sang too loudly. I will never forget him saying to
the Vienna Philharmonic, 'If you can't hear the singers whisper, then you are
all playing too loud.' With him, they never dared play above piano, and for
the only time in my life as a singer, I never had to force a single note. We all
owe him for that."[400]
   The Vienna *Rosenkavalier* performance of 23 March was filmed and released by Deutsche Grammophon. Carlos had by now reestablished terms
with that organization. He took Vienna on tour to Japan for six Strauss performances (and one more earthquake) in the fall.[401] Unknown to anyone at the
time, this was the last opera Kleiber would ever conduct.
   Its valedictory perfection has endured. Bonney thought her own work, until
one night, was not acceptable. "The other obvious vocal challenges in the role
are those very high phrases which you have to float. . . . I don't think I've ever
done it terribly well. I've *pretended* to do it, I've convinced people that I can

do it, but I know I can't. I fooled everybody and almost fooled myself. . . . Even Carlos Kleiber, who can never be fooled, was almost happy. He said, 'OK, there are some things missing, but yours is still the best-characterized Sophie I know at the moment.'"

And then, on 15 October 1994, all the wizardry in the world came together. At this one performance, "It took off in such a magical way that we all felt 'This is it!' Now we can all be run over by a truck because we have done it. This evening we made the work come alive in the way we feel Strauss wanted! Nothing can ever be like this performance. . . . There and then, I decided I never wanted to sing Sophie again."[402]

"I remember that Felicity Lott, Ann Sophie von Otter, Kurt Moll and I all looked at each other during the curtain calls, knowing that this kind of performance would never come along for any of us ever again. It was like being given the perfect gift. I never saw Carlos again after that, which I found very sad."[403]

Kleiber also felt he had nothing left to say. Aptly enough Carlos had ended his opera career with *Der Rosenkavalier*, itself perhaps the most beautiful farewell in all music.

Meanwhile, the Berlin set had been a sort of command performance. The German Bundespräsident, Richard von Weizsäcker, was stepping down from the office he had honored so ably. He served as president from 1 July 1984 to 30 June 1994 and was held in enormous esteem. At this writing he is the only German president ever elected to that office uncontested. When asked by his colleagues what he would most enjoy as a farewell, his answer came quickly: "A Berlin Philharmonic concert with Kleiber leading it. And let's make it a benefit for Bosnia." Bosnia and environs were in the middle of a civil war, with indicted war criminals in the Serbian leadership making it their business to murder as many Muslims as possible. Politically and personally, von Weizsäcker had struggled against this and tried to help its civilian victims. Kleiber sympathized completely. The management of the Berlin Philharmonic contacted Carlos, and he agreed. The date 28 June 1994 was set, two days before von Weizsäcker's retirement. When the announcement was made, the usual box office pandemonium resulted.

The concert itself was by-now standard fare: Beethoven's *Coriolanus*, Mozart 33, and Brahms 4. After it was over he seemed right proud of himself.

Would you believe it: I conducted! (A concert in Berlin with the BPH, Coriolan, a Mozart Symph and Brahms IV. I solved the Coriolan-problem by starting it off as Duke Ellington woulda done.)

—*Carlos Kleiber, 5 July 1994*

In 1995 the world's most sought-after conductor gave no concerts at all. Unannounced, he also left the opera house where he had worked most often. For years he had a personal key, a room, and a locker at the Bavarian State Opera in Munich—after May 1995, no more. He was shutting this down as well. Kleiber was now sixty-four years old.

My dear Chap!

You are gallivanting around in the world some place or other (the new secretary told me) and there's some Imperial Cake awaiting you when you return to your office. (I couldn't find any Mangos, you see.)

This AM I went to the theater, asked the "portier" (I had luck: it was the nice one on duty, the only one of them that knows me, too) for the key to the Kappelmeisterzimmer[404] *and emptied my Schrank (#6).*[405] *Then I left the Schrank Key (* it's a very small one, about this size)*[406] *with this porter with instructions to return it to whomever it should be returned to. (Now some other Stickwaver can have my Schrank, which I should have vacated AGES ago! Shame on me!) Of course I also gave the Portier guy the key to the Kappelmeisterzimmer back.*

—Carlos Kleiber, to Peter Jonas, 11 May 1995

I was not certain about the meaning of these terms, and this gesture, until Sir Peter explained them to me. Once again, Carlos had used humor to conceal abdication. In a midnight e-mail, Peter explained what I had missed.

1) He has written (rather badly) "Kapellmeisterzimmer" which is of course him being euphemistic and he means the "Gastdirigentenzimmer" in the Staatsoper, which is the dressing room in the basement for guest conductors. It was and still is a primitive, slightly dungeonesque room with shower and loo which he was rather fond of, and which was always his base of operations, and although shared with all other guest conductors he was the only soul to use it during the days, and . . .

2) In the aforesaid room there are three lockers (Schrank/plural: Schränke or Spint . . . the alternative word . . . he uses Schrank which is not so colloquial as "Spint") which are for the use of those who are not REALLY guests but more or less members of the company or the Staatsoper family e.g. the permanent ballet conductor, the first Kapellmeister (then Heinrich Bender) and, of course, Carlos, the permanent, eminent fixture!

The great significance of this is that he always kept his permanent locker there even after he stopped conducting, with his name written on a scrap of paper in his own hand slipped into the nameplate fixture. Then, one fine day, it sort of dawned on him that he would never conduct **regularly** again so he came in and on the spur of the moment emptied his locker like a baseball, football or cricket player who has just decided that it is time . . .

So you see this is a very significant detail. It was the moment when he **finally** departed the company so to speak! After that it was only (a few selected) concerts . . .

—Sir Peter Jonas, e-mail to author, 8 March 2010

The following year provided, for Kleiber-watchers, an astonishing event. In return for a new car he agreed to give a workers' concert at the Audi-torium in Ingolstadt.

This small town is located near Munich, where Carlos lived. There, Audi makes cars that Carlos admired. He liked speedy cars, period. One of the streets leading to its factory is named Furtwängler Strasse, a fact Carlos enjoyed. Ever practical, he hit upon the notion of doing a concert in return for an automobile built to his own specifications and, as he put it in a letter, "lotsa dough." Karl-Heinz Rumpf was director of Audi's corporate sponsorships, and he negotiated with Carlos personally. (Everyone else gets to go to Audi's Quattro GmbH to customize their cars.) They agreed to bring the Bavarian State Orchestra to Audi headquarters and give a unique concert. In turn, Audi would provide a car whose requirements Carlos detailed in a handwritten note, headed "LE CAR!"[407]

It was to be an "A8 3.7 Quattro, 5-speed Tiptronic," with the following exact features: "1.) Ming blue lacquer, pearl finish. 2.) Natural leather (beige). 3.) Aspherical external back mirror [etc., etc.] 16.) Leather-covered steering wheel with heating. 17.) Front and rear seat heating. 18.) Rolling shades, on the rear motor-driven, laterals manual. 18a.) Electronic protection equipment. 19.) Spot heating and ventilation. 20.) Radio installation (preferably with the antenna concealed in the rear window), with cassette player and (if possible) separate CD player (feeder in the baggage compartment not necessary)." He signed the document, and stamped his top-secret home address on it. To Kleiber's horror the note and his address became public and was reproduced in the most important German newsmagazine of the day.

Der Spiegel ran a two-page story on the subject[408] headed "Audi 8 gegen Opus 98,"[409] complete with color photographs of Kleiber in rehearsal and Rumpf posing beside the M 140,000 newly built car. The article gave prominent display to Carlos's note. Unquestionably this was his handwriting and his rubber stamp. Similar stories appeared in the *Süddeutsche Zeitung* of 9 April 1996 and *Die Weltwoche* of 15 April 1996, and were picked up by the wire services. The latter managed even to catch a candid photo of Carlos wearing white running shoes and about to get into the car. This was exactly the sort of celebrity-gawk he so despised.

Carlos had more misgivings about this odd event than the public realized, and in successive letters to his friend Peter Jonas, he disclosed them.

So you see: I'm not in a conducting mood. And, even for the love of Pete, I don't wanna "do" a Rosenkavalier in Munich nor a concert. Allerdings: the Ingolstadt idea is a <u>slight</u> temptation to my worser self, the <u>much</u> worser part I continually strive to wipe out. <u>Very</u> slight thought I'm giving it.

—Carlos Kleiber, to Peter Jonas,
12 January 1995

Re Ingolstadt: the problem would be (if I ever even get <u>serious</u> about this idea!), that Audi would need their hall and be unwilling to stop production for my rehoissals. Of which I wouldn't want <u>any</u> in Munich (!) but 4 "sur place", as the French say. . .

—Carlos Kleiber, to Peter Jonas, 25 January 1995

About the Ingolstadt-Deal I am beginning to have just the slightest of misgivings. I'll let you know if they develop into full-fledged ethical (who, me? Ha!) cramp: or anything.

—Carlos Kleiber, to Peter Jonas, 18 April 1995

I'm still 50/50 on the Ingolstadt decision. Do you think anyone would come? (I did a Staatsorchester concert in Regensburg once and almost no one went.) [410]

—Carlos Kleiber, to Peter Jonas, 1 January 1996

This evidence of Kleiber's self-doubt as conductor is irrefutable. At an event where most imagine it was a clear track ("I want Audi. Do concert. Get Audi."), it turns out to have been no such thing. After it was over, he wrote me another letter, typical of his rueful, sardonic, and self-mocking persona.

Ingolstadt was a 'Happening mit Herz' and had them rolling in the aisles before it even started. I was pronounced a whore by the press on account of I got payed with a car (AUDI A8, 3.7 liter) and lotsa dough. My public image is now blurred.

—Carlos Kleiber, 5 April 1996

The concert itself ran well,[411] and so did the Audi. Embarrassment lasted longer than either, and I wondered if Carlos told me about it as a kind of preemptive strike. If so, it would be meant to ward off questions or teasing or both. "My public image is now blurred" was the best face he could put on a private matter being made very public.

He gave only one other concert in 1996, seven months after Ingolstadt. Its repertoire was identical to the Audi affair and no less rapturously received. Billed as a "private concert," it took place at the Herkulessaal in Munich on 21 October, once again with the Bavarian State Opera Orchestra.[412] This concert had an unusual genesis. It was made to honor a man and to honor the launch of a classical music television channel. The man was Leo Kirch, founder of Unitel and a friend of Carlos. The channel was "Classica," planned as an all-digital entry in the European and Japanese television markets. It was Kirch's seventieth birthday that day. Unitel described the occasion as "a personal gift" from Kleiber to Kirch.

The distinguished film historian and producer Christian LaBrande some years ago began the restoration of important films concerned with music. He often showed these in festivals held at the auditorium in Paris's Louvre Museum. I had told Carlos about these programs and sent him material acquired because of them. He was quite interested in this sort of work. In 1997 he was the subject of a retrospective in the same series.

In September, *Classique en Images* presented Carlos's most important films.[413] The auditorium was jammed, and people were amazed to see how much film of Kleiber was available. The homage opened with his father's brief appearance in Beethoven 9, from Prague in 1949. It continued with the commercially available films of Carlos's 21 October 1996 performance with the Bavarian State Orchestra, and his 1979 and 1994 productions of *Rosenkavalier*. It also included the televised concerts he did in 1989 and 1992 with the Vienna Philharmonic on New Year's Day, and in Beethoven Symphonies 4 and 7 with the Concertgebouw Orchestra in Amsterdam.

When they showed his La Scala productions of *La Bohème* (1979), and *Otello* (1976), hushed whispers of astonishment lit the room. Kleiber was *rara avis* in Paris. He had never worked there, and Parisians were seeing for themselves how the legend gained that rank.

Even greater amazement lay ahead. That audience saw the only known films of Kleiber in rehearsal. As earlier described, each was made with the Süddeutscher Rundfunk Orchestra[414] and both disclose procedures he never again opened to the public. These televised rehearsals and performances are, quite literally, unique documents. The Louvre program booklet observed the rarity of Kleiber film performances in Beethoven. It cited the if-only prospect of his planned collaboration with Horowitz in Beethoven's third piano concerto. It also cited the absence of any film of Carlos's performances of Beethoven 5.[415]

Kleiber conducted only twice in 1997, each time at a festival and both times in identical repertoire: Beethoven, Overture to *Coriolanus*; Mozart, Symphony No. 33; and Brahms, Symphony No. 4. The first concert took place as part of European Cultural Month, at Ljubljana's Gallus Hall in Slovenia on 6 June. It too was instigated by Stanka, aided by relatives who moonlighted as doctors and nurses. It was more successful than the 1981 venture in that small country. Carlos spoke Slovenian extremely well and had no difficulty obtaining what he wanted from his players. Indeed, he had a special fondness for Slovenian culture. In Munich he actually joined the Terglau (Trglav, Triglav) Club, an association for Slovenian immigrants in Germany. The club is named for Slovenia's highest peak, Mt. Trglav in the Julian Alps.[416] With Stanka's encouragement, Carlos belonged to this organization for quite some time.[417]

According to Slovenian sources, a video of some kind was made of this concert. Many efforts have been made to track it down. It now appears to have been lost or stolen, and many fingers point at a reporter who was "hanging around for over a month, scrounging and poking his nose into everything."[418] A screen cap, evidently from the film taken of this concert, may be seen online to this day.[419]

While there, he accepted an invitation of a sort previously unknown to him: he attended a rehearsal of a youth wind orchestra and offered "a few comments." VIVA, the Zagorje Music Youth Wind Orchestra[420] was founded in 1992 and by the time of Carlos's appearance had attracted eighty highly talented young people to its ranks. Under the leadership of their conductor, Drago Peterlin, they also attracted professional coaches of the first rank. (In 1996 James Galway joined them.) To this day Carlos's name appears in all of their promotional literature. He may be seen in brief video clips leading the adult orchestra at the beginning of the *Coriolanus* Overture, and addressing the children's orchestra thereafter. These clips are held in the Conductors on Film Collection at Stanford.

Kleiber's second performance occurred in that year's Ravenna Festival on 19 June. Together with the Bavarian State Orchestra he appeared at the Palazzo Mauro de André. He would not conduct again for another year and a half, and then only to close out his career altogether.

Later in 1997 he acted on a long-held interest in the work of the child prodigy gone Hollywood, Erich Wolfgang Korngold. His most important opera, *Die Tote Stadt*, had been premiered in 1920 but has not been often seen since. That fall, at the Royal Swedish Opera, it was revived in a widely hailed production.[421] Led by the gifted eccentric Leif Segerstam,[422] with the orchestra and chorus of that house, it attracted strong reviews and a real audience. On 21 October Carlos flew to Stockholm and attended the last of those performances. I have not been able to find any record of his response to it.

Carlos did respond to an enquiry from Sir Peter Jonas. Evidently, a young conductor had been raising a fuss while doing *Fledermaus* in Munich, and Peter sought advice about handling the situation. It was awkward all round.

Dear Petrovič!

About your young BATter: it's fine to be severe and curt if that's the way you are, 24 hours a day! But if it's just reserved for rehearsal (especially the ones with our intrinsically sweet Bavarian Band), well, better not! If only because: what will you do when you want something unconductable like, for instance, music?

Con affetto, Calvin Klein

—*Carlos Kleiber, to Peter Jonas, 17 December 1997*

He gave no concerts in 1998.

It's easy to see how it happened. Come the end of Carlos's working career, his public repertoire had dwindled to two works: the fourth and seventh symphonies of Beethoven—nothing else. In 1999 he gave this pair a total of ten times, all in obscurity. For friendship he agreed to participate in the Music Festival of the Canary Islands, off the coast of Spain. Together with the Bavarian Radio Symphony Orchestra, he appeared in Las Palmas on 7 January 1999, and again at Santa Cruz de Tenerife on the 9th.

Recalled Alfred Brendel several years later, "I last saw him conduct at Las Palmas, in his final concerts. It was not inspired."[423] Carlos then appeared in Valencia on 20 February and at Cagliari on 24 and 26 February. With this final concert he was done.

It did not end well. Gerhard Koch attended and wrote perhaps the last review of any Kleiber concert anywhere. At the Lyric Theatre of Cagliari, Carlos conducted the two Beethoven symphonies. He was evidently suffering from the flu and working beneath his ordinary standard. He had been persuaded to work at the 1,628-seat Cagliari by its general manager, Mauro Meli. Himself born in that city, Meli put it on the musical map of Europe. Getting Kleiber was one of his greatest coups. He began sending Kleiber cards and letters in the early 1980s, imploring him to conduct. "He was a kind of Dalai Lama of music," Meli said. "He transmitted emotions, extraordinary waves that engulfed you." In November 2003 Meli was named director of the Theatre Division at La Scala.[424]

"He was a bit slowed in his usual élan," Koch reported. Acoustics were inadequate, energy was low, and this conductor could not summon sparks as in days of old. Although Kleiber remained "a Bird of Paradise," the performance seemed strangely old-fashioned.

Only in the encore, the Overture to *Fledermaus*, did the magic touch return. "It was all swirling and perfect," Koch said, unaware it was the final work Carlos would ever lead.[425]

Carlos Kleiber gave his first performance in 1952, and his last forty-seven years later. In almost half a century he led 89 concerts, another 620 performances in opera, and 37 in ballet. He released 12 recordings.

In the world of professional conductors, those numbers are low. His friend Herbert von Karajan gave 2,260 concerts, 1,020 opera performances, and made 91 films.[426] Leonard Bernstein made 826 recordings.[427] Wilhelm Furtwängler gave, among hundreds of other works, 240 performances of Beethoven 5 and 175 of Beethoven 7 alone.[428] Arturo Toscanini had an active repertoire of over 600 orchestral works and 117 operas.[429] Leopold Stokowski led more than 400 *premieres* of new music.[430]

By those Herculean standards, Kleiber had worked little. But for him, numbers of performances bore no weight at all. He did work through which he believed he might speak to others. Everything else lived within.

There might have been more. In 1990, a complicated scheme to lure Kleiber was conceived by Claus Helmuth Drese, then artistic director of the Vienna State Opera. He heard that one of his singers "knew" Carlos Kleiber. Tenor Luis Lima had earlier sung "Tales of Hoffmann" in Munich, and one day he found a note left for him on the artists' board near the entrance. In Spanish it read, "Dear Mr. Lima, I heard you live near to the house in which I used to spend my holidays as a child, in Alta Gracia. I would like to get more information about that. So please, write to me . . . just write to me . . . please, write to me! Yours, Carlos Kleiber."

Lima was touched and amused by the manner of Carlos's letter and replied that he would gather such information and send it to him as soon as possible.[431] Shortly after, Lima went to Vienna to sing and told Drese about the surprising note from Kleiber. Another surprise followed: Drese organized a splendid party at the home of the Chilean ambassador in Vienna. It became a celebration of Lima's career, with many exquisite dishes named after the tenor's operatic roles. After this homage, Drese came to the point: he wanted Lima to talk to Kleiber and convince him to come to Vienna and conduct anything he wished—but *Tristan und Isolde* if possible. Drese admitted that Carlos was not returning his letters and calls and believed that Lima could work some kind of miracle. When Lima returned to Alta Gracia, the then-owner of *La Fermata*, Dr. Chiotti (a personal friend to Lima), allowed him to visit the place and to collect numerous small objects that the Kleibers had left behind: press clippings, concert posters, old contracts, family photos, scores, and even a baton. Lima made up a package and wrote a letter in poetic form for Carlos, employing the style of such rhymed gaucho tales as "Martín Fierro" and "Santos Vega" familiar to children. His poem described *La Fermata*, its peculiar aura and perfumes, and the fact that to this day people can "sense" a child (Carlos) riding a horse there.

He sent the package to Munich. Carlos answered immediately, telling Lima that he went through the poem and package with his sister Veronica. They were so moved as to cry together like babies. Oddly, nothing else came of that particular scheme.[432]

Franco Zeffirelli pursued him for years. In 2001, Kleiber "almost accepted" a new production of *La Traviata* at Busseto, this in celebration of the Verdi anniversary. Then, he reconsidered and told Zeffirelli that it would be better "if I leave you in peace." Zeffirelli pressed him to do a *Don Giovanni* and got no further than Kleiber's sardonic agreement that "the beginning and end are beautiful." When he tried to create an *Il Trovatore*, Kleiber asked if the composer was Verdi. His last effort was toward *Falstaff*. Kleiber replied with a hopeless counter: "Perhaps, but it would be necessary to cut the final fugue."[433] The Teatro Real in Madrid also offered him a *Falstaff* and had, of course, no better luck. Everyone tried.

There might have been more, but it was almost impossible to divine Carlos's humor and distinguish it from his aesthetic. He was once asked at La Scala if he would like to do anything new or different there, and made an odd reply. It may be he was teasing the celebrated snobbishness of that audience. It may be he truly loved the work, and no one had asked him before. In any event, he replied, "*Adriana Lecouvreur*, of course, a most elegant opera," and the room was startled into silence. Given the disdain in which Cilea, Mascagni, and Catalani are held by certain elites, a disdain of which Carlos was deeply aware, it may have been no more than a quick dart of the tongue and a mocking of political correctness in the opera world. Or perhaps he did like *Adriana*—"because of its sophistication." We'll never know. In any case, it too never happened.[434]

An important figure from Argentina managed to get Carlos's home phone number, and in early 2000 called him with a proposal. Juan Carlos Montero is today a leading music critic, writing for *La Nación* in Buenos Aires. At that time he was general manager of the Teatro Colón and desperately wanted Kleiber to conduct there. He was aware of Kleiber's terms and had persuaded his colleagues to meet all of them. Carlos answered the phone and in perfect Spanish talked with Montero about the possibility of working in that great house. Montero offered carte blanche. Kleiber could name his own opera, cast, dates, and fees. Montero politely suggested that Carlos open the official season the following year: six or seven performances and a stay in Buenos Aires from 15 April to 15 May. "He told him that the Colón was also willing to cancel every other performance and rehearsal for that period in order to have Carlos working in perfect peace, with the entire house concentrated only on his opera production."[435]

Montero thought he detected a brief nostalgic interest, until he heard Kleiber say that he had an extremely busy schedule "all year."

He made time to send one last card to his old pal Bonnie Lynn Adelson, who had written after some long absence. It was mailed on 7 February 2001, in reply to an update from her.

Dear Bonnie Lynn Adelson, Tigress of the Tymps! I remember you well from the RTL TV shows—your verve, rhythmic bite, body language, etc! But I told you all that a 100 years ago; all that and more. --------

Happy that Hager gone with the wind; very sorry about Mr Shallon; pleased to hear the orchestra is doing so well; delighted that you sound chirpy, though a bit philosophical. Thanks for your kind, informative letter! Wishing you Health, Luck and Joy!
Yours Sincerely,
Carlos Kleiber

There might have been more music, but the death of an equal intervened. According to Harold C. Schonberg,[436] Vladimir Horowitz was playing with his television one night in 1989 when he came across a performance of Kleiber in Vienna, presumably in the New Year's concert. He had not seen Kleiber before and was deeply impressed. Horowitz told his photographer, Christian Steiner, that he had not witnessed anyone lead music with such passionate insight (excepting his father-in-law, no doubt).[437] Some months before Horowitz's death, the two met and discussed recording Beethoven's third piano concerto together. Thereafter, Horowitz made arrangements to see Carlos conduct, in person. He died two weeks after he could have seen Carlos lead *La Traviata* at The Met.

And when it was all over, Carlos retired to his home, occasional travel, and family. He read books. He wrote letters to his friends. He drove his car. He watched films and television. His world gradually became smaller. On 18 December 2003 it diminished again with the death of his wife, Stanka. Isao Hirowatari visited him toward the end, at Carlos's flat in Salzburg. "The shock of losing his wife made him appear quite aged," he said. "The young grandson was introduced to me. I was surprised that his answer was 'Erich' when I asked his name.

'When you grow up what do you want to be?' I asked. His mother answered.

'Musician.'"

When Carlos died on 13 July 2004 something amazing happened. He had wanted to keep his passing quiet, and in this, he also succeeded. The world learned nothing for another six days, long after he had been buried in Slovenia, beside his wife.[438]

They chose the Konjsica churchyard, remote from any opening night, far from any capital of music. The surrounding countryside is beautiful and rare. The cemetery of St. Jernej is crowded with trees and memorials, shining in blue and green and white.[439]

At the end there was no fuss. No spotlight. No applause. The curtain had come down years before.

NOTES

1. Carlos refers to a Russian literary character, Il'ia Il'ich Oblomov. The eponymous satirical novel, published in 1859, was written by Ivan Alexandrovich Goncharov. It describes a lounging lord of the Russian aristocracy, incapable of decision making and barely capable of leaving his bed. Oblomov is a day-dreaming visionary who has lost the ability to do anything at all. Spiritually speaking, when asked the famous question "to be or not to be," his answer was "no." This character cut so great a swath in Russian culture that it led to the currency of a new word, "oblomschina," meaning a backward-looking inertia. Samuel Beckett also referred to himself as Oblomov, a trivium Carlos probably knew. The writer Kevin Bazzana reminds me that there are two other aspects to the character. In his mind there is a logic drawn from experience. Whenever Oblomov engages with life, and especially with romance, it is a disaster. From his perspective he is entirely right to avoid contact with the outer world. It is also made clear at the end that Oblomov—though cranky and withdrawn—has a bigger heart than anyone around him.

2. Information courtesy Felisa Pinto, via Matías Bradford Serra.

3. Archipel 0089.

4. Ricardo Ortale, via Sebastiano De Filippi, e-mail to author, 3 April 2010.

5. Russell, 75.

6. Mary Ludemann, Director of Communications, Riverdale Country School, e-mail to author, 18 May 2010.

7. Carlos Kleiber, letter to author, 8 December 1992.

8. Wallmann, 127. Memories are tractable. Carlos would have been eighteen at that time. One presumes their encounter occurred somewhat before then.

9. Information from Veronica Kleiber, interviewed by Argentine music historian César Dillon. This claim is queried by Sebastiano De Filippi, who describes it as unsupported by any of that era's documents. E-mail to author, 18 March 2010.

10. Courtesy Felisa Pinto, who at the time worked for Veronica's travel agency.

11. Michael Gielen, letter to author, 22 April 2005.

12. Today, ETH Zurich, the Swiss Federal Technical University. Carlos appears on their list of famous graduates.

13. Gielen, author's interview, San Francisco, 1 October 2004.

14. "Don't lie to me."

15. Gielen, letter to author, 22 April 2005.

16. Alexander Borodin, the gifted Russian composer whose day job was research chemist at the Academy of Medicine in St. Petersburg.

17. Sebastiano De Filippi, e-mail to author, 3 July 2010.

18. Sebastiano De Filippi, e-mail to author, 3 July 2010.

19. DG 447 400-2, originally recorded in 1975 and 1976.

20. Liner notes by Peter Cossé, translation by Mary Whittall.

21. Sebastiano De Filippi, e-mail to author, 28 February, 18 March, 3 April, 7 April, 1 May, 2 May, and 6 July 2010.

22. http://books.mongabay.com/population_estimates/full/Montevideo-Uruguay.html, accessed 2 May 2010; http://countrystudies.us/uruguay/30.htm, accessed 3 May 2010.

23. Servicio Oficial de Difusión, Radiotelevisión y Espectáculos; literally, Official Service of Diffusion, Radiotelevision and Shows; more colloquially, State Service of Communication, Radio, Television and (Stage) Performance(s).

24. Sebastiano De Filippi, e-mail to author, 2 May 2010. At p. 41 in his biography, Alexander Werner cites information to the contrary, this drawn from the *Podium der Jungen* of 7 December 1960 and from work by Alfons Neukairchen appearing in the *Düsseldorf Nachrichten* of 2 December 1961.

25. Adapted from the work of Giuliana Bilotta and Robert McGinn. Erich Kleiber died on 27 January 1956.

26. Courtesy Stefanie Hagen, Sekretariat Orden Pour le mérite für Wissenschaften und Künste, e-mail to author, 7 April 2010. "In La Plata he had his first engagement."

27. Literally, "good airs."

28. United Nations, World Urbanization Prospects, 2001. Argentina itself had a population of 17,150,000. By comparison, in the same year, Canada had 13,737,000 people, the UK 49,816,000, Brazil 53,975,000, and the United States 157,813,000.

29. Gielen, letter to author, 22 April 2005.

30. Hunt, 311.

31. Matzner, 113.

32. About 183 centimeters.

33. *Atlantic Monthly*, February 1988.

34. Simon Rattle, *Charlie Rose*, PBS, 16 December 2010.

35. Reiner was crippled by heart disease and had no choice in the matter. Film of him from the 1920s, 1930s, and 1940s reveals the expansive and energetic beat of a healthy man.

36. The occasion when orchestra first meets singers and accompanies them in a music-only run of the show.

37. Jonas, e-mail to author, 11 April 2005.

38. *Kurier*, 8 February 2001. Translation courtesy Karen Mercedes.

39. "One Kleiber is enough." Michael Gielen, author's interview, San Francisco, 1 October 2004.

40. Slonimsky, 505.

41. In 2008 dollars, this was just over $115.3 billion.

42. About 310 square kilometers. By comparison, San Francisco is 49 square miles.

43. *Brandenburgische Neue Nachrichten*, 24 February 1955. Courtesy Ulrich Plemper.

44. Michael Gielen, author's interview, San Francisco, 1 October 2004.

45. William Lacey, e-mail to author, 14 April 2010.

46. Matheopoulos, *Maestro*, 447.

47. Matheopoulos, *Maestro*, 450; Mutsu Yamazaki, *Ongaku Gendai*, Tokyo, 10 May 1983.

48. *Ples čarovnic*, Slovenian Film Fund (Zbirka slovenskega filma).

49. Culshaw, 207–8.

50. *Erfolgreiche junge Musiker*, 8 December 1960.

51. Matheopoulos, *Maestro*, 451. Memories are tricky. There is no evidence that Carlos ever performed *Swan Lake*. Dr. Willnauer was likely recalling *Sleeping Beauty*.

52. Matheopoulos, *Maestro*, 451.

53. Herbert Graf was a remarkable character in his own right. He was the son of the formidable critic Max Graf, and at age four he was sent to Freud in Vienna. The precocious young Graf became "Young Hans" in Freud's famous case study. It is an Oedipal tale of puppets, Pinocchio, and giraffes.

54. *La Chauvre-Souris* ran on 28, 29, 30, and 31 December 1965, and 1, 2, and 3 January 1966. Courtesy François Passard.

55. Author's interview, San Francisco, 8 February 2005.

56. Alasdair Steven, *The Scotsman*, 21 July 2004.

57. *Daily Telegraph*, 5 September 1966.

58. Conrad Wilson, *The Herald*, Glasgow, 2 August 2004; and e-mail to author, 11 October 2004.

59. Conrad Wilson, *The Scotsman*, 29 August 1966. Courtesy Ulrich Plemper.

60. Matheopoulos, *Maestro*, 460.

61. Matheopoulos, *Maestro*, 451–52, adapted.

62. Schäfer, 216–21.

63. www.youtube.com/watch?v=FO8NEuXZio4, accessed 27 July 2010. And, www.servustv.com/cs/Satellite/Article/Spuren-ins-Nichts-011259286557317, accessed 27 July 2010.

64. Equivalent to principal conductor.

65. Stewart Kershaw, then on staff at Stuttgart, e-mail to author, 3 February 2005.

66. Another source says 7 July.

67. Letter of 4 May 1993.

68. Author's interview, 23 June 2010.

69. Heyworth, 319.

70. www.andrusier.com/prod_detail.asp?intProdID=2857, accessed 4 June 2010.

71. A Latin expression: "Quod licet Iovi, non licet bovi," meaning "What is legitimate for Jove (Jupiter), is not legitimate for Bovi (oxen)," attributed to the Roman playwright Terence. It suggests one standard for the gods and another for the rest of us.

72. Werner, 141.

73. Sir Peter Jonas, e-mail to author, 6 July 2005.

74. This production was directed by Rudolph Hartmann and would be given by Kleiber another seven times.

75. *Rosenkavalier*.

76. "Implicitness, a matter of course."

77. Bonney, e-mail to author, 6 March 2005.

78. This included 82 *Rosenkavalier*, 71 *Fledermaus*, 41 *Traviata*, 22 *Otello*, and 14 *Wozzeck*, among others. www.muenchner-opern-festspiele.de/c.php/info/aktuelles/aktuelles_festspiele.php, accessed 23 December 2004. In his public remarks of 12

December 2004, Staatsintendant Sir Peter Jonas noted 251 performances of 7 different operas and 12 orchestra concerts.

79. Wolfgang Sawallisch, fax to the author, 3 October 2004.

80. Joined by Güden, Wewezow, Horysa, Peterson, Murray, and Klarwein. It was directed by August Everding, and would be led by Carlos forty-one times altogether.

81. On 21 August 1968 the forces of Soviet liberation sent in the tanks. They stayed until Gorbachev removed them in 1989.

82. His colleagues included Hamari, Sauter, Bence, Hirte, Peters, Pfeifle, and Nurmela.

83. In this production his partners were Watson, Benningsen, Nikolov, Tipton, Hoffmann, Lenz, and Proebstl. Rudolph Hartman directed, and Carlos gave it nine times.

84. His partners included Windgassen, von Rohr, Bjoner, Neidlinger, Grefe, Freivogel, Pfeifle, Opp, and Unger.

85. Nicholas Kenyon, *New York Times*, 15 October 1989.

86. Author's interview, Vancouver, 22 March 2007.

87. Hirowatari, 11 October 2004.

88. Fine, Wewezow, Adam, Uhl, Lenz, Paskuda, Engen, Proebstl, Hoppe, and Carnuth.

89. On 27 January 1970.

90. On 22 April 1970. Both were directed by Dieter Ertel.

91. RAI Radio 3, 25 February 2008, courtesy Robert McGinn.

92. They are preserved at Stanford and may also be found through various commercial sources. TDK's version is the best.

93. KD, author's interview, 23 June 2010.

94. Matheopoulos, *Maestro*, 453.

95. "Dirigent Carlos Kleiber gestorven," *Nieuws-MA*, 19 July 2004.

96. Yet another pirate exists to allow personal judgment. The performance of 17 June 1971 has been released by Connoisseur. The singing is not perfect.

97. Courtesy Robert McGinn.

98. An Amazonian queen.

99. Herbert Wernicke.

100. Librettist Hugo von Hoffmanstahl, "help!"

101. Wagner, 161–62.

102. From *The Marriage of Figaro*.

103. For a superb introduction to her art, listen to EMI Classics' three-disc set *Great Moments of Lucia Popp*, EMI CMS5 65770-2.

104. They were joined in this triumph by Jones, Fassbaender, Waas, Bence, List, Tentrop, Evangelatos, Elchlepp, and Ridderbusch.

105. Matheopoulos, *Vanity Fair*.

106. Roughly at the level of the *New York Times* or the *Times of London*.

107. Carlos refers to Heimito von Doderer, a Vienna-born writer and poet. His most famous declaration was "My actual work consists—in all seriousness—not of prose or poetry, but of recognizing my stupidity." From "My 19 Curricula Vitae," 1966.

108. Musberg is a small town, south of Stuttgart, in the Baden-Württemberg district of Germany.

109. Podium.

110. This is a small masterpiece of genial evisceration. Kleiber was quoting Rudyard Kipling's 1892 poem, "Gunga Din":

> An' watch us till the bugles made "Retire,"
> An' for all 'is dirty 'ide
> 'E was white, clear white, inside
> When 'e went to tend the wounded under fire!
> It was "Din! Din! Din!"

111. It is possible to do so by listening to another pirate. The Haydn and Beethoven appear courtesy of "Originals" (surely a joke), an Italian label which printed three thousand numbered copies of this CD. According to my copy, I purchased number two. The sound is rather poor and was presumably taken off-air. The performance is a knockout.

112. At the Casinosaal on 22 June 1972.

113. Examine *La Bohème* as he performed it at La Scala, Covent Garden, and Tokyo, and look at Act I, 16 before rehearsal figure 26, *Allegro agitato*. He restored a measure often omitted, thus re-voicing and reenergizing the passage. My thanks to Valéry Ryvkin.

114. He omitted to mention at least one change he made in the *affekt* of the piece. Weber wrote for four French horns. Carlos used six.

115. The fearsome vocalization indicated in the score.

116. Liner notes, DG CD 00289.477.5324.

117. Gunter Rennert.

118. At the Musik Halle on 8, 9, and 11 April 1973.

119. But perhaps as nothing compared to Michelangeli's later partnership with Sergiu Celibidache. In 1982 they gave a Ravel G Major piano concerto with the London Symphony Orchestra. Even Celibidache was cowed by Michelangeli's austere majesty.

120. Klaus Wagner, "Wahlverwandtschaft von Feuer und Wasser," *Frankfurter Allgemeine Zeitung*, 16 April 1973.

121. Garben, 67.

122. Liner notes, DG CD 00289.477.5324.

123. Erich conducted just one production at the Vienna Staatsoper, giving three performances of *Rosenkavalier* in 1951. Carlos conducted there from 1973 to 1994, in a total of three performances of *Bohème*, five of *Carmen*, five of *Traviata* and eleven of *Rosenkavalier*.

124. It would also be given on 17, 23, and 30 October, and again on 1 November.

125. *Opera*, December 1973, 1079.

126. Weber, Overture to *Freischütz*; Schubert Symphony No. 3; and, Beethoven Symphony No. 5. This set was given on 10 and 11 February 1974.

127. The cast had changed. Watson, Schmidt, de Groote, Waas, Bence, Abt, Linser, Auer, Elchlepp, Ridderbusch, Kusche, and others rotated into it, as would Jones and Fassbaender, but the production remained the same.

128. On 29 and 30 March, and 4 April 1974, in the Musikvereinsaal, for Deutsche Grammophon.

129. *Time Magazine*, 13 June 1983.

130. On 12, 15, 17, and 20 June.

131. Tooley, 67.

132. Lebrecht, *La Scena Musicale*, 30 July 2004. One cites Lebrecht with some caution. In his obituary of Carlos he asserted that Erich died at age sixty. It was sixty-five. In *The Maestro Myth* Lebrecht declared, "There was only one prize Herbert von Karajan still wanted from Berlin: Furtwängler's title of artistic director. . . . When the Christian Democrats were routed in December 1989 by a coalition of Socialists and Green environmentalists, he greeted the new cultural senator with a brusque letter of resignation." Karajan died on 16 July 1989. Lebrecht, 125.

133. Truly psychic tendencies alarmed Carlos. In a PS to Peter Jonas, he wrote: "To my horror, I've discovered I'm 'psychic!' The night he died, I woke up and knew he was dying! I was so sure, I almost went to wake Stanka and say, 'Slavko died!' Turned out I was right, next day. Ich 'wusste' es als Erster! (I don't like this kind of thing at all!)" Carlos Kleiber to Peter Jonas, letter of 23 March 1998. NB: According to KD, this refers to a brandy maker with whom Carlos liked to sit around, talking and drinking, at the cottage in Slovenia.

134. General director of the Royal Opera House, Covent Garden, 1970–1988.

135. Tooley, 67.

136. Mackerras to the author, letter of 29 October 2004.

137. Author's interview, 3 June 2005.

138. Hugh Canning, *The Guardian*, 13 January 1987.

139. Gilbert, 577.

140. This included the very impressive cast of Brilioth, Ligendza, Minton, Moll, McIntyre, and Steinbach. Performances continued on 3, 6, 15, 25, and 28 August 1974.

141. Wagner, 163.

142. Matheopoulos, *Vanity Fair*.

143. Spotts, 280.

144. Courtesy Ulrich Plemper, and his vast collection of Kleiberiana.

145. Author's translation.

146. On 3 October they moved to Osaka's Festival Hall for a special performance there. Carlos's colleagues included Jones, Fassbaender, de Groote, Linser, Jungwirth, Elchlepp, Ridderbusch, Kusche, and Thaw. Curiously, *Rosenkavalier* would open Carlos's career in Japan, and close it altogether twenty years later.

147. Isao Hirowatari, "*Maestro* (Carlos Kleiber) and Incidents," translation courtesy Mako Rova.

148. "The speedy behavior of many Italians."

149. Hirowatari, "Class of 1959." Another version of the tale holds Carlos calling out to the departing donkey, "Bye bye colleague!"

150. Hirowatari, "*Maestro* as I Knew Him."

151. "Cancellation devil."

152. Weber, *Freischütz* Overture; Schubert 3; Beethoven 5; with Mozart, Overture to *Figaro* as encore.

153. On 10 and 15 December 1974, with Jones, Fassbaender, de Groote, Waas, Bence, and List.

154. With thanks to librettists Haffner and Genée. Drawn from Meilhac and Halévy, based on Benedix.

155. "Entries, editorial markings."

156. Their singers included Janowitz, Malone, Fassbaender, List, Wächter, Kmentt, Kusche, Brendel, Taub, and Fehenberger. Carlos conducted this production seventy-two times in fourteen years.

157. *Fledermaus* was presented on 8, 10, 12, 17, 22, 25, 27, and 29 January, and on 2, 9, and 11 February. Interrupted by another *Rosenkavalier* on 8 April, *Fledermaus* resumed on 8 April and continued on the 11th and 13th. *Rosenkavalier* popped up again on 15 April, and Carlos returned to *Fledermaus* on the 21st, all these in Munich.

158. On 26 and 30 April, and 4, 9, 13, 19, and 24 May, and 7 and 15 June.

159. These performances were on 13 and 24 July, under the auspices of the Munich Opernfestspiele.

160. Followed by dates on 4, 7, 19, 22, and 26 August, with a cast that included Ligendza, Brilioth/Esser, Minton, McIntyre, Moll/Ridderbusch/Mazura, Steinbach, Zednik (two roles), and Rydl/Hillebrand.

161. Recorded at Munich's Herkulessaal on 9, 10, 11, 12, 13, 14, and 28 October 1975. His chorusmaster was the esteemed Wolfgang Baumgart.

162. On 7 and 18 October, 4, 7, 13, and 19 November 1975, in the Uhrmacher, Linser, Jungwirth cast.

163. Jones, Schmidt, de Groote, 22 November 1975.

164. Janowitz, Fassbaender, Perry on 25 and 30 November, and 26 and 31 December 1975.

165. On 26, 27, 28, and 29 November 1975, and finishing up on 16 January 1976.

166. RSO Berlin, today DSO Berlin, one of the most important radio orchestras in Germany. There has been confusion about this matter. The recording was originally to have been done with the Berlin Philharmonic, but DG reconsidered. Helge Grünewald, dramaturgie, Berliner Philharmoniker, e-mail to author, 15 March 2010.

167. Garben to the author, e-mail 23 June 2005.

168. At Budapesterstr 25, near the Kurfürstendamm and other attractions.

169. Garben, 73.

170. Donderer was a superb musician, a distinguished teacher, and an artist who appeared on dozens of first-rate recordings. Those he made with the Drolc Quartet for Deutsche Grammophon are justly famous.

171. Garben 74–75.

172. Pianist Alfred Brendel once discussed the whole fiasco with Carlos and confirms Garben's account. Author's interview, Vancouver, 22 March 2007.

173. Garben, 74.

174. Bowen, 65.

175. On 3, 8, 11, 18, 22, 27, and 31 January, 8 and 28 February, and 2 and 30 March.

176. On 10 and 21 January, 5, 9, and 27 February, and 4 and 16 March.

177. On 1 February and 17 March.

178. On 23, 27, and 29 April, and 2, 4, 6, and 8 May.

179. On 24 and 29 May.

180. On 30 May, and 15 and 22 July.

181. La Scala was opened in 1778, bombed to pieces in 1943, and rebuilt for a new opening under Toscanini in 1946.

182. It was recorded with the Bavarian State Orchestra, at the Bürgerbräukeller in Munich, from 18 to 21 June 1976.

183. Richter, 121.

184. Richter, 58.

185. John Mordler, e-mail to author, 20 January 2005.

186. Wagner, 163.

187. Carlos's Deutsche Grammophon recording comes in seven minutes under four hours exactly.

188. Richter, 239.

189. David Gilbert, assistant to Boulez, via Donato Cabrera, e-mail of 15 January 2010.

190. All are at Toru Hirasawa's invaluable and ongoing website, www.thrsw .com/archives/2009/11/bayreuth_tristan_video_on_yout.html, and preserved at the Conductors on Film Collection at Stanford.

191. On 30 July, 3, 11, and 19 August; 23 and 26 August were taken by Horst Stein. Carlos had injured his wrist and couldn't work.

192. In ways reminiscent of the equally famous "Lisbon Traviata" of Maria Callas.

193. Peter Conrad, in his book *A Song of Love and Death*, devotes two pages to this recording. He determines that, among its other unique properties, Carlos takes the singers to an uncommon aesthetic. "Their dramatic preoccupation consists of listening to the music." Conrad, 317.

194. www.deutschegrammophon.com/cdnew 0734014, accessed 26 November 2004.

195. Altogether, these sessions ran on 26, 27, 29, and 31 August, and 18 to 26 October 1980, continuing from 5 to 10 February and 10 and 21 April 1981, and "finishing" on 27 February and 4 April 1982.

196. Matheopoulos, *Bravo*, 307.

197. Stephan Mösch and Celia Sgroi, *Opernwelt Jahrbuch* 1995 (29 April).

198. Munich, 24 October, 13 November, and 12 December.

199. La Scala, 7, 11, 15, 19, 22, and 28 December.

200. Zeffirelli, 294.

201. Valerio Cappelli, "A Genius Who Enchanted: Zeffirelli Remembers Kleiber," *Amadeus* 184 (March 2005), translation courtesy Robert McGinn.

202. This film is held in the Conductors on Film Collection at Stanford. It is also seen in a 2004 Österreichischer Rundfunk (ORF) television documentary produced by Landesstudio Steiermark.

203. Domingo, 142.

204. Domingo, 143.

205. Transcription courtesy Robert McGinn. Adapted by the author.

206. Fawkes, 188.

207. On 2, 5, 13, and 16 January 1977, with a cast including Cossutta, Cappuccilli, Giannella, Raffanti, Foiani, Mori, Morresi, Freni, Jori.

208. On 8 and 11 January.

209. On 10 and 24 January, and 8, 12, 18, 20, and 22 February.

210. Continuing on 10, 14, 19, and 23 May, with Szirmay, Jones, Craig, and McIntyre.

211. The productions of 1971 and 1977, not well recorded but astonishingly performed.

212. Joined by Waas, Wewezow, List, Folkert, Jungwirth, Rix, Forsman, Ridderbusch, Kusche, Thaw, Peter, Paskuda, Klarwein, Wilbrink, Fehenberger, and Chizzali, continuing the run on 15 and 31 July.

213. The publisher of the book in which Carlos's words appear declined consent for their direct quotation.

214. Domingo, 137.

215. Slonimsky, 505, et al.

216. Adler, 367.

217. On 15 September, 23 October, and 13 November. The first and third were led by singers Jones, Schmidt, and Popp, and the second by Jones, Schmidt, and de Groote.

218. They also performed on 3, 6, 12, 16, 19, and 28 November 1977. Carlos led this particular production a total of fourteen times.

219. A changed cast reopened *Otello* on the 29th and continued on 4 and 9 February. In some ways this cast was a placeholder, as Plácido Domingo returned to the role on 9, 12, 15, 19, and 24 February, joined by Mirella Freni.

220. Mio Caro Teatro, Modena: Artioli, 1990.

221. On 5, 12, 15, 19, 23, and 26 April 1978.

222. Harvey Sachs, *New York Times*, 25 July 2004.

223. Wagner, 257.

224. *Los Angeles Times*, 20 July 2004.

225. "Sir Salty," as he christened him in one letter.

226. Sir Peter served as personal assistant to Solti beginning in November of 1974. On 14 October 1977, he was appointed artistic director of the Chicago Symphony and would hold that position until 16 July 1984. He left to become general director of the English National Opera. He would go on to serve as intendant of the Bavarian State Opera in Munich, beginning there in 1993. After Jonas left Chicago, Carlos never returned.

227. Jonas, e-mail to author, 5 November 2004.

228. Sir Peter Jonas, BBC Radio 3, 26 September 2009. Transcription courtesy Robert McGinn.

229. *La Nación*, 3 July 2010, www.lanacion.com.ar/nota.asp?nota_id=1259202, courtesy Sebastiano De Filippi.

230. Fogel was appointed executive director of the CSO on 25 April 1988 and promoted to president eight years later.

231. rec.music.classical.recordings, accessed 25 November 1996.

232. *Philadelphia Inquirer*, 22 July 2004. Confirmed by Alison Ames, e-mail to author, 3 August 2010.

233. CSO press release of 28 March 1984.

234. CSO press release of 21 February 1985.

235. Obraztsova, Domingo, Mazurok, Buchanan, Kanfoush, Gall, Rydl, Helm, Zednik, and Wolfrum led a brilliant cast. The production ran on 9, 12, 15, 17, and 20 December 1978.

236. Jones, Fassbaender, Popp, Waas, Wewezow, Wirtz, Hake, Jungwirth, Sonnenscheim, Moll, Kusche, Thaw, and others.

237. On 22, 24, 27, and 30 March, and on 1, 6, 8, and 13 April.

238. Matheopoulos, *Vanity Fair*.

239. Pavarotti, 25.

240. www.facebook.com/topic.php?uid=44343327755&topic=8431, accessed and translated 7 June 2010.

241. Domingo, 152.

242. At the Nationaltheater on 1, 3, and 16 June, and on 20 and 22 July, with Jones, Fassbaender, Popp, Waas, Wewezow, and Wirtz.

243. These were given on 7, 10, 13, 16, 19, 22, and 27 November 1979, with a cast including Cotrubas, Ghazarian, Aragall, Summers, Rawnsley, and Howell. It too exists as a pirate recording.

244. Mackerras, letter to author, 29 October 2004.

245. Author's interview, 3 June 2005.

246. Musikvereinsaal, 15 and 16 December 1979.

247. M 0335166.

248. Buenos Aires is 6,916 statute miles from London.

249. On 5, 9, 12, 16, and 19 February.

250. Gilbert, 577.

251. Author's interview, 3 June 2005.

252. Alan Newcombe, DG Project Management, Hamburg, e-mail to author, 17 November 2004.

253. *iv*, from measure 191.

254. Hotel Vier Jahreszeiten Kempinski, a famous lodge built in 1858.

255. With Domingo, Cappuccili, De Palma, Manganotti, Roni, Mori, Morresi, Freni, and Malagú on 26 and 29 April, and 3 and 6 May 1980.

256. *London Telegraph*, 21 July 2004.

257. *London Telegraph*, 21 July 2004.

258. BBC3, *Who Was Carlos Kleiber?* transmitted 26 September 2009. Transcription courtesy Robert McGinn.

259. On 8 and 16 July, Bavarian State Opera, with Jones, Fassbaender, Popp, Hake, H. Jungwirth, Sonnenscheim, M. Jungwirth, Kusche, and Thaw.

260. In 1968, 1975, 1976, 1977, 1981, 1984, 1985, and 1989.

261. These latter events took place on 11, 14, 26, and 30 January 1981 with the Bavarian State Opera Orchestra and Chorus, and Cotrubas, Linser, Jungwirth, Schicoff, Brendel, Lenz, Wilbrink, Auer, Hillebrand, Craig, Goritzki, and Sapell.

262. Tooley, 71. The film, starring Peter Finch and Glenda Jackson, is a minor masterpiece. I always thought Carlos was uncomfortable with sexual ambiguity, regardless of his friendships with Bernstein and Zeffirelli. Schlesinger's film orbited on it.

263. Given 25 and 27 April, Teatro Juárez, Guanajuato; 28 and 29 April, Sala Ollin Yolitzli, Mexico City; and 30 April, Sala Nezahualcoyotl, Mexico City.

264. Founded 1554 on the wealth of nearby silver mines, located 260 miles/380 kilometers north of Mexico City, and today a university town and center of the arts. In 1886 it saw the birth of Diego Rivera.

265. I am indebted to John Kelly for his kind consent to share this letter. In an earlier letter to John, dated 8 December 1997, Carlos discussed his admiration for a Stokowski performance of *Coriolanus* he had copied himself "on a lousy cassette I made from a broadcast. It is chaotic, it 'falls apart' quite often; but I love it!, especially the opening bars, that furious first attack with no pause before the tutti ff! And then . . . oh well, it's great!"

266. On 27, 29, and 31 May, and 2 June 1981, with Garaventa, Nucci, Salvadori, Washington, Giombi, Giacomotti, Freni, Guglielmi, Porzano, Morresi, Meliciani, Romani, and Dvorsky from 31 May.

267. The date marked the seventy-seventh anniversary of the founding of the LSO.

268. On 5 June 1981, at La Scala.

269. Originally *The Manchester Guardian*, by 1981 simply *The Guardian*, but for all time *The Grauniad* in honor of its innumerable typos.

270. His company included Jones, Fassbaender, Popp, Waas, Wewezow, Anhorn, Murr, Jungwirth, Moll, and Tauboth.

271. Domingo, Carroli, Di Cesare, and Tomowa-Sintow opened the bill in *Otello*. Dvorsky, Saccomani, Salvadori, Washington, Giombi, Giacomotti, and Freni did the same in *Bohème*.

272. Presented 2, 5, and 8 September 1981.

273. On 15, 17, 19, 21, 25, 27, and 30 September.

274. Solfège, or its Italian equivalent "solfeggio," is a system widely employed to sing at sight a score or a part. The syllables *doh re mi* and so on are used as mnemonics, and every music student masters these names and intervals. Many singers use moveable *doh*, in which *doh* is the tonic in a given key area. Many conductors use fixed *doh*, in which C is always *doh*.

275. Author's interview, 16 June 2009.

276. Franz Endler, www.sankei.co.jp/mostly/0110/endler_e/2.htm, accessed 19 January 2005.

277. The concert took place 17 November 1981, in the Great Hall of the Slovenian Philharmonie. The orchestra was then known as the RTV Ljubljana Symphony Orchestra, and today the RTV [Radio and Television] Slovenia Symphony Orchestra. In a letter to the concert organizer, Dr. Henrik Neubauer, Carlos also suggested Mozart Symphony No. 33, and Brahms Symphony No. 4, in addition to the *Freischütz*. He wanted all winds doubled, "even at rehearsals," and passed along "warm greetings from my wife." Irena Lesjak, Events Manager, RTV SLO, e-mail to author, 11 August 2010.

278. And repeated it on 2 and 5 January 1982. His cast included Popp, Evangelatos, and Perry.

279. *The Gramophone*, October 1975, 170.

280. It had been scheduled for 4, 5, and 6 June 1982. Muck, 452.

281. Letter of 16 April 1982, www.facebook.com/topic.php?uid=44343327755& topic=8431, accessed and translated 7 June 2010.

282. Released in 1984.

283. Karl-Robert Danler, 31 July 1982, courtesy Ulrich Plemper.

284. Ardoin, 241.

285. The "Immortal Beloved" was likely Antoine Brentano. Beethoven's famous letter of 6 July 1812 was written some five years after the Fourth Symphony. Op. 120, from 1823, is dedicated to her. But Carlos knew history. He also referred to the Empress Marie-Theresa (1717–1780). In her reign as queen of Hungary and Bohemia, and empress of Austria, she was the greatest of the Hapsburgs. Music and learning flourished in her time. She played double bass and respected composers. One of her sixteen children was Marie Antoinette. Haydn's *Theresienemesse*, his Symphony No. 48 *Maria Theresia*, and his *Te Deum* written in her honor all testify to her stature.

286. Sir Charles Mackerras, letter to author, 29 October 2004.

287. Vienna Philharmonic website, accessed 23 October 2004.

288. In 1974, 1975, 1976, 1981, 1982, 1983, 1984, 1985, and 1987.

289. Butterworth's life, like so many others, was wasted by depraved and incompetent generalship during the Battle of the Somme in 1916.

290. Jonas, e-mail to author, 22 December 2004.

291. *New York Times*, 15 October 1989.

292. John von Rhein, *Chicago Tribune*, 27 July 2004.

293. These concerts were repeated in Den Haag on 22 October 1983.

294. My thanks to Ulrich Plemper for this discovery and to Sir Peter Jonas for his confirmation. At this writing, the entire rehearsal set has not been released.

295. Using the bow.

296. Plucking the strings.

297. Much less fast.

298. Quick, with lively energy.

299. Immediately.

300. Very loud.

301. From 29:44 to 29:56 on your DVD.

302. Clever Beethoven. It's an inversion of the dactyl from the second movement.

303. A similar problem occurred at 9:46 in the first movement.

304. A British term meaning suspenders or galluses. His friend Isao Hirowatari reports that Carlos gave him much the same advice. "Never wear a pair of eyeglasses on the podium. You might lose them by waving your arms. Never use a ready-made bow-tie with a hook. It ought to be tied manually."

305. Bernard Haitink, author's interview, Switzerland, 5 December 2004.

306. Jonas, e-mail to author, 26 August 2010.

307. RAI Radio 3, 22 February 2008, transcription courtesy Robert McGinn.

308. On 21, 22, and 31 October, in Beethoven, *Coriolan* Overture; Mozart, Symphony No. 33; Brahms, Symphony No. 2.

309. Rosenberg, e-mail to author, 14 June 2005.

310. This concert was televised by NHK on 19 July.

311. Hugh Canning, *The Guardian*, 13 January 1987.

312. "Spirit and intellect."

313. Lucas, 210.

314. At Pompei, 20 September; Madrid, 10 and 11 October; Cologne, 18 and 19 October; Rome, 23 and 24 October, 1987.

315. Gilbert, 502.

316. Fiedler, 413.

317. With further performances on 25 and 28 January and 1 and 6 February and a cast that included Pavarotti, Freni, Summers, Daniels, Howell, Hampson, and Giombi.

318. *Village Voice*, 9 February 1988.

319. www.encoremupub.com/reviews.htm, accessed 20 January 2005.

320. Marsh, 119.

321. They appeared at Osaka, 16 September; Tokyo, 20, 22, 25, and 27 September; Yokohama, 30 September 1988, all with the La Scala Orchestra and Chorus, and Freni, Dvorsky, Summers, Salvadori, Surjan, Giombi, Daniels, Gavazzi, Panariello, and Porzano.

322. This television broadcast was preceded by an identical event in the Vienna Musikvereinsaal at the Silvester Concert on 31 December 1988, with music of Johann Strauss Jr.: *Accelerationen, Bauern-Polka, Bei uns z'Haus, Die Fledermaus-Overture, Kuenstlerleben, Eijen a Magyar, Im Krapfenwald, Fruehlingsstimmen, Csardas, An der schoenen, blauen Donau*; Josef Strauss: *Die Libelle, Plappermaeulchen, Jockey-Polka, Moulinet-Polka*; Johann and Josef Strauss: *Pizzicato-Polka*; and Johann Strauss Sr.: *Radetzky-Marsch*.

323. His father appeared in just one season, on 1 and 15 February, 20 March, and 4 April 1924.

324. Approximately US$4,200 in 1975; US$1 equaled 3.5 DM that year. Prof. Robert Murdell, Columbia University, 17 April 2000.

325. Lang, 133, adapted.

326. Osborne, *A Life*, 361.

327. Osborne, *A Life*, 409.

328. Osborne, *A Life*, 457.

329. Gielen, letter to author, 18 October 2004.

330. Author's interview, 23 June 2010.

331. *Süddeutsche Zeitung*, 19 July 2004.

332. Osborne, *A Life*, 681.

333. Osborne, *Conversations*, 65.

334. Osborne, e-mail to author, 15 February 2005.

335. Osborne, *A Life*, 702, from Endler, 338.

336. Osborne, e-mail to author, 15 February 2005.

337. Grünewald, e-mail to author, 19 April 2010.

338. Gruberova missed two performances, and Shicoff missed one. Matt Schudel, *Washington Post*, 20 July 2004.

339. *Mad About Music*, WQXR, adapted, 7 March 2010.

340. Robin Young, *The Times of London*, 17 January 1990.

341. Sir John Tooley, author's interview, 3 June 2005.

342. Transcription courtesy Robert McGinn, as adapted by the author.

343. Cappelli, "A Genius Who Enchanted."

344. October 1989.

345. Alison Ames, e-mail to author, 3 August 2010.

346. That is, "shit"; "pigs"; "a bunch of bull"; "without the faintest idea."

347. As noted before, he once gave me a letter of recommendation for professional use. He may have done the like for others. In April 1991, at the request of timpanist Bonnie Lynn Adelson, he sent a letter recommending her to the Indianapolis Symphony Orchestra. They seem not to have answered, perhaps thinking it was a forgery. In any event, the following January, Kleiber wrote to Adelson, "I wrote to the orchestra you were interested in when you asked me to. Wonder if it did any good?" It did not.

348. Transcription courtesy Robert McGinn.

349. Kaiser is a well-known critic, author, broadcaster, and professor of music in Germany. His critical method often proceeds by comparative analysis.

350. Kaiserschmarren are sweet Austrian pancakes, filled with raisins or strawberries. Bernard Haitink, e-mail to author, 8 December 2004.

351. *The Mirror*, Germany's largest newsmagazine. It is politically progressive.

352. In his letters to me, Carlos mentioned Celibidache only once. It was in 1994 and in the context of praising a *New York Times* article critical of him.

353. Karl Böhm and a reference to cheap clothing material.

354. Hans Knappertsbusch, the distinguished opera conductor.

355. Furtwängler, longtime conductor of the Berlin Philharmonic.

356. A particularly bitter joke at Celibidache's expense. Until Furtwängler was formally "de-Nazified" after the war, Celibidache was the conductor appointed by the U.S. Army to serve as music director of the Berlin Philharmonic. Furtwängler eventually regained that post and certainly knew Celibidache quite well.

357. Haydn.

358. van Beethoven.

359. Brahms.

360. Bruckner.

361. "Damn" comes close. "Dreck" means dirt, and suggests droppings.

362. Celibidache long asserted that belief system and had a personal guru.

363. Walter.

364. Lieber Sergiu! Wir haben im SPIEGEL von Dir gelesen. Du nervst, aber wir vergeben Dir. Es bleibt uns nichts anderes übrig: Vergeben gehört hier zum guten Ton. Kartoffelsack Karli erhob einige Einwände, aber als Kna und ich ihm gut zugeredet und ihm versichert haben, dass er musikalisch sei, hörte er auf zu lamentieren. Wilhelm behauptet jetzt plötzlich steif und fest, dass er Deinen Namen noch

nie gehört hat. Papa Josef, Wolfgang Amadeus, Ludwig, Johannes und Anton sagen, dass ihnen die zweiten Violinen auf der rechten Seite lieber und dass Deine Tempi alle falsch sind. Aber eigentlich kümmern sie sich einen Dreck drum. Hier oben darf man sich sowieso nicht um Dreck kümmern. Der Boss will es nicht. Ein alter Meister des Zen, der gleich nebenan wohnt, sagt, dass Du den Zen-Buddhismus total falsch verstanden hast. Bruno hat sich über Deine Bemerkungen halb krankgelacht. Ich habe den Verdacht, dass er Dein Urteil über mich und Karli insgeheim teilt. Vielleicht könntest Du zur Abwechselung mal auch was Gemeines über ihn sagen, er fühlt sich sonst so ausgeschlossen. Es tut mir leid, Dir das sagen zu müssen, aber hier oben sind alle ganz verrückt nach Herbert, ja die Dirigenten sind sogar ein klein bisschen eifersuchtig auf ihn. Wir können es kaum erwarten, ihn in etwa fünfzehn bis zwanzig Jahren hier herzlich willkommen zu heissen. Schade, dass Du dann nicht dabeisein kannst. Aber man sagt, dass dort, wo Du hinkommst, viel besser gekocht wird und dass die Orchester dort unten endlos proben. Sie machen sogar absichtlich kleine Fehler, damit Du sie bis in alle Ewigkeit korrigieren kannst. Ich bin sicher, dass Dir das gefallen wird, Sergiu. Hier oben lesen die Engel alles direkt von den Augen der Komponisten ab, wir Dirigenten brauchen nur zuzuhören. Nur Gott weiss, wie ich hierher gekommen bin. Viel Spass wünscht in alter Liebe Arturo.

365. Umbach, 197.

366. Umbach, 197–98.

367. Renard Machart, *Le Monde*, 29 July 2004, referring to the *Le Monde* special issue about Pavarotti. "Dear Sir, When Luciano Pavarotti sings, the sun shines on the world."

368. Per the usual practice of *The Times*, the letter was published with its original date noted, 26 October 1998. Its text read: "Sir, The threatened closure of the Royal Opera Company for most of next year is deeply distressing. What will become of the orchestra and chorus? If these bodies are not performing they will cease to exist and cannot be recalled to life when needed. It takes a long time to build up so excellent an orchestra and chorus and no time at all to destroy both of them. If they had been responsible for the mismanagement of the ROH it would be easier to understand the present situation, but it is not they who have brought disrepute to the place. On the contrary many, many performances have been given by them which have been the envy of the world. Under the projected plan it will cost more to produce a lower standard. What do the board and the minister want? Yours Sincerely, Colin Davis, Daniel Barenboim, P. Boulez, V. Gergiev, Carlos Kleiber, James Levine, Zubin Mehta, Simon Rattle, M. Rostropovich, 39 Huntingdon Street, London N1 1BP." This is currently the home address of the Haydn Chamber Orchestra.

369. E-mail to author, via and translated by Sebastiano De Filippi, 3 April 2010.

370. "They have their face, and I have mine."

371. Gradwohl, e-mail to author, 22 February 2005. His letter has been, with permission, slightly edited for this book.

372. This 1819 opera was the first of Rossini's using stories from Sir Walter Scott. Pesaro was Rossini's birthplace and is the site of an annual Rossini Festival. Pollini conducted on 16, 18, and 20 September 1981, working with Philip Langridge and the Chamber Orchestra of Europe.

373. Courtesy Robert McGinn.

374. Gülke was kapellmeister at the Staatsoper Dresden in the period and completed that production.

375. This refers to Ives's practice of musical collage.

376. Very tricky to translate. At one level it refers to sonata form in the highest state of expansion beyond its classical origins. At a deeper level, *Hauptsatz* would be the main theme of a sonata, describing variations that occur throughout the piece, but suggesting that Carlos goes back to his "main theme" regularly.

377. *The Outdatedness of Mankind* would certainly appeal to Carlos. It is a two-volume set of literary and philosophical essays examining the impact of technology and mass media and their power to misshape human life. Anders was at one time married to Hannah Arendt.

378. Christian von Borries, e-mail to author, 24 March 2010.

379. *New York Times*, 7 March 1990.

380. Lieberman, e-mail to author, 9 September 2004.

381. Courtesy Stefanie Hagen, Sekretariat Orden Pour le mérite für Wissenschaften und Künste, e-mail to author, 7 April 2010.

382. Letter of 20 December 1992.

383. Courtesy John Stubbs, photocopy received 4 July 2005.

384. Robert Cardinalli, Tashkent, Uzbekistan, opera-l@listserve.cuny.edu, accessed 21 July 2004.

385. Tooley, e-mail to author, 14 October 2004.

386. Very politely, she declined to participate in this book.

387. Author's interview, 3 June 2005.

388. Isaacs, 222.

389. Musikvereinsaal, 6 and 7 October 1991.

390. John Mordler, e-mail to author, 20 January 2005. This report bears a striking similarity to von Karajan's talk of deep freezes.

391. Nicolai: *Die lustigen Weiber von Windsor-overture*; Josef Strauss: *Dorfschwalben aus Oesterreich, Feuenfest! Sphaerenklaege, Jockey-Polka*; J. Strauss I: *Radetzky-Marsch*; and J. Strauss II: *Vergnungszug, Stadt und Land, Der Zigeunerbaron-overture, Tausend und eine Nacht, Neue Pizzicato-Polka, Persischer Marsch, Tritsch-Tratsch Polka, Unter Donner und Blitz*, and *An der schoenen, blauen Donau*.

392. Vienna Philharmonic website, accessed 23 October 2004.

393. *New York Times*, 19 February 1992.

394. Osaka on 5 and 6 March, Nagoya on the 7th, and Tokyo on 9, 10, 12, and 13 March. Two programs were announced: Mozart Symphony No. 36 and Brahms Symphony No. 4; and, Schubert Symphony No. 8 and Strauss waltzes. Sinopoli ended up conducting this tour. Tomoyuki Sawado, e-mail to author, 10 December 2004. In a letter of 5 March 1992 to his friend Bonnie Lynn Adelson, he confirmed this version of the cancellation.

395. Slovenia, independent of Yugoslavia since 1991, has a population of 2,100,000.

396. BBC Radio 3, 26 September 2009. Transcription courtesy Robert McGinn.

397. *A Hero's Life*, written 1897–1898.

398. www.thrsw.com/ckdisc/strauss_richard_1864_1949_/ein_heldenleben_op40/, accessed 12 July 2008.

399. Chemical name for ethanol, the drinkable form of alcohol.

400. Bonney, e-mail to author, 6 March 2005.

401. Given at Tokyo's Bunka Kaikan theatre on 7, 10, 12, 15, 18, and 20 October 1994.

402. Matheopoulos, *Diva*, 6–7.

403. Bonney, e-mail to author, 6 March 2005.

404. Music director's room.

405. Locker.

406. Kleiber drew a picture of the key, evidently to scale.

407. The orchestra was paid in Tonka toys.

408. On 8 April 1996, 228, 230.

409. "In exchange for."

410. On 26 April 1986, at the Audimax University.

411. Ingolstadt, 5 April 1996, Bavarian State Opera Orchestra, Beethoven: *Coriolan-Overture*, Mozart: Symphony No. 33, Brahms: Symphony No. 4.

412. It was broadcast by NHK on 18 April 1997 and has been released as a Deutsche Grammophon DVD.

413. On 18, 19, 22, 25, 26, and 27 September 1997.

414. South German Radio Orchestra, 1970.

415. This was in error. As noted, there is such a film, made during a Vienna Philharmonic tour of Mexico in April 1981.

416. Measured at 2,864 meters, or 9,396 feet.

417. KD, e-mail to author, 26 November 2009.

418. KD, e-mail to author, 26 November 2009.

419. www.trvslo.si/kultura/glasba/v-spomin-na-carlosa-kleiberja/137604, accessed 12 June 2010.

420. Mladinski Pihalni Orkester.

421. With Sunnegårdh, Tobiasson, Bergström, Dalayman, and Jonsson. Johan Ragnevad, e-mail to author, 13 January 2005.

422. Also the composer of 116 symphonies, 30 string quartets, 11 violin concertos, but only 4 piano concerti.

423. Author's interview, 22 March 2007.

424. *Corriere Della Sera*, 8 March 2005. Translations and text courtesy Giles Watson, Giuliana Bilotta, and Robert McGinn.

425. Koch, "Auf Wundersuche," *Frankfurter Allgemeine Zeitung*, 27 February 1999.

426. Ina Gayed, Herbert von Karajan Centrum, e-mail to author, Vienna, 21 September 2004.

427. Courtesy Jack Gottlieb, Leonard Bernstein Archives, New York City.

428. John Hunt, *The Furtwängler Sound*.

429. Sachs, 341.

430. Barber and Bowen, forthcoming.

431. Author's interview, by telephone, 14 July 2010.
432. My thanks to Sebastiano De Filippi for his sleuthing.
433. Cappelli, "A Genius Who Enchanted."
434. Paolo Isotta, *Corriere della Sera*, 18 January 2000, p. 35, courtesy Opera Chic.
435. Sebastiano De Filippi, e-mail to author, 8 July 2010.
436. Schonberg, 270.
437. The gentle Arturo Toscanini.
438. The music journalist Christine Lemke-Matwey, a friend of Carlos, believes that he hastened his own demise and offers evidence. On 11 July 2004, from his home in Grünwald, came Kleiber's last known message, a handwritten fax sent to his friend Karl-Heinz Rumpf. It was transmitted at 11:04 that morning. Later that day, Carlos drove himself to Konjsica, a distance of 449 km, or 279 miles, via the A8 and A10 motorways. The estimated drive time was four hours and forty-one minutes. Carlos was but two days from his own death.

Rumpf was director of commercial and corporate sponsorships for Audi, and he led that company in tremendous generosity to the arts. Their relationship had blossomed since the deal was made for the Ingolstadt concert in 1996. Carlos valued Rumpf's opinions, trusted his discretion, and considered him a confidante. This last letter was written in a clear, strong hand; in that regard, typical of many letters Carlos had sent me over the years. What follows is the original German text of Carlos's last known letter, and its English translation.

11. Juli 2004
Herrn Karl-Heinz Rumpf
AUDI AG, Ingolstadt

Lieber Herr Rumpf, Treuester der Treuen! Innigen Dank für Ihre liebenswürdigen Birthday wishes!

Ich denke ebenfalls oft an Sie und hoffe, Ihnen und Ihrer lieben Familie geht es bestens. Der Herr Sohn macht gewiß Quantensprünge der Entwicklung und des Wachstums.

Ich umarme ihn, unbekannterweise, affetuosamente! Auch mein Enkel (8 Monate) zeigt jeden Tag ein neues Gesicht und neue, ungeahnte Krabbelfähigkeiten und Selbstständig-keitsbestrebungen. Er läuft schon fast!

Gesundheit, Glück und Freude! wünscht Ihnen und den Ihren, immer, von Herzen, Ihr Carlos Kleiber

PS Wie, dank Ihrer, AUDI mit meinem über alles geliebten alten, wunderbaren A8 umgeht, dafür bin ich unendlich froh und dankbar! Bless you all!

Here it is in English:

11 July 2004

Dear Mr. Rumpf, truest of the true or, most loyal of the loyal. A deeply felt thank you for your cordial birthday wishes.

I also think about you often and I hope you and your family are most well. Surely young Mr. Rumpf literally, Mr. Son is making quantum leaps of development and growth. I am giving him a hug, without knowing him, affetuosamente 'with much affection'.

My grandson (8 months) also shows a new face every day [an idiomatic German expression, showing a different side of one's personality] *and new, unexpected abilities to crawl and a drive towards independence. Already he almost walks!*

Good health, happiness and joy! to you and the people around you

Best wishes, always, yours

Carlos Kleiber

P.S. The way AUDI, thanks to you, treats my most beloved, old, wonderful A8, this is something that makes me infinitely grateful and happy! Bless you all!

After receiving a copy of this fax I attempted to contact Rumpf directly to ask his opinion of the matter. I was too late. Together with his wife and son he was killed by the Asian tsunami on 26 December 2004. Rumpf, age fifty-four, was drowned on Bang Niang beach, at Khao Lak in Thailand. The body of his wife, Ina, thirty-four, was found in April 2005, and that of their son Christoph, age four, was discovered in June. The language of the fax is all Kleiber. Its English translation is courtesy Julia Roever, Los Altos Hills, California.

I am indebted to Will Lacey for pointing out the haunting similarity of Carlos's text "Treuster der Treuen" and Tristan joyously addressing Kurwenal in Act III of *Tristan und Isolde*: "Kurwenal, treuester Freund! All mein Hab' und Gut vererb ich noch heute." "Kurwenal! most faithful of friends! All my goods and possessions I bequeath this day!"

439. Konjsica, population 150, is located in the Zasavje Hills Region above the Sava River, fifty-five kilometers east of Ljubljana. The area of the church, "St. Bartholomew," and its grounds occupies no more than thirty by twenty yards (twenty-seven by eighteen meters). My thanks to Tom Empson. He made the pilgrimage in September 2004.

TAKE NOTE

Dear Mr. Barber!

Tho' honestly + immensely impressed by your qualifications and accomplishments (wish I could compete!) I am sorry to say; I hardly conduct at all; so that would mean that you would be totally hors d'oeuvre (out of work) and horrified at my lack of interest, energy, initiative, and so forth. When I do venture out (about once a year) and go thro' the motions of leading an orch. in some repertory war-horse, it has to be a group that

The first letter, Grünwald 1989. Carlos Kleiber Archive at Stanford.

will play nicely any old
how — I mean, sort of
in spite of me, kinda.
If anything, I'm good
at not getting in the
way, mostly.
To avoid the embarassment
of being watched at
rehearsal by innocent
passersby, I avoid
letting anybody in.
I'm a real mess, actually.
Don't tell anyone, please.
With best wishes,
and kind regards
Yours sincerely
Carlos Kleiber

The first letter, Grünwald 1989. Carlos Kleiber Archive at Stanford.

The Big Five: Bruno Walter, Arturo Toscanini, Erich Kleiber, Otto Klemperer, Wilhelm Furtwängler, Berlin 1929. Carlos Kleiber Archive at Stanford.

Ruth Kleiber, Erich Kleiber, Tiergarten, Berlin 1929. Courtesy Zander & Labisch / ullstein bild / The Granger Collection, New York.

At one month, with mother Ruth Kleiber, Berlin 1930. Courtesy Jörg Tschenker.

The first drum lesson, Berlin 1931.
Courtesy Zander & Labisch / ullstein bild /
The Granger Collection, New York.

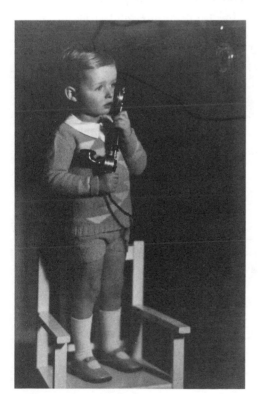

Taking a call from a soprano, Berlin 1934.
Courtesy Jörg Tschenker.

Erich Kleiber, Buenos Aires 1935. Photo by Melitta Lang Studio. Courtesy Jörg Tschenker.

Carlos, Erich, Veronica, Austria 1936. Carlos Kleiber Archive at Stanford.

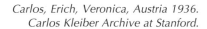

SODRE radio concert, "In Honor of Argentine Minister Dr. Enrique Ruiz Guiñazú." Ruiz was minister of Foreign Affairs, International Trade, and Worship. He was also pro-fascist, an odd companion for Kleiber. Montevideo, circa 1941, courtesy Sebastiano De Filippi.

In the pit, Stuttgart 1968. Photo by Hannes Kilian, Carlos Kleiber Archive at Stanford.

At Smetana Hall of Obecni dum, Prague Festival, 1968. Courtesy Vaclav Jirsa.

Karl Böhm, Carlos Kleiber, circa 1970. Carlos Kleiber Archive at Stanford.

Attending a von Karajan rehearsal, Salzburg, circa 1975. Carlos Kleiber Archive at Stanford.

*"Danke für die Käfer!!" (1978).
Photo by B. Jehle, Carlos
Kleiber Archive at Stanford.*

Carlos conducting as the Bhagwan, Munich 1980. Courtesy Anne Kirchbach.

Rehearsal with the RTV Ljubljana Symphony, 1981. Courtesy KD.

WIENER PHILHARMONIKER

 SAISON 1982/83

Großer Musikvereinssaal
Samstag, 18. Dezember 1982, 15.00 Uhr

Öffentliche Fernseh-Aufzeichnung

Beethoven, IV. Symphonie B-Dur op. 60
Beethoven, VI. Symphonie F-Dur op. 68 „Pastorale"

WIENER PHILHARMONIKER
Dirigent:
CARLOS KLEIBER

KARTENVERKAUF
ab Montag, 13. Dezember 1982, in der Zeit von 9 bis 12 und 15 bis 17.30 Uhr, in der Kanzlei der Wiener Philharmoniker,
1010 Wien, Bösendorferstraße 12, Telefon 65 65 25

One that got away, Vienna 1982. Courtesy Wien Bibliothek.

Chicago Symphony Orchestra, Chicago 1983. Carlos Kleiber Archive at Stanford.

Carlos Kleiber, Peter Jonas, and Reginald Goodall, the English National Opera, Coliseum, London 1986. Photo by Catherine Ashmore, courtesy Sir Peter Jonas.

A Kleibergram for the French horns, at the Metropolitan Opera, *Der Rosenkavalier*, New York 1990. Courtesy Julie Landsman via John Stubbs.

Kleiber the graffiti artist, Grünwald 1992.
Carlos Kleiber Archive at Stanford.

Dear Maestro,   14 Jan 93
You are incredibly prompt, generous, tidy,
funny, exact and all the while as Kalmus
can be. Just a short note to say thanks.
In a void, I'm working on "Ein Heldenleben"
and was just wondering about orch.
material! If all gangs agley here, I might
try Edwin in Boca Raton, and will
maybe need your help with that, then.
the trouble with using "pirate" material in
Europe is: the thwarted local yokels who
live off the fat of the point send their spies
to concerts to check what's being played
from. If they see Eggbert ditmus' stuff, they
get lawyery! Do you have any MONTEUX?
Quite a guy with a stick, eh? Good "Heldenleben".
      All the best!   Charlemagne

Thinking about Heldenleben, Grünwald 1993. Carlos Kleiber Archive at Stanford.

15 VI 93

Dear Batman!

Poster: No 1 is best, of course *!

VII Beethoven: [arco] was written
in later but not in LvB's hand.
Only Klemperer and Erich Kleiber
do (pizz). (That is correct)
NB: 1) do [♪ ! ♪ | ♩] ! and not
| ♪ ! ♪ | ♩ ! | (see (hear) B. Walter on
that. 2) do as quick a Trio as you
dare. (I regret not having done so
on my disc). At least ♩. = 84

That you were floored by Salome
is a good sign! Bravo! Ain't
it something!

* don't put the info in the white
space. Rather create a little space
under the picture. Less is more.
(#2 and #3 are no good)

Molti saluti
your Carlos Kleiber

PS What possible mistakes, or mutilations, can there be
in VII Beethoven? Other than the
misplaced cresc (< >) in 2 Mov.
(it should go: 104 106 and 227 229)
NB: Beware this piece. B. Walter says:
"never have I heard this rhythm correct:
♫ ♫ " (neither have I!)

Carlos the teacher on Beethoven 7, Grünwald 1993. Carlos Kleiber Archive at Stanford.

att. Dr. C. Barber　THANK YOU 😊 7. 9. 94

Dear Charles! Thanks for letter!
Thn off to Japan.
No, the name of the bimbo wasn't
Macgribaucx. It was Macgribauxc.
(Quite someone else, obviously.)
You ask for diagnosis re-varicose
veins? Here it is: varicose veins.
The trouble is you don't listen.
(You're a teacher, that explains it)
*Cechov's greatness was his
great, great heart* and soul* plus
talent*. All inexplicable things,
those. And overwhelming.
PS. I don't believe in "working
like the devil", even in rehearsal.
After all, it's the flaming band
that should (want to) play, no?
And Furty, well it wasn't the
tempi; it was: U and I and the
many others (though not all of 'em)
are, say, moles, poodles, warthogs,
goldfish, etc (which is OK, I guess) and
Furty + the like were, say, Giraffes,
Whales, Rhinos, Dinos, -- oh well* ALL THE BEST
from CK

* Ever notice how some have too large
the size of your thigh? Other diagnoses?
Therefore do exist. Also cerebrally. But
nothing to do or worry about. There's
room for us all. There's just no competing.

There is room for us all, Grünwald 1994. Carlos Kleiber Archive at Stanford.

A photo from Carlo the Dog, Vienna 1993. Carlos Kleiber Archive at Stanford.

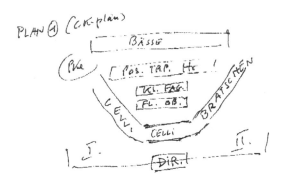

A Kleiber seating chart, circa 1997. Courtesy Sir Peter Jonas.

The last concert, Cagliari 1999. Photo by Marcello Mencarini, courtesy Blackarchives.

Carlos and Stanislava Kleiber gravesite, Konjsica 2004. Courtesy Tom Empson.

Chapter Three

Correspondence, 1989–2003

*How do you like the moose on my envelope? I think his eyes are molto espressivi.
And he has the stolid stance of the born maestro. The horns are from his girlfriend.
(She got tired of that short tail.)
Semper idem,*

—*Carlos Kleiber, 26 March 1997*

The first letter arrived in 1989, the last in 2003. This volume releases most of them, with the exception of a couple that I managed to lose and several whose content was wholly personal. These came very late in our correspondence and reflected his feelings at that stage of his life.

As seriatim reading makes clear, the rigors of consistency never troubled Carlos. His formidable intellect frequently yielded to the moment and invariably to his disdain for phoniness and preening, and to adamant certainties about musical and personal relationships. Early on he makes it clear that he *never* discusses other conductors; soon however, and "never" be damned, he is offering highly personal views of many of the most famous of his time, and not always gently. He held those he most esteemed to the highest standards of a consistency he himself could not sustain. Readers who are even now looking up famous names in the index may be quite surprised by the opinions he offered on some of the most-admired baton wielders of the twentieth century.

The pace and personality of these letters is well judged by the forms of salutation we used. He was, for years, "Maestro Kleiber." I was "Mr." or "Dr." or (absurdly) "Maestro." However, by 1993 a good deal of joking had set in. We started to assign ridiculous nicknames to one another. Soon enough they were "titles" that became part of evolving in-jokes. I will do my best to explain them. Many of his letters also included cartoons and little drawings, usually intended to illustrate his argument in whatever we were discussing at the time.

Some may be surprised by the fact and force of his views on two public figures largely revered in the world but considered by Carlos to be models of cant and hypocrisy. When he first mentioned these names to me I thought he was joking and so offered a standard defense of each. To my surprise he came roaring back, time and again in the case of Lincoln, to the subjects of hypocrisy and misuse of power. (Robert E. Lee was, to Carlos, a much more admirable human being.) He considered Gandhi part of the same class of disingenuousness.

Similarly, some may be surprised by Carlos's choices in reading overall. As much as any in the world of poetry, the American Emily Dickinson earned his highest esteem. Carlos's frequent references to her, the direct (and apparently memorized) quotation of her works, and the childlike joy he took in an Emily Dickinson T-shirt I gave him offer testimony to his regard.

He possessed a remarkable knowledge of conducting history and practice, and displayed a reverence for certain of the Old Greats. Bruno Walter, von Karajan, Stokowski, Klemperer, Furtwängler, Strauss, Toscanini, Talich, Monteux, Goodall, Mitropoulos, Ansermet, Mravinsky—all of them met his approval and served his inspiration. Among his living contemporaries, only Tennstedt and the unusual Sándor Végh seem to have earned his unconditional admiration.

And he shared his knowledge and excitement with many others. John Tooley remembers an occasion at lunch one day when Carlos was exulting over the conducting of Dmitri Mitropoulos. "Observance of tradition was very important to him," Tooley declared. "At this particular lunch he wanted to know whether or not I had ever seen or heard Mitropoulos conduct Verdi. I had not. Carlos insisted that 'we have to put that right.' After lunch I returned to my hotel, and then to work. When I returned later that day there was a package. Carlos had run around half of London looking for a recording of *Ballo* led by Mitropoulos. And there it was. 'John, this is for you,' his note read. His enthusiasms were extraordinary."[1]

Carlos also reveled in a wide knowledge of pop culture, the value of the Euro, and current affairs. Although generally a man of the political left, he was deeply mistrustful of authority under any cloak. He may have withdrawn from the public stage. He never withdrew from an awareness of the world. His letters repudiate the widespread notion that he lived in a cave. His correspondence with other friends makes the same case. This was a man of diverse parts.

Carlos Kleiber traversed a glorious career and a troubled life. Were that life not so churned by hypersensitivity and self-criticism, his concerts may have been more numerous but their power less real. In these letters we discover some of his backstage opinions and the powerful—and witty—intellect that advised and shaped them. Most important, we see what he thought about music he led. In order to make sense of his, I have compacted and paraphrased mine.

IT BEGINS

I sent my first letter to Carlos on 25 January 1989. It was mailed to him through Ron Wilford at Columbia Artists Management (CAMI) in New York City. Its purpose was simple.

> Dear Maestro Kleiber:
> I write to ask if I could persuade you to accept me as a student and assistant in the fall or thereafter of 1989 . . .

My letter rattled on for a page and a half. It praised me and talked about my practical and academic training as a musician. I was a graduate student in conducting at Stanford University ("a small private school near San Francisco"), had started piano at six, violin and trumpet at ten, and first conducted an orchestra at fifteen. The letter also described my reaction to film of his Concertgebouw concert and to his 1989 Vienna Philharmonic special. It offered "highly organized and disciplined" service to his work as conductor. All of this was tempered with jokes.

Kleiber replied two weeks later. His letter was in hand and written on two pages of paper headed "TAKE NOTE" at the top, with music staves lined beneath.

(The following letter is reproduced in the photo section of this book.)

6.2.89

Dear Mr. Barber!

Tho' honestly + immensely impressed by your qualifications and accomplishments (wish I could compete!) I am sorry to say: I hardly conduct at all; so that would mean you would be totally hors d'oeuvre (out of work) and horrified at my lack of interest, energy, initiative, and so forth. When I do venture out (about once a year) and go thru' the motions of leading an orch. in some repertory war-horse, it has to be a group that will play nicely any old how—I mean, sort of in spite of me, kinda. If anything, I'm good at not getting in the way, mostly.

To avoid the embarrassment of being watched at rehearsal by innocent passersby, I avoid letting anybody in.

I'm a real mess, actually. Don't tell anyone, please.

Yours Sincerely

Carlos Kleiber

There was no return address. Others might have taken the hint.

I replied on 5 March. Catching his humor, I made up a letterhead identical to his, headed "NOTE RECEIVED." I thanked him for his reply and told him about a lecture I had just attended over at UC Berkeley. Physicist Stephen Hawking, through the special technology he uses, talked about first cause, logical paradox, and singularity. Once again I wanted to approach Kleiber from an unexpected angle. In any case I was (like everyone) deeply impressed by Hawking's courage. I purchased a copy of Hawking's *Brief History of Time* and sent it along with the letter, all kindly forwarded by CAMI. There was no reply.

That summer I attended a classic car show in the parking lot of a former evangelical church that got that way because its preacher had an affair with the wife of somebody else. The place was now a performing arts center at Santa Rosa, a city in northern California. While at the car show I came across a large old truck and was startled by its marque: KLEIBER. I asked the owner about it, and he told me the story. He also said that a surviving relative still lived in San Francisco and ran a hardware store there.

I tracked down Paul Kleiber III, told him what I was up to, swore him to the secret, and we hit it off. He took me for a brief ride in the Kleiber automobile he owns. He then allowed me to pose in a Santa suit on its running board and took a number of photographs. Paul gave me more information about his grandfather and the company itself, as well as specs for the car. He asked if he might be related to the conductor to whom I was writing. I had no idea.

About a week later I sent the photos, specifications, and company history to Carlos, again via New York. There was no immediate reply. (Years later I would learn that, at this time, he was busy concocting a letter from Toscanini to Celibidache.)

On 2 November 1989 I sent him another letter. He was doing *Otello* at The Met in March of 1990, and I asked if I could attend his rehearsals. My plea was sad and pitiful: "Were you able to grant permission for me to sit silently in the last row during rehearsals . . ." He replied mid-month. This letter was also in hand, longer than the first, and set the tone for all that would follow.

17.Nov.89

Dear Dr. Barber

Thanks a 10(6) for the fabulous Kleiber-material and the snapshots etc! Very touching and amusing! Makes me thoughtful 'cause my father's mother came from a carriage-building family, her father (EK's grandf.) even made a carriage for the Emperor Franz Joseph who said to him: "Es fährt sich gut in dem Wagen"!² (Franz Joseph was notoriously ungarrulous so that's a lot of words, coming from him.)

As to NY rehoissals in March '90 they are <u>absolutely huis clos.</u>[3] I won't have any musicians—especially talented ones like yourself—entertaining themselves with my fumbling preparations. Plumbers, laundrywomen, bouncers, dealers, carpenters: OK, (Maybe!) * Other than that: sorry, no go! Seriously! I feel very mean 'cause you made me so happy with the Kleiber vehicles. If you therefore have any wishes that have <u>NOTHING TO DO WITH MUSIC</u> (like Austrian Candy or Swiss Cheese or something) do let me know. I'll see what I can do.
All the best from your old
Carlos Kleiber

* don't attempt a disguise, tho': my thugs will see thru' it!

Christmas intervened, and I didn't answer until 5 January 1990.

Dear Maestro Kleiber: First, happy new year to you and your family, and best wishes for a wonderful 1990. (Good wishes to your trusty NY thugs too.) Second, I'm delighted that the material I sent on the Kleiber cars and trucks pleased you. . . . I'm torn between your kind offer of Austrian candy or Swiss cheese and wonder if you would consider a hot dog at Sabrette's instead?[4] I'll be in NYC for your "Otello" on March 5 and 9, and prefer mustard, no pickles, and hold the calories . . .

Meanwhile, it's back to scores (Messiaen, "Turangalila")[5] and hockey practice. Charles Schulz, cartoonist of "Peanuts" fame, lives and built a rink here in northern California, and lets us play on it. It's a strange place, looking like what I imagine a Swiss brothel to look like (do they have such things?) but has pretty good ice. I play defense—without a helmet, as you've no doubt gathered.

There was no direct reply to this one either, save that I sent him another note and we met backstage. He joked that I was a good deal taller than he expected, and then he instructed that I tell no one he had allowed me to say hello. I thought he was kidding. He wasn't.

I meant to write him another letter after seeing *Otello*, but never got around to it. I was in the full throes of finishing my doctoral work, defending it before my committee, and starting a job. By the time I got back to the subject, jabbering about *Otello* was too late. I decided to write a book instead.

On 25 July 1991 I wrote, "to ask your participation in a project to memorialize Leonard Bernstein." I knew they were friends, went on to name eight subjects about which he might care to write, and kindly suggested that he could write anywhere from fifty to five hundred words. I put mine on Stanford letterhead.

He answered three weeks later. This time his stationery was Euro-long, and crosshatched with the blue lines draftsmen use. It was also in hand, but there was one difference. In the top left corner he had stamped his home address. I was astounded. The caveat at the bottom, marked with an asterisk, was just as important to the future of our correspondence.

22 August '91
Dear Sir
Thanks for your letter July 25, '91.
About Lenny, a year after his passing.

First: please excuse this paper. I have run out of stationery and have the flu; so please also excuse the writing. <u>This letter is just for you personally</u>. * I tried to write something in the way of an "appraisal", etc. It just won't work. But I want you to know that I made an effort.

I guess I didn't know enough about LB's work. Never saw him rehearse.[6] Never heard his compositions except West Side and a Serenade or something. Very nice, some of it. I never saw him conduct except on TV, (I loved that very early series "for young people".)

We met quite often and I felt great sympathy for him. He was always very kind. Maybe the great thing about him was his kindness. . . . (Kindness must have been very strong in him to survive that temperament every day!!)
—Thank you and kind best regards,
Yours Sincerely
Carlos Kleiber

* please note + respect. <u>Don't</u>, please, quote me! I never give opinions of any kind, specially about musicians.

This time I wasted no time and wrote back on the third of September. He was laying down the rules by trusting me with his home address. In time I would learn that he lived in one of the wealthiest towns in all Germany, about twelve kilometers southwest of München and very near the Grünwald Forest. His town had a population of almost ten thousand. Near his home at 1-A Aurikelstrasse could be found such musically inclined avenues as the Lohengrin-, Parzival-, Niebelungen-, and Joseph-Keilberth-strassen. His home was accessed directly by Kaiser-Ludwig-Strasse, named for the great patron of Wagner. What a neighborhood.

Hereafter I told very few people about these ongoing letters and swore all of them to silence.

In my reply I described the last time I had seen Bernstein. It was with the Vienna Philharmonic and Christa Ludwig in a concert of Sibelius 5 and Bernstein's own *Jeremiah Symphony*. "He led the Sibelius from memory and Jeremiah from score, an odd contrast," I told him, and then I talked about the nature of super-success and how it had damaged Bernstein. Had he been made "a cartoon of himself? hostage to his own success? The world knows him made meteor by ambition and genius; that night, something much gentler and more meditative was released. I only knew 'Jeremiah' from recordings, and hadn't seen more in it than inspired bombast (I'm sorry if that sounds snooty). But for one night, with that orchestra and that voice, it became a work of parable and prayer. At the end the crowd paid a very great compliment: it did not applaud for some long time."

I ended by thanking him for his address. He must have replied the day he got mine. This time, his was typed.

12 Sept 91
Dear Dr. Barber!
Thanks for great letter.
　　Yes indeed, I would like to have a copy of whatever comes of all this.
　　Glad you appreciated the kindness-angle. Just yesterday a TV manager and regisseur told me how he had to inform Lenny that he was forced by circumstances to stand in for Lenny's favourite for the job.
　　"I hope you don't mind" he said to Lenny.
　　Lenny, annoyed "I have no choice".
　　There was a delay of the beginning of the session. Lenny was writing a letter and would "just be a minute". It turned out to be a note to this man saying "Good luck! I love you! Lenny." (Please don't use this, though, OK?)
With best wishes,
yours sincerely,
Carlos Kleiber

Weirdly, Carlos was almost the only conductor to reply to my letters about the Bernstein book. Others may have been a good deal busier than he was or committed to similar memorials being led by others. However it happened, the so-called recluse replied and almost no one else did. It soon became clear that my Bernstein book was going nowhere.

I wrote on 30 September to thank Kleiber for his answer. "It said something definitive about his quickness to judge, to regret, to reconcile." For the first time I told him about a film I had acquired—Bernstein preparing *West Side Story*—and asked if he wanted a copy. It prefigured the central system of many years' correspondence. More or less by accident I hit on the way I would "study" with him. I ended mine with a joke about saxophones and lawn mowers. He answered with a short note two weeks later, in hand on a card.

Oct. 15, '91
Dear Mr Barber!
Thanks for yours of Oct. 1! I saw that rehearsal of W. S. Story here on TV and took it on tape; so, thank you, I won't need another copy. If ever I did need any TV

cassettes, it wouldn't matter what format, 'cause I can boastfully declare I possess a Japanese machine that converts simply everything automatically into something else and vice versa; and then some. (Just in case.)

Wishing you all the very best,
Your grateful
Carlos Kleiber

Once again the holiday season came up. I was committed to conducting concerts, visiting family, and traveling with friends. I didn't reply until 18 February 1992. I told him about research work I was doing on the Russian musician Alexander Siloti and about a new course I was teaching on "The Great Conductors" at Stanford, and I ended with, "As ever, I would be grateful for your help, and could offer in turn a large bag of cookies and a few tasteful Dan Quayle jokes." [7]

I managed to lose Carlos's reply. I recall that it was brief, declared no interest in my Siloti doings, advised that there was no film of Erich Kleiber, and expressed happiness with my Quayle joke. The next letter went out for his sixty-second birthday, on 3 July. I read somewhere that he had canceled a performance due to illness and wished him well. I also sent him the birthday present of a new book about Bernstein, just published by somebody else.

I told him about films I was collecting of Furtwängler and others for my Stanford class. I asked if he would like to see any of them. I had just shown them film of his own Concertgebouw concert, and the students were knocked out by it. Once again he seems to have replied the same day it arrived. Kleiber's letter was typed, with a handwritten PS crawling around the right side of it.

8 July '92
Dear Maestro Barber,
Thank you for your kind letter with its birthday wishes and all the exciting info re- old videos of the great dinosaurs. That you liked Beethoven 7 makes me happy!

Thanks also for the lovely Bernstein-book and the trouble you took to mail it. VERY cheering and revitalizing, indeed. I have a question about that Concertgebouw Beethoven 7: if it was a rehearsal and not the performance, would you let me know? because if that is the case, I'd like to have a word with my company 'cause they know I don't relish having my inept rehoissals in circulation and I didn't know they were being taped.

You are a <u>very</u> busy man, I know. But if you ever have time, here goes with some "wishes" which of course you can ignore.

I would love all the Furtwaengler bits and pieces. I have seen (on TV) a little of "Till", mercifully sans ballet, though. His beat (what a word!) always seemed to me to be extremely clear there and when I saw him conduct in Buenos Aires. Are you in cahoots with the Japanese or something? Otherwise I can't imagine where you got all the rest of your stuff. A friend in Paris, you say. Boy! If he is not Japanese, I might eat my hat, a Bavarian model and tough to chew.

Blech, Klemperer, Knappertsbusch, Mengelberg (unless it's just Oberon Ouv. which I have already) Mitropoulos, Nikisch (unless it's the 5 Beethoven without any sound), Talich, von Schillings, Schuricht and "others" (!?) would interest me no end. I can play any VHS video-tapes of any known type on my miracle-machine unless it goes bust.

Remember, it's your fault for mentioning these wonderful things! Richard Strauss would be great but you don't mention him. All I ever saw of RS was a tiny bit of Rosenkavalier and I thought he had the most beautiful "three" I ever did see.[8] It would be interesting to see how Mitropoulos managed to have different sections of the orchestra playing different tempi at the same time and making it sound together and just right.

I'm tickled to death to hear that your class liked the Beethoven 7 with Concertgebouw. At the time, I felt very frustrated because they were so stolid and uninterested and because my hair was flying every which way (I had forgotten the hairspray, the most important thing for a conductor right after knowing how to tie your own bow-tie, having shirts the right size and wearing braces that don't shrink when they get humid) and the clarinet was taking deep breaths where I told him not to, etc. But who cares, eh?

Did you ever see the tape of Danny Kaye with the NY Philharmonic? I believe that some of the conducting that evening belongs to the best I know.

Well, I'm digressing and getting garrulous (Garrulous Kleiber) so I'll stop now, thanking you again for cheering me up so much!

With best wishes,

your

Carlos Kleiber

PS: About 7 Beethoven, the trio of the scherzo. Later I decided it SHOULD be about 84 per beat and that LvB's idea (I think) was for it to be funny and not . . . well, just not the way we do it. If it has religious connotations, maybe they are of the sort that would belong in Don Quixote? Just an idea to explain the MM.[9]

[In hand around the margins:] *The eggheads feel sure his metronome was bust when it was too fast. Too slow was never a problem for any of them.*

Over the next decade I mailed Carlos videotapes of conductors in rehearsal, concert, and conversation. These were edited from a collection I was assembling for private study, for my classes in the history and aesthetics of conducting, and for what became the collection Conductors on Film held in the Archive of Recorded Sound at Stanford. At this writing, our collection has more than three hundred conductors from 1897 to the present, seen in more than twenty-five hundred hours of film and videotape.

I answered his two weeks later, and reassured him that the Concertgebouw material was not, in fact, a rehearsal. I would learn how important were these matters to him. For the first time I asked for his advice about a problem in an opera I was rehearsing. "How do you deal with sopranos who can't control vibrato? Lovely woman, weird wobbling. She sounds like a Theremin."[10]

I also told Kleiber about a Furtwängler conference I was to address in October and about the problem endemic to old film of old conductors— synchronicity. Sound and picture often failed to correspond. Bowings were wrong, fingerings were impossible, and the beat patterns ran against the meter. This was by way of apologizing for the technical quality of some of the antique stuff on the videos I was now sending him. In my letter I included all the Furtwängler I had yet located.[11]

Carlos's reply was typed, included numerous handwritten corrections, over-writes, underlines, and even more postscripts running up and down the margins. Many of his letters looked like that.

29 VII '92
Dear Maestro Barber,
What to do about a wobbling soprano? Well, Lao Tse would act one way and Toscanini another way. In the long (sometimes too long) run, I reckon Lao Tse wins hands down.[12]

About Danny Kaye's video with the NY Phil. I taped the show when it ran here on TV years ago. If you want it, I'll send it. I didn't do a very good job, tho, taping it. And it is in the local system, not your kind of VHS-system. It is on sale in the US (I saw it in a shop under the MET) your system, in presumably better quality, too. But if you want mine, say the word.[13]

Why are the historic tapes 99% of the time non-synch? My son works part time and freelance for a TV company here (UNITEL) on the classical stuff. He is very knowledgeable re-technical things like cutting and dubbing or whatever. Pity he isn't here right now. He explained to me and I'll try to pass on the little I understood of what he said.

It appears that the people who did the transferring from the old films to video-tape should be boiled in oil after extended exquisite torture and then drawn and quartered. (See also Osmin's suggestions in "Entfueh-rung")[14] What they should have done and didn't do was to use the same apparatuses with which the filming was done in those days, or rather, the equivalent projectors they had then. If they couldn't dig anything like that up, they should have built some exactly like the old ones. Those (old) machines had less pictures per second and our machines run the films "too fast" (I hope I'm not muddling things).

To save time and bother, the bastards doing the transfer let the film run any which way and then some untalented person attempted to synchronize the sound to it, posthumously, so to speak. This gives you Furty conducting AFTER the orchestra, when, in fact, what he did (a grand old Boche tradition which avoids tailgating and bent bumpers) was conduct AHEAD of them.

In the WF videos you have the orchestra, at best, coming in on the beat. Admittedly, this is something some conductors insist on. * But it was not Furty's cup of tea. Incidentally, even the interview with that concertmaster was not synch.

But, what the hell, I THANK YOU AND A MILLION TIMES AND FROM THE BOTTOM OF MY HEART FOR THAT WF TAPE!! You don't know what emotion and excitement it gave me! Please keep up the good work. And send me a bill for expenses, please!

The Furtwaengler widow is a dear and sweet lady. So is Klemperer's daughter. But (between you and me and the gatepost) they do what they believe the Master would have done, namely: not give a damn what happens to the orchestral parts. Or scores. They say, or think: "Furty and Otto are dead and all that paper is lying around. In their (Klemp and Furt's) present state, surely they wouldn't worry (they don't worry!) about what becomes of it. So we girls won't, either!"

"Now and then," say widows and orphans of the Great, "we'll make some nerd of a simpatico musician happy with part of a material or a marked score." That's about it. Chè miseria! The only consolation is this: you can have all the parts, all the bowings, all the markings and still make an Unfurtwänglerish or Unklempererian mess of it, conducting-wise. Make your OWN damn mess, is what they are telling you. Maybe there's something to that.

Hey, this has turned into a silly, rambling letter and I apologize. What I really wanted to say was Wow! Just look and listen to THAT! (WF!) Thanks again and again!

With best wishes and regards,

yours sincerely,

Carlos Kleiber

* a big mistake in my view. Though there are some exceptions where it's ok. But very few. Especially in opera. (You don't want the soprano's bumpers dented, now do you? So don't tailgate. Like the fellow said.)

A word about Lao Tse, he of the many spellings. It is clear that Carlos was deeply familiar with his work. One time only did we discuss in person his verses. My own ignorance paralyzed that conversion. My friend and colleague Will Lacey reminds me of other lines that may have had idealizing influence on Carlos. From Verse 22, in the translation by Stephen Mitchell, clues about Carlos's views of mastery.

> The Master, by residing in the Tao,
> sets an example for all beings.

Because he doesn't display himself,
people can see his light.
Because he has nothing to prove,
people can trust his words.
Because he doesn't know who he is,
people recognize themselves in him.
Because he has no goal in mind,
everything he does succeeds.

And from Verse 38,

The Master does nothing,
yet he leaves nothing undone.[15]

I answered Carlos's letter on 12 September. His enthusiasm for these old films fired mine, and I began trawling archives, libraries, and private collections around the world. The Internet was just opening up and proving a powerful resource. For an upcoming concert I asked him about the highly specialized (and largely European) practice of conducting "ahead of the beat," and for his instruction in that weird art. His how-to reply changed my understanding of the technique.

I sent over Tape No. 2, film just acquired of Blech, Borchardt, Busch, some "new" Furtwängler, Knappertsbusch, von Schillings, and Bruno Walter. This was an encyclopedia of conducting technique, and I asked him to tell me what he saw. In this letter I initiated the practice of sending along a separate sheet with information about timings, content, and provenance for each of these films. I also began to number them.

Provoked by his comments about breathing, I ran off and read Chang Tzu,[16] and told him about finding this: "The breaths of the Perfect Man come from his heels, while men generally breathe from their throats." I meant it as a bit of a joke, but also as evidence that I would respond like any student might to readings and references.

19 sept 92

Hi there, maestro!

Mille grazie for the tape with all the old guys on it. And for your wonderful letter.

I have a Zhuang-zi or Chuang-tzu in Italian, Adelphi Edizioni, a cura di Liou Kia-haway which is absolutely marvellous and my greatest joy. Then also a complete edition, 1968 Columbia University Press, in an (english) translation by some <u>*horrible*</u> *guy named Burton Watson, addicted to idiotic, mock-erudite footnotes, the victim of an emetic style, in short, uno stronzo. (Stronzo is a word <u>I</u> translated from english into italian 'cause it sounds better that way)[17]*

Chuang, spell it whichever way, is really the greatest of them all. I have little scraps of paper with sayings of his stuck to the walls of my garret with scotch tape. One of my favourites is "chi rispetta la sua vita non deve danneggiare il suo corpo per conservare i mezzi con cui lo mantiene."[18] And also "E deploevole che tutti considerino le proprie capacité come un tesoro."[19]

I was familiar with the quote you flung at your soprano, but it isn't on my wall since I felt that an effort to breathe through my heels was incompatible with smoking cigarettes. By now, you will have "opened" with Miss Wobbly and I am sure it went well.

You misunderstood me, incidentally. The idea was not "to conduct ahead of the audible pulse" as you put it; but rather to have the band play <u>behind</u> the <u>visible</u> beat, the one which the singer would be expected to think he/she was following. No matter: no one ever looks anyhow. It is only a polite gesture they make when they gaze at you now and then. Even then it can be very unsettling. Don't ask for it.

Your tape. Bless you for sending me these exciting and often pleasurably irritating items. The Fidelio-bit couldn't be Furty. He would never give so many superfluous cues to the singers. Must be Boehm.

*Schillings * looks like some degenerate bon vivant out of an Erich von Stroheim film. William Tell isn't his cup of tea, and he ruins it and murders the flautist, all the while maintaining a poker faced bleary-eyed pose of hypnotic trance. What struck me throughout (Blech, Busch, Kna and, even, Bruno, most of the time) was the amount of bar-beating done. Like they hadn't rehearsed or were afraid that, if they left one out, it wouldn't be played at all. Furty is quite another matter. <u>He</u> could <u>truthfully</u> sing "I got rhythm" if he cared to. Blech with Meistersinger Ouverture is maybe the worst offender, a real hectic tempo-bender.*

Yes, Danny Kaye was a genuine fish in the waters of conducting. We've talked about that, haven't we? Nowadays I recommend only Boulez and (this only works when the orchestra can take over genially) Sándor Végh. Those are the ones to look at if you get a chance. <u>Sound</u> good, too! (Fringe benefit?)

Watching your tape and the faces and gestures of the audience and musicians, an uncanny feeling overwhelmed me at the thought they were all now dead as doornails. It would take Proust to put it in words, but you'll understand.

I tremble in joyful anticipation of what your next VHS will bring. And am ashamed that I have nothing to offer in exchange. But the moment I do, you'll get it.

All the very best,
your grateful old
Carlos Kleiber

* His wife was a famous, big, horse-faced soprano, Barbara Kemp, with a devastating temperament and an irrepressible sex-drive. A legendary punchbag she was, and Max was proud of the fact! Does this explain the bleary eyes?

More film material continued to arrive at my end. As soon as I had an hour or two ready, I mailed it over, along with my learned commentary. On 6 October I told him about film of Ansermet, Blech, Fricsay, Keilberth, Klemperer, Knappertsbusch, and Mengelberg acquired and shipped, and about two films of the remarkable Václav Talich.[20] I also described a rehearsal I had just attended of Boulez preparing his *Répons*, and how fascinated I was by his "awesome articulateness," his spell "worthy of a Merlin," and more clichés of that character. I thanked Kleiber for his advice about Miss Wobbly and his jokes about von Schillings.

I told him that I had been asked to do my first *Fledermaus* and hinted that I might come to him for advice. Finally, I asked him to recommend reading sources for the "conducting ahead" practice I wanted to try out, and I joined his feelings about musicians now passed on. "It is an honor to be able to share this spelunking with you." His reply was in hand, over two long pages, with four measures of music written out at the bottom of it, and more text running up the sides and margins—obiter dicta.

19 X '92
Dear Maestro!
*Just back, jet lagged, from Japan. Found your marvellous (thanks!!) TAPE. Klemperer in IXth absolutely great (interpretation a matter of taste, but THE GRAND MANNER! WOW!!) ***
Take care approaching "The Bat". Listen to Clemens Krauss and fix your orch. material + or - by what you hear there. Take out a lot of the "fortes" and reduce them to "pianos". Don't do the ballet which is in the score. Never beat the "3" in a Waltz. Rosalinde's Csárdás is difficult 'till you know it well. Krauss is great there. Take it seriously, it's a HOMESICK piece, the Csárdás. Hey, look at me, giving advice to a Maestro! What nerve!
*About the "after the beat playing", I know of no literature. It's a subject indelicate and universally avoided. ** Maybe you do it anyway and don't know it. That's best. The thing is to keep the boys in the band listening to each other and to the singers.*
However good your reflexes are, theirs are better. You can sense the places where it's WISE to let them take charge. They have to know you want them to, though! Aw, shut up Carlos!
All the best and keep me wrapped in great old tapes, God bless you!
Your grateful old grey
Carlos Kleiber
* In the IInd Movement, bar 44 etc, he's fixed something extra in the horns (III + IV). Sounds great; but I can't find it in the score. He plays [musical notation appears here] *or maybe it is done the trumpets "A"? I don't think so.*
** Maybe because it makes 50% of the rehearsals unnecessary?

I wrote back a few weeks later, and told him about the recent Stanford Symphony tour of Japan. I had made an orchestral arrangement of the song "Akatombo," and we presented it as a surprise encore after our performance of Beethoven 9 in Kyoto. The response was very touching: stoic, silent Japanese tears across the whole audience.

More tape of Abendroth, Kempe, Knappertsbusch, Konwitschny, Krips, Kubelik, von Matačić, Nikisch, Strauss, Stravinsky, and Walter was sent winging over to Grünwald. I also bragged about all the work I had done to locate a 16-mm film of Mitropoulos in rehearsal, and made jokes about a Richard Strauss look-alike "in the Krips re-make of The Maltese Falcon." (It was a very dark version of Krips performing Schubert 8 with the Vienna Philharmonic, "Samuel Spade, concertmaster." The film was quite odd and full of noirish images of statues.) The Strauss was from 10 June 1949, leading a dress rehearsal of *Rosenkavalier*, and very moving. It was the last known film of Strauss, who died at eighty-five three months later.

I also told him about a 1913 film of the great Artur Nikisch conducting the Berlin Philharmonic. Even though it was silent, and "maddeningly ill-matched to the score he was supposedly conducting," it was still a wonder. "It is as heart-stopping as if there suddenly appeared a newsreel of Lincoln giving the Gettysburg Address—even though the sound track is Mao Tse-Tung." I also thanked him again for his conducting advice. He replied ten days later, once more in hand on Euro-long paper.

17 XI 92

Dear Maestro!

Bless you for letter and tape! Loved the touching story about the Japanese encore!

   Stravinsky + Mitropoulos VERY interesting and exciting!!

   Abendroth, Kempe, Knappertsbusch, Konwitschny, Krips, Kubelik and Matačić are at double speed on my tape (were you breathing down the engineer's neck?), but, mercifully intelligibility (the correct speed) returned with Nikisch to last "al fine". (Never mind about A, the 5 Ks and Matačić, OK? They're not my special cup of tea, anyhow.)

   !!THANK YOU!! for the (very important) rest of the tape which made me extremely happy and still does and always will.

   I loved Fricsay leading Strauss to the podium amidst the joyous clamor.[21] And that unfathomably canny look on RS' mongolian features. And the left hand on thigh, thumb on outside, left. And the glance the players got (remember "Back to Methuselah" where the youngsters (and "teen" aged centenarians) have to avoid meeting the eyes of the 300, 500 etc year-olds 'cause such a look would kill them instantly?)[22]

   Well that look Strauss gave the band when they played the "a tempo" (after Ochs finishes) without following his beat, that look gave me an idea of what GBS had in mind, nicht wahr?!

Yours letters, in fact <u>everything</u> Barberian, are/is full of humour, order, know-
ledgeability and kindness. Great! Thanks!
    Shamelessly looking forward to more, in gratitude and friendship.
Yours truly,
the ancient
Carlos Kleiber

I replied on 2 December, with apologies and analogies. "The engineer on the last tape was your brain-stem-only correspondent." I described the new film enclosed as being rather bizarre: Albert Coates with Gracie Allen on the piano (yes, *that* Gracie Allen), followed by Stokowski, Reiner with Heifetz in the Tchaikovsky violin concerto, and Charles Munch leading the Boston Symphony in the Franck D-Minor Symphony. I asked Carlos how he read Stokowski, in rehearsal, at age eighty-eight.

I also asked him to recommend a performing edition of *Die Fledermaus*, as I had finally signed a contract to do it next season. My letter was signed with an illiterate's X, and underneath in type "Ten Thumbs." His reply was typed, with more hand-written emendations running in the margins and through the last two paragraphs.

8 XII '92
Dear Santa!
    Guess this will have to be gushy and disorganized and full of typing mishaps. Don't have time to write a decent, short letter, like the fella said.
    But I must catch the impulse while it's rampant. Being one of gratitude immense, it might not last long. Or do you believe that a drug addict will be grateful for a shot eternally? But the comparison limps, as the Germans say, and you just can't imagine the joy you have given me with Tape #5, so I won't even try to tell you.
    Here, however, go some comments.
    Skipping Coates, Le Beau Charles is next. Now, the trouble is, This Franck piece is <u>the</u> one piece in the <u>world</u> I thoroughly hate from beginning to end, the themes, the developments, the flat(ulent) Tuba, the composer's every intention, in short, the whole bloody piece. But one can learn a lot from Münch.
    He is not fishing in troubled waters and his stick means what it says. Even in the bits where he gets flamboyant for his fans, the gesturing is still professional and committed to the players, though it may look (then) free. What helps, too, is that he obviously likes the piece, a confession of execrable taste (to my mind) but . . . a help. The ensemble playing is perfect. The stick is surgically precise. The face is fine, showing no emotion to speak of or get disgusted with. <u>More</u> Munch (+ a <u>decent</u> composition) is very <u>welcome</u>, yes!

Next, Reiner with the ineffable, the super, the one and only, the over-whelming, the divine Heifetz. Oh, HEIFETZ! Can one talk about him at all? So let's not.

Reiner disgusts me on this tape and I'm glad Heifetz almost never gives him a look. Or gives ANYTHING a look, for that matter. The ensemble is so-so, considering the rather broad look-no-hands, look-no-feeling Reiner suggests. But he <u>does</u> "move". You're right. There goes the famous anec-dote, eh?

Then comes Rodzinski, entirely wooden and pathetic and, yes, unmusi-cal. Wie der kleine Moritz sich einen Dirigenten vorstellt, kinda.[23]

Then, Ah! THEN comes (MERRY XMAS, Carlos Kleiber) Stokey, the GE-NIUS! Isn't that SOMETHING? The rehearsing is fabulous, he isn't present with aches and pains and hopes of a little "Atempause"[24] like us mortals. No, he's there and nowhere else, but he disappears by being there so completely.

He wants to hear what he wants to hear and he doesn't care how they do it. His beat is having a revival with Boulez, I feel. Anyhow, it is a great, great experience. And that juggernaught unremittingness is overwhelming. And there's passion in there, too. (His Tchaikovsky 5 is a letdown after that, a lot of posing, cold, mystery-lighting, tricks with the hair, the works. Ugh!)

No, I haven't different speeds on my machine. No Matter, though, I don't think I missed anything I would have <u>liked</u>, by your hitting EP. Maybe just in time, as a matter of fact.

No, thanks, no Bernstein required right now.

If you are going to read Methuselah, I hope that my memory of the play didn't deceive me and that what I <u>said</u> was in there, <u>IS</u> in there, o my God!

FLEDERMAUS

Score: Johann Strauss (Sohn) Gesamtausgabe

Herausgegeben von der Joe Strousses (sorry) Gesellschaft, Wien

Serie 2: Buehnen- und Vokalwerke. Band 3: Die Fledermaus.

Wien, Im Gemeinschaftsverlag Doblinger/Universal Edition.

What I don't know is whether or not they have also printed orchestral Material and vocal scores. * I used the material by the [expletive] Kalmus, which I had already prepared with lots of Eintragungen (by me) before the above-mentioned score was on the market. The score (see above: score) is big, thick, heavy, well-printed, etc, but uninspiring in lay-out, somehow. However, I believe it is the only full-score extant. Look carefully at the Kalmus <u>parts</u>. They are seething with mistakes.

I had my own private parts (OK, OK) fotocopied once and they are lying around somewhere, weighing a ton or more, dusty and completely loose (unbound, I mean).

Now listen. If you are a real artist (whatever THAT is) then 1/2 the fun will be marking the parts (bowings, dynamics, etc) yourself according to what you think you want to hear. Saves a lot of rehearsal time, if you don't happen to be a Stokey or a Karajan.

If you take someone else's material, the flight of your genius will be hampered. You will be confessing to laziness disguised as willingness to learn. Furthermore, you will have to look at the orch. parts ANYHOW, if only to figure out what the guy who arranged them wanted. Then you will have to "want" it too or rehearse like wild to get all the work the other guy did OUT.

BUT, BUT, BUT!

IF you want two tons of flying leaves containing Fledermaus, arranged to death, here's what, out of extatic gratitude, I might just offer. If you send someone over to Aurikelstrasse 1a, W-8022 Gruenwald (outskirts of Munich) who will collect the unwieldy carton with his grubby little paws and get it over to you, somehow, undamaged (if possible) and then (you) take over my markings (I won't tell) or those of them you think are any good, that's OK.

But my gratitude (unending gratitude) is not such that I can go to the post-office lugging this stuff after packaging it properly (a thing I just can't do, even to save my life), doing the Customs-ritual, etc.

Do you understand what I mean? Whatever you decide, be aware of the fact that I have never made an indecent proposition of this kind to anyone in my life before. So I want you to make a big show of being very moved, OK? Let's see some abject gratitude. (Just kidding)

I COULD send you my score (very heavy, as I mentioned above) but there is almost nothing in it except what Joe S. composed (or what has been relayed to us as such). You will want to mark your own score according to your intentions (like the young girl's father said to the boy who was courting her "what are your intentions?" The boy: "do you mean I have a choice?") <u>if</u> you are able to focus on any intentions you will later be capable of remembering, which is <u>the</u> great difficulty in this business, I feel.

But I am wandering again; Alzheimer (how merciful it is that, having it, one forgets it) is looming in my Smith-Corona "Silent". (I bought it at Wanamakers, NY, in 1947 and it's loud as hell)

Finally, let me repeat how grateful I am for the exciting things you send. Picture me as doing the kind of dance a dog will do when you come home or get ready for a walk with him. Got it?

All the very best from an old, retired stick-waver,

Merry Xmas!! Carlos Kleiber

PS: First time I did "The Bat" was in Geneva and in French. ("La Chauvre-Souris") Of course you know that the original <u>play</u> was a French one, "Le Reveillon". That's not important to know, however.

Second (and last) time I did it was in Munich.

* I used a vocal score (that is, the singers + repetitors did) which I vaguely remember being by one Anton Paulik and containing a gruesome English translation of the text, beside the original German text.

Astounded by Carlos's offer, I replied on 17 December. "When I came down from the ceiling Hilde asked me if I had been snorting helium again." I went on to acknowledge how rare a gift he was making. Then, "I must, with respect and affection, decline your fabulous and wonderful and stunning offer." I babbled on and asked if—after I had learned the score independently—I might get back to him with interpretive and technical questions and hinted that I might ask to look at his full score.[25]

I was quite shocked by this sudden turn. It had never occurred to me that he would propose such a thing. I told him about new Munch I had been able to find (now with Beethoven, Brahms, Mendelssohn, Ravel, Schumann, and Wagner). I also thanked him for his comments about publishers: "I don't know if you've ever been to that house in Florida, but I think every employee has a parrot on his shoulder." I ended by saying that his offer made me feel "like the most flattered guy on the planet." Letters crossed in the mail. The day after I sent my reply, a postcard arrived.

9 XII 92
Dear Maestro:
I forgot to mention in yesterday's letter: "My" parts (the kind "ready to play from") of Fledermaus don't belong to me, but to the Bavarian Opera, where they continue performing from them, sans me. What I do have is/are the Photocopies (flying and disorganized) I mentioned in my letter.
All the best
Carlos

I went out of town with Jason on a ski trip, and when I got back another letter was waiting.

20 December '92
Hi there, Maestro!
By the time you get this, it won't be the Year that Was anymore. But: HAPPY NEW YEAR, anyway!

Thanks for your kind letter and the Muench tape. I'll resist the temptation to go into Muench at length. Suffice it to say that there is a great deal of orchestra-conditioning, hire-and-fire-power[26] and Crustymony Proseedcake (excuses to Pooh) involved,[27] else it wouldn't function so smoothly solely on the basis of the "beat".

About the Bat: you didn't get me about my score. There's nothing in my score, so no point in comparing. I have always, maybe mistakenly, had the notion that, since the PARTS are what the players play from, the parts have to be perfectly in order.[28]

Scores, I believe, are irrelevant. UNLESS you mark the score and give it to a copyist with instructions to transfer the markings to the parts. This is not my method, though.[29]

With "bat", if the players are Viennese it's less important to mark and/or bow everything. But with a Senegalese orchestra it might be a good idea. (No offence meant!)

Where the REAL difficulty arises is when the dear, talented conductor, armed with his precious, marked score hasn't grasped the style. If he has, OK, It takes a few seconds to mark a cresc. or a p or a gliss or a spicc. in a part; but it takes minutes to ask for such things in rehearsal. The conductor has to talk and (at least hereabouts) every word is a nail in his coffin.

Regarding ORIGINALITY: the warm glow one gets from growing things from scratch on one's own dungheap IS gratifying, though I'd hate to have to re-invent the telephone, for instance. Remembering that the BAT is a supremely persnickety piece, I'd therefore suggest that the best bet would be to listen to Krauss (now on CD, even) and consider "marking" well-nigh accordingly.

I'd love to visit Kalmus and his pirates and parrots. Do you think Mr. Kalmus ever turns red when people get sour at him? No, I guess that's Litmus.

All the very best, and affectionate regards to your wife, hoping you have fun in Canada or wherever you are!

Your very grateful and amused old coot,
Carlos Kleiber

PS Be-Ware-offsky Swar-offsky! He may have been a good conducting teacher, but he is wrong on pretty near all counts on Joe Strauss. Keep off![30]

PPS Would you give me Mr. Kalmus' address + telephone Nr, please? I think (no joke) I need his pirates for another (non-Bat) project, honest. Thanks!

I replied to all this with a quick note on 6 January. I sent over the whole Kalmus catalogue and asked what "another project" might be. I signed off "Enchanté, Le Beaujolais Charles." He seemed to like the joke, as thereafter we made up various odd names for one another. His reply was very exciting. Here was the prospect, for the first time in years, of Carlos doing repertoire new to him. Evidently, he didn't want people in Europe to know about it.

(The following letter is reproduced in the photo section of this book.)

14 Jan 93
Dear Maestro,
You are incredibly prompt, generous, tidy, funny, exact and all the while as Kalmus can be. Just a short note to say thanks.

In a void,[31] *I'm working on "Ein Heldenleben" and was just wondering about orch. Material. If all gangs agley here,*[32] *I might try Edwin in Bocà Ràtón, and will maybe need your help with that, then. The trouble with using "pirate" material in Europe is: the thwarted local yokels who live off the fat of the print send their spies to concerts to check what's being played from. If they see Eggbert Litmus' stuff, they get lawyery.*

Do you have any MONTEUX? Quite a guy with a stick, eh? Good "Helden-leben".

All the best!

Charlemagne

I got around to his several on 15 January 1993. Mine was lengthy but tedious. I told Carlos I had read Shaw's *Methuselah*, and that he gotten the story right. I asked about the name's etymology and mentioned locating "man of the dart" or "man of Selah," but little else. I suspected that the genetics of a word would interest him too.

I went on to describe the Beecham and Jochum films in the tape for that week and Koussevitsky and Nikisch (complete) as well. There was a German film scholar who proved that Nikisch was actually conducting Tchaikovsky's Symphony No. 6 when Oskar Messter made the film in 1913. Its provenance was a very long story and included the U.S. Army of Occupation. The highlight of the latest video anthology was Strauss himself doing the whole of *Till Eulenspiegel*. It took me months to find but there it was—entire, with the Vienna Philharmonic, filmed in June 1944. A great discovery.

The letter brought him up to date on my own *Fledermaus* studies. I wanted to know what he meant by the "persnickety-ness" of the piece, and talked about the Clemens Krauss recording. I also told him Hilde was not my wife: "She's a PhD in chant and plays gamba. You'd like her. Smart and warm." I closed by telling him about my new job with a regional orchestra nearby. "Their resident conductor took off for a job in Memphis and left them stranded. Must have been a hell of a close relationship."

He replied sympathetically and was especially bowled over by the 1944 film of Strauss. His was in hand, on two very long pieces of paper. In one "side note" he first mentioned his antipathy to Abraham Lincoln. I think he buried it there to see if I would bite. Speaking of biting, he also mentioned for the first time his sardonic belief that he was the reincarnation of Emily Dickinson's pet dog.

20 Jan 93

Dear Maestro,

Wonderful, ./., ./., ./. Richard Strauss video!! Thanks a 10 (18)[33] for that "Till". That's the stuff! The orch. Must be the WPH[34] which was doing a lot of RS with RS for disc in '44.

Just imagine the scenario! The war had come hard to Vienna. Conditions were chaotic. Prof. Strasser who is now 91 or 92 (and chirpier than anyone around) tells about it. I think I recognize Strasser as leader of the 2nd Violins, which are, quite rightly, on the right where they belong, opposite the 1st Violins.

Methuselah? All I have is Webster's, like you do. But you must know some ineffable etymologist-egghead at your College for the real low down?

Beecham (I'm a great fan of his. Best "Carmen" and "magic Flute", etc.) is pretty damn muscular with Mozart in Montreal. But he seems to have a concept, no?

Yes, Jochum is a sweet one. As a person, he was very much a goody two shoes/ gloves. His DGG Bruckner discs (Berl. Phil) are great stuff. Later he did ditto with Dresden on EMI: not 1/8 as good as the DGG set. He had Jesus Christ's unlisted tel. number, they say, and called Our Lord constantly, even during recording sessions. (Jochum's)

I'm relieved that we've ended all BATinage and that you are, admirably, independence personified, ready to build the better mousetrap all by yourself. (Kalmus and Carlos: eat your hearts out!) Seriously: you have the right spirit, yeah!

Just what passages of "Pathètique" Nikisch was conducting I couldn't figure out. But the gestures were beautiful and relaxed.

The Meistersing-Prelude-project sounds exciting, though a little contrived, kind of cloning around, sort of. Incidentally, the best M-prelude known to man is (to my mind) R. Strauss' disc. I don't own it, though, just heard it on the wireless. (I love the word "wireless".)

Koussy (on the video) is "wie der Kleine Moritz sich einen Dirigenten vorstellt,"[35] all perse and poisonality, kinda.[36]

Ain't watched Igor S. yet 'cause Jochum is taking too long with his Bruckner celebration.

Yes, the Clemens Krauss Bat is the one you have. Re—style, I'm in the dark. But it seems that the devil is hidden in details and that which details demand insistency isn't ever clear. Krauss and his crew are by turns committed and distanced, never pasteurized or bent on proving anything.

It's dry like VERY fine French Champagne, which, as we know, doesn't "taste" as "good" as cheaper imitations. Maybe it's a dialect!? I, for one, can't bring it off; nor that style. But I'm "Japanese" and can do a pretty good . . . imitation? Maybe.

Yes, I got the Furt and Klemp documentaries and enjoyed them no end! If I didn't comment, I intended to do so before Alzheimer struck again. Merci, belatedly! All the very best from your grateful colleague, Carlo *

* Did I tell you I was E. Dickinson's dog * in a former life? Sure I did. How I adore(d) that lady!! Something good about America, unlike Mr. Lincoln! (Sorry!).

I got back to him on the 19th "with greetings from the 20th Century" and told him that the *Heldenleben* score and parts were also available from Luck's in

Detroit, and that both Kalmus and Luck had taken theirs from the first edition of F. E. C. Leuckhart in Leipzig. I declared that I'd be happy to get them in my own name, if that would help preserve the secret of his interest. "I'd be honored (knighted, practically) to help you obtain these materials, anytime. It's WONDERFUL that you might be doing Heldenleben. . . . Salut, Beaujolais."

29 January 1993

Dear Maestro,

Thanks for the lowdown on Heldenleben. I went to Leuckhart directly (they're here in Munich) armed with a bottle of Cognac and they put at my disposal a virgin rental material, complete. I now await a surge of energy. When and if it comes, I'll mess the parts up to my liking and use them, maybe, when the prospect of a performance crystallizes.

Hereabouts, it works thus: If the band I do the work with has its own (rental or acquired—one used to be able to buy it legally some 30–40 years back) material there is no $ due to the publisher as long as the performance is one the orchestra organizes. If there is some other person or group doing the organizing, they pay the cost of rental per performance.[37]

Thanks a lot for offering help and for sending the Apfelmus-Catalogue!

You say you don't breathe any air in LA. But "Mountain View" sure sounds very scenic and ozonic to me. It is a misnomer?

Dear Emily Dickinson's magical

"And the Mountain to the Evening

Fit his Countenance—

Indicating, by no Muscle—

The Experience—"

comes to mind with your home address. Also, funnily enough, Richard Strauss, while conducting Till Eulenspiegel! Did you register what he said to the applauding WPH? "Wir brauchen uns nicht zu bewundern: wir sind einander wert!"[38] *Lovely serenity, s'truth.*

Well, someday you must tell me about what exactly it is you do beside taking over concerts for conductors who suddenly flee when no man pursueth.[39] *And sending endlessly appreciated letters and videos to a crazy retired Kapellmeister, namely, your very*

Sincere and grateful

Carlos Kleiber

PS: This is impertinent, OK, But, anyway: love to Hilde with whom, I hope, you live in sin and happily, to boot. (The only way, really!)

I got caught up with Kleiber on 22 February, thanking him for his last two letters and for his description of wartime Vienna. I was surprised by how many people he knew from that era. He had asked for Monteux, and I began a search but so far had nothing for him. I did offer a zany story about Madame Monteux requiring bald men in the San Francisco Symphony to cover their shiny heads with wigs, so as not to cause glare in her eyes. (A true story, evidently.) And once again, I told him how important and welcome would be his *Heldenleben*.

I reassured him that I lived near Stanford, nowhere near LA, though I often worked down there: "Best of all, we're 45 minutes from the rolling Pacific and its glorious wild beaches. Next time you're in California I'll take you surfing. Don't worry about sharks. They don't eat conductors—professional courtesy."

I also alerted him to the recording project I had been researching and organizing, "American Classics," a new series for Naxos. I ended by telling him about my own interest in Dickinson and asked if he knew the poet Theodore Roethke and his "Meditation at Oyster River," a personal favorite. "Hilde loves your impertinence. So do I." His reply came in hand, decorated with three very American icons.

15 III 93

Caro Maestro:

Yes, I love Roethke. Especially "the pensive gnu, the staid aardvark . . ." a poem I once copied and sent to an American lady to whom it really applied, by God!

Your letter + the tape: Great Joy! I laughed at your expert delivery of the Zoot-shoot! Smirked at Mrs. Monteux's allergy to shiny pates.

Am so glad you wrote because I was afraid my Lincoln-remark had scared (shocked) you away. I realize I am alone in loathing that man, his kitschig oratory, his brutal pragmatism, etc. but I'll shut up about it. Shut up, Carlos, you inveterate seccessionist, you! Incidentally, I also loathe Gandhi . . . (here I go again!) Don't mention it, OK?

Talich is great, yes!! But I kinda freeze*, watching + listening. Guess I'm so crazy about Szell with those dances. (One of the best records I know of.)

Beecham is irresistible! (Peter Brook is irkingly interruptive, getting his 10 cts in while Sir T. has started talking. But at least he provoked that wonderful outburst about conductors!)

I get less + less addicted to Munch, tho'. A little Munch goes a long way, huh? Admired your reviewing work![40] Glad you breathe fresh air in M View. Am too old to surf, unfortunately.

I'm afraid I'm no good on SILOTI. If I weren't so apprehensive, I'd have to admit that either I never heard of him or Alzheimer's has erased him from my, well, brain! Hey! You conducted Grofé's Gr. Canyon, did ya? Toscanini loved that piece and there is an Arturo T. recording of it. It just goes to show, irregardless.

Am relieved that Hilde looked not askance on my impertinence, whew!
Well, I guess that does it for today.
THANK YOU ☺
THANK YOU ☺
THANK YOU ☺
Again!
We are very much in snow here, –10 degrees C (14 degrees F, I think that's it).
The sun is shining bright on my old Grünwaldy home.[41] *As Emily said "The Flake*
the Wind exasperate / More eloquently lie / Than if escorted to its Down / By Arm
of Chivalry." Woof! Woof!, Sez I.
Cari Saluti!
Carlos

PS. Met with Sándor Végh (my conducting-idol) unexpectedly in Salzburg. (His
daughter has an apartment in the same apt.-house I do, over there.) He is great,
wild, Asiatic. Over 80 and very bent. I didn't get a word in edgeways, thank God.

* There was that cartoon in the New Yorker, two cows and a farmer with a
milking-pail approaching them. One cow to the other "here comes old icy fingers".

I was coming to realize that our correspondence, ridiculous as this may
sound, meant something to him. Here was one of several occasions on which
he expressed concern that I might stop writing him (my own concern was
quite the reverse) and expressed gratitude that I hadn't.

In mine of 31 March 1993, I began, "Cher Maître. Appologissimo. Delay
had <u>nothing</u> to do with old Abe. . . ." and went on to say that I had been awaiting arrival from the Czech Republic of more film of Talich, and I made a joke
about "heat-sensitive cows." I argued with him about Lincoln. Unorthodox
political views don't spook me in the least, "especially when they come from
someone whose friendship I enjoy so much." I enclosed a recent essay by
Garry Wills on the genealogy of the Gettysburg Address, on the evolution
of Lincoln's thinking within, and on the brilliant sleight of hand whereby
Lincoln used the text of the Declaration of Independence to promulgate an
(ideal) reading of the Constitution that followed.

"Lincoln moved where he could, conceding inessentials, unyielding in
his single goal," I said. (Two months later Kleiber would quote Dickinson's immortal line, "A Bayonet's contrition / Is nothing to the Dead," and
thereby make the moral case against Lincoln—and all warriors—as well
as anyone ever has made it.) "If the North had failed, slavery would have
endured another 50 years. I think Lincoln is owed this much, regardless
of Original Intent. (Did Gorbachev really intend to dismantle the USSR?
Bayern go Bragh!)

"My own impractical heroes are people like Kropotkin and Bakhunin and Paul Goodman. . . . If sentimental fondness for 19th C Russians repels you, send me a postcard: 'Stop writing rubbish. Just send videos,' and I'll do it. But you'll miss my jokes." I rattled on about a 190-minute silent film I had sent him of conductors at the Hollywood Bowl from 1929 to 1936. I had done the digging at UCLA, and written their catalogue. They own a Treasure Island of buried rarities. The letter ended by asking about *Heldenleben* and volunteering the services of my orchestra in California, "but you wouldn't like the oboes. I'm afraid they sound like sheep. Sweet, paraplegic sheep. Baaa, Charles."

His reply was on one big typed page, pleasantly combative, with handwritten margin notes running up and down every side of it.

April 3, 1993
Dear Maestro Pipistrellatore,[42]
Million thanks for the silent tape with all those time-beaters on it. Unfortunately, couldn't identify any but the ones I knew and the ones that were mentioned in the titles. Particularly revolting is Rodzinsky whom I feel like shooting at.[43] Anyway, I had a lot of fun watching those guys waving.

I should have warned you that I am the proud owner of the whole, beautiful "Lincoln at Gettysburg" BOOK by mr. Wills. Thus I could have saved you the trouble of sending the Atlantic excerpts.

The book is, for me, a Marcus Antonius (Lincoln is an honorable man) which rests quite safe in the assumption that the Amurricans won't get the point. I'd kinda hoped Canadians might, tho'. But then again they speak such deplorable French, I shoulda known better. Just kidding.

I also have the whole Burns "The Civil War" on Video. There's plenty in there to turn your stomach, but my "favourite" bit is when Abe wants to see <u>Richmond</u> (!) (with his wife, who predictably went off her rocker) when the Union had finished devastating it. But let's keep off Abe: nothing in the world will ever convince me he wasn't a louse, sorry. (Slavery? <u>Ended</u>??? My foot! A ploy, sez I.)

I'm glad you're happy with the huge, unwieldy Fledermaus score. Be careful: there are mistakes in there galore. I love the censored couplet at bottom right of page 541 which has the Dame von Paris looking for a new Adolf to replace the one who got shot in the gizzard by the Marquis!

If the oboes sound like sheep, maybe they are realizing the erstwhile ideal of the Viennese Oboe, before Yamaha took over. Quién sabe.[44]
All the best!
Your grateful old,
Confederate
Carlos K.

PS I did manage to identify Toscanini (he's the one trying to push a poodle off the balcony ledge) and Einstein (looking very mischievous and chirpy) but they didn't conduct, unfortunately.[45]

PPS Maybe you should read the <u>whole</u> book by Mr. Wills, especially the fine print and Abe's unsent and sent letters. Like Ogden Nash's pigeons when moulting: they're pretty revolting. At least <u>MRS</u> Lincoln has my sympathy for doing the only sane thing the wife of such a louse could do: go nuts.

PPPS If it's any help, I'm inordinately fond of Lee. Though all that military mawkishness—going to one another's funerals, taking off one's hat and catching cold, etc—IS also tainted with the ubiquitous US-Kitsch. At least, as far as I know or remember, HE didn't go right smack off to slaughter the Indians when there wasn't enough fighting left to keep his adrenaline flowing.

Incidentally, the preoccupation with the cosmetic necessity of keeping one's endorphins up (use 'em or lose 'em is the motto) drives Murricans, young and old, to do their "thing" at any, preferably some one else's, expense.

[In hand around the margins:] They have exported this trait so successfully, it is no longer exclusively endemical by any means. But they are <u>better</u> at it than anyone else. (If one can be good at a trait; which, of course, one can't. Furthermore, dear Carlos Kleiber, you can't even export a trait. Oh god . . .

I waited two weeks and considered carefully how to reply. The Lincoln-thing could be a poison pill, or a test, or some sign of trust that I wouldn't be horrified and fly the Kleiber coop. I wrote back on 15 April.

"Cher ami du Robert E: <u>Damn</u>! I should have known you'd read the book. . . . I am open to irony (Marc Antony, Jonathan Swift, Mother Theresa) but I drew none of it from the Atlantic Monthly miniature," and I promised to read the whole book that weekend. I made jokes about the *joual* of Québec, and the English of Lawn Gyland. Defending Americans, I told him about the extraordinary warmth of folks Mark and I had met on our bicycle trip from Stanford to Los Angeles.

Then it was time for a 1966 film of George Szell and an observation about the "poodler." "You're right about the identity of the poodle-pusher, but could you identify the poodle?" My PS provided the answer: Shirley MacLaine. It was a joke about her own beliefs in reincarnation and Kleiber pretending to be "Carlo the Dickinson Dog." All very elaborate. The letter ended mockingly. "Hilde offers love and spring wishes to you and Mrs CK, and asks that I join her in these regards. Well, I do. So there. Yours, M. Chagrin."[46]

His next letter had no date, but was received in California on 19 April. Its box included a PAL VHS of his latest film, this with the Vienna Philharmonic.

On its plastic cover he had drawn graffiti on his own face. The letter ran two pages, in hand, separated by a musical instruction.

Dear Maestro!

This just came in today. In case you also want VHS's (our system, unfort.) of the 2 New Years concerts that I did once upon a time, just yell. In Mozart + Brahms, (between you and me) I kinda overdid the "look, no hands!" gag because a distinguished (shitty) colleague was in the box to my left and I wanted to show off, damn me!

But there are a few nice things in it 'cause the WPH, mercifully, didn't LOOK at me. You'll like (?) the chaotic bowing and the 2 Violins on the right. Where they belong! V.S.[47]

The other day someone called "Tennstedt" (?) was on TV with Brahms I.[48] I liked him, 'cause he looked helpless and unpretentious AND the orchestra (NDR)[49] played for their lives! Quite astounding!

A lot met the ear that didn't meet the eye. . . . And isn't that what it is all about? Quién sabe. My only quarrel with his performance was that he took the Protestant "Chorale" slow (everyone but Arturo T. does, nowadays) in the last movement. (For Calvinists and Puritans and their Hymns I unenthuse like for Abe and Mahatma. I think I may be mentally ill, though.)

Regardissimi, Your old and senile,

Carlos

Confident we were still friends, regardless of Lincoln, I replied on the 23rd. Letters once more crossed in the mail. Carlos had been deeply antagonized by events in Waco, Texas, where the FBI believed that its proper business was to murder children and set them on fire, though not necessarily in that order.

19–20 April, 1993 (Fed. Tanks storm the sect in Waco*)

Dear, great Past—and Futuremaster of word and stick!!

Yet ANOTHER TAPE!!! WOWEEE!

You are so generous, I have decided not to go into the 'Murrican Dream, no more, no more. PAX! Nevertheless, behold Waco!*

Szell: great and humble. Humble (humble) for the camera? Anyway, there's an awful lot to learn there. BASIC things which, paradoxically, beginners fear to touch on because the orchestra just won't take it from them. Stickwise, GS is molto stodgy; but it works, I guess.

My Gripe: the placement of the camera. One hardly sees the stick (particularly the all-important POINT of it) and arms. Just, mostly, glasses, sweat, nostrils, lips. The family's aversion to outing this reportage would be understandable for that sole reason. And also for the <u>*TERRIFYINGLY*</u> *uncharacteristic # patience GS shews with the orchestra. And with the young nerds "thirsting for knowledge" breathing down his neck.*

I'm glad you identified the reincarnatable poodle. I'm glad Hilde is glad I gotcha on Mr. Wills! Is she occasionally irked by your all-encompassing erudition and well-founded <u>*convictions*</u>*?*

Women! (<u>*How*</u> *I would like to imagine that Hilde, at least* <u>*Hilde*</u>*, might just possibly share my near-Krishnamurtian disgust for the kitschig Gettysburg hot air and for the brutality, the stubbornness it romanticizes!) (Stop right there, Carlos! Freeze!)*

After all, dear Maestro Charles, you have a great sense of humour and your velocipede-trip from SF to LA does warm my cynical old heart; the unadulterated outdoorsiness of it catches the CAMEL in me. . . .

As my adored Emily says: "If your soul seesaw—/ Lift the Flesh door—/ The Poltroon wants Oxygen—/ Nothing more—" (#292) (I had to look that up, though I know it by heart. My eye fell on #1227 and off I was to Gettysburg again. I told you I'm nuts. . . .)

I am thankful to the powers that be for your escaping unscathed (?) that horrific Baseball-bat-episode you mentioned. Not only for exclusively and tape-hungry reasons, no Sir!
Very gratefully and affectionately,
the old Carlos K.

PS: A ridiculous, apocryphal story of mine: The French take-charge-guys musta been a crumby, motley crew and, in Canada, the mess they spoke curdled into what it is today. Dégueulasse![50] *Whereas the Mayflower-gang exported "English as she was spoke" at the time. It was wonderful English. (And I like it, despite Abe's "artistic" efforts with it.)*

 # Alas, poor Szell! I knew him well. . . .

I got back to him on the 23rd, having watched his new video several times. On the third page of mine, I asked him a number of technical questions, gave him an A+, and signed it "Mohandas Beckmesser PhD." Tape No. 13 included Toscanini's edited version of Brahms's First Symphony. I wrote out the great chorale tune from the fourth movement and added the parody words "Hail to the Chief" to its nonexistent text. Page one thanked him for the new video and talked about the tradition of gearing down at the entrance of the chorale. I signed off "Salutissimi, Your Young and Prehensile Charles."

He sent another speedy rejoinder. It rambled in hand up and down the margins even more than usual. His spellings are deliberate. The envelope had two stamps bearing the likeness of Georg Christoph Lichtenberg, whose face looks remarkably like that of one of the Founding Fathers. On the back, Carlos wrote, "The guy on the stamp is <u>not</u> G. Washington."

3 May 93
Hail to Thee, prehensile Maestro,

I didden no about the chorale's relating to Dear Abey; [51] *but I always disliked it instinctively and will <u>not</u> <u>hear</u> (of it) from <u>now</u> on!*

Thanks for your comments on the VHS I sent. One hears the faggot and hoboe(e) in Mozart Trio 'cause we had just a <u>couple</u>* of fiddles and gamberoni scratching there. [52]

The long [CK draws a quarter-note here] *upbeat in Menuett (small menu?) is a steal from Bruno Walter.*

Always hated the "clean" image Arturo T. was labelled with. See, for instance, Coriolan Ouv. He (AT) was a distorter in monk's skin. But . . . I LIKE HIM. 'Cause he makes you feel: the <u>moment</u> is all-important, <u>every</u> moment. No matter if Katzenjammer sets in soon after: It <u>mostly</u> does, anyway. I <u>hate</u> Rodzinski! Do you mention him to get my goat? If the RS Rosenkav. Isn't synch and RS is invisible, just the music would do (on a Musicassette) if you find time. . . .

Confession: you are the <u>only</u> person that ever writes to me! I have successfully alienated (spelling?) all other would-be correspondents. If they are American, I do it with Abe. With other countries . . . well, I find a way!

My specialty (or, British, "speciality") is mocking serious young letter-writers à propos "MUSIC". They give up PDQ, pouting. "Theory" is what you don't understand and "Praxis" is what you can't explain, eh? (That's cute; but someone else said it, damn him.)

Listen to Don Quixote (RS) (with fabulous Mainardi!) [53] *by the composer. (1933, Staatskapelle Berlin). Try to follow with a score. . . .! Well? If you don't get lost twice a second, you're a better man than I am, Gungadin.** Sheer genius, music-making wise! A blow in the schnozzle of us poor stick acrobats from which I, for one, never recovered. Thank God, by 1944 RS was a <u>little</u> reduced. But not much.*

Let's all go to hell, shall we? Taking along lotsa colleagues and eminent shits. Like Injuns, the only good conductors are . . . yes. And even of those stiffs only 2 or 3 are good ones. Hey, did you know this disgusting "joke"?: "Who killed the most Indians"?

Answer is under this sticker. [sticker when lifted revealed "Union Carbide"]

Hey, don't you just <u>adore</u> Clinton's grin?

Love to Hilde!
All the best,
Your CK

(* An olde Furty tricke, also good—in places—for J.B. and <u>L.v.B.</u>!!)

** *Incidentally, from 1 before* [35] *to 2 before* [42] *(for me, the loveliest RS ever wrote. And that for the "insula Barataria!")*[54] *No earthburger ever, ever did (or will) get <u>near</u>, <u>anywhere</u> near, the way that orchestra was enchanted, hexed. (This sentence doesn't work, but you'll know what I mean. Compare, for instance with, say, G. Szell, etc)*

PS Trick in Brahms II: the <u>two</u> bars before A: do in <u>one 3/2 bar.</u> Then (+ or less) the [CK makes dotted half-note] *at A becomes what the last* [half-note] *of that 3/2 became. Or <u>something</u> like that. . . . Makes life easier, in a way. No?*

Next day he sent a two-page PS to his letter above. My replies were getting seriously out-of-synch.

4V 93
Dear Maestro:
A PS, (to yesterday's letter)
   An unarmed, unpremeditated word re—Tennst. With Mahler I. (Just watched it a min. ago)[55]
   I don't love Mahler, but this time I succumbed, thanks to Tenn. He is a most sympathetic conductor, never "clever" or perfunctory, never <u>self</u>-conscious, his love for the piece makes it irresistible (the piece), there are plenty daemonic ghosts around him (as were around Gus Mahler), nerve, lilt and grit, body language sans exhibition, it's all there, GENUINE, enough of it for other "eminences" to cut big pieces off without diminishing Tenn's funds.
   In short: at last someone to admire! The orch. (what this says about them!) appreciates and does wonders. It is love. I hope Tenn. Is OK healthwise? It seems that his sensitivity and openness makes him, physically, psychically, a victim of many influences which "our" (?) elephantine hide shields "us" from.*
   (Mahler created lots of jobs, though. Lincoln, vacancies and graves.) (and bullshit)
   I hate going overboard like this. I hope it won't last. Nothing fresh does. Fruit, Bread, Meat, epiphany, all that jazz. Long live those Chicago musicians!! Just look at their faces!! And, of course, listen to that . . . er . . . that whatever it is we wait for and, mostly, don't get. Don't tell anyone that I liked a conductor! (of Scheisse, Mann!)
The old C.K.

PPS. An idea for your class. Have them take a baton and a score of "Don Quixote" (RS) and play them RS' disc of the piece, asking them to beat time to it whilst following the score. Chè bel pasticcio! (May take them down a peg, eh?)

* *(I hear he is almost always ill?) But then, the eleph. Hide, though helpful living-wise, would not allow Tenn. To make music like that.*

On May 10 I finally replied to his of 19 and 20 April, in which he had talked about the well-planned tragedy at Waco. I told him I couldn't find the 1227 reference, and asked him to send over a copy. He had asked if Hilde ever tired of my so-called all-encompassing erudition. That was an easy one: "Thanks to Hilde, I learned to distinguish Josquin Desprez from his better-known cousin Jacqueline Du Pré."

I too found the federal government's reckless attack on Waco despicable. "100 TV cameras and no firetrucks . . . every time the feds raid a building, it burns down." I answered Carlos's question about my encounter with a drugged-out sociopath and his baseball bat, and thanked him for his concern. Then it was time to get serious. I reminded him of his "confession."

"I'm a bit disoriented by what you said about our letters. Corresponding with you is an incredible delight. You ALWAYS make the best challenge: to reconsider, to read, to trace, to come at something from an original vantage. Your jokes, your language, your upfrontness—I love it. I've always presumed that many others connect with you this way. If 'musicians' are so easily put-off, something is quite wrong, lacking boldness or wryness or whatever. Who can make strong music with a weak heart?"

I was beginning to learn about his rules, his trust, his exclusionary zones. I became convinced that others may have failed with Carlos because there was a want of humor, a poverty of sardonic distance in their dialogue. It would be easy to take offense at his wit. But it was unnecessary to do so. As I read and reread his letters, a pattern emerged. Greater vulnerability on his part was invariably prefaced by a test and a joke. If I failed the first, or failed to get—and trump—the second, it seems that I would soon be relegated. Our correspondence succeeded, in part, because he enjoyed friendly contest.

I asked again about the status of *Heldenleben* and offered a joke even more terrible than his last, "in gracious reply." I closed by telling him that Hilde and I had seen Bill Clinton at a rally during the summer. "The grin's for real. So's the intelligence of the man." I PS'd confirming the stories about Tennstedt's great talent and poor health.[56]

"I have other films of Tenn, if you'd like to see them. And Chicago does seem to adore him. Love, as you say. Your friend and admirer, C."

29 V 93

Dear amigo and collega,

Once again tapestried by you, I shall do my tape-dance this PM. Delightedly as always. It is AM right now and I'll attempt to "answer" your great letter, at least in part.

I was surprised some time ago to learn that Stan Laurel was the brains of the Laurel + Hardy team. That Hilde is the brains of the Hilde + Charles team gives me similar pause. Waddya know! I'll be more careful from now on, yessir.

There's a smallish pocket-book (faber + faber, London—Boston) edited by T. H. Johnson called: E. D. The Complete Poems. But I'll copy the second 1/2 of 1227 for you.

Here goes: "What is to be is best descried / When it has also <u>been</u>— / Could Prospect taste of Retrospect / The tyrannies of Men / Were <u>Tenderer—diviner</u> / <u>The Transitive toward.</u> / A Bayonet's contrition / Is nothing to the Dead."

But I'm not going to push ED on you no more. It is, I guess, a personal love-affair of my very own. (The underlining is mine) (Written c. 1872)

Yes, re—Waco, we got all the (<u>very</u>) low-down. Loved your description of the park in Napa. Love RLS.[57] Home is the sailor home from the sea + the hunter home from the hills is such <u>music</u>, one freezes; if* ["if" appears in a box, like a rehearsal letter] *one is a tuning-fork.*

Yes, Mr. Tennstedt will understandably tend to be perishable like fresh things do, always.

"Heldenleben" went OK with WPH in Vienna (15 + 16 May, Musikverein) and when and if there is a "live" CD of it (coupled with the Mozart Symph #33, B flat Major) you'll get it from me, OK? #

Incidentally, here's an address (don't say I gave it to you, just in case he's as fuddy-duddy as I am): <u>Sándor Végh</u>, TÖRRINGSTR. 11/A, A-5020 Salzburg, Österreich. (That man is pure music, <u>a monster</u>)

Am horrified at the outcome of the baseball-bat encounter, 80 stitches, etc. Don't want to think about it, golly! <u>Get</u> a Brinks truck, por favor!

How is "The Bat" going, huh? Do tell, sometime, please. (If ya wanna, that is)

Please take care, thanks, bless you, be happy, love to Stan[58] Hilde,
your old
CK

* Possibly, I'm misquoting. If so, excuse, please
 # "'Tis Glory's far sufficiency / That makes our trying poor." (#1229)

I saw my first performance of Richard Strauss's *Salome* on 4 June[59] and the next day sent Kleiber a note telling him about it. I had never studied Strauss in a comprehensive way, merely moving from an opera to a tone poem to a song, all at random. It was time to approach the music more rigorously.

On the 10th, I sent another note, having just received his of 29 May. I promised to reply at length, and soon, but meantime wanted his advice about three prospective posters for our upcoming performance of *Fledermaus.* I sent him color copies of each version. I also asked about the pizzicato ending in Beethoven 7, second movement, as I had a concert coming up in October. I ended by telling him how happy I was that *Heldenleben* actually happened.

(The following letter is reproduced in the photo section of this book.)

15 VI 93
Dear Batman!
Poster: No 1 is best, of course. *60

VII Beethoven: arco ["arco" appears in box, like reh nos] *was written in later but not in L v B's hand. Only Klemperer and Erich Kleiber do pizz.* ["pizz" appears in a circle] *(That is correct)*

NB: 1) do [musical notations appear here] *and not* [more notes] *(See (hear) B. Walter on that.)*

2) do as quick a Trio as you dare. (I regret not having done so on my disc). At least [dotted half-note] = *84*

That you were floored by Salome is a good sign! Bravo! Ain't it something!

• *don't put the info in the white space. Rather create a little space under the picture. Less is more. (#2 and #3 are no good)*
Molti saluti
Yours Carlos Kleiber

PS What possible mistakes or mutilations can there be in VII Beethoven? Other than the misplaced cresc [CK makes hairpins within brackets] *in 2 Mov. (it should go:* [more notations]*)*

NB: Beware this piece. B. Walter says: "never have I heard this rhythm correct: [see original for his printed rhythmic figures] *" (neither have I!)*

On 20 June, I tried to catch up to everything in his latest letters and to tell him about a recent adventure above Santa Cruz, a beach community in northern California.

"Dear Emily O'File: What a glorious Monday last week. A huge unseasonal windstorm rolled in, and I rolled over to the coast to watch it. Black rain squalls pounded on locomotive-sized waves, salt flew a thousand feet from the beach, lightning flashed over the sea, and wise birds sat it out on the cliffs. Wonders made visible. (Learnedly thinking of *phantastikos*, ahem.) Felt ionized, and did a fast bike ride to burn off excess energy. . . ."

I babbled on to thank him for 1227, shared his admiration for RLS, talked about Hart Crane, and told him I was re-reading Robert A. Caro's masterful biography of Robert Moses and the New York City he built and ruined. I have long been fascinated by the idea of cities. Years earlier I had written Moses a letter, and I got to spend an hour with him one afternoon. What a formidable character.

My letter continued with complaints about the appalling and ridiculous errors in the *Fledermaus* orchestral parts.[61] I had taken his advice, done my own markings, dropped the ballet, and would insert "your Donner und Blitz, four bars to a beat." I asked about his summer plans and enclosed a birthday present (a T-shirt of Emily Dickinson), with instructions not to open until 3 July, when he would turn sixty-three. His reply zoomed back, typed, except for the salutation, which he wrote in a large hand.

26 VI 93
Charlemagnanimous!
What a joy! Of course I couldn't wait to open my boithdee present. It is beautiful! How well the cartoonist caught those eyes, the mouth, the hair, from the only photo (as far as I know) that exists, with the exception of those childhood group snapshots. And it's done lovingly, too. I'll WEAR it, yessir, when the weather gets less chilly here again.

Much enjoyed your unseasonal-windstorm vignette. And it truly befits a professor to think learnedly of phantastikos, ahem. I looked it up and it was, as I expected, a Greek I of fantasticks opf coarse.

With ED, I'll stick to incipits when compulsively quoting from now on.

I must confess that I am not acquainted with Hart Crane's poetry. Like those people whose only knowledge of Richard Wagner are details about his silk robes, my mind has MR. Crane identified solely by his wish not to get any older than Jesus did (an obsession shared by Kierkegaard senior and junior) which he managed to avoid by jumping off a boat just in time.*
I envy him for cheating the undertaker like that. Flippancy aside, OK, I'll try and find Bridges.

Neither have I an inkling of Moses and Caro. But the wrecking of neighbourhoods flourishes all over the place, here, too.

I like to imagine you correcting parts for the Bat. There's nothing like it for penetrating a work. Glad your band consists of wonderful folks and your idea of giving them the lyrics to the numbers is great. My father used to do that with new operas. Gives those miners in the pit some knowledge of what they're digging for, it does.

In case I didn't make myself clear, here goes again: I am truly touched and happy and tickled to death by your kindnesses, tapewise, letterwise, T-shirt-wise (Yabbaddabbadooo! Fabulous! Phabulostros!) und ueberhaupt! Every happiness to you, too! And to dear Hilde, of course!
Your old Carlos.

PS (no incipits, tho: these are from letters)
"Be sure to live in vain and never mingle with the mouse."
"The Ear is the last Face. We hear after we see."
"While there is anything so sudden in the world as lightning, no event among men can seem anything but slow."
"I hope you are safe and distinguished. Is the latter the former? Experience makes me no reply."
Emily

* . . . not with a bang, but a . . . splash?[62]

PPS   As of July 1, 1993, we have a new Zip code:
C.K.
Aurikelstr. 1A

| D-82031 | Grünwald

Out of synch yet again, I wrote Carlos on 24 June "to thank you for yours re Batposter and Beetpizz." Playing defense I told him about going to the Beethoven Center in San José, where I found Altman quoting Beethoven dissatisfied with the first edition Steiner, "as both score and parts contained many mistakes." I also told him that I had corrected the hairpins and would, as instructed, try to conduct the "Trio" at MM 84.

My letter mostly talked about the Strauss Festival continuing at the San Francisco Opera and how I was seeing *Daphne* and *Capriccio* for my first time. I told him about a superb performance of *Rosenkavalier* led by Sir Charles Mackerras and featuring von Stade, Schaefer, and the incomparable Felicity Lott as the Marschallin. "A gradual acceptance of loss, her gathering dignity, the final glance over her shoulder, the way the colours of her voice caught and intensified these emotions—how *attuned* she was. The orchestra was positively heliotropic, following her to twilight." It ended by describing Jason, a friend of mine who saw it for the first time, eyes shining in the dark.

I wrote him again on 15 July, and we got back into step. This letter congratulated him on the XL fit of his Dickinson T-shirt, and described "a famous picture of Moses, blueprints in hand, standing on a girder high over the East River, Ozymandias at the summit. Caro got the Pulitzer for the book. Someone should have gotten it for the photo."

It also brought him up to date on casting, chorus, and rehearsals for *Fledermaus*, and various public speaking projects of my own, allegedly in the field of music education. The same letter included film of a few more conductors and an apologia: "I really do appreciate the thanks you express for the junk I write, and for the films I xerox. . . . It's an honor to serve someone who serves music the way you do. Besides, I like your jokes, even the ones Stan has to explain to me." His answer came fast.

20 VII 93

Hi!

Regarding the photo of Master-Builder Moses-Solness,[63] high up on a girder: Is there a Hilda looking on from below? #

I got tape Nr. 15 but haven't watched it yet. Would you send me the number of your bank-account so's I can ease my conscience by transferring some dough to it? (Your CK expenses are a weight on me I'd lighten if you'd allow. Pretty please!)

The postage for US has long gone up and I didn't notice till yesterday. But my letters seemed to get there anyhow.

Here is something someone from the MET sent me. I liked lots of it.⁶⁴ Specially the cellists zipping up kid's snowsuits.

Yeah, coulda told Mr. Tilson would talk + talk! (He thinks he's Lenny reincarnated.) Glad you got paid for your lecture despite Tilson's efforts at redundancy. I have a Fricsay "Moldau" rehoissal + perf. He talks + talks and, yes, there's plenty of Anouilh on the faces of the players, who immediately realized he's addressing the camera. (If only he'd admitted it, they could all have taken it smilingly.)

32 chorus! Wow, that's really a lot, no kidding. Congrats! By your description of the Falke I would guess he's Afro-American. Is he? The "Hotters" (not so hot, they) were obviously whiteys, n'est-ce pas?

About ED I can say what I don't appreciate:

1) All the Bible bits (except "the lillies")

2) The whims(e)y, when it gets real heavy

3) The grovelling, mock-abject tone of some letters to the "Master"

4) The 2nd versions of the poems.

5) 6) 7) etc; other things. ("Immortality", etc.)

What I love about her? Well, it's love; so I won't expose it to scrutiny or discussion. Regarding 1), 2) + 3): even in these, there's the saving astringency of that two-timing sadism Ms. Paglia cleverly recognized. * One has to listen carefully, tho'!! Keeping in mind that ED wasn't silly, by any means. (As I told you: Carlo, the dog, was me!)

Now, to leave Shirley MacLaine (Arturo's poodle) to lie where she was layed (Remember the Lays of Marie de France?)

I turn to your remark about "the junk I write" (CB). YOU DON'T WRITE JUNK! And I'm always happy to read you. I enjoy!

☺ ☺ ☺

I bought this in NY. Isn't it horrible? But, in this case it brings the message across colourfully enough. Good luck with everything, especially "The Bat".
Always your grateful old dissident and recluse
Carlos K

PS What does Chomsky say about Lincoln and/or the Civil War? If he is of my opinion, I'm interested. (If not, I'm not. Ha!)

 # Was he goaded onto that goider by a goil?

* Stan will explain if necessary.⁶⁵

He wrote again the next day to talk about Tape No. 15, which I had sent him earlier. Boulez, Fricsay, and Knappertsbusch were the subjects of that dub, and so of his letter. As with almost all of his quick replies it was written in hand, with numerous underlines and marginalia.

21 VII 93

Hi!

(After consuming tape #15 ☺)

1) BOULEZ. I tried to anagramaticize "I COIN VARESE" into "VARICOSE VEIN" but found there was a "V" de trop. God! What a crashing [sffz on "crashing"] *bore! Stalwart Boulez's poker face implies that the silly noise neither surprises nor bothers him. Determined professionalism. It's a job, you see.*

2) Fricsay. I never liked this guy nor his music-making. But now . . . I loathe him! The only part I enjoyed was when his left cuff (x tra long) got stuck up the sleeve of his monkey-suit. (Do watch that bit again! Jerry Lewis, eat your heart out!) Some conductors used to scare the shit out of orchestras. Fricsay bored the shit into them, additionally. And look at that chain! Look at the "Legion d'horreur" in his lapel! What a prick! Oh yes, and he murders Dukas; with relish.

• *Knappertsbusch: if you can overlook the "Grosses Bundesverdienstkreuz"[66] around his neck, the meticulously cute hairdo, the disinterestedly twitching baton and the fact that the band is playing lousily, why then . . . it's OK, I guess.*

What, my son, do we learn from these 3 guys on Tape #15? Speak up, don't mumble! What? That's right: They know exactly who the hell they think they are! Bravo!

Molti saluti from (care canem)[67] Carlo who won't bite the hand that feeds him tapes, tho'! Never!

I was working out of town that summer, and I regretted not telling him so. He had made it clear that he felt a bit hurt, overlooked if there was no speedy reply to his letters. There was about Carlos an abiding insecurity in matters where logic would declare cause for none. No matter how often I declared my gratitude for his correspondence, he seemed hurt not to hear from my end of things, and quickly too. On 13 August I sent a long, two-page typed letter, as friendly as I knew how to put on page.

"Dear Wonder Dog," it began. I declined his transferred dough and said that I would rather have a signed photograph. (It came quite soon.) I thanked him for the Lutheran essay, told him about various writing projects of my own, and answered questions about our "Bat" casting by telling him that our Falke was actually white as a refrigerator. I also told him about my scheme to use holograms and asked his advice about employing (or not) *stringendo* in the "Friska."[68]

His stamp was truly goofy, and I tried to top it by using one my mom had given me. I played along with his invitation to anagram ("severed raga" was the best I could do) but it was pitiful. I asked if he had ever written anything for print himself and offered noms de plume he might use (Leon Trotsky, Mike Tyson), and then I asked, "Are <u>you</u> Camille Paglia? Stan PhD wouldn't answer, citing doctor-recluse confidentiality."

For the first time I wanted him to consider conducting a specific work. I put it as a joke proffered as a bribe. This was a tactic I had been contemplating for some while. Surely it would be a very good thing if he could be persuaded to work in new territory. I had no influence, of course, but felt secure enough to give it a try.

"Have you got anything in mind for your next project? Do you accept bribes? For a Brahms *Requiem*, one bag of cookies. For a *Ninth*, two. For a *Peter Grimes*, three. Oatmeal or chocolate, your choice." Jokes always provided the safest avenue.

That letter's tape included Boult, forty minutes of old Czech film (including his father, and Mravinsky, Munch, Shostakovich, Ançerl, Talich, etc.), Schuricht, and a film of himself doing the Overture to *Freischütz*. In my film notes I attributed the latter to one "E. D. Caninus," and his dates 1920–1967. His reply came rapidly, in two pages of tight writing on long paper. He was still a bit annoyed I wouldn't let him pay me for my efforts.

n.d.[69]

Dear Oliver Batman,

Should I remain uneased or should you feel mercantile? What is more painful? I shall cogitate and ruminate and come up with something or other.

A couple of things in your letter were beyond me.

1) What is a B of A?

2) I don't get "Bolto". Am I dense? (don't tell)

3) Couldn't solve the anagrams (Severed Raga, etc)

4) Why was Caninus born in 1920 and why did he buy the farm in 1967? (He'd be 73 today) Now, with a great big [here he stamped his happy face "thankyou"]

Boult is adorable! Great! Have always loved him! ["Boult," "adorable," "always loved him" inside thick lined boxes]

Borenboim is a bar; but he's better here (less of his usual School-girl over-phrasing) than he is toady.[70] *("Toady's special" was an item on the menu of an ocean liner I was once on.)*

Don't know what Scherchen was conducting but the Czech commentator indistinctly said what it was. Find a Czech who don't bounce and he'll tell ya. EK was conducting the Bohemian Suite by (spelling?) Vitscheslav (Viçeslav?) Novak who is the old guy stumbling around with EK in Prague.[71]

I liked Shostakovitch telling the pianist something in no uncertain terms! The rest of the conductors got on my noives, tho' each of them, like O. Nash's benighted Hindu, does the best he Kindu.

Hated Caninus, the dirty dog!! Schuricht was posing for his death mask, seems like. He's good at Brahms, tho' Was, I mean.

I _Never_ have written _anything_ for print. Paglia on ED ("Amherst's Madame de Sade") is loopy and sexes things up for what she correctly estimates the 'Murrican polymorph-perverse, puberty stuck public to hanker after. But, for me, the fact that she _loves_ ED excuses the bull ~~cow~~shit she exudes and sells.

Marko, my son, would like to explain to you how he did the multicoloured address. But I said no, he shouldn't: Es ist ein Betreibsgeheimnis.[72]

Friska—is that the last of the Csardas? [they] mislead people, who at all costs want to appear Hungarianer than the Hungarians, like to start that reprise _real_ slow and build it up. Me, I _don't_ like that. Aarrgh!

Who is _Blomstedt?_[73] Wasn't he the bad guy in the James Bond films?[74] I know Previn is still alive, but is he kicking?

I liked the stamp your Mom gave you. I gather she saw you as très sportif.

For the Ninth I would require 5 to 9 bags of cookies (oatmeal, of course). The other two pieces you mentioned are _definitely_ not my cup of tea. (The cookies would crumble. . . .)

Yes, Mengelberg was _the_ most talkative of all conductors. They say.

*Good luck with "Così"! (Yeah, go ahead, rush in where angels fear * to tread!)*

* I'll change that to "feared" on account of there ain't no angels around no more, far as _I_ can see. (Don't listen to me, please!)

Speaking of angels: If your Gabriel is getting cold feet, get a reserve-guy just in case he chickens out. Someone who is possibly better loitering in the wings is very motivating for the stage-frightened!

I _greatly_ enjoyed Karajan's 1 1/2 minute rehearsal of the Dvořák G-Major symph!!! It was typical of him to lead the last rehearsal into a shambles (on purpose, of course) and make like he didn't notice or care two cents. And yet . . . there was more music there than (with the exception of Adrian's contribution) anywhere else on the VHS. I _think_ I know. . . . Do you think I know? Who cares?

Affetuosi saluti, anche per Stan-Hilda, from your old (63) and mangy mutt, Carlo

I answered on 20 September, thanking him for his comments on the technique seen in the films and for his advice about my own conducting projects. We had to dismiss our first Gabriel, I told him, even though "the stage director, aware of his troubles, had reduced his movements to iron lung level."

The same letter "explained" that I found Caninus, the son of Norma Desmond and Rumpot McBride, in *New Grove*. "After a career in restitution, Caninus took up conducting, studied with Frodzinski, and died of rabies in 1967. It was all very sad. I don't like to talk about it." I also told him that friends of mine in the San Francisco Symphony were anxious he come over to lead them in a concert or two.

Hilde made the promised cookies, which we mailed over to Grünwald. "If you need one bag of cookies per symphony, let's forget about Haydn, OK?"[75]

He sent over his photo, inscribed to Stan and Oliver. I thanked him for it and explained that "it's on my little shrine (well, on my diskette box). When studying score and about to commit some wretched excess, I look at you and see you waggling 'NO!' and return to taste and normalcy." PS: "Ein betriebsgeheimnis, you say? Come on. It was woodpeckers with colored beaks."

But before I could mail it we did the Sitzprobe for *Fledermaus*, and I wanted to tell him about it. The Sitz had gone very well indeed, but "it's infuriating when one clumsy egotist sings into the silence and defeats the achievement of 40 others." It ended by telling him, "We move onstage tonight, and open Saturday. Next to hearing the first A in the pit, there's nothing like walking behind the curtain and seeing a whole new world aborn, eh?"

In the next mail came a postcard.

n.d.[76]

Dear Maestro!

Hope all's well with you, haven't heard any news for so long. If I have inadvertently incurred your displeasure, that's preferable to the thought of your maybe having trouble with bats (baseball or other bats) or with existence in general.

My best wishes accompany you steadily,

Yours Sincerely,

C.K.

He stamped his home address at the bottom, as if to suggest I had misplaced it. On the same day I received his card, I wrote back, enclosing a tape with Ansermet conducting *La Valse*, and Szell in Beethoven's Piano Concerto No. 5, with pianist Friedrich Gulda and the Vienna Philharmonic, from 1966. I asked Carlos what he thought of Ansermet's Ravel. (It seemed wonderfully eloquent, but I still didn't have the nerve to venture my opinion first.)

Our *Fledermaus* had now ended, enjoying a very successful run, and I took the occasion to thank Kleiber for his contribution to it. "Much credit was given for its 'Viennese-ness.' I hereby deflect it to you." I rattled on about the Beethoven 7 I would be conducting and about a recording project that had gone bust. Thanks were also given for the home address of Sándor Végh; it resulted in film of that maestro, and I asked Carlos if he'd like a copy.

His next note—startlingly—asked if he still remained in my good books. Every time he spoke like that I shook my head in disbelief. To me our friendship was wholly lopsided. I was in a state of deep obligation to him. None-theless, concerned that he might be misinterpreting my own desire not to burden him with letters every day, I fired off a quick card the next afternoon: "Everything's fine. Wrote in September with book and cookies. Love from Hilde, and a hearty masculine handshake from me."

To demonstrate the perfection of my goodwill I also wrote the following day, on the 22nd, and told him about a delightful first meeting in San Francisco with Sir Charles Mackerras and his wife, Judy. We discussed Václav Talich, whom I knew to have been Mackerras's teacher. It was a fascinating encounter with two remarkable people talking about a third.

"I asked Sir Charles who he thought was the most important conductor working today. He didn't hesitate. 'There's no contest, really. Carlos Kleiber. He is the greatest conductor of our time, I believe.'" This was typical of Mackerras's humility and honesty.

I finally responded to Carlos's repeated concerns that I might "abandon" him. "Incurred <u>my</u> displeasure? Not possible. It remains an honor to share these little diggings with you, and to enjoy your company and imagination and jokes." I signed this letter "Ex Cathedra, Charles, Prince of Rome," and made a little cartoon sign of the cross. At the time, I did not know he was Catholic.

26 Oct 93
Dear Dottore! Just an ultra-quickie. Received today the Ansermet tape. Will react in the next few days after hearing. Congratulations on your success with Bat, and thanks for saying I helped. Makes me feel good! The book you mentioned never arrived: this Ansermet etc tape is the first I've heard from you for ages.

I thought I had annoyed or offended you and wrote, a few days ago, a short note referring to that possibility. Glad I'm still in your good graces, wheew!
Kind regards and greetings, love to Hildestan, keep well, be happy,
le crotchety vieux fard,
Carlos K,

For whatever reasons of weird mail delivery, mine seem to have arrived on his doorstep in a bunch. His next letter had more of his smiley faces of it, a new home address stamp (in color), and shrewd insights into the work of the great ones.

27 Oct 93
Dear Barbieri!
Never rains but it pours. Or is it (ad for salt) when it rains it pours?[77] A shower of letters and a tape, Whee!
THANK YOU ☺

Re-Mackerras, he chose me because I never conduct, which is a comfort to all and sundry <u>and</u> me. Nice of him 'tho.

TAPE: Just heard and watched. Skipped some of the German history: I have the insane notion that they change history around all the time. Soon as I've caught on to one purportedly genuine version, next thing I see is a different one. This is probably wishful musing, an excuse not to bother with history at all. Of course,

<u>Lincoln</u> is the <u>real</u> criminal: look at the fate of secessionists today . . . but I'm boring you . . . that yawn . . . OK, OK.

You write: "Ravel, La Valse, rehearsal and concert." It is a magnificent performance, old answer-me is out of this world! But, sorry, there ain't no rehoissal on the tape*, that's for sure. After La Valse comes snow, snow, snow. I watched it snowing dutifully (I mean I WATCHED dutifully) for about 20 minutes. Then the phone rang and I turned it off.

Gulda and Szell were fascinating, if somewhat rigid and didactic. There was a positive lack of pottery,[78] sort of, hovering over it all. Gulda tried a couple of times for humour, but was squelched subliminally in the act by Szell. The WPH rose to the dehydrated occasion seriously and note-bent. But, hey, it's easy to be critical when one just sits there and gripes as I do. At least it had a sort of juggernaught rhythm. It's the way YL, that thug of the podium, would like to do things, no? <u>If</u> he <u>could</u>! <u>Muscular</u>!

The Crawl-singers[79] interviewed were all-but-dead, a sight to turn away from, felt I. But they obviously revered the Klemp. Incidentally, about Cosí: there is a surrealistic but ben trovato[80] story about Boehm, who was considered good at the piece: Before a Cosí, guy comes out and announces: It is my sad duty to inform you that Prof. Boehm has just passed away. But, unwilling to disappoint the audience, he will nevertheless conduct this performance. Thank you.

Very glad I didn't incur (woof woof) your displeasure, as I told you in my card.[81]

My typewriter has been in repairs for so long, I've lost the touch as you can see. Will mention Heldenleben when and if anything comes of it ever.

Is it as exciting, living near or in LA, as the people on German TV will have us believe? Do you drive right through red semaphores to avoid getting mugged, murdered and/or raped? They make a big thing of that over here where it doesn't happen often: Wie langweilig.[82]

All the best from

Carlos

* before <u>or</u> after.

On the 29th I sent him a postcard from my Beethoven 7 engagement, and on the second of November, I sent a much longer letter, telling him about the concert itself. I had taken his advice, especially concerning the downbeat ornamentation in the slow movement and the dotted figures he warned me about. "The 'modelling' of these signature rhythms always worked best start-ing with the woodwinds," I told him, endorsing the obvious. "Strings were the last to get it right. They over-bow, believing it shows Enthusiasm, which I suppose it does." I seated them the way he had instructed and sent along a copy of a very forgiving review that saw fit to mention this novelty.

I reiterated my reassurance: "I'm glad it's clear that I was not (and could not be) unhappy about anything between you and me. I cherish our letters, and your friendship, very much." I apologized for snow on the last tape, explaining that it had been transferred at a commercial lab, and promised that I would personally preview every tape I sent over in the future. (I did. It took hours.)

Because he had complained about his typewriter I suggested he get a Mac-intosh and have son Marko teach him how to use it. I also reassured him that I still lived four hundred miles north of Los Angeles and was in no danger. Even so, I agreed that gun-nuts have far too much clout in our politics. After a massacre at an office building in San Francisco, I sent a letter to the papers, offering comfort to the survivors. "Your relatives did not die in vain. Sac-rifices must be made to protect our Constitutional right to bear arms." The irony did not fly, nor did the letter.

The package included tapes of Kubelik, Frühbeck de Burgos, and Sto-kowski. I ended by defending the United States. "This country also produced Stanford and Harvard and stunning advances in medicine and the Chicago Symphony and Whitman and Dickinson and her little dog Spot. How's by you?" His next letter arrived a couple of days later. We were out of synch, again. It was typed more carefully than any other letter he sent.

Nov. 4, 1993
Dear Concer(tat)o(re) Grosso!
    Here's dashing of a stream of undisconsciounableness.
    Just received cookies and Moses-book (haven't started on book yet) plus delightful letters of yours dated September 20, '93. Cookies (still) delicious! Yummy!
    First: LA is on fire right now. We are trying to feel sad about Barbra Stry-sand's villa in ashes. Difficult. But our pyrophily ends at Mountain View: is your diggings OK? We hope so. Your fired, "unnoted" Gabriel: we've heard of great singers who couldn't read notes. They were only a bother for the repetiteur. Also heard of singers who could read all notes,* even in tenor-clef, who were no good at all. Such is variety—or varietée, huh?[83]
    Yeah, sure, send me your BofA, now that I know what it is.[84] OK, let us forget poor Caninus, whom-by hung a tail.
    Congratulations, once again, on your Bat!! I adore Boult, yes. Don't know about resemblance to Nikisch though. I like the way AB defends

seating the 2nd Vls. On the right of the conductor, the place where they belong, as I discovered far too late.

When the weather gets better, I'll put on my ED-T shirt and send you a snap of me thus attired.[85] Bet you can hardly wait! It's good to hear that you enjoy the slings and arrows of (outrageous?) conducting so much! About those 2 little-bitty notes in the andante of the 7th you should have cited Bruno Walter (instead of me!) (there's a tape of a rehearsal) insisting on doing it that way. (Like Frankie, he did it his way)[86]

Tickled to death you enjoyed the Met Otello (was it the Met one?) am basking in the glow of your kind remarks about it. I confess to not being moved, personally, by "the first A in the pit". Maybe because, for all I know, it could be any other flipping note of the scale. Always have envied people with perfect pitch and I squirm when they pretend it's a handicap— the way pretty girls pretend they'd prefer to be plain.

This also applies to photographic memory. But I believe only Dimitry M. had THAT truly, genuinely.[87] But what good would it do us to see the page if we couldn't read it? Mitty could, of course.

Do you think he could sight-read from memory? What a thought! Anything one can do, someone else can do better, yes they can! (Annie's Law).[88]

This is a silly letter—please to excuse—but I am quite vacant at the moment. Seems to be turning into my definite state of mind, gallopingly.

Am enjoying some old discs of Cortot's. Did you know the Japs made him a present of an island—Cortotshima? I heard him in Buenos Aires (1950?) when he was way, way past his prime. He looked like a spider and left out all the notes we would leave out, but still played quite a few we couldn't have managed, ever.

Many affectionate good wishes 2 U 2 Mountain Viewers, a rave review for the cookies, grateful greetings galore,
your
Charlie Heartburn #
from too many cookies

PS: rereading this whimsical epistle, I see I've used "we" and "us" now and then. Doesn't mean you and me. Well, maybe me. But it's not pluralis majestatis,[89] non plus. Just refers to an imaginary, indefinite bunch of more or less endearing ineffectuals, windmilling on the rivers of the music? Of the mind.[90] Now come on, Carlos, shut-ye up. Au reservoir!

* There's also people can "read" notes but haven't a clue to what they sound like!

His next letter caught me before I had a chance to answer his last. It was back to the usual: typed, with corrections in hand. However, this time the marginalia were also typed. It must have taken some labor to line them up as neatly as he did.

11.11.93
Mon cher Charles,
Again, molti congrats on your 7th and your Bat! Your seating is OK; but celli at 1100 and violas at 1300. (With, of course, secondi at 1500.) <u>Many</u> good reasons for that; the most human one: primi hate sitting next to the—traditionally benighted—violas. AND vice versa!

No Macintosh for me: things you gotta plug into an electric circuit before use I like not. Nor can I take to four-cornered keys.

Yes, Stanford*, Harvard, the Chicago Symph, ED and (with some reserve) great advances in medicine: these "You-night-as-tates"? things I will follow you in effortlessly enthusing about. But Whitman I hate, loathe and despise. I won't go into why, because you obviously like ? him. Just don't mention him or Lincoln again unless you enjoy watching me run amok, OK? If you do, I'll know you're rattling my chain. A dog's chain, remember.[91]

Found Mountain View on my map. And, in <u>much</u> finer print, there's also Bonnie Doon, Coyote and Stanford. For these one needs a magnifying glass. *Stanford <u>is</u> ON the map. And I guess you, Maestro, <u>put</u> it there. Otherwise, what's <u>it</u> doing there?

Am relieved at the distance of Mt. View from the fires of LA. Feared you might be getting toasted last week. (You WERE getting toasted, of course, but it was because of your Beethoven, no arson involved.)

Moses-book is fascinating. Later more. Stokowsky <u>fabulous</u>, thanks a million for letting me have that! I'll tell you what I think of Kubelik and Burgos another time. (Non troppo, that's for sure!)
Frau Hildestan einen Handkuss; affectionate, grateful regards
and wishes to both of you,
all the best,
Your
Carlos Kleiber

PS: Szell had a great sense of humour, off-rostrum. Very selective, though. And guess who did the selecting? Right!

PPS: know the story about Klemperer who went to a concert with La Mer conducted by Szell? Asked for an opinion, he quipped: "Das war nicht La Mer. Das war hoechstens Szell am See." (In case you didn't know this, Zell am See is a small lakeside resort)[92]

PPPS: Sorry about "pottery". I intended "Poettry". Just like Smith-Corona to dunk it in whimsy. Maybe Macintosh . . .

Carlos wrote again five days later. He had evidently been watching the latest video. He was still using that multicolored hand stamp for his return address.

16.11.93

Caro Maestro,

Re your *VHS*, just consumed your *Kubelik* and *Fruehbeck*, I had skipped them in favour of Stokowsky, remember. *Kubelik* is a delightful person. This said, I'll confess that, with me, a little *Kubelik* goes a long way. Particularly his conducting. The way ensemble falls apart at the seams bothers me and I wonder if it isn't maybe because of 2 things.

1) He has less rhythm than the orchestra.

2) The body-language of his head-movements contradicts that of his hands.

Maybe the Czechs, as Czechs, always want to make a big thing of "making music", a quality they are famous for and irritatingly intent on living up to, willy-nilly. Then there's all that talk, talk; all that ingratiating would-be poeticizing. It's eerie to feel the guy overstaying his maudlin welcome with just a sentence or two. At least, that's my impression.

Mr. F. de B. (with Schumann #3) is a wonder: one wonders how anyone could ever have wanted to let him loose on any orchestra known to man. He's infra-dig, bush-league; at least, that's my impression.[93]

THE MOSES BOOK; have started on that bulky tome and am quite carried away.[94] Amazing it ever went to print during Moses' lifetime. While I work through it in my spare time (most of my time is spare, by dint of procrastinating), spellbound, my one-track mind keeps comparing the protagonist and his many personalities to other famous people who went out and did things. Like Hitler, Gandhi, Abe, Nero, etc. and my stubborn intent on proving what a mistake it was is gratified alround. (What kind of a sentence was that, if any? I'll let it stand 'cause I'm too lazy to correct this letter, please excuse.)

Here, today, winter "ist endlich eingebrochen",[95] as the Boches and Bavarians say. Everything is white and would be glistening were there any sunshine. Cars are gliding elegantly, slowly off course; undeterred cyclists keel over with a sheepish grin; old folks at home who were careless enough not to stay there are fracturing their brittle bones with falls that wouldn't leave a bruise on you or—perhaps—me.

For comfort, I went through the Romeo and Julia Stokowsky thing again. Loved the poker-face Stokes maintains in the face of some of the intonation and ensemble; moments where Arturo T. would have broken into his well-known tarantella of hate and murder? Isn't Stokey's reaction so much preferable?

Well, dear Maestro, I stop this nonsensical letter and wish you and Hilde all the best: luck, health, peace and all that jazz very sincerely and from the heart,

Your CK (* musique du vingtième siècle)

Gran Cassa

Allegro feroce [musical notation appears here]

On the 23rd I sent him Tape No. 18-B. It contained great material. "Wanted to rush these new films to you ASAP. Legible letter to follow. Allegro dolce, Charles." It was the BBC's splendid film documentary *Art of Conducting*, for which I had supplied some of the material and much unsought advice.

4 Dec 93

Charlemagnanimous!

Gramercy for BBC-VHS! Lots of good stuff on it. Karajan—as usual—misunderstood. Remarks about conducting and conductors by Mr. Grubb (?),[96] *Menuhin, a fat guy in a brown sweater,** Mr. E. Gardiner, Jansson, Szell etc etc all silly and/ or gushy.*

  But that's the way even the professionals talk about the profession-du-baton. Soon as they open their mouths, they turn into house-wives. (Worst: the BPH tympanist!)[97]

  Mon cher Charles: thanks a 10 (6) for the videos! It's always a FEAST when one of them arrives!

Affectionate Yuletide noises

from CCC#

* a bush-league take-charge guy!

 # Crotchety Coot Carlos

I answered his several letters on 1 December. Apologizing for my slothful replies, it was three pages long, typed, with no marginalia at all. "Dear Micetro: this is the letter that should have accompanied the last tape. I thought I'd answer November 4 and 11 at the same time. And then along came yours of November 16 . . . so, here they is."

Re the BBC film, "I asked why you weren't in it, and they said that they were going to end the series with you as a symbol of continuity with the great conductors of the past. Then, they got worried about hurting Solti's feelings, and decided that the series would only show holy ghosts."

I put questions about how he memorized a work, thanked him for the Szell joke, expressed regret on the death of his friend Lucia Popp, and appreciated his lyrical lines about Grünwald in winter. "When it falls below 55 F degrees here, California weather-wimps run inside and put cats on their noses." I also got to more serious business, expressed as silliness.

"Are you <u>really</u> as lazy as you pretend? I had sort of hoped that my cookie-bribes would encourage more music. Hmmm. Maybe all these films falling from the sky have created some kind of cargo cult, and Grünwaldians spend all their time watching them instead of . . ." It ended by telling him that I had just agreed to do *Magic Flute*.

A few days later I mailed over a sarcastic review of a concert recently given by an American conductor, one more famous for his ego than his skill. Kleiber must have replied instantly, using the paper at hand—the verso of a blue resumé for one Arno Raunig, "Sopran, Alt." He scribbled fast and enclosed an elegant, embossed Japanese business card.

10 December 1993
Dear Maestro!
Thanks for KLM clipping. (What a jerk!)
Merry Xmas
and a
Happy New Year!
Your
Carlos Kleiber
PS: This is my visiting card!

A week later another letter came in.

17.12.93
Dear do do [musical notes drawn above "do do"]
A quicky in answer to yrs. Of 1 December. This here is Boult on seating.⁹⁸ I also have a book, very erudite, on all opera and concert seating from "adam" to Solti; incl. Haydn, of course, and Verdi, Mozart, Weber, Nikisch, Stokey, Vienna till 1940 and after, the works. But I've lent it to a WPH violinist and he hasn't returned it.* An Ammurican in some University wrote and illustrated it, can't remember his name. That book + Boult + videos of the giants made me change. If that weren't enough, just look at any score.

Incidentally, never did I have violas at 1100 except in opera where I once had 1 at 0900, Violas at 1100, Celli at "1200–1300" and all "Blowers" on the right; Basses across the back is always best when possible. In the olden days, says the murrican book, they had Contrabassi dispersed all over the orchestra so's all could hear them!

"Doing" a piece "from memory" is something your Aunt Sally would have no trouble with. Knowing exactly what is (supposed to be) going on is something, I believe, only Mitropoulos could honestly claim to. With the right band in a good, condescending mood, there'd be no audible difference between Sally and Dimitri, if Sally had digested the overall ductus.

Yes, Lucia Popp was, for many years, an extremely close friend.⁹⁹

Kubelik wanted the Furty brand of inexactness; but, as I said, he didn't have F's rhythm so "all he ever got was 5 salted peanuts."¹⁰⁰

Seeing as the "Russians" are waxing nostalgic for the erstwhile cat 'o nine tails they used to have, I guess Arturo[101] <u>was</u> loved for

1) being honest and spontaneous and

2) for not being ingratiating in the slimey manner we all have to affect nowadays, a thing that goes down small with, especially, older players who weren't raised by Dr. Spock. But, maybe, "all you need is love".

Love to Hilda, complicated or not. Sometimes I feel that what makes women seem so complicated is that they're so simple. (Simple in the right sense, of course) We hanker for intricacy.

I'm off, Merry Xmas,
all the best,
Your old CK

* the bastard

This letter was written on the back of four pages of material xeroxed from Sir Adrian Boult's well-known book *The Art of Conducting*, pp. 144–147. Carlos never relented in his opinion about proper orchestral seating, and many times he told me about the significance of this. Although I began reseating my own orchestras according to his instructions and even sent him video to prove it, he seemed to think I was not convinced. Kleiber was adamant that the seconds belonged downstage, to the conductor's right, opposite the first violins. Here, he drew lines under and boxes around assertions made in Boult's fourth section, "Arranging Orchestras," to wit:

I have heard it said that the right plan would be to let everyone sit where he wishes. . . . I am personally not inclined to try this bold plan, <u>exciting though the results might be!</u>

Boult goes on to consider numerous other options. One of them, phlegmatically put, draws Carlos's amusement:

There are two things here which I dislike intensely.*

Carlos adds, "* Boult in a rage"

This principal of tonal balance also affects the position of the second violins, <u>about which I feel most strongly, although I am in a small minority.</u>
The seconds thus share the front of the platform instead of being tucked away behind the firsts, where, I maintain, their tone is largely lost. Indeed, <u>the practice which I so dislike</u> came in only about fifty years ago. . . .
True, it is easier for the first violins to have the seconds near them, and for the violas to be placed between the seconds and the 'cellos, <u>but is ease</u>

of playing and convenience to be the chief criterion? Surely the result is what matters, and I can assert that on many occasions in many halls I have heard the give-and-take answering passages, which occur in all music from Mozart to the present day, sound completely ineffective when the answer comes as a pale reflection from behind the first violins instead of springing up bravely from the opposite side of the platform.

Carlos was quite emphatic about this last passage. It was double-underlined, and in red, and introduced with a large exclamation mark. The final passage he wanted me to note concerned seating for choral music with orchestra, and appears to refer to Beethoven 9.

> it is indeed often better for most of the audience to have the solo quartet near the chorus; the orchestra, of course, must keep their accompaniment discreet. Once again I say, as on previous occasions: trust the orchestra. *? They can actually hear the soloists, and judge the balance for themselves, far more easily than if the soloists are singing away from them with their backs turned.

Carlos does not concur, and thinks Boult has contradicted himself. He adds a "*" and a "?" in the text, and at the bottom of the page adds, "??? * see p. 146: 'is ease of playing and convenience . . .'" Alas, we cannot know what he would have done. Carlos never led a *Ninth*, save in his reading of the score. He knew the work profoundly but never gave it outside his study.

Mine of 12 January offered cheery Christmas tales, further condolences on the loss of Lucia Popp, "a long-distance hug" for same, and film of Leinsdorf; Knappertsbusch and Nilsson in the Wagner *Liebestodt*; the corrected version of Ansermet rehearsing *La Valse*; and, an astounding film of Heifetz at the peak of his form playing the "Hora Staccato." "This latter includes a down-bow technique which is not physically possible." I also enclosed a New York Times review not sympathetic to conductor Sergiu Celibidache.

22 Jan. 1994
Hi there!
Thanks for great tape!
 Nilsson, Ansermet—(loved the part about "Valse" and "Vienne", little towns in France!) and HEIFETZ with O. Staccato and what a staccato, V or M. [up and downbow marks] WOW!!! (Pianist drags a little) At last the guy from Vienna Phil. Has returned my copy of the following book. It is a sensational book, a MUST!
 "Orchestral Performance Practices in the 19th Century" subtitle: Size, Proportion, Seating. By Daniel J. KOURY. UMI Research Press. Studies in Musicology, No. 85

Revision in author's thesis (Ph.D.)—Boston University 1981
ML 1 1200.K68 1986 785? 09'034
85-16345.
ISBN -0-8357-1649-X (alk paper)
(I add all those funny signs to help (?) you* find it. It is a flabbergasting work!!!
Read!!!)
Boult and his words about 2 Violin-seating is in there, too
Enjoyed the N. Y. Times assessment of Celibidache! Exactly right, sez I!
Are you OK despite the QUAKE? What a horror! Watched CNN in anguish.[102]
Also—40 [degrees] in Washington. Crazy!
Fond regards, auch au Hilde!
The ole gray Karl.[103]

Getting speedier in reply I answered on 29 January with an all-Klemperer letter and video care package. I had made friends with Lotte Klemperer, daughter of Otto. She was a very generous woman who wanted Stanford to have a
safety set of her father's films. Over time, she gave us all of them, including
the 1964 Ninth and a 1985 BBC documentary that I passed along to Carlos.

I whined about a music competition I had recently judged. "All notes, no
music. Merde. I expect a brief word of sympathy." Running slightly ahead, I
wrote again on 1 February and sent *Everything You Always Wanted to Know
about Conductors—But Were Afraid to Ask*, a 1993 documentary. It was one
of those snide efforts interested in the offstage lives and back-stage gossip
of the trade. Its tone was groveling and sneering at the same moment. Think
Basil Fawlty in the presence of Lord Melbury. The film, however, included
some rare work of podium greats.

His letter of 1 February referred to earlier films I had sent him and answered a number of questions posed about technique and display and how he
achieved the results seen in his own films. I wanted to know what of his own
semaphore he practiced in advance.

1 Feb 94

☺

Dear Charles
*Recovered more or less from the FLU, allow me to answer, ramblingly and unelec-
tronically, your kind and perfect letters; and to thank you* for the great pleasure
you give me by sending those very fascinating and controversial VHSs. I haven't
dealt with Klemp yet, but the one about "what you always wanted to know about
conducting etc" I have consumed.*
*The bottom line always seems to be: no one on earth can tell you anything ac-
curate or intelligent about conductors or conducting, least of all musicians, critics,*

and . . . CONDUCTORS, including yours sincerely. Why? Because all and sundry don't have the faintest, including, again, me. Mehta, that benighted thug; Christoph von Dutch Nanny, the slob-snob; why even Sir Salty—who oughta know better—and, to my horror, my revered Tennstedt: they all shoot off their mouths to pitiable effect.

The "montage" Karajan / Nazi-parading is in the worst possible taste. Nobody ever seems to get around to Karajan as a musician and conductor (in which rôles he swam circles around other stickwielders like a dolphin around oceanliners) 'cause they are all caught in the commercial part of his image. I feel very deeply that you can only (and even that is very difficult) talk about Maestro X doing Piece Y. Not Maestro X as such. One performance at a time, no generalizations, no anecdotes, no "he was a Nazi", no nothing.

I was glad that Tennstedt got a lot of appreciation. I think he is really very special. To say (as some a..h..e does on the Video) that "he has no technique" is so absurd, it sets my teeth on edge. He has a splendid "technique"; it just isn't (Gott sei Dank!)[104] the kind that any idiot can "learn". But the fact that people don't understand the least little bit about the whole thing at least keeps the discussions going, inane as they are.

It was a relief to find no mention of the earthquake in your bouncy missives. I guess you maybe didn't even notice? That's the real artist! Immersed in his work, dead to the squalor of the purportedly "real" world around him. Great![105]

Wanna hear bout me? I actually conducted something! The Gypsy Baron Ouverture. It was for the opening of the Vienna Philharmonic Ball. It is a great piece and I love it and people seemed to like our rending rendering. (About 4 minutes) (Rent-a-Rendering?) The Ouvert. Is kinda like a TV spot, every couple seconds it jumps to another picture. First, in come the Gitanos,[106] crashbang. Then: careful! Don't sing that tune too loud: it's a forbidden tune. Then, something jolly, then something brutally ethnic; then a blind seer, age 99 1/2, telling (monotonously) the gruesome future; then a cry of "what the hell, who cares", then a lilty walzer, und so weiter. What a genius, old Johann Jr!

I got a decoration, quite a nice one, too. I am now exteriorly decorated. But my interior decoration leaves everything to be wished. I am a silly, empty old coot; but I do still enjoy my food and, yeah!, <u>drink</u>! You betcha! (Evviva C2H5OH!)

Now, seriously: I do so very much hope that you and Hilde are in robust and rambunctious good health and that all your best laid plans flower into what you hoped they would and that life is treating you swell.

Your grateful old penpal and Video-Tapeworm

[address stamped]

Carlo(s)

(le pooch d'Emilie)

My reply went over on 8 March. I was disturbed by his "silly, empty old coot" comment, but didn't know how to reply. I wanted to address the insecurity within. The furthest I could go was

> Your remark hit home. I didn't know if it was a throwaway line or something you wanted to talk about. If it is a trespass to ask about such personal things, please forgive it and I'll forget it.
>
> But if ever you need / wish to know how deeply you are admired and honored, please hear it from me and ten hundred thousand others. And if you don't know how you have conjured the warmest affection, well, just ask. Cause your wonderful letters, heart and humor have done so. You had my greatest respect the first moment I saw you work. Now you have friendship too, if you want it.

I invited him to visit us in California, promising to pick him up at the airport in an actual Kleiber automobile and run him around "the Napa and Sonoma valleys for wine and champagne, around San Francisco for the spectacle, and down to Monterey, Carmel and Big Sur for paradise. After that you may see whales in the wild, condors on the fly, or monkeys in tuxedos. It's all here."

I reasserted cookie bribes and told him about a brilliant composer friend, Jason Sherbundy, whose latest work was stolen from his car. I had to help him reconstruct it in time for a recording session.

This long letter offered to write a song for him. "Hilde will play it for you on her gamba. I will accompany on harmonium, and you can sing the German translation. How's your German, anyway?"

31 III 94

Dear Charles,

Foist of all, flippantly, to avoid my everready tendency toward maudlinness (I know there's no sech woid) I'll take a rain cheque on your affectionately offered spiritual support. Merci beaucoup, mon ami.

Second: your sleepy young composer's adventure reminds me of a cartoon I saw in a British paper. A shop, selling antiques, has been burgled. The policeman inspecting the scene says: "They must have been experts. They didn't steal a thing." How proud your Student must be . . . unless of course his thieves weren't experts . . .

Thoid: it's beyond me that you, after having purportedly studied KOURY, made all those surprised noises some time ago re-orchestral seating. You know, seconds to the right of them, firsts to the left of them, into the valley of death . . . theirs is not to reason why, theirs but to do or die, and so on . . .[107] I just wonder, where do you deposit your frontal lobes when you read that kinda stuff, huh?

I thank you ever so much for the noo VHSs (Goiman Raydiow Orchs. Et al) and wonder, again, what they tell you; unless your German is as good as mine. Mine's wonderful, incidentally. Enjoyed old Isserstedt and (a lot) Adorno who, as you know, did all the music bits in Mann's Dr. Faust. Of course Tommy put the poetry and mystery in, sans which it weren't worth the trouble reading.

I answered your missives so late, on account of I was in Vienna until yesterday, doing 3 Rosenkavaliers at the Grand Old Opera. A fun thing we will re-do in Japan in Sept-Oct 1994, 6 times, to the elation of the natives.

Am happy and relieved to hear that you were not seismologically jolted in your log cabin, far from the madding mob.[108]

Your scenario: CK arrives in CA, climbs into a Kleiber and is given the VIP treatment, scenic routes, madrigals, gambas, etc by Hilde and Charles. I think I will take you up on that. Sounds out of this world!

Woof, Woof, says Carlo, frantically wagging his tail instead of his baton.

That's all folks. I'll be back. Take care.

Don't forget me. Love to Hilde.

Be good.

Affectionately,

Der Alte Karl

Carlos

I replied a few weeks later, saying little, but for reasons I no longer recall sent along the first page of Chicago Symphony and Carnegie Hall programs from 1904. Hearing nothing in reply, on 4 April I sent a postcard asking if everything was OK. I followed with a "Hot Damn" on 19 April, congratulating him on his recent *Rosenkavalier*s. I also played defense about the Koury, telling him that reading K was good but asking CK was better.

This letter's films included the whole of the remarkable Hearst-Metrotone Newsreel archive, and asked his comments about same, per usual. The same reel included Szell rehearsing Brahms 3 from 1957 and Munch leading Beethoven 4 with Boston in 1961. It also included a very funny (and impressive) sequence wherein Munch lost his baton during Mendelssohn's "Scottish" Symphony and retrieved it out of the air. This sort of mishap occurs with conductors all the time, but I've never seen anyone play fetch quite so well. I also pursued the idea of Carlos's visit to California, tossing in allure talk about Yosemite and Jack London's house in the Valley of the Moon.

On 25 April I sped over a Far Side cartoon of Dog No. 24 working at "Anderson's School for Seeing-Eye Dogs." The critter was leading a blind man up a ramp toward a Boeing, and one of the adjudicators says, "Well, scratch No. 24. He did pretty good, though—right up to the jet engine test." On 2

May I posted a photograph of skater-muggerette Tanya Harding autographing a Wheaties box.

3 May '94

Dear Charles!

Thanks for tape #24. Hey, incidentally, do send me your fax Nr.: I occasionally have access to a machine and might send a letter off that way sometime. Well, re-tape 24: Szell's speech was ugh! His rehoissal = 0.

Hearst-Metrotone Archives: Sorry, didn't identify anyone you didn't. All in all, a tape to fast-forward, no? Then Munch with L. v. B. #4. (I loved the bit) in the Hearst-tape where, by din't of waving too crazily, his baton takes off and he just barely manages to catch it! (Serves him right!) With the IVth he, or rather the band, does some good, straightforward things with the music. Sometimes, at least. He must, however, have taken a lot of time and patience to get used to.

PS Trumpets and Tymp too loud. But OK.

Your defence of your frontal lobes is pathetic*!!!* ["pathetic" in box]

Who cares about CK's "opinion" when the seating was "written for" by the composers? I was (thanks for the NY Times reviews) never very rattled by Simon; but at least he put the seconds on the right, like the fella (Mahler) said.

Boodle (I rhyme him with poodle) is an asshole if there ever was one. I can't bitch about Bitchkough, tho': never heard (of) him.[109] I took it on 'cause we will (if God wills) go to Japan with it. And Japan (especially the food and the Shiatsu) appeals to me.

Will think about going to California, gee, thanks! I'd love to eat stomped grapes in a mud bath while listening to an opera. That's a polyphonic dream*! Re-Zauberflöte: the only decent disc is Beecham's. (1/2 way, at least.) But everyone drags the tempi + or -. Beecham's OK + singers!!!*

All the best,

Yours, Charlie

Affectionate noises also to Hilda.

P.S. do the "Geharhischte" in [sign for cut time]*, meaning 2x as fast as usually done. (Father's advice) dann stimant der übergang "mich schreak + Kein Tod"*

PPPS: of course Jason's thieve's wasn't no experts: they kept the music! (And sunk the car in a canyon PDQ.)

PPPPS Le Boeuf Dutoit ("Von den Dach") is pretty shitty. But nowadays anything goes.

Mine of 15 May contained a film I had been searching out for a long, long time. I knew it would excite him, and so I began with "Dear Carlos, Good news—skip my letter and head right to the tape." It was Pierre Monteux at eighty-five leading the Chicago Symphony in Beethoven, Berlioz, and Wagner. Once again I asked Kleiber to teach me what there was to be learned from Monteux's work, his baton, his eyes.

I confirmed that the Hearst material included the earliest known sound film of Klemperer, from 1936. Because he seemed to want to speed up our conversations I arranged a fax machine and gave him the number. It ended with thanks for his advice about *Magic Flute* and offered a Karajan rehearsal from 1965. His next was the first of numerous faxes.

Attention Dr. BARBER

24 May 94

Dear Friend!

What a JOY! GEE WHIZZ! Thanks, thanks, thanks!

> *I've always adored Monteux but had never seen him conduct. I can't tell you what this has meant to me. It has overthrown so many preconceptions of mine that my mind is literally littered with debris, flotsam and jetsam, pulverized securities, etc.*

> *To make this bearable, I'll rationalize ruefully for a miserable minute or two.*

> *Well, OK, in France (where the guy comes from) the orchestra plays on the beat, yeah, even almost BEFORE the beat. And then there IS this tremendous respect and vitality the Chicago-gang offers him with heart and soul and the almost Mafioso understanding between professionals (in the best nuance of the word) namely 3 professionals, the composer, the CSO and PM.*

> *I just can't get over it. Guess I'll drink some Schnaps and wish I'd been a violin virtuoso once and were 86 years old today and had a walrus moustache and a clear beat and some idea of what I conduct.*

> *Incidentally, H. v. K. conducting a rehoissal of Schumann 4 in 1965 would be awfully welcome.*

> *Love to Hilde! All the best to vous deux. And remember Blaise's: le coeur a ses raisons que le raison ne connaît point.[110] That's always worth considering. Like blazes! (sorry)*

> *toujours vôtre ancien ami*

> *Carlos*

I replied on 3 June, "Sehr ancient ami" and congratulated him (and son Marko) for the fax machine. Tape No. 26 was enclosed, von Karajan rehearsing Schumann 4 with the Vienna Symphony Orchestra in 1965. It is a superb illustration of that maestro's way of hearing, of matching timbre, and of creating the special sound with which he was so identified. (It's required watching for every conducting student of mine.) I also blathered about having just done some recording work in Los Angeles, and then sent along a U.S. supermarket tabloid.

It was (until the Internet) the most peculiar source for U.S. political news. The cover story featured an unretouched photograph of several U.S. senators standing with their fellow space aliens. Mine ended quoting Emily Dickinson's "In the name of the Bee . . . Amen!"

10 VI 94

Hi, Friend!

Loved the Aliens. Note: don't buy Beecham. (Flute) I've discovered it ain't so hot. (Often mannered and kitschy.)

Herbert in rehearsal: Ain't that something? One point always gets me: how he avoids (or don't it occur to him at all?) correcting the obvious things "you and me" would harp on. And he don't get flustered, ever!

I'm in a hurry, but will digress another time, OK?

This is to say

THANKS!

All the best to U + Hilde!

Your old

Carlos

I sent Tape No. 27 and No. 28 on 14 June, with a little "hi" note and nothing else. On 23 June I sent Tape No. 29 and No. 30, graced by "hi2."

5 VII 94

Dear Maestro!

Thanks for the great tapes! Especially enjoyed Mravinsky (Old Smokey) who is irresistible when he smiles. Which ain't too often, by gum.

Would you believe it: I conducted! (A concert in Berlin with the BPH, Coriolan, a Mozart Symph and Brahms IV. I solved the Coriolan-problem by starting it off as Duke Ellington woulda done.)

Maintenant I am practically not here no more: off (if all goes well) to Sardinia for a coupla weeks. Take care, be happy, love to Hilda, most affectionate and grateful regards,

your

Carlos

Out went Tape No. 31 on 12 July, all-Szell, and another very brief note. He sent a thank-you postcard in reply. My next letter, *senza* tape, was written on 1 August. I congratulated him on his work in Berlin and queried the Ellington reference. The letter also rattled away about my work on Siloti, included a copy of his famous B-minor Prelude, and a cartoon about the "Crustacean Liberation Front" at Christmas.

I wrote again on 12 August, with Tape No. 32 and Beecham in Chicago: "You can hear him say 'no repeat' under his breath in the Mozart. Guess he *really* didn't like rehearsing." I also told him about new Furtwängler material, the recent purchase of a powerful new Mac SE computer (whoo!), and a small disagreement with Hilde. I also asked him for a professional contact and offered, in return, "more cookies. Or dog biscuits, if you'd rather." The letter closed with talk of a bike ride to the coast with Mark and of my writing liner notes for a Naxos Berlioz set we recorded in San Diego.

Quoting me, I wrote "On learning that a funeral oration was to be given him by the composer Antoine Elwart, Berlioz on his deathbed is supposed to have said, 'If you must make a speech, I'd rather not die.'" I PS'd mine with "Great exit. On my deathbed, I think I'll listen to the Beethoven cavatine awhile, then repent." His reply answered my last two.

25 Aug 94

Dear Charles,

Thanks galore. Loved "Felix Navidad" etc. Am not well so this is short, OK? BPH extremely responsive.

Re-Coriolan: The Duke and I whipped a downbeat sans upbeat out of nowhere for the start and similar "starts", making it sound like running into a wall at 60 MPH with a Rolls Royce, OK? Orchestras love the challenge if explained. "The Chef's Secret."

Mravinsky's nickname "Old Smokey" was invented by me on account he's a chain smoker. Am enjoying Beechy; but not as much as expected cause he drifts into perfunctoriness too often.

Guessed I missed class when they were doing SILOTI. (If he is a contemporary of Vivaldi, include me out.) Amazed that V. Cliburn is still alive. The hell you say! I didn't go to Sardinia after all. Excuse brevity of missive: the veins in my leg (left) are acting up and I can't sit still for long.

Loads of gratitude and affection to you and Hilde. Get in there and fight if that's what you want. Keeping busy is universally praised. Everyone likes praise for some obscure reason. So? Furthermore it is recommended as a cosmetic and rejuvenator. And there are worse things to do or not to do, no question, eh?

Your old CK

I answered his on 26 August, expressed concern about his vascular problem, and asked for (too many) details. I sent the introduction to an article I had written about Siloti for the *Journal of the Conductors' Guild*. It described Siloti's life at the famous Ansonia Hotel on the Upper West Side of Manhattan. I also told him about plans to convert the Conductors Collection to CD-ROM "so that anyone with a Mac and a mouse can download it." Tape No. 33 included some rare film of the pianists Cliburn, Cortot, and Myra Hess, as well as five obscure conductors.

It went on to describe a recent lecture I gave about old conductors and asked about tempo relationships in *Magic Flute*. It ended by talking about an orchestral parody I had composed (under an assumed name, "Carlos T Sweeney") and performed at school: "Paralysis 29." We gave it in a concert of new music one night. It involved every cliché in the new music/new age catalogue, and then some. We ended the performance by introducing the composer's widow. "She came dressed like a Spanish whore, veiled and fingernailed in black, and ran out of the hall sobbing." The chairman of the department congratulated us on a good joke, and "two composers were really, really pissed and didn't talk to me for a week. I have matured considerably."

6. Sept. '94

Hi! Thanks!

Vein of humour. Humour of vein. Vein, vein go away, come (don't) again some other day. Veiny, Weedy, bitchy.[111] OK, So Siloti is/was great and not Vivaldy synch. Liked the place at table for Liszt. Pity he lacked Kleiberesqueness, póbre hombre. Thanks for the great Cortot article. Herbert v. K, also always warned against "waiting" before the next "one".

Ansonia, o Ansonia! I was (shh!) in love once with a blonde bimbo who lived there. A ghostly apartment that was! Those corridors, endless, empty, spooky. The place almost burnt down once. "Gothic", in the US sense of the word. Shudder!

Ah, the Russians. How come they knew everything? I'm doing Chekov right now (life, times, work) and: WOW! "Wow" goes, too, for Pushkin, Gogol and the rest. Is it squalor does it? Hoo nose . . .[112]

I'll listen to/watch the new VHS when I get back (end of October) from Japan. Ain't got the time right now. Incidentally, Beechy with "Fingal's Cave" is SUPER!

Liked very much the "Bang the Drum" piece from Classical Pulse. What shits conductors are, eh? Except you and me, natch.

Molto Affetto + Grazie

from the old

Charlot

Before I could reply he faxed a PS to his own.

6.9. '94
PS. To earlier fax:
1) no thanks, no Popp.
2) Haven't a clue to M. Flute tempi. Thought I had, once. Illusion. Now sadder and weiser. Sorry.*
3) Musta been great, your P29! Congratulations! The widow! <u>Wonderful</u>!
Relationships, even (+ especially) tempi relationships, give me the creeps. And isn't it, after all, the creeps who declare one tempo for one Mozart opus and derive all the other speeds from it? There aren't enough 4-letter words to describe those guys.
Ah, well . . .
All the best!
Charlemagne

The first reply went out on 5 September and included Tape No. 34, this of Mravinsky conducting the Leningrad Philharmonic in Schubert 8 and Shostakovich 5. The second was mailed on 11 September, and expressed further concern about his vein problems. I also joked about the woman at the Ansonia: "Was she a blonde bimbo about 5'6", tough as cheese, and named Macgribaucx? I met her once, but she never mentioned you." Mine also talked about Russian writers and about Tolstoy's wonderful short story "How Much Land Does a Man Need?" which I first read in junior high school and have never forgotten.

I asked my usual questions about how Carlos found tempi, how they create character and mood, and how "Furtwängler seems to have led not by the bar but by the hour." I then asked about the contradiction involved in "how to study hard in every detail, work like the devil in rehearsal, and then keep it new and robust and unexpectable every night." It closed by wishing him well in Japan.

(The following letter is reproduced in the photo section of this book.)

17.9.94
☺
Dear Charles! Thanks for letter!
I'm off to Japan.
No, the name of the bimbo wasn't Macgribaucx. It was Macgribauxc. (Quite someone else, obviously.)

You ask for diagnosis re-varicose veins? Here it is: varicose veins. The trouble is you don't listen. (You're a teacher. That explains it)

Chekov's greatness was his great, great heart* and soul* plus talent*. All inexplicable things, those. And overwhelming.

PS. I don't believe in "working like the devil", even in rehearsal. After all, it's the flaming band that should (want to) play, no? And Furty, well it wasn't the tempi; it was: U and I and the many others (though not all of 'em) are, say, moles, poodles, warthogs, goldfish, etc (which is OK, I guess) and Furty + the like were, say, Giraffes, Whales, Rhinos, Dinos,—oh well.*

—ALL THE BEST
from CK

* Ever notice how some have forearms the size of your thigh? Other dimensions therefore do exist. Also cerebrally. Ain't nothing to do or worry about. There's room for us all. There's just no comparing.

On Halloween I sent him a "Welcome Home" card and Tape No. 35, with a 1972 documentary about Bruno Walter and Willem Mengelberg performing in 1931. As was usually the case now, he replied by fax. (Cartoons and postcards continued to arrive by mail.)

Att. Dr. Charles Barber
3.11.94
Hi!
Thanks for Mengelberg and B. Walter. The Walter VHS drove me nuts with anger. All those beautiful, interesting documents of Bruno conducting—only to be seen + heard in fragments interrupted by history and slobs talking bullshit. How sad that no one wants to hear, say, the Brahms II rehearsal from beginning to end. Or any other item for that matter. Don't we have enough yacketty-yacking all day + night?

Anyone talking about music or musicians makes a fool of himself/herself, even Lotte Lehman and the unbearably impy Yehudi; not to mention Böhm*, etc.

Mengelberg: the stuff isn't his best, is it? The Oberon (too fast and stiff) skips a beat or 1/2 half a beat and old Mengly is almost dopilly self-conscious. But they DO play! And how!

I was in Japan with Rosenkavalier. (This is me, in Japanese [japanese stamped imprint])

Ate so much fish I grew fins and turned to MacDonalds for comfort.

Back here, we have an Indian Summer of sorts; but the cold is hovering in the wings, ready to pounce. How's things with you? OK, I hope.

I'm jet-lagged and weary. I'll stop now. But with best wishes, gratitude and affection, always,
Your
Carlos
* He loathed BW![113]

My reply went over on 13 November. I argued a bit: "I agree with you about the down-side, but here's the up of those talkety documentaries—they often contain *unknown* snippets of beautiful stuff. I think of them as tracer bullets. They help locate the real target." Tape No. 36 included the whole of the extant Brahms 2 rehearsal led by Bruno Walter in Vancouver in 1958 and passed along the usual good greetings from Hilde.

22 Nov. 1994
Hi, Charles!
You've made a tapeworm very happy with Bruno + Brahms II. Just as happy as can be! If I have any "complaint", it's nothing you can do anything about. I'll say it anyway:

1) Pity it's too often non-synch
2) Instead of Bruno's solemnities and sermons, aided and abetted by the idiot ("a ferry goot frend") critic, they could, timewise, have given us the 2nd and 3rd movement, eh?

Oh, well, just 1 and 4 was wonderful.
THANKS A 10 (6)!

No, I ain't been operated on yet (legs) and I may chicken out for the duration. The Viennese have invented a new operation, simpler than "stripping", less damaging. I'll wait till they've perfected it, sure. (at least)

Take care! Be happy! Love to Hilda! Many cari saluti e grazie!
Your
old
Carlos K.

I replied on 7 December with a longish letter and Reiner in Chicago conducting Beethoven and Berlioz in 1962. I was also working up the nerve to ask Carlos for a letter of reference, meant to push along my own career. I told him about a recent all-strings concert in Sacramento, where I had them standing and playing Mendelssohn from memory. On behalf of my tenor friend Richard Margison, I asked if he'd be willing to listen to a tape and told him about Hilde giving a paper on tropes at George Mason University.

It closed by asking about his Christmas plans, and then telling him to "Pick a number from one to ten. Multiply by eighty-seven. Enter figure above my signature. Know that this is the actual number of heartfelt good wishes currently winging your way from California. Enter number here: _____."

On the 9th I sent over another quick note, and Tape No. 38, the extended version of *The Art of Conducting / Great Conductors of the Past*, a BBC project to which I had contributed.

20.12.94

Dear Chas:

Foistofall: Merci for 2 VHS (Reiner, etc)!!

Then: MERRY XMAS ET TOUT LE JAZZ!

 About your tenor (R. Margison) I'll be Frank and Ernest (as always): interest: 0.

 Now to your appeal for "Help". Could you please let me know + or—what it is you'd like me to write? I haven't seen/heard you conducting, now have I?

 As a matter of fact I know you only thru your letters. But, from what I have learned, reading you, you are knowledgeable, witty, generous, kind, dedicated, eager to learn, etc. So tell me what kind of a "to whom it may concern" you have in mind and I'll see what I can concoct honestly, OK?

 Give Hilde my love, too and I hope her paper on tropes just rocks the Masons in the aisles. Thanks for the (I chose 10) 870 good wishes which I echo heartily from Grünwald! (adding 130)

Tout le meilleur (all the best)

from Charlemagne!

"Dear Charlemange," mine of 2 January 1995 began. "Thanks for not being grossed out by my request. . . ." It rambled on about conducting aspirations and the like, and then offered to make contact with specialists at Stanford Hospital who might be able to recommend surgical alternatives for his leg. It continued on about the serious illness of my Los Angeles mentor, Marty Paich, and the passing at eighty-three of Maria Siloti, one of my principal connections to Alexander and his family.

I also told him about a book by Molly Ivins, the cracklingly funny and acute Texas columnist. I quoted her on Gib Lewis, newly reelected Speaker of the House. "'I am filled with humidity,' he said. Then he looked at all the handicapped folks who had wedged their wheelchairs into the gallery, and said, 'And now, will y'all stand and be recognized?'" Great stuff.

The letter also included a *Chicago Tribune* article about Boulez and Tape No. 39: Bernstein, Stokowski, and fifteen immortal minutes of me on the podium, which "I include *only on condition that this horror show will not jeopardize our friendship.*" It included excerpts of me in Beethoven, at a pops concert rehearsal, guest-conducting in Tokyo, and leading *Fledermaus*, "where I made love to Rosalinde from the pit of doom."

Time passed, anxiety arose, and I sent a card on February first asking if he had received Tape No. 39. I was worried that he was not amused.

20 Feb. 95
Dear Charles!
Just back from Milano. Before I left (over a week ago) I received a letter from you in which you seemed very anxious to hear my reaction to "your work," which I would be able to see on a VHS you had sent. Dear Charles, no VHS with you rehearsing or performing has arrived here yet. As soon as it does (if ever) I will rush down to my engine-room, lock myself in with the VHS, and watch and listen, and re-listen and re-watch over and over again; and then run upstairs and write a fax to you, OK?
    I do so hope that all the floods, earthquakes and Simpson-trials (We all know he did it, so what's the fuss?) etc that shook and drenched your neck of the woods have not affected you and Hilda (alias Stan Laurel) at all!
With affectionate greetings and wishes,
Your old Carlos

I replied to his on 22 February. No tape had gone missing before, and I had put a lot of work into it. I asked about La Scala, told him about U.S. media carrying O. J. Simpson all day long, and said Hilde was to be giving a paper on things medieval at a Kalamazoo conference. "She sends best wishes, regards, love, as does her friend."

1 March 95
Dear Charles,
Either the #39 never arrived or yours truly misplaced it instantly and can't find it no more right now. If it's here, it'll pop up only when and if I am not searching for it. THEREFORE: if you are still a glutton for punishment, go ahead, make my day.
    Send 15 min. rehearsal and 15 (continuous) minutes conducted by [musical notation appears here] *poissonally and await an honest appraisal (subjective but forthright) by a recognized hater of 99.5% of all stickwavers. When you send the VHS don't hide CB under a nom de plume, else he'll be misplaced 'cause I'll think it's someone else who can wait, or is dead, or doesn't care a hoot what CK thinks of him.*

Glad you agree Orange Juice done it. I know 'cause Jay Leno* sez so. Love and congrats to "Rin-tin-tin" Hilde![114]
All the best!
Your ole C. K.

P.S. No, I didn't work at the Scala. I received a baton of gold from R. Muti. Nice buffet lunch afterwards.

* Stand-up stuff! I see him almost every evening at 22:30 on Super-Channel. An example: "There was (this is true, no kidding) this guy in hospital to have his left leg amputated; but they cut off his right leg by mistake. Now he's hopping mad!"

I got back to him on 4 March, "impressed with this talk of gold batons. I was once given a baton by a grateful orchestra, but that was in lieu of a fee and weighed three pounds. I donated it to the Museum of Lead." Mine lamented the loss of Tape No. 39 and hinted that the "Tokyo" material was of special interest. "You will even get to see a bit of Hilde." I told him I would send over the "15 + 15" he requested of me at work. "However, Der Alte, I think you're the glutton for punishment in this case—but it's damn nice of you to offer."

14 III 95
Dear Maestrone!
Gramercy for your multiple, cute (and acute) signs of life! Hope the floods, like the earthquakes, have left you high and—not all too—dry?
Sorry, but I can't reveal the fax-# 'cause it isn't MINE and cause the owner of the machine allows me only sending, not receiving. I'm sure you (or, at least, Hilde) will understand?
Kind greetings from
your inveterate secessionist,
Confederate Carlos

P. S. To Confucious it seemed much better to be human-hearted than righteous. (What a loser!)

Because he raised the subject of Lincoln yet again, on 7 March I sent over a little package. Carlos had just faxed an article from *Time Magazine* on Lincoln, obliquely endorsing his own views. He wasn't going to give up, but I was. My package included a white flag on a stick and a fancy card emblazoned with the words "Re Abe—Manus Dedo."[115]

In his reply he had finally seen the AWOL Tape No. 39. Its "Tokyo" sequence was a trick. With the help of my friends Ann, Kay, and Larry Byler, and a fancy editing console in their Silicon Valley home, I sent Carlos a color sequence of himself conducting Beethoven 4 in Japan. However, we made a black-and-white xerox of my own head, in three different sizes. We put that head on a stick and very crudely superimposed it on his own. If he was going to start critiquing my own work, which I welcomed, I wanted to preface it with a visual joke. His was a long letter, single lined, in hand, by fax.

Tuesday 28 III 95
#39 arrived while I was away in Slovenia. Just now I went thru it. By the Lenny Shosti V bits I was (maybe I'm ill or something, in my dotage et al) moved to tears, a rare thing with me re-conductors. His patience with these coolissimo players, his loving and demanding and knowing way with that wonderful music (John Williams' treasure chest, eh?) really got me where it hurts, yeah!

Stokey, on the other hand, was a let-down; but I do like his using a score and beating a clear beat, very tight, only when of use to the players. Yet here he is disappointing because, as so many of the "old guard", he has become a caricature of himself.

Now I move on to the USA and its commendable efforts to lead the next generation into the concert hall and towards so-called classical music. Personally, I don't believe there ever will be a dirth in lonely, pimply youths and spectacled, homely young ladies who will find the classical kick on their own, even in Podunk and unguided! And I believe that it is the unguidedness and the chance (!!) epiphanical encounters (Radio, etc) that turn into genuine love for the great (dead, white) music.

The youngish man, strongly in need of a haircut (!),[116] doing Sousa, Ludwig van, Bat and "the raiders of the lost ark" by Dimitri Williamowitsch (and a pretty lousy IVth L v B in Tokyo,) has my sympathy. The VII andante is too slow, the [musical notes appear here] *shoulda been* [more notes] *according to Walter and yours truly, and there's too much motherly care and concern for stuff that goes all by itself (when unhindered!) involved. But the old CK finds fault with internationally accepted, nay, venerated stick-wavers who also do just that, so not to worry!*

In the Czardas, stylistically, it should always be more [musical notes appear here] *than* [more notes] *I feel. And, when beating 4/4 anywhere, anytime, it should never fall into a calisthenic rut (like Piglet, saying "look at me swimming" sort of thing, if you get me.) but rather follow the phrasing and line.*

Video. I would have needed lots, lots more rehearsal and performance to form an opinion. But "Mr. W!" is sympatico, that he is! That's it for today, folks!

Love to you and Hilde!
Your old
CK

"Dear Carlos E Lee," I answered on 28 March, "the youngish man is grateful for your critique, and is putting together the 15 + 15 you requested three faxes ago. 39 was made pre-Kleiber. What follows will have the gain of post-Kleiber advice." (All very smarmy.)

I argued with him about public school music education. It would be a wasteland without, I said, passed on more hints that he should buy a Mac, and asked what he might want for his sixty-fifth birthday due in July. I thanked him for a package he had mailed over about a conducting competition he wanted me to enter. (I never did.) I also asked permission to quote him describing Richard Strauss's baton technique in a journal article I was writing. It included Tape No. 40, with Beecham and Stokowski.

5 IV '95

Dear, Barberous, Charles

Thanks a 10^6 for good letter, Tape #40 and misc. clippings. I'll look at the #40 soon.

Info: my typewriter is bust. No, I can't manage anything electronic re-typewriters. I've tried, you see.

2) There are no bad orchestras.

3) All orch. go off track when engineered.

4) No cookies, pretty please and no nothing for 65 if you want to stay in my good graces, OK?

5) Knussen had a nice time buying the ranch, I reckon![117]

6) Don't (I believe) believe in bringing Brahms or The Bard or T. Mann or ANY-THING to meet ANYONE; but maybe it's because I hate teachers and teaching, however cunningly disguised. Some Kindheitstrauma, I guess.[118]

7) Please DON'T quote me on RS' beautiful 3. (Incid. it wasn't a dress rehearsal and it wasn't "RosenK". It was some fragment in 4/4.) The remark was silly anyhow, so don't, please.

8) I'd love to see Hilde waving as you type.

9) I'm off to London for a coupla days. Might buy a typewriter there 'cause they have the "Y" where I want it. Here, they have a "Z" there instead, and a "Y" where the "Z" should be. That makes for "How are Zou todaz?" or "I'm a verz layz guz," using as I do the 10-Finger-blind-system. Stress on "blind". That's one of the reasons I can't do computers: the kezs are too lumpz and react too quicklz or doublz or not at all. And I hate being connected to anzthing or (almost) anzone. Oh, well. Affectionate regards from

old Charlz

On 5 April I sent over a bizarre item from Herb Caen in the *San Francisco Chronicle*, apparently true, about a truckload of Roget's Thesauruses being dumped on a freeway nearby. "Police Chief Jim Cost reported that witnesses told officers they were astounded, shocked, taken aback, surprised, startled, dumbfounded and caught unawares."

Meantime the Conductors on Film Collection was growing rapidly. On 22 May I sent Kleiber Tape No. 41, an extraordinary interview of Dmitri Mitropoulos on CBS television, with Edward R. Murrow. The same film included Mitropoulos rehearsing De Falla's *Homenajes*, a film from Australia about Riccardo Muti, and a film of Klemperer conducting Beethoven 6, in stereo and color no less.

I also told him about the recent acquisition of a film of Kleiber himself conducting in Mexico. Would he like a copy? I ended by telling him I had just signed to do *Merry Widow*: "I was scared at first, but once I realized that all the big tunes begin soh-doh-re-mi I figured I could probably learn that stuff real easy."

29.5.95

Dear Charles,

Thanks for the Mit- Mut- and Klemp-video. The orchestra seemed very uninterested, even surly with Mitty.[119] The piece "Homenajes" aint so hot. Funny no one pronounced it right, not even M. Guess there were no hispanics around, eh?

Muti is a sweet guy and my personal friend. So I won't think of anything snide to say about him. (Now isn't THAT something, Carloswise?)

Though Klemps temps (I've only heard the first two movements of the "Pastorale") are slow to the point of near standstill, the attention of the orchestra and the sound they produce are lovely. I particularly like the fact that Klemp seats the strings like it should be. A rarity nowadays, unfortunately for the composer.

London was just a holiday kinda thing. No music, merci. The veins are holding up OK, thanks. Thanks for reminding me of Napa, Sonoma, Twain, etc. It has set me thinking about it again. Maybe I'll accept your kind hospitality sometime when you're least expecting it.

Oh, please, YESS! DO send me the Juárez thing. (It was 1981, incidentally) And, when you have edited yourself to smithereens on your "Barberconducts" VHS, send that too. The Franck symphon. in D minor is one of my most hated pieces. I loathe it. But maybe you made it work, quién sabe.

If there was a blonde bimbo in that Mexican thing, then it wasn't the WPH. By the way, how's your eyesight?

"Lustige Witwe"[120] is NOT easy, mein Freund!

Please give my love to Hilde, will you? And you, you take care, don't worry, be silly!

affettuosamente,

Carlos

His last had been typed, and my reply of June first began "Dear Carlossus: Whoa!! Is the Smith Corona Silent back?" I talked about Klemperer, Toscanini, and the interconnection of age and tempi. Much of the letter was teasing. "My eyesight is great and highly imaginative. I'm convinced our blonde bimbo is in the flutes, fourth from the right, winking like a pulsar." I told him he'd have to give a bit of notice if he wanted to be picked up at the airport in the old Kleiber autocar.

There was no reply. I had been worrying about his leg and whether or not anything as deadly as a thrombosis might be developing. I wrote again on 13 July asking if everything was OK. "If you've done the surgery and are feeling too punk to write, phone me collect at . . ." It PS'd with the promise of a film of Lucon with the Berlin Philharmonic, in wonderful shape and dating from 1931.

20 July 95

Esteemed + erudite old pal!

Goddamn, I thought I'd faxed you ages ago about the Mexico thing. Didn't I tell you, for instance, that the date was wrong on your menue, the paper that goes with the VHS? I wish it was YOU, for a change, whose sclerosis beat mine. Did it? Confess! Well, OK, just in case: thanks for the Mexico VHS in which I didn't like the conductor, nor the tempi nor the garrulous Hispano-lady; BUT: it is a souvenir and, as such, very appreciated, thank you!!

Now to your letter of 13.7.95. Who the hell is LUCON? (Berl. Phil. 1931)? I'm getting too dense for all but the most transparent whimsical abbreviations, don't ya know.

So you're reading the Lustige Witwe. From what? In my days of yore, there was no such thing as a score of anything by Lehár. Apparently he didn't want scores of his pieces in circulation cause he was afraid his orchestration-secrets would be stolen. But you have a score, do you? Wow! Maybe some Kalmus slave one day sat down with the orchestra parts and reconstructed a score therefrom, hoo nose. I had to do with the vocal spartito, poor me. I hated "hoppa, hoppa Reiter" but otherwise the piece isn't so bad. I love the "Koenigskinder" bit where Danilo goes all gooey-proud-offended-debonair.

Listen, Charlie, don't constantly rattle my chain about my leg, OK? If and when there's any news de ma jambe, I WILL let you know. Just forget about it til then, like I do.

I was in Sardinia (Torre delle Stelle, near Villasimius—accent on the mius— east of Cagliari), for the better part of 3 weeks. Crystal-clear ocean waters, sunshine, pasta, fruit, wine and all that jazz, staying at a millionaire's wonderful, secluded villa with 2 pools and direct access to la mer. I am now ready to buy the farm:[121] nothing better will ever happen to me. AND I've seen Naples, but that was nothing to write/fax home about in comparison.

I was flown back and forth in a huge, brand-new private jet worth 25 million dollars (eat your heart out, s'il vous plaît) with just me and a lucious, 20 year old blond (don't mention it) de mon choix (OK, so I am a Dirty Old Man) Grisette. Arriving in the land of Sardines, I was dismayed to find there were no cars with automatic transmissions for rent. Then what? I never drive those clutch-and-shift things. BUT I DID!! (bravo, Maestro!) And as soon as I stopped shifting from second into fifth gear (it was a tiny Alfa Romeo) and wondering at how feeble the Macchina was, all went well and I felt positively youthful, kinda like The Last of the Red-Hot Lovers, you bet!

Music? Pah! Scores? Get out! Work? . . ., . . ., . . ., . . .!

Now don't get me wrong, please. I am a serious person. An intellectual, in fact. Hahahahahahahahahahahahahahahahahahahahaha! Una risata di cavallo! (a hoarse laff) Then, at this incredible place, there was a cuppca cook (right out of one of those post-war neo realistic Italian films, de Sicca etc) and a slightly soused gardener (Not John Eliot) to take care of (almost) everything with Sard(on)ic good humourdness.

And the FOOD! Le FODDER! (It's a wise child that knows its fodder) OUT OF THIS LE MONDE! Now here I am, back in Greenwood. . . . Was it all just a Dream? Did it really happen? Are those funny little books scores? Oh my God! Don't DO this to me again! Don't worry, be silly

(At this point the Maestro flipped out. Finis.)
Carlos doldrums

I got his fax on the 20th, and answered the same day. Confessing to envy, I corrected the Mexico material, told him about Lucon in Berlin and pioneer German filmmaker Oskar Messter. The same letter also asked his advice about projecting the Humming Chorus in *Merry Widow*, and included Tape No. 43. In my notes I purported that Gualtier Maldé was the soprano in "Caro nome." Big mistake.

I closed by congratulating him on the Alfa blonde in Sardinia and the importance of driving "Babemobiles" in particular ways. It ended by giving him my new fax number and advised that I was off to work in Maine for a while.

After I got back from New England I told him, on 7 August, about my "work" at the Monteux School for Conductors in Hancock. I had shown film of the "portly one," and every student (together with about half the town) showed up to see it. There was a tremendous response.

"Best part: ended up sleeping diagonally in his bed (I'm 6'3" and he wasn't) at the family home, and spending time in his study, itself a museum.

Pictures, albums, scrapbooks, diaries everywhere. Actual batons on a table.
And scores. Not 'Le Sacre.' Lost years ago. But: his own Symphonie
fantastique, La Mer etc etc. Like touching pieces of the True Cross. Great
fun, holy ground, wonderful visit. Your friend, admirerer, and anecdotalist,
Marco Polo."

Fr. 11.8.95

Dear Charles

*Just back from a trip to Ravenna (Italy). I find your kind letter, the VHS and
(not from you) a huge pile of mail, bills, misunderstandings, death-notices (always
the good people, natch), declarations of love (It's a 4 letter word) by 70 yr. old US
ladies, postcards illegibly signed, tax-stuff, etc ad. And so it'll take a while 'ere I
react to the VHS, OK?*

*About the melody "Lippen Schweigen" (Lehár) I can only say: my Dad was at
the première and often told of the hypnotic effect this toon had on the audience,
how they swayed like stunned chickens, etc. Though I've conducted the piece a coupla times, I didn't realize it was HUMMED. . . . The hell, you say? Always. But
my memory is fading, anyhow. Meanwhile, let me remain in your good graces, OK?
Take care!*

Love to Heidi!

PS. Gualtier Maldé is not the name of a singer!!!!! (It's the DUKE's alias.)

I answered his on 1 September. My letter made jokes about Ravenna and
copied out parts of an appallingly bad English translation (Chappell, 1907) of
Merry Widow. I told him about new film finds (Bernstein in 1947, Ansermet
in *La Mer*, Monteux in concerto) and passed along the rotten news about the
death in Los Angeles of Marty Paich. I had worked for and learned from that
mentor over almost a decade. Marty was one of those extraordinarily catholic
musicians able to work in every style and every period. He asked me to come
down to help him and the family at the end. I did so, moving in for a week,
and told Carlos about all of it. This was the first time I had seen anyone die.

On happier topics I offered to trade stalkers and told him about a married
woman who was coming on to me pretty regularly. "Do you wanna exchange
love ladies?" The letter also included a hilarious clipping from the *New York
Times* about Stefan Zucker, the self-described "world's highest tenor."

In the same vein, I wrote about a talented and engaging conductor in the
States, surrounded by a relentless publicity machine that debases his reputation by crass promotion: "In all of history only two conductors have been
named conductor of the year twice. One belongs to history. The other belongs
to . . ." I joked with Carlos about this nonsense and noticed that "when this
conductor walks in daylight, he casts no shadow." Kleiber despised the ma-

chinery of marketing but liked to gossip about it. "Howdy receives your love gratefully, and returns it emphatically," I told him. "You couldn't get out of *my* good graces even if you tried."

The fall passed without reply. I was concerned again that he was unwell, or annoyed at something I said or failed to say. I wrote again on 2 November asking what was up, sending along Tape No. 42-B (his Mexico work, in better condition), and declaring that I had very carefully "proof-read this letter for doctrinal and spelliong error." It turned out he had sent me a fax I never received.

Nov. 7, 1995
Dear Charles
Dya meanta say ya never got heartrending fax regarding my broken foot? (ankle)*
And how it hoit so much I can't write, hardly? Thanks for the Mexico Tape (I'm terrible on it!) and for your great letters and so weiter!
Very affectionate greetings and wishes from the tired, sad, old, bedraggled, foot-
[word unclear], *useless*
Carlos

* May be you sent condolences and I forgot. . . .

[marginalia unreadable]

I answered on 9 November.

"Dear Hopalong," it began, "Nope, I never got no heart-rending fax about broken foot (ankle)*. Yours is the second fax that got eaten by evil electrons. . . . Could you fax it again?" I commiserated about his injury. Because he said he was writing hurt, I made up a questionnaire, asking about the cause of his injury.

I fell down.	Yes___	No___
She fell down.	Yes___	No___
Her husband came home.	Yes___	No___
I respectfully decline to answer on the grounds that . . .	Yes___	No___

I enclosed Tape No. 44, ostensibly meant to cheer him up, and offered "affectionate greetings and fast-heal wishes. Your consoling friend, Jack Kevorkian."[122]

Sometime thereafter he sent along a fax with cheery jokes and greetings. I loaned it to a friend, who never returned it, and so cannot reproduce it here. I recall it being silly and sentimental.

"Dear Carlossus," I replied on 16 January 1996, "your Xmassy fax came just in time. I was about to call the Mounties and send Saint Bernards after you." I prattled on about a concert I had given, the "world premiere" of a clarinet concerto, and told him about a fire at their apartment building that had driven my parents into the night.

He replied on 14 February with a four-page fax that included a lengthy book review from *The [London] Spectator* of 20 January 1996, written by Thomas Fleming. Fleming served as editor of *Chronicles, A Magazine of American Culture*, a journal that tends to take conservative but contrarian views of public issues. He reviewed *Lincoln*, by David Herbert Donald. Fleming's essay was headed "A Duplicitous, Incompetent Racist." Carlos never gave up trying to convince me.

"It is as easy to write critically of Lincoln today as it would have been to attack the memory of Lenin in 1940," Fleming declared. Lincoln "turned the peaceful republic of Jefferson and Jackson into a plutocratic empire."

Carlos's views on the sixteenth American president may be the subject of controversy. He was deeply offended by racist remarks Lincoln made during the Lincoln-Douglas debates, including these: "I am not, nor ever have been in favor of bringing about in any way the social and political equality of the white and black races. . . . I am not nor ever have been in favor of making voters or jurors of negroes, nor of qualifying them to hold office, nor to inter-marry with white people."[123]

Often omitted from this citation is Lincoln's view that slavery was a moral wrong, and so too the Dred Scott decision that legitimized it.[124] Even so, Carlos remained persuaded that Lincoln was a racist and hypocrite.

He agreed with Fleming's sentiment: "I have often thought 'Honest Abe' was bestowed on Lincoln as a frontier example of *lucus a non lucendo*—like calling a tall man 'Shorty.'"[125] Carlos was repelled by fake piety, by moralizing and deceit. For many historians, Lincoln's pragmatism was evidence of smart politics practiced in the service of the nation. For Carlos, it was unprincipled, and intellectually dishonest, beginning to end. No room, even conceptually, was allowed for growth on Lincoln's part. No room, even tactically, was allowed for the methods Lincoln actually employed to win the war. For Carlos it was all butchery. The butcher was not remotely admirable.

Carlos's fax also included a ridiculous letter from one "WBA" of Costa Mesa, California, sent to the Vienna Philharmonic. They gave it to Carlos, and he gave it to me. I suspect he offered it as counterweight to the very dark item about Lincoln.

Mr. WBA had apparently watched the most recent New Year's Day concert broadcast from Vienna. He had a few suggestions. "Strauss," he said, "never wrote an angry note, a melancholy note or a note suggesting of mental imbalance. . . . May I suggest you bring in a bit of the hofbrau haus into the concert hall? You could feature Alpine types in liederhosen and feathered hats; you could have some Fraüleinen with big smiles, big bosoms and big bottoms. Carlos Muti, I think, should be your choice of conductor, for I sense that he is the most experienced in the rollicking, jubilant atmosphere of the hofbrau haus. Most cordially yours . . ."

14 II 96
A 4-Page fax from Charlie Chan
Dear old C Club,
Here something to amuse you. (Motto: God bless America)
 I've given up music, incidentally. But I'll still maybe conduct. That would make me . . . what? a professional?
Love to Heidi,
your
Zubin Maazel

PS This is Valentine's Day or something

Kleiber always drew attention from curious nonprofessionals. They made him laugh and cringe. He was deeply aware his fanatics were out there, although he would sometimes pretend otherwise. I occasionally sent him some of the odder material. One piece stands for many others. "Romy the Cat" advised, "I will just note that to me watching Carlos Kleiber conducting is a pleasure that can be only compared with eating of the skin of a freshly roasted duck."[126]

I wrote back on 26 April to "Zootkin Mehta." "Loved the letter praising Carlos Muti. Awesome tribute! You will not be surprised to learn that its author lives in Orange County, southern California's cathedral of crackpots." I reminded him re Abe that I had mailed an actual white flag of surrender many months before. I also offered to send him a CD I had recently coproduced, this of Bach-Siloti transcriptions performed by pianist James Barbagallo. (Jim died, age forty-four, during the sessions, and the album was left incomplete.)

I sent over Tape No. 45, *The Quest for Reginald Goodall,* a 1985 BBC documentary about a man whom I knew Carlos admired very much. The letter brought him up to date on my *Merry Widow* rehearsals and early preparations for *Magic Flute,* and asked my usual questions about tempi. My offer of armistice about Abe was to little avail.

4.5.96
Hi, Charlie, ya big old facetious ray of sunshine, you!
 Your Siloti and my Abe: we shall have to get used to each other's running irritants, I reckon.
 Bach, all by itself, is already a leaky water faucet to listen to. Busoni and Co. merely intensify the bleep bleep charm. Playing it oneself (trying to,

even) is, on the other hand, wonderful fun. But when some whizz rattles off the welltempered, what just barely keeps one awake is the exciting thought "this is very difficult and I'll never be able to do it. But I'd enjoy doing it if I could. Which I can't." Don't quote me, I'm NEKULTURNY.[127]

Goodall Video (THANKS A 1000000) made me happy and thoughtful. The sweetest man and a great conductor! Perhaps he could only achieve if venerated; and had luck in finding the right ensembles and orchestras for that. He was 100% pure. This quality he shared with nobody. Personally I loathe Pears, "Grimes" and Benjamin B. But if Reggie liked that gay kaboodle, well, more power to him, bless his soul.

Thanks also for sending me the best-seller list with ME (!) on top. WOWEEE! Look at me swimming, as Piglet would say![128]

Ingolstadt was a "Happening mit Herz" and had them rolling in the aisles before it even started. I was pronounced a whore by the press on account of I got payed with a car (AUDI A8, 3.7 liter) and lotsa dough. My public image is now blurred.

I wish you a great "lustige Witwe" and the right tempi* for "Zauberflöte". (* If you can guess the right tempi and have the courage to DU them,[129] that will be a world première, Gunga Din!)

Love to Hilda! AND REMEMBER: ABE WAS A LOUSE!!!
YOUR COMPLEAT MUSICOLOGIST,
CK

"Dear Compleat, just got your fax and many thanks for it," I rejoined on 12 May. "I will send you the Siloti anyway, and at the very least we can admire Bach's sheer survivability, ok? Besides, if I can keep an open mind about Abe you can keep an open ear about Al."

I consoled him for the nonsense in Spiegel about the Audi concert. "They could pay you in monkey paws for all it should matter to the critics," and asked if he had gotten a new typewriter. "Your latest fax looks like an electric." I talked about Abendroth, offered a catalogue of rare pirates, and I talked about Tennstedt and his very poor health. (He would be dead within two years.) I also asked about his current T-shirt size, and thanked him for his good wishes about *Flute* tempi. "I have worked out a complex equation which guarantees accuracy in all such matters. Leibniz."

OK, OK!! YEAH! YEAH! YEAH!
20 V 96 Information
this typewriter is a present from my son and goes by the name of SHARP Q1-110. You make a mistake and notice it, you gotta correct it right off. Mostly I don't unless I write to a King or something. The Spiegel thing (there was worse in the same vein and not as witty, either) didn't bother me a minute.

Pity about Tennstedt; but he doesn't / didn't belong to the cliques that play an exclusive shuffleboard with the available jobs and positions.

No, I don't think I ever got excited about Mr. Abendroth. Hans Rosbaud, perhaps. Both begin with R, maybe that caused the confusion.[130] Yes, Reggie was great. Pity that pipsqueaks like F.S., by observing the miracles of Reggie got the notion that it would be enough to keep your head in the score and beat time. My T-shirt size is XL and/or XXL. If it's an "I Love Bach" ad, don't do this to me.

Incident-ally (oops, I pushed "return" once too often there) assuming everyone is right about Bach except yours truly, that would mean he certainly is a "lily", huh? Now why would anyone want to gild him? Unless they were composers run out of ideas, like Liszt (you can't imagine the spellings I've seen, especially in S. America: Litzs, Lizts, etc) doing all those unplayable whirligiggs with poor dear Schubert and other innocents, Wagon Lits Cook. But please, I'm really interested in the catalogue you mentioned. Arlecchino, was it?

Hey, old chap, give the long-suffering (she MUST be that!) Hilde a big abbraccio from me; and you, get back to your flutes and widows et al, OK? And about Abe, well, I don't believe you are converted yet. So I will proselytize over and over till I get bored with it. That'll be soon, I guess. So rejoice!
—XXX

My answer was dated 3 July (his birthday) but was actually mailed a week earlier, so that the Merry Widow T-shirt would get there in time. "Dear Robert E Incorrigible," it began. "I like the new typewriter. Marko did good. Makes it a wee bit easier to read your faxes, as sometimes they come over a bit faint and I have to ask the young ones to read them to me in the flickering light of churches burning down." This was a reference to a recent spate of church torchings. I told him about our opening night of *Merry Widow* and that a couple of Viennese-accented ladies came up and praised it as being in "the spirit of Boskovsky and Krauss, and 'not at all Amerikanische.' This was evidently meant as a great compliment. I kissed their hands with my international teeth."

Attention Mr. Dr. Charles Barber[131]
Howdee!
Thanks for the beautiful WITWE t-shirt![132]

Please excuse me for reacting so belatedly; I couldn't get at my typewriter because new windows were installed during which period I found my room impenetrable. As I am no longer capable of writing by hand, this delayed me.

You are probably conducting all sorts of things, constantly, and giving lectures to your students and anyone prepared to listen. And all the while

I am as idle as Oblomov. In fact I am Oblomov. My son has become a Doctor of Philosophy, thesis and exams and all that jazz, and we are very proud of him.

I hope you and Hilda are well and happy!

For my birthday I also was presented with 20 VHS cassettes of TOM & JERRY.[133] Some of the musical sequences were breathtaking!

Take care, enjoy life and don't forget me, OK?

your old
Charlie

I answered the same day I got his fax, congratulated Marko on his PhD, asked what its topic was and whether or not it would be published. Per usual, I put a few technical questions, these about balances between pit and stage, and offered more cookies in order to learn more secrets. I pressed to know whether or not his handwriting was a genuine problem or a metaphysical joke.

I also pressed about a performance: "Any chance that Oblomov might consider doing the *Ninth* we talked about a couple of years ago? He could even do it in Russian, for all the world would care. The impact would be stunning. . . . Charles and Hilde would make up special t-shirts for the occasion. Any size, any color." I also offered a Klemperer Beethoven film series, hoping it would inspire him along those lines, and concluded by reiterating the California invitation. "The Kleiber car remains available for touring, and I promise not to sing."

12 VII 96
Dear Charles!
Congratulations on your great WITWE-success!

About balances: I didn't understand the question/problem. But balance, I think, consists of letting (forcing) the orchestra (to) listen to the singers which is done by not conducting clearly. This makes the singers their only help. Please, even had I deserved them, no cookies: they don't travel well, like Italian wine, etc.

Marko's diss: "'Kunst und Mythos' bei Georg Picht: Ihre Bedeutung für die Frage des Menschen nach Wahrheit und Wirklichkeit."

ISBN 3-86064-468-8 (Verlag Dr. Kovac)

Order it PDQ or you'll be on a long waiting list, for sure. . . .

My handwriting is OK by me. Like the doctor turned kidnaper, but who failed because nobody could read the ransom notes, I'm getting illegible for others.

Any films of Klemp, providing they are absolutely sync, are welcome. Thanks for renewing your invitation to California! Quién sabe . . . merci!

Regarding Zauberfloete, I don't relish ANY translations of anything. Never heard A. Potters. (sorry, Porter's) Which reminds me of the two-liners: opera in English is a fine idea. It helps you understand what's boring you.

Yes, the T-shirt fits and gives me cachet and self-confidence. It's a little cold right here now; but I'll wear it without a raincoat when the sun comes out. If ever.

Thanks for the clipping about "my" Beethoven 5 & 7. Guess they go over big on account of they're cheap or something, huh?

Do take good care of yourself and Hilde (The Barbered Bride) & be happy, don't worry (actually, I think you don't worry ENOUGH! Musically, that is.) Take it easy
with the affettuosiest salutis,
Carlos

My answer went back on 1 August. "Dear Wunderkleiber . . . thanks for all things and info," and asked if Marko might consider depositing a copy of his dissertation at the Library of Congress. "It would certainly guarantee the widest possible audience—assuming M actually wants anyone to read it." I talked about a project I had just written on Oscar Levant and his concert music, several mutual friends, my upcoming *Magic Flute* and its splendid Sarastro, Andrew Brumana, and I enclosed Tape No. 46, Klemperer conducting Beethoven Symphonies 1 and 2 in 1970. It is astonishingly slow and noble stuff.

I also made the mistake of telling him that Hilde was off to a boring medieval music conference, "sponsored by Sominex."[134] The letter ended by delicately dancing around the subject of a newly discovered film of his father conducting *Blue Danube* in the early 1930s. I had been asked by Warner/ Teldec to sound him out on granting permission for its release, and I was testing roilable waters.

24 VIII 96
Dear Charles,

Thanks for interest in Dr. Marko who will send copy soon (you asked for it!) and feels very important 'cause of your ideas. It is in Deutsch though, NB.

*Klemp is a delight, like dictation to a slow typist. His secret: * he has worked on the orch. parts and wants what he wanted when he did.*

Hilde's activities are NOT boring, you BOOR! Who is Mackerras? (Don't tell me, please.) No, no Sardinia and no Grisettes this year. (CK pouts. . . .) Glad your Sarastro has good voice. Don't schlepp, tho'. Try doing the Geharnischte in [sign for alla breve]. (EK did) It results in the "right" (but almost never done) TEMPO for what comes later. . . .[135]

Looking forward to Blue Danube![136]

All the best from your CK who is trying, like Yeltsin, to give the impression he isn't dead!
Affetto,
Carlos

I got totally ensnared by *Magic Flute* and didn't answer that letter of Carlos until after another arrived. He also mailed a copy of Marko's dissertation, in book form. Carlos's own letter was typed with uncharacteristic neatness, and only one marginal emendation.

17.9.96
Dear Charles,
This has been a lousy summer, cold, rainy, triste; except, maybe, in Barbados or Athens or something. Here, it was: see above. I've just read a depressing book by one Lebrecht "When the Music Stops", I think is the title. I can only recommend the interesting bits about the days of Adelina Patti and the likes. After that it gets tiresome.[137]

Also I am reading a book by Fernando Pessoa, a dead white Portuguese writer, which would be just one more book by a student of his own navel, were it not for the fact that the man was intelligent and, practically, sexless. The latter is something I appreciate, considering the way sex is flung in one's face partout. Well, this book ("The Book of Disquiet") is all the more depressing for not being dumb, if you know what I mean. So here we are with the bloody weather and 2 slightly nauseating tomes.[138]

I have orders from Dr. Marko Kleiber to send you (without making any silly remarks, he said) his dissertation.* Because, as I had told him, you had expressed interest. Now that the book is released, he likes very much your idea of having it put in the Library of Congress. AND, he says, it would interest him to know if it would be possible for an assumedly interested person in the US to order it under the ISBN number.[139]

I have written the above paragraph rather tremblingly. Tremblingly, because there is no rage (even that of a woman scorned, or what have you) comparable to that of one's offspring when one doesn't do exactly as they say in matters concerning their affairs. I am sure you know how touchy offspring can be when parents, doting or otherwise, mix in, yes? So I just wrote exactly what he asked me to write and left out all my famous charm and wit.

(He particularly hates my charm and wit: he maintains it just isn't, period)

Poor me!

Anyway, you'll do the right thing, I know. And I am grateful, as always, whatever you do, OK?

I hope you and Hilde are in great health and enjoying life!
All the best,
affectionately,
Yours,
Carlos
* Which I think is great, incidentally

On 1 October I sent a long reply to both of his letters, full of *Flute* information and a list of distinguished libraries to which Marko might send his book. I told him I was reading the dissertation ("together with my Langenscheidt") and would send it on to the Library of Congress, which I did two weeks later. I answered his questions about ISB numbers and advised about getting it online. I also told Carlos that the film of his father would be transferred in due course and that I would send it over. Finally, I said that I was now contracted to do *Tosca* in the fall and asked for his advice about problems in it.

The letter included Tape No. 47, *The Art of Singing—Golden Voices of the Past*, to which Hilde and I had contributed a bit of research.

16.10.96
Dear Charles
Thanks a million for:
   1) VHS with singers of yore
   2) your interest and activity in and for Marko (just what the Doktor ordered!)
   3) Your news and good wishes!
   Be sweet to Hilde, take good care not to get run over by a truck or Scarpia or such-like.
All the very best from
your old Carlos!

PS. I have never "done" "Tosca". But I am sure, as always with Puccini (those fast bits you can't read in performance, those heart-rending bits everyone (but you?) knows "by heart" and which don't allow for a look in the score for a clue as to "what's next") it is best, nay, indispensable (spelling?) to LEARN THE WHOLE DAMN OPERA BY HEART.

Always your
Curmudgenous

I went home for Christmas that year, only to have my dad announce over dinner that he had lung cancer, and it had already spread to the lymph system. My letter of 3 February 1997 dealt with such personal matters. It went on to revive the subject of my request for a letter of recommendation. "Also, sprach Barbathustra, I need to ask your help," it began. I was still very hesitant and put it in the most casual terms I could.

The letter included Tape No. 48, with a film of Horenstein (a friend of Erich Kleiber), and remarkable film of Leopoldo Fregoli from 1897 impersonating Rossini, Wagner, Verdi, and Mascagni. On the same video was Willi Merkel from 1911, impersonating Wagner, Johann Strauss Jr., and John

Philip Sousa. The same video included Mengelberg and Mravinsky in identical repertoire. I ended by telling him about recent conducting assignments.

16 II 97

Dear Charlemaître,

Thanks! For letter and VHS! Liked Mascagni (of the impressions) best. What Sousa was conducting was certainly no march; or one by Stravinsky, perhaps? Sorry, but I dislike Horenstein whom I met in Buenos Aires in my teens. I know that "Smelly" (Humperdinck also was, my father told me) is no artistic verdict. But Horenstein was smelly in the non-olfactory dept., too. (Personal opinion, of course)

Sorry about your Dad. Maybe the medical expert is wrong. They usually are, you know!! Can't imagine WHY they have to give the patient such (possibly mistaken) news if the patient feels OK, It could kill a cancer-less person, even. Shitty, stupid doctors!!

Hey! You are doing a lot of conducting. More power to you, sez I!

Charly, dear pal, we've gone thru this before: How can you expect me to say (write) anything about you as a DIRIGENT when I ain't seen or heard you at it?

All I can say at the moment is that you are the most amusing, garrulous, knowledgeable, erudite, friendly, funny, generous, etc etc etc etc person imagineable and that your French is probably emetic, but your English is OK,

But, listen, re-conducting: you are doing such a lot of it already, you can't be lousy at it, certainly not lousier than X, Y, Z and Co. And isn't that what it's about.

"Look at me swimming!" said Piglet. Or was it Roo? Anyhow, THERE'S the rub! By the way, 2 Years ago I gave + or - the same answer and YOU never came up with anything USEABLE in the way of VHSs of you conducting!! Just, mostly, silly-funny Photo-montages, remember?

Loved old Mravinsky! Didn't love Mengelberg.

Spent Xmas and Noo Yeer heer.

"Tosca" do listen to 2 CDs, Sabata and Karajan (the latter, sadly, has the LOUSY tenor Whatsisname) either or both, lying in bed, the whole piece through, often.[140] (No phone calls, lunch calls, interrupts of any ilk). You can conduct to it, mentally or with a finger or two. It'll give you the FLOW and some surprises: you'll run back to the score. But later!

Love to Hilde!

Your old Carlos

Things got worse with my father, and I didn't reply to Kleiber until another arrived in early March. However, I did send over a film of myself in rehearsal and concert with two professional orchestras in California.

12 III 97

Dear Charles

I've been thinking. What with that and the coals you keep heaping on me, year in and year out, and your latest feat: getting my son's tome into the Kleiblary of Kongress, hey! Unless you're sour at me, here's an indecent proposal. To wit:

1) YOU write my letter of recommendation regarding the conductor Dr Barber.

2) You send it to me.

3) I copy it on my typewriter or, better, in handwriting.

4) I sign it.

5) I send it back to you.

Now, how ABOUT that, eh? What the hell, you must be a good conductor or they'd have lynched you by now, surely. Be nice, old chap, and do it MY WAY! Are we friends, or what! Love to Hilde and U, take care!

Your Carlos

PS. If you don't hate me, try to get one of your College slaves to send me "If you love me, don't love me" by MONY ELKAIM, New York: Basic Books, 1990 (I can't get it here and it sounds good.)

PPS I'll be away from Grünwald for 2 weeks beginning 13 III 97

I wrote back on March 20 with more bad news about my father's health, and family news about family complications. I took his *Tosca* recommendations and found de Sabata the most convincing. I sent over the book he requested, brought him up to date on the restoration work being done on his father's *Blue Danube* film (by far the longest film of Erich Kleiber in existence), and also did as he asked re the letter of recommendation. The letter he actually sent, written out by hand, turned out to be a distant cousin to it.

Naturally, I thanked him profusely for doing such an extraordinary thing, and "Hilde thanks you too, hoping that it will lead to my being out of town much more in the near future." His letter of recommendation came in a truly silly envelope he had made up. It featured a large brown cartoon moose in the lower left corner. Inside was a Garfield Cat "Just a note" on a musical staff, and on it the words

How do you like the moose on my envelope? I think his eyes are molto espressivi. And he has the stolid stance of the born maestro. The horns are from his girlfriend. (She got tired of that short tail.)

Semper idem,[141]

CK.

The letter itself, in hand but written with uncommon legibility, follows.

26 III 1997

To Whom It May Concern:

This is a letter of recommendation for the conductor Dr Charles Barber of California.

Years ago, he wrote to ask if he could study with me. I politely said I had nothing to teach; but he persisted anyway. Since then, we have communicated many times about conducting, scores, opera, old conductors, recordings, tempi, phrasing, and personal matters. We have become friends, and he pretends to believe that I have taught him something.

Charles Barber is a scholar and a conductor who adores and understands music. He is also a most amusing, garrulous, knowledgeable, erudite, friendly, funny, generous etc etc etc etc person.

I never write letters of recommendation, so this is an exception. Charles Barber is becoming more active in opera. He also now wants to do a recording series of rare 19th century concert music. I am writing this letter because I want to help him do that.

When you meet him, I think you will feel the same way.

Yours Sincerely,

Carlos Kleiber

[home address stamped]

I wrote back on 16 April, thanking him in particular for the ribald moose. The letter told him about the new phenomenon of websites devoted to him. "There are more than 325 references to you. . . ."[142] He replied with cheery sarcasm.

April 24, 1997

Caro Barberone,

Grazie per fax! Am glad to see my opinion confirmed inter-net-tionally: "CK is the greatest!" (Huh?) No, Dear Charles, don't send no more of those things. Thanks anyway! Yeah, AUDI is great and I enjoy much it. (Anglais?)

Hope you and Hilde are well and happy!

THANK YOU ☺

Semper idem,

vôtre Charles

[home address stamp]

Mine of 27 May thanked him for his, enclosed Tape No. 49, brought him up to date on Hilde's doings and on my own preparing of the "new" Gershwin musical, *Crazy for You* that I would be doing with Jason. (I did not ask his advice about that one.) Tape No. 49 included more of my own rubbish on it and a performance of Takashi Asahina (age eighty-eight) doing Bruckner 5 in Chicago. I thought he would like it. I was wrong. I also asked questions about *Magic Flute* and for criticism of my own work on video.

Unfortunately, a fax transmission problem removed some of the text of his reply. Carlos "shredded" the original, he said in his next letter, and so what follows is an approximation of what he wrote.

> *9 VII 97 (what a date!)*
> *Dear Charles!*
> *Finally I took a gander at the horrible old Jap ruining Anton and,*
> [unreadable] . . . *YOU.*
>
> *"Zauberflöte" bit was undifferenziert in mood (it should change with every mood) and too overtly im Takt. (As opposed to Rhythmus, which is the thing to go for. (Don't we all!)) Beethoven VII, 2. Mov. overphrased like piano teachers want poor little* [unreadable] *kids to. (Sorry, I'm being Frank,* [unreadable]. *The rest of the tape (it breaks off very suddenly) you should look carefully at and watch how the orch. reacts (how sweet of them!) to each of your movements in this rehearsal. If you're perceptive and observing you will see what not to do. (That's about 90% of what you did)*
>
>   *AND: never ask things like "has anyone a B natural at bar x?"*
> [unreadable] *you asked for it!*
> [unreadable] *Trotzdem: affettuosi Saluti to you and Hilda from*
> *your old* [unreadable: could be "conductor"]*-phobic Carlos*

Mine went back over on 7 October. It included an art print of Furtwängler, long overdue for his birthday, and a photo of Hilde and me at Marty's ranch near Santa Barbara. "Hilde is the short one with the sun-burned face who knows how to smile properly." I told him about a most-moving "Vissi d'arte" in our production of *Tosca*, and then pursued an earlier question about "takt and rhythmus." I was not sure about the distinction he was making.

Because the fax he last sent was largely unreadable I mailed it back, asking for a reconstruction.

> *12 X 97*
> *Dear Charles,*
> *Thanks for returning what became of my fax on its way to you. Now I will know better than to fax anyone ever again: I can't make head or tail of it and, as I've shredded the "original", reconstruction is out.*
>
>   *The question about what the difference between "Takt" and Rhythm is, is a tough one even when one recovers from having been* <u>*asked*</u> *to, at all.*

"Takt" is a German word. When applied to music (as opposed to behaviour) it means "Time", usually in the sense of "im Takt bleiben" (staying in time). There's Zwei Viertel Takt (2/4), drei viertel Takt (3/4), Vier Viertel Takt, etc etc. "Im Takt bleiben" means meeting (more or less exactly) on what is being beaten by the conductor (or the metronome) on the [musical notes appear here].

Whereas rhythm is what happens (should happen) "in between"! One can proudly sing/say "I got rhythm" (if one does!!) but "Ich bliebe im Takt" isn't something to brag about! One can almost say that "takt" is a dead thing and Rhythm a living thing. But then again, Rhythm can bring Takt to life. (Vice versa: no go!)

This is the best I can do in answer to your question, assuming I know the answer. Which I most likely don't. (Please don't ask me again about such things. It gives me the creeps!)

Thanks for the snapshot of Mr. and Mrs. Barber! Very "gemütlich"! (And don't ask me to explain "gemütlich", OK? Nobody has ever succeeded in translating that word correctly)

Take care, good luck with "Tosca the Tearful" (I hope she giggles when she's stabbed Scarpia. Through the tears, of course!) and many affetuosi saluti to you both!

Before I could reply he sent another.

28 X 97
DEAR CHARLES!
THANKS FOR THE
FURTY POSTER!
HE KNEW ABOUT
RHYTHM! YESSIREE!
HE ALWAYS SAID:
"ES BEDEUTET NICHTS
WENN ES NICHT RHYTHMUS HAT!"
LATER, AN AMURRICAN
TURNED THIS INTO:
"IT DON'T MEAN A THING
IF IT AIN'T GOT THAT SWING"!
ALL THE BEST!
YOUR OLD
CHARLES K.

"Dear Carlos, I'm glad the Furty poster arrived," I replied on 21 November. "Stayed up to walk in a midnight storm. Thanks too for the letter about *takt und rhythmus*, and sorry my question gave you the creeps. . . . Tosca was a knock-out. I know the teary spectacle must seem ghastly / preposterous in cold print but—no kidding—it was terribly moving at every performance.

The audience was struck dumb by the truth of her sobs, and I had to wait until Cynthia gathered herself. The silence was stunning."

Gunther Schuller had just published *The Compleat Conductor*. "Jump to the next para **immediately** if you don't want to know that he describes you as an utterly unique and 'perfect conducting machine.' . . . There. Enough." I ended by offering film of himself conducting *Otello* and *Bohème* in Japan, and "the usual haystack of good wishes from California."

He replied five days later with another postcard. This was of a lovely Japanese pond, The An-min-taku, a pond "for pondering," he wrote.

Caro Barberino and Co. Ltd!
Congratulations re- Tosca! (Puccini always said "Main thing is: everybody sobs!")
Please send no CK videos, Japanese or otherwise! ("ALL I NEED IS LOUVRE")
  Incidentally: Bless Mr. Schuller's heart! Yeah!!
  MERRY XMAS AND A HAPPY NEW YEAR!
Dies wunsche Ihnen und den Ihren,
Ihr Carlos, die perfekte Dirigiermaschine.

Meantime, my father's illness was nearing its end. He asked me (and my sisters) to come home and be with him at the end. While making those arrangements, we learned that my mother's cancer had returned. Each was given only weeks to live. I drove back that fall and stayed for five months. During this period Carlos and I exchanged wholly personal letters. He was very kind. I also brought the Mac and my research boxes and started writing the long-delayed Siloti book. I wanted to do something more pleasant than hearing my parents cough to death. I kept Carlos apprised and appreciated his warmth and sympathy.

After both funeral services we closed up the estate. I drove back to California and returned to conducting. I next wrote him in May, bringing family updates and news about the prospect of doing Offenbach. I also told him about an all-state orchestra I had been asked to lead and the extraordinary talent of its members.

24 V 98
Dear Barbiere,
  1) Nice to hear from you. (18 V 98 letter)
  2) Very Sorry about your parents.
  3) Hope it's Orpheus in the Underworld you're doing, and not . . . . . oh God!
  4) Re-Cal. Honor Orch: What!? 1300 applicants for 110 positions!? And how many applicants for the one position at the rostrum? "Not a dog in the bunch".
  . . . Hmm.

5) My interest in Siloti knows bounds. (The little you once sent went the whole way!)

6) Don't, please, send Mengelberg, Klemperer, Art of Cond II, nor Carmen 1978. Thanks!

7) The AUDI is still rolling along, singing a song. Also the 3 BMWs.[143]

8) Family contented and well. Weather so-so.

Best wishes to you and Hilde,

molti cari saluti,

yours truly,

(in a hurry)

Carlos Kleiber

PS. The European Union and the impending Euro (currency) are one big pain. Except for the industry and the banks.

For the next many months I worked flat-out on the book. I was reliant on Russian translators, and spent countless hours with them. At the same time, I was making a publishing deal with Carl Fischer to release Siloti's music in a new piano anthology. Similarly, I negotiated with Klaus Heymann at Naxos Marco Polo for copies of the Bach-Siloti CD we had recorded. It all came to pass, but took much—much—more time than I had planned. I wrote Carlos to tell him about all this, but he expressed little interest. We then corresponded on another personal matter.

In May 2000 I came across a contrarian essay about Lincoln I knew he would enjoy. I sent it to him, with a little note of remembrance and good wishes.

28 V 2000

Caro Carlo!

Thank you!

A valuable addition to my "Lincoln was a Louse" collection!*

(I can still use a little help on another louse: Mohandas Karamchand Gandhi.)

Kicking against the pricks (Apostles 9:5) may be hard; but it's fun, hey![144]

Wishing you all the best,

Curmudgeony Carlos

* Just imagine the American Indian in Africa!

PS. Tried to fax this note: didn't work.

Barberfax: 001-650 967-5———

I answered on 25 July 2000.

"Dear Curmudge: Thanks molto for yours, and sorry to be a turtle in reply. I just got off a ten-week stint doing 'Grafin Mariza,' the old Kálmán thing you may know or even have done in your forbidden youth. We had a very good time with it. And before I forget, but with no further reference to the day, happy July 3. Hope you stayed inside—cold sober—the whole time."

I then told him I would be "working" on my first *Rosenkavalier* in the fall, with Sir Charles Mackerras at the San Francisco Opera, and asked questions about tempi, character, performing editions, and the like. "Any heads-up from you about Rosen-dangers would be most welcome." And a hint: "If you've got a moment go see Woody Allen's 'Small Time Crooks,' a feverishly silly and funny film. You'll love the joke, Lovitz to Allen: 'They were being sarcastic!'"

1.8.2000

Dear Charles,

Thanks for your letter and for your good wishes!

ROSENKAVALIER. Assuming you've bought the score revised by Clemens Krauss (copyright assigned 1943 to Boosey and Hawkes) and are following Mackerras' rehearsals with that in hand: there are many mistakes in the score, but there are 1001 times more [underlined in red ink as well] *mistakes in the orch. parts!* [also underlined in red ink, including the exclamation point]

In most of the "played" orch. materials some of the worst mistakes have been corrected, but never [also underlined in red ink] *all of them! (Unless—ahem!—I* [again, underlined in red ink] *have used the materials. . . .) There are also many (also text.) differences twixt the vocal and the full score. (The latter is "right.")*

A little "joke": Just for fun, take a furtive look at the part the 1. bassoon is playing from. If, in the last bar of Act 1 the [musical illustration] *isn't there (and nobody has pencilled it in), say to the conductor: "I can't seem to hear the bassoon's B flat in the last bar of Act 1" He (the conductor) will hate you instantly! (It means he's deaf!)*

Good luck with Siloti, love to your spouse, take care of yourself!

Yours ever, Carlos

P.S. [running vertically on left margin] *No need for any more lowdown on Mahatma and Abe: I have enough already to despise them thoroughly! (Thanks anyway!)*

P.P.S. [running horizontally at bottom of page, and then running vertically on right hand margin] *The last note (Trumpet solo) of the second bar after |31| in Act II should be E flat. And, 4 before |33|, Sophie's last note: D flat! Only musicologists choose E* [natural] *and D* [natural] *(sounds awful!) And there's no # on the last note of the horn, 2 bars after |34|, eh? Ha!*

In his letters Carlos often included cartoons, weird newspaper clippings, and the like. A typical example? In this envelope Kleiber included material from *The New Yorker*. It consisted of a Booth cartoon on one side and a Sipress cartoon on the other. The Booth older lady addresses her uninterested, newspaper-reading husband and their vaguely interested dog: "I am going to SoHo. My doshas are all out of balance. Well, my kapha is hunky-dory, but my pitta and vata are out of whack. Today the practitioner is going to get rid of all the stress with geranium, ylang-ylang, bergamot, and patchouli, and, of course, a little time in the steam tent."

The Sipress cartoon was set in a Middle Eastern locale, on a bench, in current times. A seemingly Jewish fellow addresses an apparently Arab fellow: "Why is it we never focus on the things that unite us, like falafel?"

I wrote back on 13 November with photos of me and my new car (a glorious old white Jaguar) and an update on Rosenkavalier. The bassoon's B-flat was, indeed, missing and "I won a smile from the bassoonist because he likes that note and dutifully entered it in his part." I also told him about the wonders of Susan Graham as Octavian and that I had just opened a nine-night run of Sondheim's *Merrily We Roll Along*, his musical that runs in reverse, opening in the present and unfolding backward over twenty years. "A typically difficult Sondheim score, full of sustained syncopations. Jason has been very helpful, per usual. Very kind audiences are coming, thank gawd. I will not send you a video." I ended with automobile jokes, and "I hope this finds you exceedingly well and whistling a happy tune where 'ere you walk."

My PS consisted of "A joke to equal your cartoon."

Q: Why did the Siamese twins move to England?
A: So the other one can drive.

Another brief and personal note followed. Then on 20 February 2001, I told him about my newly acquired fax and phone numbers and that I was shortly doing *Gianni Schicchi* and *Pagliacci* in a double bill.

My concern is the Commedia in Act 2, and how to communicate the looming reality of the play-in-play. I want to show the horror of it. There must be a moment when Nedda *knows* that there is *no way out,* that all previous charms can no longer save her. . . . I don't know if you've read about it in the München press, but there's a dreadful story in SF about a young woman who was killed by two vicious dogs in the hallway of her own apartment building. There must have been a moment when the victim knew she was not going to survive. In Pagliacci we need to convey the same fear and inevitability. This, at least, is how I read the story and want to lead its music. Any ideas?

He didn't reply. I wrote again on 25 June 2001.

> Dear Carlcurmudge: A video I've been searching out for years has finally come in, and I want you to have a copy. You'll have to accept it as a birthday present: Von Karajan in Tokyo, with the Berlin Phil on tour, 1957, complete, in a surprisingly good kinescope, though a few missing seconds from the top of Beethoven 5 are covered by stills. His reading is surpassingly wonderful. And wow! What line and form and fashioning in this man's stick. I remember you telling me he was like an ocean liner among dolphins. The image remains. His transitions, especially in the Strauss and the Beethoven at the end of ii, and from iii into iv, are miraculous. Anyway, yowsa from me to you, and I hope you enjoy these religious artifacts.

I also brought him up to date on other conducting activities, present and planned.

> *3 VII 2001*
> *Dear Charles,*
> *Thanks for the excellent Herbert v. K. tape and for your kind birthday wishes.*
> *Congratulations on your Jaguar and all that conducting! (When you do an opera at the SF Opera or a concert with the LA Philh., do send me the reviews. Would interest me. . . .) Re—the ocean liner versus the dolphins, you misunderstood: for me HvK was the fish, not the boat! The point was . . . oh, what the hell.*
> *Wishing you and Hilde all the Best,*
> *Yours,*
> *Carlos*

In the fall I sent along an essay about Dickinson and a few meaningless jokes. The same package included an absurd article on "How To Opera."

> *4 XII 2001*
> *Dear Charles,*
> *Many thanks for the lowdown on Austin + Mabel![145]*
> *Anything that has anything to do with ED is always more than welcome here. Hope you are well and happy, and wish you all the Yuletide joy possible!*
> *Always the same old*
> *Carlos*

I took up work on a number of conducting and several recording projects, and more writing work. It was months before we corresponded again.

On 3 December 2002 I sent over Monteux in his only known film of Stravinsky, leading *Petroushka* with the Boston Symphony. It was a long time in the finding, and I hoped he would enjoy it. I also told him about its provenance and asked him to tell no one I had given him a copy. The same note included Christmas greetings and a few words about things family and personal. I also told him about helping plan a new opera house in northern California and about concern for the pit and the hall's acoustics.

His reply had two return address stamps on the envelope, one of them upside down. He even indicated (apparently) the time of day he wrote it.

10/12/02, 15:40
Dear Charles,
Yuletide is upon us and waking towards Xmas—the which I wish you and Hilde merry and bright.

Thanks ever so much for the Monteux VHS. Monty was one of the genuine Dinosaurs and certainly one—of the 2 or 3—most adorable and simpático. Performance: precision breathtaking. Orchestra superb. Pity they didn't (the filming team) focus more on the beloved walruss.

VHS: big secret, eh? But the Japanese will come out with a "Best of Monteux" PDQ, wanna bet? And Petrouschka will be on it.

Kill me if you wish, but the piece itself doesn't do to me what it is probably supposed to, je regrette infiniment. (Anyway, I couldn't dance to it unless you fired a six-shooter at my boots.)

My Audi, now 7 yrs old, is doing great except until today, when he refused to start. Looks good, tho'. If you can tell what does (and doesn't) work in concert hall architecture, you must be the only person in the world.

Take care, keep well, try to conduct like Monty (if at all), and don't underestimate "Cosi". . . .
All the Best!
Carlos

In early 2003 I sent Carlos a note: "Dear Carlos, As you long suspected . . ." I had been in the local supermarket and had seen by the checkout scanner a tabloid "exclusive." In large type, with an authentic unretouched photograph from the 1860s, ran the lead story: "ABRAHAM LINCOLN WAS A WOMAN!" Inside, over two pages, more photographs of this long-suppressed fact and a set of explanations from "leading historians" accounting for Abe's ruse. I sent it over by the fastest mail possible.

17 II 2003
Dear Charles,
Thanks for the adorable Lincoln-article!

Hope you are well and contented!
All the Best,
Carlos

P.S. Dontcha have no fax # anymore?

Included in his reply was a clipped *New Yorker* cartoon, by Gregory, with a balding executive behind a desk, talking to a speakerphone: "I don't want to hear 'can't'—you find out where the Special Forces are deployed, and you send them some goddam muffin baskets!"

Toward the end of June 2003 I sent a birthday card, planned to arrive 3 July, and the present of a magnificent sweater with Wilhelm Furtwängler on it.

A brief note from him followed. Thereafter, our correspondence was wholly personal, and unrelated to music. And then, no more.

NOTES

1. Author's interview, 3 June 2005.
2. "Riding is good in those cars."
3. "Closed door."
4. A hot dog stand at Columbus Circle, near The Met. Kleiber would know this. I wanted him to be impressed that I did too.
5. I was doing my doctoral work on Messiaen's symphonic masterpiece at the time.
6. This might not be so. John Tooley reports that he and Carlos together attended a rehearsal of Bernstein leading *Tristan* in Munich. Tooley's memory has a zany angle.

> I saw Lenny in his room, and he asked me to come to his rehearsal. When I got there Carlos was also present. We sat together, but I told him I couldn't stay long as I had a plane to catch. "Don't worry," insisted Carlos. "I have this great new watch. It has an alarm. I'll set it, then you'll know when to leave." "I'll do no such thing," Tooley answered. "It will make a big noise and bother Lenny." Carlos thought a moment. "All right, I'll sit at the end of the aisle. When the alarm goes off Lenny will turn around and see you getting up to go. He won't blame me at all!—Tooley, author's interview, 3 June 2005.

Further to the relationship between Bernstein and Kleiber, in Box 32 of the Leonard Bernstein Collection at the Library of Congress, there are two items of correspondence preserved. The first is dated 17 October 1989. In this note, Kleiber tells Bernstein that his son Marko is a great admirer of Bernstein and is busy translating Bernstein's tapes/commentaries on *Romeo and Juliet* into German. He then asks Bernstein to autograph a CD of *West Side Story* that was apparently sent with the note and return it to him either at the Metropolitan Opera or the Carlyle Hotel on East Seventy-sixth Street. The note is on Carlyle stationery. The second is a note from Bernstein's assistant dated 21 September 1990 saying that Kleiber had stopped by Bernstein's apartment at the Dakota, but no one was home and he sends his best wishes and hopes for a quick recovery. James Wintle, Reference Specialist, Music Division, Library of Congress, e-mail to author, 3 January 2011.

7. Vice President Quayle was, until the ascent of Sarah Palin, considered the dumbest person ever to seek national office in America.
8. Kleiber is referring to the standard beat pattern used in the trade to show time. For an excellent discussion of the matter, see "Conducting" in *New Grove 2000*, or essays on same in the *Cambridge Companion*.
9. MM = Maelzel's Metronome, the first device (patented 1814 by Johann Maelzel) which reliably set musical pulse. Beethoven used it, retrospectively.
10. A very early electronic instrument, developed by Russian scientist Lev Termen/Leon Theremin in 1920. A recording by Theremin's student Clara Rockmore, released as Delos CD 1014, is the best ever made. Stokowski once gave a concert with twenty of them.
11. This appears as Tape No. 1 in appendix C.

12. I believe that Carlos refers to the natural and modest style advocated by Lao Tse and compares it to the imperial style of Toscanini.

13. Carlos notes the differences between the Euro-PAL/SECAM and North American-NTSC systems.

14. Mozart's opera *Abduction from the Seraglio*, 1782.

15. Will Lacey, e-mail to author 21 June 2010.

16. Known in history by several names, including Zhuang-zi.

17. "Stronzo" means exactly what you think it does.

18. "Whoever respects life should not damage the body that preserves the means to maintain it."

19. "And deplore that all consider their own capacity like a treasure."

20. Talich was the teacher of Sir Charles Mackerras.

21. It was Solti, not Fricsay, but in those days they looked alike.

22. *Back to Methuselah (A Metabiological Pentateuch)* consists of a preface and five plays by Shaw, and is a massive work written between 1918 and 1920.

23. "How little Moritz imagines a conductor."

24. "Breathing-space."

25. The core document employed by conductors, containing every note written for every player and singer.

26. Carlos refers to the authority conductors had, in those days, to hire and fire at will—especially in Boston, the last major orchestra to be protected by a union.

27. Owl explaining to Winnie the Pooh the "customary procedures." The Bear of Little Brain mishears. Cathryn Johns, e-mail to author, 30 November 2004.

28. Read aloud to catch his irony. This would not be the last time he made fun of my literal-mindedness.

29. This is truly astounding. I had never heard of a conductor who marked directly in the parts. It was unimaginable to me that one could do so without the advantage of the full score open on the desk. How else could a conductor assert bowings, balances, accent, phrase, and the rest without the whole thing laid out in front of him? Carlos carried the score in his head to such a degree that he didn't need it when it came to marking parts. This remains one of the most startling aspects of his genius. I don't believe that even Mitropoulos worked this way. However, in the failure of the *Emperor* with Michelangeli, Kleiber's score evidently resembled a Jackson Pollock.

30. This is a reference to the conductor, and better-yet teacher of conductors, Hans Swarowsky, pronounced "svaroffski."

31. Another pun. Aloud, "woid" (word), as spoken by someone from the Bronx.

32. He refers to a poem by Robbie Burns.

33. Ten to the eighteenth power is a lot.

34. Wiener Philharmoniker; that is, the Vienna Philharmonic.

35. "How little Moritz imagines a conductor," the same phrase he used to describe Rodzinski.

36. "Perse" is clearly what Carlos wrote here. I never did figure out what it meant. It might be a misspelling of "purse," referring to the vast wealth of Koussevitsky's wife. Bruce Herman suggests it is a play reversing syllables and should be understood as "poise and personality."

37. From "Hereabouts" to "performance" Carlos bracketed his text with the word "uninteresting" in the margin.

38. Strauss was modestly asking the players not to be in awe of him. "We don't have to admire each other. We are worthy of each other."

39. Carlos is quoting from Proverbs 28:1, or its earlier iteration in Leviticus 26:17, and refers to a wicked man in either case.

40. I had been sending him concert reviews I wrote for an online journal in San Francisco.

41. He alludes to the American ballad, "The Sun Shines Bright on My Old Kentucky Home," by Stephen Foster.

42. Colloquial Italian for "bat-maker."

43. Kleiber refers to the legend about Rodzinski carrying a revolver to rehearsal, afraid that his players would actually kill him.

44. "Who knows . . ."

45. Carlos refers to a Toscanini sequence in the UCLA film.

46. This was the only time I mentioned his wife, Stanka. He never followed up on it.

47. *"Volta subito,* or "turn quickly," a standard instruction telling players to turn the page speedily.

48. Yet another joke. Carlos knew perfectly well how to spell "Tennstedt" but preferred to pretend he was some sort of stranger.

49. North German Radio Symphony.

50. "Disgusting people."

51. A conflated reference to the American advice columnist "Dear Abby," and President Lincoln.

52. "Fagott" is the German term for bassoon. "Gamberoni" is a goofy reference to cellos.

53. Enrico Mainardi, Italian cellist.

54. Referring to the beautiful island of equality promised to Sancho Panza. W. S. Gilbert used the same symbol in *Gondoliers.*

55. This refers to the performance Tennstedt gave with the Chicago Symphony Orchestra. I had sent it to Carlos. It's a glory.

56. Like Bernstein, he smoked himself to death.

57. Robert Louis Stevenson. I told him about a camping trip we had made to this lovely, nestled park in California's upper Napa Valley. There, we met Ranger Bob. I later found out that they're all called Ranger Bob.

58. "Stan" is carefully crossed out.

59. At the San Francisco Opera's Strauss Festival, with Maria Ewing, Tom Fox, Robert Tear, and Leonie Rysanek.

60. It's the one we finally went with.

61. Any conductor will tell you who publishes these wrecks. They're cheap.

62. As usual, Carlos knows more than he lets on. He refers to the manner of Hart Crane's suicide, jumping from the SS *Oribaza* off the Florida coast just before noon on 26 April 1932. Crane wrote the epic poem *The Bridge,* a work now central to American literature of the era. ee cummings declared that "Crane's mind was no big-

ger than a pin, but it didn't matter, he was a born poet." Years later, Robert Lowell declared that Crane was "less limited than any poet of his generation." Kleiber well knew the Brooklyn Bridge, the central image of Crane's finest work.

63. Halvard Solness, the "Master Builder" in Ibsen's 1892 play.

64. This was "The Young Lutheran's Guide to the Orchestra," a sweet and silly essay.

65. Carlos had read Camille Paglia's *Amherst's Madame de Sade: Emily Dickinson*.

66. Great Order of Merit Cross of the Federal Republic of Germany.

67. A play, suggesting "expensive dog."

68. *Stringendo* describes the gradual speeding up of a musical line. It is a long form of *accelerando* and means literally "a tightening."

69. Received 25 August 1993.

70. Pianist Daniel Barenboim was piano soloist in the Boult film.

71. "EK" refers to Carlos's father.

72. "It is an operating secret," suggesting a trade secret of some arcane sort.

73. Conductor Herbert Blomstedt, then music director of the San Francisco Symphony.

74. Ernst Stavro Blofeld.

75. Haydn wrote 104 of them.

76. Received 20 October 1993.

77. He refers to the old slogan for Morton's salt, a perennial in US advertising: "When it rains, it pours."

78. I later found out that he meant "poetry."

79. Members of the Kroll Opera.

80. "Apt, even if untrue."

81. A horrible pun on curs (dogs) woofing, and another allusion to Carlo the Dickinson dog—that is, himself.

82. "How boring."

83. I had been whining to him about illiterate singers.

84. Bank of America account number. I never did.

85. He never did.

86. Referring to Sinatra.

87. Dmitri Mitropoulos. It is a common belief that he had an eidetic memory. William Trotter, in his exemplary biography, demonstrated that he did not. It was all brutal, hard work.

88. A reference to the Irving Berlin song in *Annie Get Your Gun*.

89. The "royal we," identified with Queen Victoria.

90. Another elaborate play, here on "Windmills of Your Mind," a 1968 song made popular by Dusty Springfield.

91. He was still loathing Whitman in a 2 February 1998 letter to Sir Peter Jonas. He commented on a production of Michael Tippett's opera *The Midsummer Marriage* and somehow managed to work in further disparagement. "You can always count on me to dislike 98% of everything and everybody, so you won't be surprised by what I think of Mr Krellmann's hefty "Heft" re-Tippy's "Marriage." 1) If he (K) printed (p8) Mr. Whitman's stupid*, mock-macho original and the Boche-translation on p9, why

didn't he do the same for some of the <u>good</u> poems? In German, poor Donne, Eliot, Valéry etc and Auden's "If I could tell you I would let you know" (which turns into "Ich würd's dir sagen, wenn's zu sagen ware" (sic!) look like something by Wolfgang Schreiber = <u>unreadable</u>. (And <u>HEAVY</u>!) * I <u>LOATHE</u> Walt Whitman!"

92. I didn't. Here's Klemperer's pun: "That was not La Mer. At most, it was Szell by the lake."

93. "Infra dignitatum": beneath one's dignity.

94. Carlos refers to a book I had sent him, Robert A Caro's magisterial *The Power Broker: Robert Moses and the Fall of New York*. It was the best political biography I had ever read.

95. "Is endlessly unbroken" or, more colloquially, "finally upon us."

96. Suvi Raj Grubb, record producer and protégé of Walter Legge.

97. Werner Thärichen, longtime timpanist of the Berlin Philharmonic and a great admirer of Furtwängler.

98. He enclosed a photocopy of four pages from Boult's book on conducting.

99. So close that rumor claimed Carlos and Popp had been secretly married, in Chicago. It was nonsense.

100. I have no idea how Carlos knew this song. It's beyond obscure. Written by Charlie Abbott in 1945, the first verse runs "I put a penny in the slot / And all I ever got / Was 5 salted peanuts." If you have to hear it, check out Tony Pastor and His Orchestra. They recorded the song as fox trot on a Victor 78. So did those other hit makers, The Counts and the Countess.

101. Toscanini.

102. Cable News Network. He refers to the 17 January Northridge quake in Los Angeles, Richter 6.7, which cost fifty-seven lives and $15 billion in repairs.

103. His allusion to an American vernacular song, "The Old Gray Mare."

104. "God be thanked."

105. CK refers again to the Northridge earthquake in Los Angeles, four hundred miles south of my home. He alludes to his own experience conducting during an earthquake and not even noticing it, all the while others were scrambling for cover.

106. Gypsies.

107. He refers to Tennyson's "The Charge of the Light Brigade."

108. Another literary reference, this to Thomas Hardy's *Far from the Madding Crowd*.

109. Russian conductor Semyon Bychkov.

110. "The heart has its reasons of which reason will never know." Pensées 277 of Blaise Pascal, a French mathematician and philosopher.

111. Veni, vidi, vici: "I came, I saw, I conquered."

112. A horrible pun on Gogol's brilliant 1836 satire, "The Nose." The tale includes talk of a barber, which Carlos probably thought I would get.

113. Bruno Walter.

114. A reference to an American television dog. I didn't get it.

115. "I raise my hands": that is, I surrender.

116. That would be me.

117. Referring to the passing of bassist Stuart Knussen, father of Oliver and a friend of mine. I had told him the backstory.

118. "Childhood trauma."

119. No question. The New York Philharmonic gentlemen treated him with open contempt. Homophobia was the least of it. Szell referred to them as "murderer's row" not without reason.

120. "Merry Widow."

121. American slang, referring to a fatal accident.

122. An American doctor who was busy in those years helping people commit suicide.

123. From the verbatim record of the debates at Charleston, Illinois, 18 September 1858.

124. On 6 March 1857, the majority of the U.S. Supreme Court held that no black person of African descent could become a U.S. citizen, and therefore lacked standing to sue in federal courts. The opinion, written by Chief Justice Roger B. Taney, held that the Missouri Compromise was unconstitutional and that the federal government did not have the power to prohibit slavery in its territories. Lincoln responded by giving his famous House Divided speech on 16 June 1858. He argued, "Slavery is founded on the selfishness of man's nature—opposition to it on his love of justice."

125. The Latin, attributed to Honoratus Maurus, or to Quintilian, is an etymological absurdity, a self-contradiction.

126. www.goodsoundclub.com/Forums/ShowPost.aspx?postID=14116#14116, accessed 28 July 2010.

127. Russian, "uncultured, uncouth."

128. Another reference to Winnie the Pooh.

129. A pun in reference to a chorus in *Merry Widow*.

130. A hard joke to explain. "Abend" means evening. "Abendrot" means sunset and sounds very like "Abendroth." He was trying to tease me into thinking that the conductor's real name was "Abend Roth." Typical Carlos name play.

131. Received 6 July 1996.

132. "Widow."

133. An American cartoon series for children, featuring antagonistic cats and mice.

134. A brand of sleeping pill.

135. Another reference to the "Armored Men" sequence in *The Magic Flute*.

136. This was his granting of consent, or so we took it.

137. After Carlos's death, Lebrecht wrote an obituary under the charming title "Carlos Kleiber: Not A Great Conductor." *La Scena Musicale*, 30 July 2004.

138. I had never heard of Pessoa until Carlos's letter. He was a Portuguese poet of peculiar but influential character. Dickinson-like, he was largely housebound in Lisbon for almost thirty years, writing in obscure poverty and only "discovered" after his death. Pessoa published almost nothing in his lifetime but is today the subject of a wide following in Portugal. He wrote as four distinct personalities, each with his own name, using the heteronyms "Alberto Caeiro," "Ricardo Reis," and "Alvaro dos Campos." After I learned all this, Carlos's interest in him became self-evident.

139. International Standard Book Number, a machine-readable global cataloguing system.

140. Saving curious readers the trouble, Karajan recorded *Tosca* twice: in 1962, with di Stefano, and in 1980, with Carreras. Take your pick.

141. "Always the same."

142. Imagine—325. At this writing there are 181,000.

143. He quotes a 1925 song by Harry Woods: "Oh, we ain't got a barrel of money, Maybe we're ragged and funny, But we'll travel along, Singing a song, Side by side."

144. "And he said, Who art thou, Lord? And the Lord said, I am Jesus whom thou persecutest: it is hard for thee to kick against the pricks." Bible scholars differ on the meaning of "pricks." One holds, "This is an ox-goad. An ox-goad is not meant to kill an ox, but meant to be unpleasant enough to get the ox (or other animal) to move the way his master wants him to go." Another asserts, "This is a proverb which is spoken of those who through their stubbornness hurt themselves." An early version is attributed to Euripides. No one thinks it refers to "pricks of conscience," an expression so contemporary as to be impossible. The entire passage refers to Saul's conversion to Christianity.

145. Emily Dickinson's brother William Austin Dickinson and his married mistress, Mabel Loomis Todd.

Epilogue

A question put to Carlos Kleiber:

> "Do you live alone?"
> "No . . . I live à la carte."[1]

A belief engine propels the mystery of Carlos Kleiber.

That engine asserts charisma without limit, success without industry, rehearsals without end, and vast reputation built on little accomplishment. Like every self-generating theology, such beliefs enjoy just enough factual foundation to keep the engine combusting.

How he gained his vision and how he achieved his unique results are central questions of this book. So too are issues of reception history and personal influence in his own profession, and in the careers of the artists around him. Few were left unmoved, unchanged. While he worked, his gravitational attraction was enormous.

Because he never granted interviews, no self-explanation is available. There will be no more second thoughts in the evolutionary record. The central documents of films and recordings are his permanent inscription. The memories of friends and colleagues, "Kleibergrams" given to his players, the rhetoric of his performances—these are the only evidence of his working art. The letters in this volume add one dimension to the complexity of his character but do little to explain its origins.

The name "Carlos Kleiber" is even now assuming a magical significance. In many ways this is because of his lifelong silences, his unorthodox humility, his startling methods.

Regardless of near-universal acclaim, there has always been controversy. A few of his colleagues describe him as a sort of confidence trickster, doing it all by remorseless drill and repetition. I once showed film of Kleiber rehearsing the *Fledermaus* overture to a large audience of professional conductors. All marveled at the process. More than a few grumbled at the extravagance. "If I had forty-five minutes to rehearse a five minute overture, I could do that too," one of them asserted.

This is the commonplace of envy. It answers nothing. Other great conductors raised monuments of oracular speech. Bernstein, von Karajan, Beecham, Stokowski, Klemperer—even Mravinsky—left explanation for their art. Kleiber left nothing. Other conductors welcomed Pliny and Carlyle and Caro.[2] Kleiber threw them out. He didn't want witnesses. What he did was private, personal, and past scrutiny. When a rehearsal went badly, it was a matter of personal shame. When a performance went well, it never went well enough.

How could he retaliate against such enervating forces?

The first curtain wall in Carlos's castle was always humor. So was his last. Those who never met him find it difficult to grasp the central importance of Kleiber's humor to Kleiber's life. Anyone wishing to understand it should study his two filmed rehearsals from 1970. Look at them closely. No one else found such high purpose in such wicked wit. His reference to "crocodile tears" is better than a joke. It is a dazzling proclamation of independence from cliché.

His allusions were vivid and comic. "You have to play as if you are a bit drunk, but not too much. You still have to be able to drive a car." Or, "Play with nicotine." Or, "Like a veil of snow, spread over a Christmas tree." Or, "How would a Rolls-Royce, moving on grass that has just been cut, sound? That must be your sound." Or, "It must sound like the whisper of a feather, which falls down on a layer of scented powder." Or, referring to the snakes and ladders of Iago, "You're playing this too beautifully. A little bad taste, please!" When rehearsing the Overture to *Der Freischütz*, he asked his players, "Do you believe in ghosts? Very good! That's of great importance! Please believe in ghosts at least as long as it takes us to play the overture." In rehearsal for *Die Fledermaus*, and referring to the snare drum: "This has to sound like a conspiracy." And preparing *Tristan* in Bayreuth: "Please play this a bit more maidenly. Just imagine that Isolde feels like a girl on the day of her first communion. For her, dying is wonderful. Only the audience must weep." Many of these images were drawn upon his wide knowledge of pop culture and high literature. A clever grad student will soon obtain a PhD by compiling "The Sayings of Carlos Kleiber." Every conductor will buy a copy.

Consider the film of his 1989 New Year's Day concert in Vienna. Watch the "Bauern Polka." Players and conductor alike "sing" part of its music.

During the applause, follow the gesture that Carlos makes, fingers to throat. Watch his eyes. Everything about his sardonic laughter, his survival in the trade, is illuminated in an instant.

Or measure the costumes. Assisted by his good friend Martha Scherer,[3] Carlos would occasionally appear on the podium dressed up as someone else altogether. He would usually do this at the Fasching[4] performances of *Fledermaus* in Munich. He once conducted that comic opera dressed as Boris Becker.[5] Another time he appeared as a workman from the industrial firm MAN.[6] This company had installed a stage hydraulic, which was malfunctioning. Carlos's appearance as a repairman elicited much wry laughter from his colleagues. The audience was mystified.

Wolfgang Sawallisch himself conducted *Fledermaus* one year, at a Rosenmontag[7] performance. He looked up during the party scene. There onstage was Carlos, dressed as Johann Strauss Jr.[8]

Carlos's weirdest impersonation came during the 1980s. Kleiber once conducted *Fledermaus* while dressed up as Bhagwan Shree Rajneesh, he of the many limousines and leader of a bizarre cult in Antelope, Oregon. Rajneesh[9] gathered headlines while managing the Big Muddy Ranch. His many disciples labored in the fields but were gratified when Bhagwan rolled by in one of his dozen Royces and waved at them. After being deported for immigration violations, Bhagwan became "Osho" shortly before his death in 1990. Kleiber's white raiment must have bewildered the audience.

Regardless of such zany and provocative wit, some human flaws were crushing to him. Regardless of self-deprecation, so too were his own. He saw those flaws better than anyone. We cannot count the occasions Kleiber mocked Kleiber. On that ground he was unreachable. Richter got it right: "Such a Titan, and so unsure of himself." With every nerve exposed to failure, it is astonishing he worked as much as he did. So how did he do it? How do we account for such singular performances?

As I got to know him I came to believe that part of his genius lay in his hearing. He heard differently. Like Mitropoulos and Boulez and de Sabata, Kleiber had an immense musical imagination. He conceived sound perfectly. This desired state of perfection arose from study and fantasy. It lived "Before the Fall" of real rehearsal, actual acoustics, fallible artists. It passed to him unmediated, from the composer and the score—with all its own imperfections. But at the moment his dreams were shouted to the world, they echoed back imperfectly. It is always this way, of course. But for Kleiber, these human deficiencies were almost unbearably painful. He could not stop hearing them, within or without.

Some proof of his unmatched hearing rises in the way he prepared music for his players. Marking parts is a commonplace in the trade. Every serious conductor does it, and in a standard order. We read the full score in detail, and thereafter enter the bowings and breathmarks and dynamics and slurs and phrases in it. This master document allows us to see (and hear) at once all the instruments, presented vertically, and to adjust the individual parts accordingly. A marked full score is then transferred into individual parts.

In a display of almost "Mozartean" facility, Carlos usually marked the parts *directly*. With rare exceptions, he did not mark the score first. He didn't need to. He heard those parts within, completely. He transferred the detail of his instructions straight to the parts themselves. I discovered this when asking to see his full score of *Fledermaus*, to test my markings against his own. There was no point, he said. The markings existed only in the parts. There was nothing to see in his score.

And he worked differently on the podium. This claim requires almost no further proof. Five minutes in the deposition of that baton and its graceful conviction will persuade any musical person. But his work went well past mere eloquence.

Conducting is semaphore. It must be seen to be understood.

And so a word about Kleiber's stick technique. It begins with the now certain fact that he was self-taught. It continues with the quiet fact that learning to show time is as easy as learning to blink. Any gibbon can be taught how to show a "four." However, Carlos's semaphore—in hands and eyes and body—was so original, so logical, and so musically aware as to make him stand alone. Entirely alone.

Tennstedt transmitted kinetic electricity, Klemperer a granitic grandeur. Bernstein could be nearly orgiastic, and Mravinsky nearly monastic. Boulez found rhythm in every bar, and Furtwängler conducted without reference to the bar at all. Mackerras's baton was immensely practical and particular, as was that of Szell, Reiner, Talich, Ançerl, John Barbirolli, Bruno Walter, and Adrian Boult. Von Karajan could be elegant as white swans and thunderous as Niagara. De Sabata was all song, living in the longest of lines. Mitropoulos knew every note and could show the place of each of them. In their great careers, each of these master conductors developed a baton technique suitable to their analyses and energies, their repertoire and ventriloquism.

Carlos Kleiber stood alone in this regard: his semaphore could do *all* of these things. He could show *any* of these things. He could convey *every* mood and character, conflict and fear and ordination. Other great conductors mastered a given domain. Kleiber seemed to have no expressive boundaries. The filmed record of his work could not exist in any other hands.[10]

Study the tidal passacaglia in his Brahms 4, the backbeat in the finale of his Beethoven 4, the living hesitation and rich space in his *Blue Danube*, there in the first measure of the "Big Tune," there as he runs *doh-mi-sol* and—wait for it in the harp!—*sol*, and only then does he re-engage time. . . . This is all his territory.

Domingo was once asked, as master singer of our age, what he wanted from his conductors. He named several attributes and several conductors whom he counted upon to provide each of them. It is a good list, and ended with a universal coda: "But from Carlos Kleiber, I would want . . . everything."[11]

And Kleiber had an astonishing gift for rehearsing in small forms and large forms simultaneously. Every good conductor can do this, to some extent. Carlos did it to a degree surpassing any other. In a special regard, it was signature to his respect for the formularies of science.

Kleiber's art in rehearsal was an example of fractals in geometry. Benoit Mandelbrot coined the term in 1975, referring to objects built using recursion. One aspect of the object at hand is infinite. Another is finite. Some piece of the object is a scaled down version of its previous self. Today, the idea of fractals is a visual one. For Carlos, it was aural.

When he heard a piece in his mind, he saw each phrase in all its iterations moving nearer to the originating code of conception—perhaps just a single note. His rehearsals operated the same way, always moving toward an infinite point of truth just over there, just past the visible horizon. And he worked in the *opposite* direction, simultaneously.

For at the same moment of particulars, Kleiber was *also* building toward the great design, the view from space of a whole globe, a gigantic apparatus of line and balance and arc. In this, he had the same gift as Furtwängler: when he beat the first bar of a great work, in his mind he was already in the last.[12]

Carlos was a master of language. His images served as vivid mnemonics, inspirational jolts. When assiduously marked parts would not suffice, his baton went into expressive overdrive. Should that fail, he launched into a special discourse of simile and folk tale, of rhyme and pictograph and silliness. Kleiber would try anything to make his conception a commonwealth.

And his genius was catalytic. He could ignite energy and excitement in every part of a great house, across every instrument of a great orchestra. Players, singers, producers, directors, and the best-attuned critics always understood this. When Kleiber was around, he was not the only person to invest everything he owned. It was part of his achievement that everybody did the same. To that exact degree did he always credit his colleagues. To the same degree, they echoed his applause and returned his faith. Blowups, walkouts, no-shows and all, it was a unique set of catalyzing relationships. And of constant cross-examination.

"There is a danger with this sort of man," Bernard Haitink declared. "He was quite naughty, you know. He would sometimes test you. I think if you failed he would cut you off."

Was Haitink ever tested?

"Yes. It was at the Royal Opera House. I had offered him the use of my office, which he accepted. He was getting ready to go out and conduct 'Otello,' which he did better than anybody else. Just before he left to enter the pit, he asked me a question. 'Bernard, how should I conduct the beginning? In 2 or in 4?'"

Haitink instantly understood what Kleiber was getting at. The question was, of course, ridiculous. Kleiber knew perfectly well what he was going to do, and how, and why.

"No no no. I'm not a fool," Haitink told Kleiber, and refused to play along. In this manner Kleiber always made it hard to get close. Even such a man as Bernard Haitink would be kept one step apart. There was, for Carlos, no point in glad-handing. He generally treated his players with tremendous respect and affection. They loved him in turn. But they too never got near. To my surprise, Haitink said that he never, even once, "dared to get close to him."

Conductor Michael Gielen knew Carlos and his family from childhood in Berlin and Buenos Aires. Both he and his wife knew Carlos for many years thereafter, but in the 1980s that friendship fell away.

"I never knew why," Gielen told me. "It was never clear why he stopped seeing us. We knew him all those years, he had been a witness at our marriage, and then it ended. Finally only my wife could see him, but he refused to give her his phone number. She had to leave messages for him at the Bavarian Staatsoper. Even then we never knew if he would get back to us. Finally he did no more and we stopped trying. It was painful."[13]

When I met Gielen to discuss all this, in a restaurant near the San Francisco Opera House, he wanted to see and hold some of Carlos's letters. I brought half a dozen from home. He opened them, very gently, and turned them over in his hands, reading slowly. He finally looked up. "I don't understand. He stopped seeing so many of his friends. Without explanation. Now here he is writing all these letters to someone thousands of miles away." His eyes glistened as he finished the last of them.

As earlier described, the well-known music administrator Sir Peter Jonas knew Carlos from the Chicago Symphony days in the 1970s. Jonas made those concerts possible. Together with Sawallisch at the Bavarian State Opera, he helped make those performances possible. Kleiber's professional accomplishments would have been different—and the lesser—without the support and friendship of Peter Jonas.

When I first asked him to participate in this project, he sent back several very thoughtful replies. In them Sir Peter declared that he and Carlos, some years ago, "became somewhat estranged." The breach was never repaired.

He declined to discuss its cause or content. On that basis, he suffered the tremendous regret and remorse of an important friendship lost. Although he kindly agreed to read this manuscript for error, he chose not to talk publicly about his friend. "I must admit to you that I even felt a little guilty about what I wrote concerning him in our own Staatsoper Magazine."[14] Happily for history, by 2009 Sir Peter had changed his mind and has helped immensely with this book. Like most of us who knew Kleiber, he resents the endless disfigurement of the real man within the public caricature.

Sir John Tooley also found himself excluded and never forgot the pain of it. Several other friends acknowledged similar loss, but would not allow their names to be used in this book. It still hurts.

I suspect that Carlos had a hard time with the idea of forgiveness. This may have descended from his father, whose own character suffered the same trait. Erich took out hard feelings on others. Carlos generally directed them inward.[15]

Carlos rarely forgave mishaps in his own music, few as they were. But his perfectionism did not end when he stepped off the podium. It rang everywhere in his life. Quarrels that others would discuss and mend became, time and again for him, an emotional abyss that he would rarely confront directly, or cross at all. This abyss was deepened by the power of Carlos's phenomenal memory.

If forgiveness was not an option and forgetfulness was impossible, what to do? Carlos chose atrophy. And so friendships could end, unremarked over time. So too a whole career.

And yet, to my certain knowledge, he often expressed concern that he had given offense or feared that someone had decided to cut *him* off. Several letters and postcards published in this book give proof of it. Other friends have told me the same. It was a weirdly schismatic set of traits, disarming and sweet, troubled and troubling.

There is a wonderful story of Kleiber at his best. It is told by soprano Renée Fleming. She once wrote him a letter, asking his advice about whether or not to accept a particular role that she had been offered. He replied, strongly, urging, "Don't even think of doing [it]. Don't give any reasons, just say no! Don't argue, don't apologize, just say NO! N.O."[16]

He followed that with an unexpected phone call in early 2001. Fleming was getting ready to take her place onstage following a difficult rehearsal process for Richard Strauss's late opera *Arabella*, being produced in Munich. The designer had built a Matterhorn of hills for the singers to climb. It was all rather awkward and rickety. During rehearsal, Fleming ended up in bed for two days, suffering back pain.

"On opening night[17] Carlos Kleiber called me on his cell phone," Fleming wrote. She was preparing to go onstage. He said, "Do you know where I am?"
"No, where?"
"'I'm in Garmisch,' he said quietly. 'I'm holding my cell phone up now. Can you hear the church bells? I wanted to tell you we wish you well tonight,' Kleiber said. By 'we' he meant himself and Richard Strauss, for he was standing at Strauss' gravesite in the cemetery in Garmisch."[18]

Carlos may also have remembered a childhood encounter with Strauss himself, also at Garmisch. When he was very young, his father took him to meet Strauss at his home. Young Karl was given to understand that this was a very great man and a major figure in his father's life. Strauss greeted father and son at his door, and welcomed them inside. Decades later, he recalled that Strauss had "kind, blue eyes," and treated him with great warmth.[19]

It was not easy to be Carlos Kleiber. His operational tactics included silence, charm, and retreat. He exploited his celebrity and wealth for the sake of working standards and artistic desire. He held his success a contemptible joke.

Fame was a tocsin to him. It warned of time wasting, the wreckage of privacy, false attention, all a diversion from music itself. He took those warnings quite seriously. Retrospectively, we now see that, after periods of great acclaim and tremendous industry, he would scurry away from the spotlight altogether. He knew what was coming and despised it. His friend Peter Jonas described the "camp followers, pimps, leeches and vultures" of the music industry. They "pick at the flesh of musical and operatic life [and] met with his blistering scorn."[20]

And fame was toxic to him. The world knows what he did to avoid celebrity. His friends knew the ways he dealt with it. (His critics thought it merely self-promotional.) One of those ways, at least with me, lay in leaving clues about deep feeling—disguised as self-deprecation. Let me pursue one of them. It deals, elaborately, with the place of fame in his life. It is built on his profound reading of Emily Dickinson, her work and life and hermitage. It derives from his reading in the secondary sources as well.

Carlos pretended to be the reincarnation of her dog Carlo. He referred to this "fact" in five different letters, from 1993 and 1994.

On 20 January he wrote, "Did I tell you I was E. Dickinson's dog in a former life? Sure I did. How I adore(d) that lady!!" In July we talked about her again, and on the 20th he wrote, "What I love about her? Well, it's love; so I won't expose it to scrutiny or discussion. Regarding 1), 2) + 3): even in these, there's the saving astringency of that two-timing sadism Ms. Paglia cleverly recognized. One has to listen carefully, tho'!! Keeping in mind that ED wasn't silly, by any means. (As I told you: Carlo, the dog, was me!)" On

21 July he signed off "Molti saluti from (care canem), Carlo who won't bite the hand that feeds him tapes, tho'! Never!"

In November I was talking about Walt Whitman, whose work I imagined he would also admire. On the 11th, he replied, "But Whitman I hate, loathe and despise. I won't go into why, because you obviously like ? him. Just don't mention him or Lincoln again unless you enjoy watching me run amok, OK? If you do, I'll know you're rattling my chain. A dog's chain, remember."

In February 1994 he signed a letter "Carlo(s), le pooch d'Emilie." In March he said that he wanted to come visit Hilde and me in California: "Woof, Woof, says Carlos, frantically wagging his tail instead of his baton." And when he gave me a photo of himself, reproduced in this book, he signed it "ED's Carlo."

So why this absurd fantasy about being a reincarnated canine? Kleiber was walking in his own woods, leaving a trail for anyone invited to follow. I did. Here goes.

Carlo was given to Emily Dickinson by her father during the winter of early 1850. The dog was a Newfoundland, "as large as myself, that my Father bought me," she wrote.[21] "They are better than Beings," she added, "because they know but do not tell."

Carlo was named after the dog in *Reveries of a Bachelor, Or A Book of the Heart*, a set of romantic short stories first published in book form in 1850 and much admired by Dickinson.[22] "Whom my Dog understood could not elude others," she observed.

Within her poetry, Carlo makes his most famous appearance in "I started Early—Took up my Dog." He figures more frequently in her letters, most prosaically as "dumb and brave," most importantly as Confederate, Preceptor, and Instructor. When Carlo died on 27 January 1866, after sixteen years of devoted companionship, Emily wrote a strange letter to her friend Thomas Wentworth Higginson. In it she asked, "Carlo died. Would you instruct me now?" In multiple regards, she identified Carlo as interlocutor and balm between a noisy world and her intimate self.[23]

Kleiber also read a letter she wrote to Higginson on 7 June 1862. He knew I would eventually find it, and gather its meaning toward him.

"If fame belonged to me, I could not escape her—if she did not, the longest day would pass me on the chase—and the approbation of my dog would forsake me then. My barefoot rank is better."

How Kleiber ached for retreat from the world that made his artistic life possible. How painfully ridiculous that he chose a career that required him to stand in the center of its glare. His conflict was permanent and irresolvable. Better to be Carlo, loved and silent.

Kleiber's defenses also included retreat, even from the face and arena of his friends. He greatly liked and respected Plácido Domingo. And Domingo adored him. Kleiber turned him down, many times.

> One of the unbelievable things that I remember is to see the public at the beginning of "Otello." He was conducting and I was about to come to sing the "Esultate." I was going from the side of the boxes in Covent Garden and I could see that nobody was paying any attention to the stage. Everybody was looking at Carlos, what he was doing. And that's really unbelievable. And that was really so special that the people they were captivated, they were really, absolutely hypnotized by what Carlos was doing, and that I will never forget as long as I live . . .
> I said, "Carlos, why don't you work more, you know?"
> And he said, "I'm happy with what I do, you know me, I'm demanding, and people won't be as prepared as they should, and so I prefer not to work that much. I prefer now and then to take my rest." The big, big tragedy and loss for the world of music is that he was not working so much. I said, "Carlos, can you come next month to conduct?" "Where?" "Los Angeles." "Ahh . . . I . . . it's so far."
> Everything that you ask him he will say "no." So, it was his own choice. He really picked his own destiny, you know. Absolutely, absolutely.
>
> —Plácido Domingo, BBC Radio 3, 26 September 2009[24]

Beyond every other dimension of his talent, Carlos Kleiber was an ecstatic.

There is within traditions of faith and literature such a personality. An ecstatic experiences the world distinctly. Qualities of prophetic vision abound. In ecstasy lies a unique capacity to see one's own name from a distance and to read it aloud with tremendous cold objectivity, with brutal self-doubt. For the Greeks, *ekstasis* meant "to stand outside oneself, in trance."

Kleiber had that merit. He fused it to an artistic energy that was Blake's "eternal delight." While combining distance from his own ego with that ecstatic urgency, he made his unique art. Across his whole career Carlos lived an intensely integrated theory of music. All forces were codeterminate, correlate, all bent toward a burning sufficiency. No wonder he was so often disappointed. Few others of his time played for such stakes. Callas and Vickers and Stratas certainly did. Furtwängler and Gould, unquestionably. Add Argerich, Oistrakh, Richter, Kissin, Tennstedt, and a few others, and the list soon emaciates. A trait common to most of these personalities is that they belong to a subculture of secession. Periods of retreat, departure, disappearance were essential—and sometimes gained by dissolving into a role. In time, Kleiber exfiltrated into public shadow.

Carlos was no theologian. The manufactured evidence of belief amused and repelled him. The shoddy politics of organized piety disgusted him. He shared Emily Dickinson's view of God as "a noted clergyman."

But he understood the practices of an aesthetic faith. The tenth-century poet and mystic Al-Ghazali made sense to him: "The purpose of music, considered in relation to God, is to arouse longing for God, and passionate love for Him, and to produce states in which God reveals Himself and His favor, which are beyond description and known only by experience. These states are called ecstasy." It was a state Carlos sought in every performance. It could only be gained through the disciplines of study and imagination and an insatiable desire for proximity.

He came closer to these intimate visions, this molten awareness, than any conductor of his era. But when told so, when praised for it, he would shrug or laugh or ridicule. It was his pain that he—almost alone—could see how much further there remained to travel. He once listened to one of his own recordings, declared that it was "ok," and then decided he made a mistake. "It must have been by Karl Böhm." That could be read two ways.

I regret never talking with him about William Blake. Carlos's own states of innocence and indifference were announced there. So too was his anxiety and belief. Emily Dickinson anticipated Carlos's own desire for that special state. They understood one another. Like Blake, she foretold the cost of Kleiber's achievement.

> For each ecstatic instant
> We must an anguish pay
> In keen and quivering ratio
> To the ecstasy.
>
> For each beloved hour
> Sharp pittance of years,
> Bitter contested farthings
> And coffers heaped with tears.

There will, inevitably, be a recalibration of his reputation. It began to occur before he died. Even now it accelerates.

Although (of course) no formal announcement was ever made, Carlos in the mid-nineties started telling his friends that he had retired. It was an erratic retirement, to be sure, as he several times agreed to work in remote arenas.

Every major house and concert organization in the world tried to attract him to return. Political and artistic leadership in Bavaria attempted—repeatedly, failingly— to induce him to take the Munich Philharmonic after Celibidache died in 1996. They finally begged him to become honorary director of that orchestra, but he fended that off too. The Met offered carte blanche if he would accept a *Falstaff* there, and he did express some interest. After 11 September several of its leaders tried to induce him to lead a benefit or memorial event connected. He considered the possibility, but nothing came of it.

As above, on 19 July 2004 word was released that Carlos had died six days earlier and was already buried. It was a shocking announcement, most especially where Carlos lived. Even the president of Austria shared in the sad declaration. As it happened, the 19th was important for another reason as well. It was the night of James Levine's farewell concert as music director of the Munich Philharmonic. His program was Mahler: *Das Lied von der Erde*, and the Symphony No. 2. Its coincidence was unnerving. *Das Lied* was the only Mahler that Carlos had ever conducted, externally.

When word was given to him, shortly before the concert began, Levine shook with disbelief. He had no idea his friend Carlos was ill, much less gone. Word soon passed to every artist preparing to take the stage.

It is said the evening offered some of the greatest music making in the history of that city. Singers Dorothea Roeschmann and Johan Botha surpassed themselves. But Anne-Sofie von Otter in the "Urlicht" was, by every account, beyond perfection. She had sung with Carlos in *Rosenkavalier* and remembered. Backstage at intermission Levine declared, "Carlos is dead. This concert is for him." And so it was. And, like Carlos, matchless.

Since his passing, tributes have been offered in music and in print, worldwide. He has been memorialized by almost every organization and artist with whom he worked.

In October 2004, at the Musikverein's Gläserner Saal in Vienna, conductor and friend Riccardo Muti spoke at a public memorial for Carlos. Interviewed by Thomas Angyan, he discussed matters of personality, artistic integrity and independence, and the career overall.[25] Afterward, the film of Carlos rehearsing *Freischütz* with the RSO Stuttgart in 1970 was shown to an astonished assembly.

Two weeks later he was admitted into the very structure of the Vienna Staatsoper. On 2 November, General Director Ioan Holender declared, "Nobody in the State Opera's long history has conducted here so rarely and influenced the house so profoundly and lastingly as Carlos Kleiber." At this ceremony, a large work space in the opera house was officially renamed "Carlos Kleiber Rehearsal Stage."[26]

In an interview surveying his long career as a producer and intendant of opera, Holender was asked to name his all-time conductor.

I have a favorite for a man, who was so near to the absolute where we never arrive, in art and in no other connection, who tried to touch the absolute. Only God can touch it. And the fight from this man, all his life, to come as near as possible to what music is, to what is behind the notes, what is written—is and stays for me: Carlos Kleiber, absolutely the biggest, without comparison.

I knew him from a very, very, very long time ago, when I auditioned as singer, '66, I think, in Düsseldorf, where he was engaged as a repetitore. I accompanied myself at my audition. They didn't give me the job. In the last three years of Kleiber's life I was, I think, perhaps, the nearest person. People don't know so much about this. His daughter knows it. I have a lot of Kleiber letters, very important letters I think. We met in München, in Grünwald, and we walked and we spoke and we didn't speak.

And we ate. I was not able to get him back. I tried, in the way I thought it was good to try. The six performances of Rosenkavalier in Tokyo that he did at my direction, and the three Rosenkavaliers in Vienna, remain something that we will never hear again. We corresponded also after the death of his wife. I felt very near to him."[27]

The conductor Mariss Jansons is another such man. In a radio interview with Gilbert Kaplan, he considered the question.

"I think he was one of the most interesting and wonderful conductors in history. This man had enormous imagination, intelligence, enormous charisma, everything. Of course, his repertoire was limited, but I don't think it's so important the quantity of pieces that you are doing. The most important is how you are doing and he did everything completely fantastically."

Jansons was asked if he had ever seen Kleiber work.

Yes! I even met him. He came to my rehearsal. You know, I wrote him some letters because my father[28] played in Riga Opera Orchestra when Erich Kleiber was the conductor there. My father played under his father. And I wrote Carlos Kleiber this letter, that my father thought so much about his father, and he answered me. He always doesn't answer in letters, he answers in cards, very small cards. And he wrote me two cards and I was very happy.

When I became music director in Munich, the Radio Symphony Orchestra, Carlos Kleiber came to meet me at my rehearsal. I was so happy to see him. He came before rehearsal, we talked 45 minutes. He was an extremely interesting man and very knowledgeable, very, very sensitive, incredibly sensitive. And this, I think, sensitivity, helped him be really such a wonderful musician.

Carlos Kleiber had enormous talent, plus all other things of the highest level: intelligence and everything. To have this talent from God is not enough. You must be educated in many things. He had everything.[29]

Riccardo Muti conducted a concert in Ljubljana, on 4 November 2009, in honor of Carlos and his Slovenian-born wife. The Slovenian Philharmonic, Slovenian Chamber Choir, and Consortium Music Chorus performed Schubert 8 and the Brahms *Alto Rhapsody*. Milan Kucan, former president of Slovenia, gave Kleiber's niece Brigita Drnovsek a document in which the Slovenian Philharmonic Society posthumously named Kleiber an honorary member.

The Bavarian Staatsoper was the nearest he ever came to a home company. On 12 December that year they too offered a public memorial and a concert that consisted of the exquisite English idylls of George Butterworth. The event also included excerpts from Carlos's films of *Fledermaus*, Brahms's Fourth Symphony, and *Der Rosenkavalier*.

The concert was performed without a conductor.

Carlos's baton lay on the podium. Who could touch it?

* * *

The Ear is the last Face.
We hear after we see.

—Emily Dickinson

NOTES

1. Bernard Haitink, author's interview, from Switzerland, 5 December 2004. Carlos may have been quoting his own father. The same line is attributed to Erich in conversation with Hans Gál, recorded in chapter 9 of Russell.

2. Pliny the Elder, early Roman encyclopedist; Thomas Carlyle, nineteenth-century Scottish historian and biographer; Robert A. Caro, contemporary American historian.

3. Longtime member of the Bavarian State Opera's makeup department.

4. Carnival time, especially popular in Catholic and southern Germany and in Austria. It officially begins at 11:11 a.m. on the eleventh day of the eleventh month.

5. A German tennis star.

6. Maschinenfabrik Augsberg-Nürnberg, dating from 1844. "It's a Man's World," according to their advertisements.

7. The climax of Carnival and the Fasching period.

8. Sir Peter Jonas, e-mail to author, 30 December 2004. My thanks to Carrie Fischer for her archaeology.

9. Né Rajneesh Chandra Mohan, later known as Acharya Rajneesh.

10. If you want to see a ludicrous example of a conductor trying to imitate Kleiber, but without the art, watch www.youtube.com/watch?v=l2gRbs9Vlw8. He even manages to copy Carlos's holding the railing with his left hand, but that's about it. The conductor shall be nameless. Wisely, the players pay him no attention at all.

11. Matheopoulos, *Maestro*.

12. All credit to Josef Krips for this wonderful phrase, conceived in memory of Furtwängler.

13. There was a brief flare of collegiality. Carlos watched Gielen, on television, lead the Mahler Youth Orchestra in Mahler's Symphony No. 6, on the first night of a Salzburg Festival. Kleiber told Gielen, "Well done, Michael, you don't shake your ass when conducting, as so many colleagues do!" Gielen, letter to De Filippi, 5 March 2010.

14. Jonas, letter of 20 October 2004.

15. Save for unhappy encounters with waiters and record producers. Bernard Haitink told of an embarrassing set-to in a Munich restaurant. "The waiter had made a small mistake, and Carlos berated him terribly. The poor man was a servant, and couldn't say anything or he would lose his job." Author's interview, 5 December 2004.

16. Fleming, 147.

17. 12 March 2001.

18. Garmisch-Partenkirchen, Strauss's home and burial site. Fleming, 173.

19. KD, author's interview, 23 June 2010.

20. Jonas, remarks at the Kleiber memorial concert, Munich, 12 December 2004.

21. This is a massive and exceptionally sweet-tempered work and rescue dog, with a heavy double coat and large webbed paws. Its average height is 28 inches and its weight, 140 pounds.

22. These stories were written by Donald Grant Mitchell, under the pseudonym Ik Marvel, and were extremely popular in their day. Carlo the dog first appeared in

September 1849, in "Smoke, Flame and Ashes," the first of four "sweet and pensive fantasies" that make up *Reveries*. Biographer Alfred Habeggen believes that Carlo may have been named for St. John Rivers's dog, appearing in *Jane Eyre* in February 1850.

23. Dickinson's father chose Emily's dog wisely. Lord Byron viewed his Newfoundland dog Boatswain as possessing "Beauty without Vanity, Strength without Insolence, Courage without Ferocity, and all the Virtues of man without his Vices."

24. Transcription courtesy Robert McGinn.

25. On 22 October 2004, at 6 p.m. The room seats 380. The interview was conducted in English.

26. Press release of 15 November 2004, Office of the Federal Chancellery, Austria.

27. *Mad about Music*, WQXR, radio interview, adapted, 5 April 2009.

28. The well-known conductor Arvid.

29. *Mad about Music*, WQXR, adapted, 7 February 2010.

Appendix A

Discography

So much about Carlos Kleiber was made poignant by the great "If Only." Nowhere is this more so than in the story of his recordings—complete, fragmentary, and suppressed. In his day, there was much talk of recording *Wozzeck*, *Otello*, a *Ring Cycle*, and any Mozart opera he wished. Nothing came of it.

This material is divided into "Suppressed" and "Published." He was exceptionally, ferociously determined to release only recordings that met standards of hearing and perception possessed by no one but him. I own all the pirates listed, as do all Kleiber devotees. Most of them are in very good sound. All are fascinating.

RECORDINGS SUPPRESSED OR LEFT INCOMPLETE

1975

Beethoven, Piano Concerto No. 5
Arturo Benedetti Michelangeli, pianist
  As recounted in chapter 2, an effort was made to finish this recording after Carlos walked out at the end of the first day of recording in Berlin. The recording has not been released.

1979

Puccini, La Bohème
  This opera was to have been recorded at La Scala, Milan. Kleiber disappeared on the third day, leaving behind only the first act. These sessions were

scheduled to start on 23 June at 3:00 p.m. They did not begin well, due to impossible air traffic the day before. Only Kleiber and Ileana Cotrubas had been able to arrive on time.

On the first day of rehearsal, a recording of sections not requiring the three leads was made. On the following day, the start time was set for 10:00 a.m. Domingo was still unable to make the morning session. Kleiber appeared at 10:05 a.m. and started rehearsal just five minutes after his arrival. His sudden start stirred up a tension that shot through the hall. The recording tape was activated moments later. Even the red lamp showing the recording session was under way was not yet in place.

None other than Kleiber himself was heard through the monitor. Even though "singing" Rudolfo's part at the top of the first act, he was relentless with the orchestra. He made the harp redo one sequence more than ten times. It was over by 10:45 a.m. The afternoon session resumed at 3:30 p.m. with Domingo. Kleiber took no break in the next hour. There were no playbacks—only rehearsals and repetitions. Then, saying nothing to anyone, he left on the third day. Deutsche Grammophon tried for years to persuade him to finish the project.[1]

1981

Beethoven, Symphony No. 7
Schubert, Symphony No. 3
Weber, Overture to Die Freischütz

This was to have been the BBC broadcast of a live concert with the London Symphony Orchestra, given on 9 June 1981. As noted earlier, the reviews were largely vitriolic. Carlos was deeply offended, ordered the BBC to destroy the tapes (they did), and promised never to conduct concerts in London again (he didn't). Luckily, the repertoire here exists in several other recordings. No pirates have materialized.

1982

Wagner, Tristan und Isolde

This recording, although eventually released, represents one of the strangest and most heart-breaking experiences of Carlos's life. Although officially published by Deutsche Grammophon two years after Kleiber left its sessions, the recording itself is a patchwork of rehearsals. As recounted in chapter 2, Kleiber walked out of this project. When he did so he thought the recording would never be released.

1983

Beethoven, Symphony No. 6

For many years there was talk about his once-only performance of Beethoven 6, given on 7 November 1983 with the Bavarian State Opera Orchestra. That event became part of the Kleiber mystery. There was supposed to have been a phantom recording, but it was never released. Only in 2003 did the family make it available to the public. Carlos himself had no direct hand in its publication.

1989

Beethoven, Piano Concerto No. 3
Vladimir Horowitz, piano

Also reported in chapter 2, Kleiber and Horowitz met in the last year of the great pianist's life, and agreed on a recording of Beethoven Piano Concerto No. 3. Horowitz died before the sessions could be organized.

1993

Mozart, Symphony No. 33
Strauss, Richard. Ein Heldenleben

These concerts actually took place. Carlos appeared at the Musikvereinsaal with the Vienna Philharmonic on 15 and 16 May 1993. Sony recorded the concert, and worldwide distribution was arranged. *Heldenleben* was new to Carlos's public repertoire, and there was enormous interest in hearing what he would do with it. All the Vienna concert reviews were stunning. Carlos forbade release of the recordings. At this writing there is rumor in the industry that it may, after all, finally be made officially available. Pirates have been around for years.

Although suppressed as a Sony CD, it was broadcast by NHK in Japan on 15 August 1993 and again on 9 January 1994. It is not clear why he would allow the one and not the other. Carlos's *Heldenleben* is a glorious performance, and it is impossible to tell to what he could have taken objection— save to imagine that he heard something even more magnificent internally.

RECORDINGS PROPOSED

There are innumerable stories about projects proposed to Carlos that he eventually declined—or simply ignored altogether. Here, "what if" becomes "if only."

Berg, Alban. Wozzeck

Dvořák, Antonin. New World Symphony

In the October 1975 issue of *The Gramophone*, under "Recording News," at p. 170, the following item appeared: "The conductor Carlos Kleiber has recently signed a recording contract with EMI which includes Berg's opera Wozzeck (to be made in Dresden), a concerto disc with the Russian pianist Sviatoslav Richter and some orchestral repertoire."

Five years later, in the December 1982 issue of a leading German magazine for record collectors, *FonoForum*, writer Stefan Mikorey reported on the collapse of a plan to have Kleiber record both *Wozzeck* and the *New World*. Dr. Mikorey himself was well placed to know about such matters, as he produced Bruckner recordings for Günter Wand with the Berlin Philharmonic and the Bertelsmann Music Group, among many other projects.[2]

Wagner, Ring Cycle

Carlos studied these works (*Das Rheingold, Die Walküre, Siegfried,* and *Götterdämmerung*) deeply. In his career, he conducted none of them. The distinguished producer John Mordler put on a full-court press to persuade Kleiber to undertake this massive project. Here's how he recalls the effort.

"Our dream, at EMI, was for Carlos to record the Ring Cycle. Both my colleagues and I spent much time chasing after him, whether in person or by correspondence, to try to persuade him. Unfortunately, to no avail. While I believe that the project tempted him, he must have felt too unsure, if not actually daunted by the prospect. . . . Besides, he hated people trying to pressure him and this is why he was always so elusive."[3]

RECORDINGS PUBLISHED

This is a selective list, based on my personal collection. For a complete list, please visit Toru Hirasawa's superb—and current—website, http://www .thrsw.com/kleiber.html. For accuracy and completeness, it stands above all others.

Anthology, 1989 New Year's Concert
Vienna Philharmonic
Vienna, 1 January 1989 [live]
CBS / SONY MK2 45564

Anthology, 1992 New Year's Concert
Vienna Philharmonic
Vienna, 1 January 1992 [live]
Sony SK 48 376

Beethoven, Symphony No. 4, Op. 60
Bavarian State Orchestra
Munich, 3 May 1982 [live]
Orfeo C 100 841 A

Beethoven, Symphony No. 5, Op. 67
Vienna Philharmonic, 1975
DG 415 861-2

Beethoven, Symphony No. 5
Chicago Symphony, October 1978 [live]
Artists FED 013.14

Beethoven, Symphony No. 6, Op. 68
Bavarian State Orchestra
Munich, 7 November 1983 [live]
Orfeo C 600 031 B

Beethoven, Symphony No. 7, Op. 92
Cologne Radio Symphony Orchestra
Cologne, 27 May 1972
Memories ME 1011/12

Beethoven, Symphony No. 7
Vienna Philharmonic, 1976
DG 415 862-2

Berg, Wozzeck. excerpts
Gwendy Fine, soprano
WDR SO, Cologne, 1972 [live]
Artists FED 045.46

Borodin, Symphony No. 2
Stuttgart Radio Symphony Orchestra
Stuttgart, 1972 [live]

Documents LV 905/06
Memories HR 4410
Mediaphon 75.103
Hänssler 93.116 [with Erich Kleiber, NBC Symphony Orchestra,
20 December 1947 broadcast of Borodin]

Brahms, Symphony No. 2, Op. 73
Vienna Philharmonic, 1988 [live]
Artists FED 013.14

Brahms, Symphony No. 4, Op. 98
Vienna Philharmonic, 1981
DG 400 037-2
DG 00289 477 5324

Butterworth, English Idyll No. 1
Chicago Symphony, June 1983 [live]
Artists FED 045.46

Dvořák, Piano Concerto, Op. 33
Sviatoslav Richter, piano
Bavarian State Orchestra, 1977
EMI CDC 7 47967 2

Haydn, Symphony No. 94 (Surprise)
Cologne Radio Symphony Orchestra
Köln, 27 May 1972 [live]
Originals SH 813

Haydn, Symphony No. 94
Bavarian State Orchestra
Munich, 7 November 1983 [live]

Haydn, Symphony No. 94
Vienna Philharmonic
Vienna, 28 February 1982 [live]
Exclusive EX92T13
Artists FED 013.14

Mahler, Das Lied von der Erde
Ludwig, Kmentt

Vienna Symphony
Vienna, 1967 [live]
Documents LV 905/06

Mozart, Symphony No. 33, K319
Vienna Symphony
Vienna, 7 June 1967 [live]
Memories HR 4410
Nuovo Era 2296

Mozart, Symphony No. 33
Vienna Philharmonic
Vienna 1993 [live]

Mozart, Symphony No. 36, K425 (Linz)
Vienna Philharmonic
Vienna, 20 March 1988 [live]
Exclusive EX92T13
Artists FED 013.14

Nicolai, Overture, Die lustigen Weiber von Windsor
Zurich State Theatre Orchestra, 1966 [live]
(NB: This is in error, and, in fact, it is taken from the Vienna Philharmonic
   concert of 1992.)

Offenbach, Die Kleine Zauberflöte
Treskow, Diekmann, Gester
Orchestra of the Rhine Opera House, Düsseldorf
Düsseldorf 1963 [live]
Golden Melodram GM 4.0051

Offenbach, Die Verlobung bei der Laterne
Sommer, Wien, Kaspar
Orchestra of the Rhine Opera House, Düsseldorf
Düsseldorf 1963 [live]
Golden Mclodram GM 4.0051

Puccini, La Bohème
Cotrubas, Pavarotti, Cappuccilli, Popp, Giorgetti, Nesterenko, Porzano, Giombi
La Scala Orchestra and Chorus
Milan, 22 March 1979 [live]
Exclusive EX92T01/2

Puccini, La Bohème
Cotrubas, Pavarotti, Popp, Saccomani, Nesterenko, Giorgetti
La Scala Orchestra and Chorus
Milan, 30 March 1979 [live]
Golden Melodram 5.0038-2

Puccini, La Bohème
Freni, Pavarotti, Daniels, Summers, Howell, Hampson, Giombi
Metropolitan Opera Orchestra and Chorus
New York City, 1 February 1988 [live]

Schubert, Symphony No. 3, D 200
Chicago Symphony, October 1978 [live]
Artists FED 013.14

Schubert, Symphony No. 3
Vienna Philharmonic, 1979
DG 415 601-2

Schubert, Symphony No. 8, D 759
Vienna Philharmonic, 1979
DG 415 601-2
DG 00289 477 5324

Strauss, J. Die Fledermaus
Varady, Popp, Prey, Rebroff
Bavarian State Opera, 1976
DG 415 646-2

Strauss, J. Overture, Gypsy Baron
Zurich State Theatre Orchestra, 1966 [live]
(NB: This is in error, and, in fact, it is taken from the Vienna Philharmonic
concert of 1992.)

Strauss, Josef. Dorfschwalben aus Österreich
Zurich State Theatre Orchestra, 1966 [live]
(NB: This is in error, in fact, taken from the Vienna Philharmonic concert of
1992.)

Strauss, Josef. Feuerfest!
Zurich State Theatre Orchestra, 1966 [live]

Strauss, Josef. Jockey Polka
Zurich State Theatre Orchestra, 1966 [live]

Strauss, Josef. Sphërenklänge
Zurich State Theatre Orchestra, 1966 [live]

Strauss, R. Elektra
Mödl, Steger, Tarres, Windgassen, Wildermann
Stuttgart Staatsoper Orchestra and Chorus
Stuttgart, 17 June 1971 [live]
Golden Melodram 6.0011

Strauss, R. Elektra
Szirmay, Nilsson, Jones, Craig, McIntyre
Royal Opera House Orchestra and Chorus
London, 6 May 1977 [live]
Golden Melodram 6.0001

Strauss, R. Ein Heldenleben
Vienna Philharmonic
Vienna, 16 May 1993 [live]
Great Artists GA4-10
Memories ME 1003/4

Telemann, Tafelmusik
NDR Sinfonieorkester
Hamburg, 7 December 1960 [live]
We Love Carlos Society 1-709

Verdi, La Traviata
Cotrubas, Domingo, Milnes
Bavarian State Opera, 1977
DG 415 132-2

Verdi, La Traviata
Cotrubas, Aragall, Bruson
Bavarian State Opera, 1978 [live]
Artists FED 045.46

Verdi, La Traviata
Gasdia, Dvorski, Zancanaro

Maggio Musicale Fiorentino
Firenze/Florence, 9 December 1984 [live]
Exclusive EX92T42/43

Verdi, Otello
Domingo, Price, Carroli, Leggate
Royal Opera House Orchestra and Chorus
London, 19 February 1980 [live]
Golden Melodram 5.0028

Wagner, Tristan und Isolde
Vorspiel and Liebestod
Stuttgart Radio Symphony Orchestra
Stuttgart, 1972 [live]
Documents LV 905/06

Wagner, Tristan und Isolde (highlights)
Hopf, Ligendza, Baldani
Vienna State Opera Orchestra, 1973 [live]
Documents LV 905/06

Wagner, Tristan und Isolde
Price, Kollo, Fassbaender, Fischer-Diskau, Moll
Staatskapelle Dresden, 1982
DG 413 315-2
DG 00289 477 5324 [excerpts]

Weber, Der Freischütz
Janowitz, Mathis, Schreier
Stattsakapelle Dresden, 1973
DG 415 432-2

Weber, Overture, Der Freischütz
Vienna Philharmonic, 1979 [live]
Artists FED 013.14

Weber, Overture, Der Freischütz
Bavarian State Orchestra
Munich, 7 November 1983 [live]

NOTES

1. My thanks to Yasuo Chikaku for his account of these sessions, at which he was in attendance.

2. Mikorey may have been telescoping a bit. The *Wozzeck* recording had been planned for 1975–1976. Correction courtesy Ulrich Plemper.

3. John Mordler, e-mail to author, 20 January 2005.

Appendix B
Filmography

The following materials are held by the Conductors on Film Collection in the Archive of Recorded Sound at Stanford University. None of these materials is in the public domain. All may be viewed, by appointment and without charge, at Stanford. Film materials commercially available are noted under each heading.

The commercial catalogue numbers below refer to NTSC VHS, the North American and Japanese standard. Materials released in PAL and SECAM formats, otherwise identical, have slightly different catalogue numbers. At this writing, many of these videos have been released in the DVD format. These too are made available in PAL, SECAM, and NTSC standards.

CARLOS KLEIBER

Beethoven, Overture to Coriolanus
Bavarian State Orchestra
Herkulessaal, Munich, 21 October 1996
DG DVD B0003841-09

Beethoven, Overture to Coriolanus
Vienna Philharmonic
Teatro Juárez, Guanajuato, GTO, México, 25, 27 April 1981

Beethoven, Symphony No. 4
Bavarian State Orchestra
Tokyo, 19 May 1985
NHK television production

Beethoven, Symphony No. 4
Concertgebouw Orchestra
October 1983
Unitel 070 200-3, Philips DVD B0003880-09

Beethoven, Symphony No. 5
Vienna Philharmonic
Teatro Juárez, Guanajuato, GTO, México, 25, 27 April 1981

Beethoven, Symphony No. 7
Bavarian State Orchestra
Tokyo, 19 May 1985
NHK television production

Beethoven, Symphony No. 7
Concertgebouw Orchestra
October 1983
Unitel 070 200-3, Philips DVD B0003880-09

Bizet, Carmen
Obratzsova, Domingo, Masurok
Vienna State Opera. Zeffirelli. ORF, 1978
TDK DVD DVUS-CLOPCAR

Brahms, Symphony No. 2
Vienna Philharmonic
6–7 October 1991
Unitel 070 161-3 (PAL)

Brahms, Symphony No. 4
Bavarian State Orchestra
Herkulessaal, Munich, 21 October 1996
DG DVD B0003841-09

Mozart, Symphony No. 33
Bavarian State Orchestra
Herkulessaal, Munich, 21 October 1996
DG DVD B0003841-09

Mozart, Symphony No. 36 (Linz)
Vienna Philharmonic

6–7 October, 1991
Unitel 070 161-3 (PAL)

1989 Vienna New Year's Day Concert
Vienna Philharmonic
1 January 1989
Unitel 072 246-3

1992 Vienna New Year's Day Concert
Vienna Philharmonic
1 January 1992
Philips PHI B000388209

Puccini, La Bohème
La Scala, 1979
Pavarotti, Cotrubas, Popp

Puccini, La Bohème
La Scala production
Bunka Kaikan, Tokyo, 15 September 1981

Strauss, Johann. Die Fledermaus
Bavarian State Opera, 1987

Strauss, Johann. Overture to Fledermaus
Bavarian State Orchestra
Tokyo, 19 May 1985
NHK television production

Strauss, Johann. Overture to Fledermaus
Vienna Philharmonic
Teatro Juárez, Guanajuato, GTO, México, 25, 27 April 1981

Strauss, Johann. Overture to Fledermaus
rehearsal and performance
RSO Stuttgart, January 1970
TDK DVD DOCCK

Strauss, Johann. Thunder and Lightning
Bavarian State Orchestra
Tokyo, 19 May 1985
NHK television production

Strauss, Johann. Thunder and Lightning
Vienna Philharmonic
Teatro Juárez, Guanajuato, GTO, México, 25, 27 April 1981

Strauss, Richard. Der Rosenkavalier
Bavarian State Opera, 1979

Strauss, Richard. Der Rosenkavalier
Lott, von Otter, Bonney, Moll
Vienna State Opera and Chorus
23 March 1994. ORF-1 television broadcast
(NB: There is a version of this performance in which Kleiber appears in the
    lower right corner of the screen. He is seen conducting Act III only. There
    is another version in which his image occupies the whole of the screen.)

Strauss, Richard. Der Rosenkavalier
Lott, von Otter, Bonney, Moll
Vienna State Opera and Chorus
December 1996
3-SAT television broadcast

Verdi, Otello
Domingo, Freni
La Scala, 7 December 1976
RAI television broadcast

Verdi, Otello
La Scala production at NHK Hall
Tokyo, 2 September 1981

Wagner, Tristan und Isolde
Three sequences exist: orchestral Prelude to Act I; Act II, Scene II; and, 6:46
    from the Liebestod. All may be found at Stanford and online.
Bayreuth, 1974–1976

Weber, Overture to Der Freischütz
rehearsal and performance
Stuttgart Radio Symphony Orchestra, 1970
TDK DVD DOCCK

Compilation

Carlos Kleiber—Die Legende
This compilation DVD includes many of his most important performances:
Beethoven, Symphony No. 4 and Symphony No. 7, Concertgebouw Orchestra
Brahms, Symphony No. 2 and Mozart, Symphony No. 36, Vienna Philhar-
  monic
Beethoven, Overture to *Coriolanus*, Brahms, Symphony No. 4 and Mozart,
  Symphony No. 33, Bavarian Staatsorchester
New Year's Day Concert 1989, Vienna Philharmonic
New Year's Day Concert 1992, Vienna Philharmonic
Philips/DG 074 308-0

ERICH KLEIBER

Beethoven, Symphony No. 9
rehearsal
Czech Philharmonic Orchestra and Chorus, Smetana Hall, Prague
Hearst-Metrotone Newsreel
23 August 1949

Mozart, German Dances, K605, No. 3 [Schlittenfahrt]
Berlin Staatsoper Orchestra, 1931

Novak, Bohemian Suite
Czech Philharmonic Orchestra, c 1949

Strauss, J. Artist's Life
Concertgebouw Orchestra, RAI Hall 1949

Strauss, J. Blue Danube Waltz
Berlin Staatskapelle Orchestra, 1932
The Art of Conducting: Legendary Conductors of a Golden Era (1997)
Teldec 0927.42668.2 (DVD)

Appendix C
Films Sent to Carlos Kleiber

As previously described, I hit on the idea of asking Carlos for his comments about the work of great conductors on film—in rehearsal, concert, opera, and conversation. Many of my letters included a video and questions about its contents as might be analyzed by him. Below is a list of the fifty-three videos sent to Grünwald over twelve years. (Numbering errors on my part account for the apparent discrepancies. Cataloguing errors were eventually corrected.) Some of the most interesting films are not available commercially. All may be studied at Stanford.

Tape No. 1, 20 July 1992

FURTWÄNGLER, Wilhelm (1886–1954)
Schubert, Symphony No. 8, 1st movement, opening, 4:30
Rehearsal, Berlin Philharmonic, December 1951

Wagner, Prelude to Meistersinger, opening, 3:00
Concert, Berlin Philharmonic, December 1951

Strauss, Till Eulenspiegel, 14:00
Concert, with film of ballet inserted, Titania Palast
Berlin Philharmonic, December 1951 (ballet only, 2:20, cut)

Brahms, Symphony No. 4, 4th movement, rehearsal, 5:10
measures 113 (E) to end; Berlin Philharmonic
Empress Hall, London, 2 November 1948

Interview with Siegfried Borries, 1:00

Wagner, Prelude to Meistersinger, complete, 9:30
Concert, Berlin Philharmonic, AEG Factory, 26 February 1942

Mozart, Overture to Don Giovanni, 5:40
Vienna Philharmonic, Salzburg; color, August 1954

Beethoven, Symphony No. 9, 4th movement, finale, 4:40
Concert, Berlin Philharmonic, 19 April 1942
Hitler Birthday event; Berger, Haengen, Roswaenge, Watzke; Kittel Chorus
WF embarrassed when required to shake hands with Goebbels

Wagner, Prelude to Meistersinger, 2:24
Concert, Berlin Philharmonic, December 1951

Tape No. 2, 12 September 1992

BLECH, Leo (1871–1958)
Wagner, Prelude to Meistersinger, 7:50
Berlin State Opera Orchestra, 1933

BORCHARDT, Leo (1899–1945)
Strauss, Overture and Suite, Fledermaus, 15:00
Berlin Philharmonic (?), 1936

BUSCH, Fritz (1890–1951)
Wagner, Overture to Tannhäuser, 13:25
Saxon State Orchestra, 1933

FURTWÄNGLER, Wilhelm (1886–1954)
Beethoven, Fidelio, 2:00
Vienna Philharmonic, Vienna State Opera Chorus; Salzburg, 1950 (?)

Beethoven, Symphony No. 9, 4th movement, 1:35
Vienna Philharmonic, Vienna State Opera Chorus
Seefried, Wagner, Dermota, Greindl; Salzburg, 31 August 1951

KNAPPERTSBUSCH, Hans (1888–1965)
Beethoven, Symphony No. 9, 4th movement, 4:25
Berlin Philharmonic, April 1943, Kittel Chorus

SCHILLINGS, Max von (1868–1933)
Rossini, Overture to William Tell, 9:40
Berlin State Opera Orchestra, 1932 (1933?) [Singakademie]

WALTER, Bruno (1876–1962)
Beethoven, Symphony No. 9, 4th movement, rehearsal, 1:05
Vienna Philharmonic, 1948

Mozart, Symphony No. 40, 4th movement, 5:20
Berlin Philharmonic, 17 March 1930 [25 September 1950?]

Weber, Overture to Oberon, 8:20
Berlin Philharmonic, 1931 [Singakademie]

Tape No. 3, 6 October 1992

ANSERMET, Ernest (1883–1969)
Haydn, Symphony No. 99, 4th movement, rehearsal, 4:00
Orchestre de la Suisse Romande

BLECH, Leo (1871–1958)
Bizet, Carmen, Act IV ballet, 1:30
Staatsoper Berlin, includes Blech in conversation re Carmen, 1949

FRICSAY, Ferenc (1914–1963)
Rossini, Overture to Italian Girl in Algiers, 6:20
RSO Berlin (?), c. 1960

KEILBERTH, Joseph (1908–1968)
Rossini, Overture to Magpie, 6:45
Bavarian State Orchestra, Cuvellies Theater, Munich, 25 December 1959

KLEMPERER, Otto (1885–1973)
Beethoven, Egmont, rehearsal, 1:30
Philharmonia Orchestra, in Musikvereinsaal, Vienna 1960

Beethoven, Symphony No. 9, 90:00
New Philharmonia Orchestra, Royal Albert Hall, 1964
Agnes Giebel, Marga Hoffgen, Ernst Haefliger, Gustav Neidlinger
New Philharmonia Chorus; 27 October 1964; BBC, 8 November 1964

KNAPPERTSBUSCH, Hans (1888–1965)
Beethoven, Symphony No. 9, 4th movement, 4:25
Berlin Philharmonic, April 1943, Kittel Chorus
    NB: Same performance as on Tape No. 2, but much better synchronicity

MENGELBERG, Willem (1871–1951)
Beethoven, Egmont, extracts, 1:30
NSDAP rally, November 1940; ibid.

Bizet, L'Arlesienne Suite No. 1, 2:00
Concertgebouw Orchestra, Paris, April 1931

Weber, Overture to Oberon, 2:50
Concertgebouw Orchestra, Paris, April 1931
    Author to CK: Is the one you've already seen?

Tape No. 4, 7 November 1992

STRAVINSKY, Igor (1882–1971)
Stravinsky, L'Histoire du Soldat, rehearsal, 7:15
CBS chamber orchestra, 1958/1959, New York. Film by Nina Lean

MITROPOULOS, Dmitri (1896–1960)
Liszt, Faust Symphony, 3rd movement, rehearsal and concert, 11:22
New York Philharmonic, Carnegie Hall, December 1949

ABENDROTH, Herman (1883–1956)
Beethoven, Symphony No. 3, 1st movement, 2:35
Leipzig Gewandhaus Orchestra

KEMPE, Rudolph (1910–1976)
Wagner, Die Walkure, Act II, *Overture*, rehearsal, 1:40
Bayreuth Festival Orchestra, 1960

KNAPPERTSBUSCH, Hans (1888–1965)
Wagner, Parsifal, Act I, entry into sanctuary, pit rehearsal, 1:00
Bayreuth Festival Orchestra, 1959

KONWITSCHNY, Franz (1901–1962)
Beethoven Symphony No. 5, 4th movement, 2:30
Leipzig Gewandhaus Orchestra

KRIPS, Josef (1902–1974)
Schubert Symphony No. 8, 1st movement, 11:50
Vienna Philharmonic, 1948. Samuel Spade, concertmaster

KUBELIK, Rafael (1914–1996)
Beethoven, Leonore No. 3, 1:40
Concertgebouw Orchestra, c. 1960 television broadcast

MATAČIĆ, Lovro von (1899–1985)
Brahms, Symphony No. 1, 43:00
NHK Symphony Orchestra, 1984; NHK television

NIKISCH, Artur (1855–1922)
God knows. *Berlioz, Roman Carnival Overture,* on soundtrack, 1:00
from Oskar Messter film, with "Blüthner Orchester," 1913

STRAUSS, Richard (1864–1949)
Strauss, Alpine Symphony, 1:00
Bavarian State Opera Orchestra, 1941

Strauss, Daphne, at piano, 00:45
Garmisch-Partenkirchen, c. 1949

Strauss, Rosenkavalier, Act II, dress, 2:30
Bavarian State Orchestra, Prinzregen Theater, in RS Festival, 10 June 1949

WALTER, Bruno (1876–1962)
Wagner, Prelude to Meistersinger, 2:45
New York Philharmonic, Carnegie Hall, 1947

Plus preview of coming attractions: Vaclav Talich, Czech Philharmonic

Tape No. 5, 2 December 1992

COATES, Albert (1882–1953)
Concerto for One Note; Gracie Allen, piano, 4:00
from *Two Girls and a Sailor*; studio orchestra; MGM, 1944

MUNCH, Charles (1891–1968)
Franck, Symphony in D Minor, 36:00
Boston Symphony Orchestra, 14 March 1961

REINER, Fritz (1888–1963)
Tchaikovsky, Violin Concerto, 1st movement, 11:00
New York Philharmonic, Carnegie Hall, 1947
Jascha Heifetz, violin

RODZINSKI, Artur (1892–1958)
Beethoven, Symphony No. 5, 4th movement, 5:00
New York Philharmonic, Carnegie Hall, 1947

STOKOWSKI, Leopold (1882–1977)
Rehearsal—With Leopold Stokowski, 60:00
Barber, Adagio for Strings, rehearsal, 9:00
Rachmaninoff, Rhapsody on a Theme of Paganini, rehearsal, 38:00
Jerome Lowenthal, piano
Schubert, Symphony No. 8, 1st movement, rehearsal, 11:30
American Symphony Orchestra, Felt Forum at Madison Square Garden
Fanfare, NET/PBS TV, 1971

Tchaikovsky, Symphony No. 5, 2nd movement at M108, 6:30
New York Philharmonic, Carnegie Hall, 1947

Tape No. 6, 7 December 1992

FURTWÄNGLER, Wilhelm (1886–1954)
Furtwängler, 65:00
Bavarian Television Production, Florian Furtwängler, director
German version, c.1964
English version, BBC Omnibus series, 1971

Tape No. 7, 10 December 1992

KLEMPERER, Otto (1885–1973)
Otto Klemperer's Long Journey through His Times 96:00
TV documentary, Holland/Germany 1984
Philo Bregstein, director; German with English subtitles

Tape No. 8, 17 December 1992

MUNCH, Charles (1891–1968)
Beethoven, Symphony No. 4, 30:30
Boston Symphony Orchestra, 18 April 1961

Brahms, Symphony No. 2, 38:00
Boston Symphony Orchestra, 12 April 1960

Handel-Harty, Water Music, 1st, 2nd, and 3rd movements, 12:00
Boston Symphony Orchestra, 12 April 1960

Mendelssohn, Symphony No. 3, 34:30
Boston Symphony Orchestra, 1 December 1959 (loses baton at 17:30)

Ravel, Daphnis and Chloe Suite No. 2, 17:00
Boston Symphony Orchestra, Sanders Theatre, Harvard; 17 April 1962

Schumann, Overture to Genoveva, 10:00
Boston Symphony Orchestra, 18 April 1961

Wagner, excerpts from Act III, *Meistersinger*, 16:00
Boston Symphony Orchestra, 8 March 1960

Tape No. 9, 15 January 1993

NIKISCH, Artur (1855–1922)
Tchaikovsky, Symphony No. 6, silent, 5:00
Oskar Messter film, complete, sideways-split screen, 1913

STRAUSS, Richard (1864–1949)
Strauss, Till Eulenspiegel, 32:30
complete film, raw footage, with retakes
Vienna Philharmonic, 11 June 1944

BEECHAM, Thomas (1879–1961)
Mozart, Symphony No. 38 (Prague), 23:30
Montreal Symphony Orchestra; CBC Concert Hour, 1956

JOCHUM, Eugen (1902–1987)
Bruckner, Symphony No. 7, adagio, 27:30
Concertgebouw Orchestra, Japan; NKH TV, 17 September 1986

KOUSSEVITSKY, Serge (1874–1951)
Beethoven, Egmont, dress rehearsal, 6:00
Boston Symphony Orchestra, Tanglewood film, 1949

Thompson (Randall), The Last Words of David, 5:00
Boston Symphony Orchestra, Tanglewood film, 1949

STRAVINSKY, Igor (1882–1971)
Stravinsky, Firebird (1919), excerpts, 5:20
NHK Orchestra, Japan, 1959; Japanese TV program

Tape No. 10, 22 February 1993

TALICH, Vaclav (1883–1961)
Dvořák, Slavonic Dances, Op. 46, entire, 60:00
Czech Philharmonic Orchestra, 1955
Television broadcast, remastered in 1980; Vaclav Holzknecht, narrator
   Author to CK: The music starts at 20:00. I left in the first 19:00, in case
you want to practise your Czech. Nazdar.

MUNCH, Charles (1891–1968)
Tchaikovsky, Romeo and Juliet, abbreviated, 23:30
Boston Symphony Orchestra, 1956
From RCA promotional/engineering film, *The Sound and the Story*

BEECHAM, Thomas (1879–1961)
Sir Thomas Beecham at Lincoln's Inn, 30:00
Granada TV program, 1958, black-and-white

Gounod, Faust, ballet music, rehearsal and concert; interview with Sir T by
Peter Brook
Royal Philharmonic Orchestra

ZOOT, Rebozo von (1959–1988)
Bernstein, Suite from West Side Story, 11:00
   Author to CK: This last is a bizarre excerpt you should only watch between
meals, con vino. Zoot did it on one "rehearsal" and died in a peculiar hunting
accident less than a week later. He was out in the woods with several orchestra members and was shot by all of them. They testified in court that he was
a moose. The jury awarded the players $15,000 "in gratitude."[1]

Tape No. 11, 31 March 1993

Kahgan Collection, UCLA, 2:30:00
Silent films from 1927–1947. Conductors and soloists in rehearsal, chiefly
   at the Hollywood Bowl: Altschuler, Ansermet, Bakaleinikoff-Constantin,

Bakaleinikoff-Vladimir, Barbirolli, Chavez, Cimini, Coates, Damrosch, Finston, Gabrilowitsch, Ganz, Golschmann, Goossens, Richard Hagemann, Howard Hanson, Harty, Hertz, Iturbi, Janssen, Kindler, Klemperer, Konoye, Koussevitsky, Krueger, Lert, McArthur, Molinari, Monteux, Ormandy, Rapée, Reiner, Rodzinski, Schelling, Schoenberg, Sevitzky, Slonimsky, Steinberg, William Grant Still, Stock, Stokowski, Stravinsky, Wallenstein, Walter, Henry Wood, Eugene Zador.

ALSO: Harold Bauer, Elizabeth Sprague Coolidge, Richard Crooks, Nelson Eddy, Mischa Elman, Raya Garbusova, José Greco Dance Company, Roland Hayes, Heifetz, Kahgan, Lotte Lehmann, Mischa Levitsky, Josef and Rosina Lhevinne, Ernst Lubitsch, Queena Mario, John McCormack, Kathryn Meisle, Louis Persinger, Piatigorsky, Pro Arte String Quartet, Ruggiero Ricci, Albert Spalding, Olga Steeb, Akim Tamiroff, John Charles Thomas, and Victor Young.

Tape No. 12, 15 April 1993

SZELL, George (1897–1970)
One Man's Triumph, 60:00
Bell Telephone Hour documentary, 1966; Nathan Kroll, director
includes studio and conducting class; Irving Kolodin, narrator

Beethoven, Symphony No. 5, rehearsal and concert
Cleveland Orchestra, 1966

Berg, Violin Concerto, rehearsal,
Rafael Druyian, violin; Cleveland Orchestra, 1966

Brahms, Academic Festival Overture, rehearsal
Cleveland Orchestra, 1966

ZOOT, Rebozo von (1959–1988)
Cage, 44:33
(Edited by von Zoot) Orchestra of the Err, 1988[2]

Tape No. 13, 21 April 1993

TENNSTEDT, Klaus (1926–1998)
Mahler, Symphony No. 1, 64:00
Chicago Symphony Orchestra, live, 31 May, 1 June 1990; EMI

TOSCANINI, Arturo (1867–1957)
Brahms, Symphony No. 1, 46:00
NBC Symphony, telecast 3 November 1951, Carnegie Hall
   Author to CK: Given your admiration, I thought you might want to see the whole thing on film. And so much for the NBC publicity machine re total fidelity to the score; timpani added in iv, measures 407–416 and 447–449, for example.

Tape No. 14, 24 May 1993

HADLEY, Henry (1871–1937)
Wagner, Prelude to Tannhauser, 10:00
New York Philharmonic; Warner Bros Vitaphone, 1926
   Author to CK: This is the first known document of any conductor anywhere in sound on film.

KLEMPERER, Otto (1885–1973)
Concertgebouw Orchestra, 12 May–1 June 1958, 25:00
Beethoven cycle, rehearsals; silent black and white

SCHERCHEN, Hermann (1891–1966)
Bach, Art of the Fugue (arr. Scherchen) rehearsal, 30:00
CBC Toronto Chamber Orchestra, December 1965

Beethoven, Wellington's Victory, rehearsal, 8:20
Stuttgart Symphony Orchestra [RSO Stuttgart, 1962]

STRAUSS, Richard (1864–1949)
Strauss, Der Rosenkavalier, silent film, 11:20
Robert Jacobsen, narrator; NYC TV; Richard Strauss conducting new pre-
   title music
Augmented London Tivoli Theatre Orchestra, on separate audio track (13–14
   April 1926)
Robert Wiene, director; Pan-Film Wien, 1925
   Author to CK: I couldn't make a two-track from VHS to audio cassette, as you requested. Don't know what I was doing wrong, so I just dubbed the excerpt you wanted onto the video.

Tape No. 15, 15 July 1993

BOULEZ, Pierre (b. 1925)
Varese, Amèriques, 23:00
Vienna Philharmonic; Salzburg, 1992

FRICSAY, Ferenc (1914–1963)
Ein Ungar in Berlin—Zum Gedenken an den Dirigente, 60:00
Bartok, Concerto for Orchestra, rehearsal, 3:00
Radio Symphony Orchestra of Berlin, 1960

Dukas, Sorcerer's Apprentice, rehearsal; ibid., 9:00

Kodaly, Hary Janos Suite, rehearsal and concert; ibid., 43:00

Mozart, Overture to Don Giovanni, live in pit; ibid., 3:00
[Berlin, German Opera, 24 September 1961]

KNAPPERTSBUSCH, Hans (1888–1965)
Wagner, Siegfried Idyll, 8:30
Vienna Philharmonic, 22 May 1963

Tape No. 16, 13 August 1993

BOULT, Adrian (1889–1983)
Beethoven, Piano Concerto No. 4, 34:00
New Philharmonia Orchestra; Daniel Barenboim, piano; LWT, 1969

Czech Philharmonic Orchestra Archive, 43:00
Kratky Film Archive: Erich Kleiber, Mravinsky, Munch, Shostakovich et al.,
    Munch, Ançerl, Talich, Abendroth, Scherchen, Mravinsky, Munch, Cluy-
    tens, E. Kleiber, Ançerl, Stokowski, von Karajan, Ançerl
    Author to CK: Do you know the names of the pieces EK and Scherchen are
doing? The name of the composer with EK?

SCHURICHT, Carl (1880–1967)
Stravinsky, Firebird (1919), 20:00
Stuttgart Radio Symphony Orchestra; Liederhalle, Stuttgart, c. 1957

CANINUS, E. D. (1920–1967)
von Weber, Overture to Der Freischütz, 9:40
Stuttgart Symphony Orchestra, 1970[3]

Tape No. 17, 20 October 1993

SZELL, George (1897–1970)
Beethoven, Piano Concerto No. 5, 40:00
Vienna Philharmonic, 1966
with Friedrich Gulda, piano

Die Deutsche Mitte Kroll, 57:00
A history of the Kroll Oper, featuring Klemperer and his circle
Jorg-Moser Metius, director

ANSERMET, Ernest (1883–1969)
Ravel, La Valse, rehearsal and concert, 15:00
Hamburg Philharmonic Orchestra, ZDF, 1963

Tape No. 18, 2 November 1993

KUBELIK, Rafael (b. 1914)
Rafael Kubelik and his Fatherland, 52:00
1991 German television program
Smetana, Ma Vlast, rehearsal and performance, excerpts
Czech Philharmonic

FRUHBECK de Burgos, Rafael (b. 1933), 33:00
Schumann, Symphony No. 3
North German Radio Orchestra, 1985

STOKOWSKI, Leopold (1882–1977)
Tchaikovsky, Romeo and Juliet Overture and Fantasy, 20:00
Radio Orchestra della Swizera Italiana

Tape No. 19, 12 January 1994

LEINSDORF, Erich (1912–1993)
Schubert, Symphony No. 8, 21:00
SWF RSO, Baden-Baden

KNAPPERTSBUSCH, Hans (1888–1965)
Wagner, Tristan, Vorspiel, and Liebestodt, 30:00
Vienna Philharmonic, 31 May 1962, ORF; Birgit Nilsson
(includes 12:00 interview with Nilsson, 1992)

ANSERMET, Ernest (1883–1969)
Ravel, La Valse, rehearsal and concert, 15:00
Hamburg Philharmonic Orchestra, ZDF, 1963

Tape No. 20, 19 January 1994

KLEMPERER, Otto (1885–1973)
Beethoven, Symphony No. 9, 90:00

New Philharmonia Orchestra, Royal Albert Hall, 1964
Agnes Giebel, Marga Hoffgen, Ernst Haefliger, Gustav Neidlinger
27 October 1964; BBC broadcast 8 November 1964; Anthony Craxton, director

Omnibus—100th Anniversary of Otto Klemperer, 52:00
BBC, 1985; Keith Cheetham, producer

Tape No. 21, 1 February 1994

*Everything You Always Wanted to Know about Conductors—But Were Afraid
to Ask*, 60:00
BBC Omnibus documentary, broadcast 23 November 1993
Critics, commentators, and Esa-Pekka Salonen, Gilbert Kaplan, Franz
Welser-Most, Janssons, Tennstedt, Abbado, Klemperer, Masur, Bernstein,
Toscanini, von Karajan, Rostropovich, Maazel, Slatkin, C. Kleiber

Tapes No. 22 and 23, 8 March 1994

A History of German Radio Orchestras, Parts One and Two
A Film by Klaus Lindemann and Klaus Geitel

Tape No. 24, 18 April 1994

SZELL, George (1897–1970)
Brahms Symphony No. 3, rehearsal, 10:00
Cleveland Orchestra, Severance Hall, 1957
WEWS-TV, Cleveland

Hearst-Metrotone Archives, 1934–1966, 60:00
Stravinsky, Lange, Stokowski, Kodaly, Haitink, van Beinum, Munch, LA
Phil 1936, unknown Russian, unknown Czech, unknown Pole, unknown
Rotterdam, Ormandy, Kondrashin

MUNCH, Charles (1891–1968)
Beethoven Symphony No. 4, 30:00
Boston Symphony Orchestra, 18 April 1961

Tape No. 25, 15 May 1994

MONTEUX, Pierre (1875–1964)
Beethoven, Symphony No. 8, 26:30
Chicago Symphony Orchestra, 1960; WGN-TV

Wagner, Prelude to Act III, Meistersinger, 6:00
Chicago Symphony Orchestra, 1960; WGN-TV

Berlioz, Roman Carnival Overture, 9:00
Chicago Symphony Orchestra, 1960; WGN-TV

Tape No. 26, 3 June 1994

KARAJAN, Herbert von (1908–1989)
Schumann, Symphony No. 4, rehearsal, 60:00
Vienna Symphony, 1965

Schumann, Symphony No. 4, performance, 25:30
Vienna Symphony, 1965

Tape No. 27, 14 June 1994

ROZHDESTVENSKY, Gennady (b. 1931)
David Oistrakh Cycle [Acts II and III], 90:00

Beethoven, Romance in G, 7:00
David Oistrakh, violin
Moscow Radio Symphony Orchestra, February 1966

Locatelli, Caprice, 4:00
David Oistrakh, violin
Moscow Philharmonic, 1968

Sibelius, Violin Concerto, 30:00
David Oistrakh, violin
Moscow Radio Symphony Orchestra, February 1966

Tchaikovsky, Violin Concerto, 36:00
David Oistrakh, violin
Moscow Philharmonic, 1968

Tape No. 28, 14 June 1994

History of the Gewandhaus Orchestra, 60:00
German TV documentary
Masur, et al.; rehearsals, interviews

HINDEMITH, Paul (1895–1963)
Hindemith, Symphony in E Flat, 2:00
Berlin Philharmonic, rehearsal, Titania Palast, 18 February 1949

Evgeny Mravinsky and the Leningrad Philharmonic, 59:00
Television documentary; Russian film; ZDF, 1988

Beethoven Symphony No. 4, 1st movement, rehearsal, 10:00
Leningrad Philharmonic; in Russian, with German voice-over

Brahms, Symphony No. 2, 4th movement, rehearsal, 8:00
Leningrad Philharmonic; in Russian, with German voice-over

Brahms, Symphony No. 4, 4th movement, rehearsal and concert, 10:00
Leningrad Philharmonic; in Russian, with German voice-over

Shostakovich, Symphony No. 5, 1st and 4th movements, rehearsal, 9:00
Leningrad Philharmonic; in Russian, with German voice-over

Tchaikovsky, Symphony No. 5, 1st movement, rehearsal, 10:00
Leningrad Philharmonic; in Russian, with German voice-over; ends abruptly,
  incomplete

Tape No. 29, 23 June 1994

Knappertsbusch 100th Anniversary, 45:00
ORF documentary, 1988

Beethoven, Symphony No. 9, finale, 3:10
Berlin Philharmonic, 1942

Wagner, Siegfried Idyll, 8:00
Vienna Philharmonic, 1963

LEINSDORF, Erich (1912–1993)
Schoenberg, Chamber Symphony, Op. 9, 36:30
SWF RSO, rehearsal and performance

SCHERCHEN, Hermann (1891–1966)
Beethoven, Wellington's Victory, rehearsal, 8:20
Stuttgart Symphony Orchestra [RSO Stuttgart, 1962]

Tape No. 30, 23 June 1994

MASUR, Kurt (b. 1927)
Beethoven, Overture to Leonore No. 3, 15:00
New York Philharmonic; 17 May 1994, PBS

Beethoven, Piano Concerto No. 1, 36:00
New York Philharmonic; 17 May 1994, PBS
Emanuel Ax, piano

Beethoven, Symphony No. 5, 38:00
New York Philharmonic; 17 May 1994, PBS

Tape No. 31, 12 July 1994

SZELL, George (1897–1970)
Mussorgsky, Overture to Khovantchina, 5:00
Chicago Symphony Orchestra, 1961; WGN-TV

Beethoven, Symphony No. 5, 32:00
Chicago Symphony Orchestra, 1961; WGN-TV

Berlioz, Roman Carnival Overture, 8:30
Chicago Symphony Orchestra, 1961; WGN-TV

Tape No. 32, 15 August 1994

BEECHAM, Thomas (1879–1961)
Haydn, Symphony No. 102, 23:00
Chicago Symphony Orchestra, 1960; WGN-TV, color

Mozart, Symphony No. 38, 25:00
Chicago Symphony Orchestra, 1960; WGN-TV, color

Mendelssohn, Fingal's Cave, 10:00
Chicago Symphony Orchestra, 1960; WGN-TV, color

Delius, Florida Suite: On The River, 4:30
Chicago Symphony Orchestra, 1960; WGN-TV, color

Saint-Saens, Omphale - Spinning Wheel, 9:30
Chicago Symphony Orchestra, 1960; WGN-TV, color

Handel-Beecham, Love in Bath Suite, 22:00
Chicago Symphony Orchestra, 1960; WGN-TV, color

Tape No. 33, 26 August 1994

Pianists

Van Cliburn
Schumann/Liszt, *Widmung*, 3:15

Alfred Cortot
Debussy, *Children's Corner*, 5:00
"Serenade for the Doll"; "Golliwog's Cake-Walk"

Dame Myra Hess
Beethoven, *Appassionata*, 1st movement, 9:00

Conductors
HEGER, Robert (1886–1978)
Wagner, Overture to Flying Dutchman, 10:15
Paris Symphony Orchestra, c. 1935

GAUBERT, Philippe (1879–1941)
Berlioz, Roman Carnival Overture, 9:00
Paris Symphony (Conservatory) Orchestra, c. 1935

ELMENDORFF, Karl (1891–1962)
Wagner, Prologue and Postlude, Gotterdammerung, 5:20
Frida Leider, Max Lorenz
Bayreuth Festival Orchestra, 1934

SCHERCHEN, Hermann (1891–1966)
Bach, Art of the Fugue (arr. Scherchen) rehearsal, 30:00
CBC Toronto Chamber Orchestra, December 1965

GRAINGER, Percy (1882–1961)
silent conducting sequence
Traditional, "Maguire's Kick"

Tape No. 34, 5 September 1994

MRAVINSKY, Evgeny (1906–1988)
Schubert, Symphony No. 8, 29:00
Leningrad Philharmonic, 20 November 1983, Minsk
"Maguire's Kick"

Shostakovich, Symphony No. 5, 44:00
Leningrad Philharmonic, 20 November 1983, Minsk

Tape No. 35, 31 October 1994

MENGELBERG, Willem (1871–1951)
Willem Mengelberg, 21:00
MusicArchive documentary, Christian LaBrande, 1993

Berlioz, Hungarian March from Damnation of Faust
Concertgebouw Orchestra, 1931

Bizet, Adagietto from L'Arlesienne
Concertgebouw Orchestra, 1931

Weber, Overture to Oberon
Concertgebouw Orchestra, 1931

WALTER, Bruno (1876–1962)
Bruno Walter—The Face of Music, 60:00
BBC Omnibus, 13 February 1972; Robert Vas, producer
Brahms 2, Beethoven Leonore 3, Wagner Meistersinger, Mahler 3, Mozart 40
with McClure, Lehmann, Bohm, Solti, Bernstein, et al.

Tape No. 36, 13 November 1994

WALTER, Bruno (1876–1962)
Brahms, Symphony No. 2, rehearsal, 59:00
Vancouver Festival Orchestra, 1958; CBC-TV Vancouver
complete, with interview

Tape No. 37, 7 December 1994

REINER, Fritz (1888–1963)
Beethoven, Symphony No. 7, 37:00
Chicago Symphony Orchestra, 8 April 1962

Berlioz, Overture to Le Corsair, 8:00
Chicago Symphony Orchestra, 8 April 1962

Tape No. 38, 9 December 1994

The Art of Conducting/Great Conductors of the Past, 1:58:00
IMG/BBC Television documentary, January 1994
Bernstein, Beecham, Barbirolli, Nikisch, Weingartner, Busch
Strauss, Walter, Klemperer, Furtwängler, Toscanini
Stokowski, Koussevitsky, Reiner, Szell, von Karajan, Bernstein, Klemperer

Tape No. 39, Parts I & II, 2 January 1995, 11 March 1995[4]

BERNSTEIN, Leonard (1918–1990)
Workshop—Bernstein in Rehearsal, 1:05:00
Shostakovich, Symphony No. 5, 3rd and 4th movements
London Symphony Orchestra, 1966

STOKOWSKI, Leopold (1882–1977)
Stokowski in Budapest, 30:00
Hungarian television documentary, 1967

Bach-Stokowski, Toccata and Fugue in D Minor
Stravinsky, Petroushka, rehearsal and performance
Beethoven, Symphony No. 7, rehearsal and performance
WARNING! WARNING! WARNING! 15:00
  Author to CK: The coda of this Kleiberkino consists of me on bad video. I include it so that you may say you've seen me "work," but only on condition that this horror show will not jeopardize our friendship. If you hate the coarse amateurism that follows, you must please erase it from cassette and memory, ok? I include trash from my efforts in music education; at Stanford before meeting you; at a pops concert rehearsal; from "Fledermaus" where, heroically miscast as Conductor, I made love to Rosalinde from the pit of doom; and, me in Tokyo.

Tape No. 40, 28 March 1995

An Affectionate Portrait of Sir Thomas Beecham, 65:00
BBC Omnibus, producer, Herbert Chappell; 26 March 1968
Faust, Goldmark, anecdotes by and about Sir T

Stokowski—60 Minutes interview, 18:00
Dan Rather, CBS 1976 (includes recording session of Sibelius No. 1)

Tape No. 41, 22 May 1995

MITROPOULOS, Dmitri (1896–1960)
DeFalla, Homenajes, rehearsal and concert (excerpts, i and iii), 30:00
New York Philharmonic
includes interview with Edward R. Murrow
See It Now, CBS, 2 March 1954

MUTI, Riccardo (b. 1941)
Muti—*60 Minutes* interview, 17:00
(from Australian *60 Minutes* original)
CBS, 21 May 1995
   Author to CK: This was broadcast last night, and I thought you'd like to
see it. Not at all sure I agree with him about agéd conductors—witness Das
Klemp below, a film I've been meaning to send to you for some time anyway.
Burn-out is burn-out at any age, n'est ce pas?

KLEMPERER, Otto (1885–1973)
Beethoven, Symphony No. 6, 48:00
New Philharmonia Orchestra, Festival Hall, London
9 June 1970; BBC, color, stereo

Tape No. 42, 1 June 1995

KLEIBER, Carlos (b. 1930)
Beethoven, Overture to Coriolanus, 8:00
Vienna Philharmonic, Teatro Juárez, Guanajuato, GTO, México, 1981

Strauss, Johann; Overture to Fledermaus, 6:30
Vienna Philharmonic, Teatro Juárez, Guanajuato, GTO, México, 1981

Strauss, Johann; Thunder and Lightning Polka, 3:00
Vienna Philharmonic, Teatro Juárez, Guanajuato, GTO, México, 1981

Beethoven, Symphony No. 5, 28:00
Vienna Philharmonic, Teatro Juárez, Guanajuato, GTO, México, 1981 [in-
   complete]

CURIOUS SURPRISE
Wagner, Prelude to Walküre, 1:20
Grant Park Symphony Orchestra, 1941; Grant Park, Chicago
with James Caesar Petrillo introducing; Paramount Newsreel, Volume 1, No. 8[5]

Tape No. 43, 20 July 1995

LUCON, Arturo
Verdi, Rigoletto, Prelude, 2:00
Berlin Philharmonic, 1931
Caro Nome; Gualtier Maldè, soprano, 6:30
Miei Signori; Carlo Galeffi, baritone, 1:40
La donna è Mobile; Primo Montanari, tenor, 2:30
Undì, se ben rammentomi; Lina Pagliughi, Carleffi, 6:30
Primo Montanari, Maria Castagna-Fullin

One Hundred Years of the Bayreuth Festival, 1:40:00
from 100 Jahre Bayreuther Festspiele, 1976; Werkstatt Bayreuth 1965
with Ernst Bloch, Böhm, Boulez, Cluytens, Willy Haas, Kempe, Knappertsbusch, Maazel, Pitz, Sawallisch, Horst Stein, Suitner, Tietjen, Wieland
Wagner, Wolfgang Wagner

Tape No. 42-B,[6] November 1995

KLEIBER, Carlos (b. 1930)
Beethoven, Overture to Coriolanus, 8:00
Vienna Philharmonic, Teatro Juárez, Guanajuato, GTO, México, 1981

Strauss, Johann, Overture to Fledermaus, 6:30
Vienna Philharmonic, Teatro Juárez, Guanajuato, GTO, México, 1981

Strauss, Johann; Thunder and Lightning Polka, 3:00
Vienna Philharmonic, Teatro Juárez, Guanajuato, GTO, México, 1981

Beethoven, Symphony No. 5, 28:00
Vienna Philharmonic, Teatro Juárez, Guanajuato, GTO, México, 1981

Tape No. 44, 9 November 1995

KLEMPERER, Otto (1885–1973)
Beethoven, Symphony No. 3, 57:00
New Philharmonia Orchestra, Festival Hall, London
26 May 1970; BBC, color, stereo

Twenty-One Great Conductors, 60:00
Nikisch, Mascagni, Strauss, Toscanini, Blech, Walter, Stravinsky, Furtwän-
gler, Papst, Knappertsbusch, Munch, Schmidt-Gentner, Lucon, Böhm,
Krips, Karajan, Solti, Kempe, Kubelik, Sawallisch, Maazel, Cluytens

Tape No. 45, 26 April 1996

GOODALL, Reginald (1901–1990)
The Quest for Reginald Goodall, 65:00
BBC Omnibus 1985 documentary, Humphrey Burton, director
Wagner, *Die Walküre*, excerpts

Tape No. 46, 1 August 1996

KLEMPERER, Otto (1885–1973)
Beethoven, Symphony No. 1, 27:00
New Philharmonia Orchestra, Festival Hall, London
26 May 1970; BBC, color, stereo

Beethoven, Symphony No. 2, 36:00
New Philharmonia Orchestra, Festival Hall, London
9 June 1970; BBC, color, stereo

Tape No. 47, 1 October 1996

The Art of Singing/Golden Voices of the Past, 2:00:00
IMG/BBC television documentary, TCR version September 1996
Volume 1 [Singers on Film]: Gigli, 1927; Mary Garden, 1917; Geraldine
Farrar, 1915; Caruso, 1905, 1919; Caruso, Daddi, Journet, Scotti, Sembrich, Severina, c. 1924; Martinelli, 1930, 1931; Gigli, 1933; Schippa, 1929; DeLuca, 1927; Tetrazzini, 1929; Conchita Supervia, 1934; Rosa Ponselle, 1936; Tauber, 1933; Chaliapin, 1915, 1933; Lily Pons, 1936; Flagstadt, 1938; Tibbett, 1935; Rïse Stevens, 1941; Melchior, 1958; Ezio Pinza, 1953
Volume 2 [Singers on Television]: Victoria de Los Angeles, 1962; Sutherland, 1963; Björling and Tebaldi, 1956; Leontyne Price, 1962; Boris Christoff, 1956; Magda Olivero and Almino Misciano, 1960; Fritz Wunderlich, 1961; Jon Vickers, 1974; Franco Corelli, 1963; Guiseppe di Stefano, 1958; Callas, Lisbon Traviata, 1958; Callas and Gobbi, Tosca, 1964[7]

Tape No. 48, 3 February 1997

HORENSTEIN, Jascha (1898–1973)
Espansiva—Portrait of Carl Nielsen, 55:00

Nielsen, Symphony No. 3
New Philharmonia Orchestra
BBC Music on Two, 18 January 1970

Fregoli, Leopoldi
Impersonations of Rossini, Wagner, Verdi, Mascagni, from 1897, 1:30

Merkel, Willi
Impersonations of Wagner, Johann Strauss Jr., Sousa, from 1913, 3:00

MENGELBERG, Willem (1871–1951)
Tchaikovsky, Symphony No. 5, finale, 1:00
Budapest Symphony Orchestra, c. 1939

and for the sake of comparison . . .
MRAVINSKY, Evgeny (1906–1988)
Tchaikovsky, Symphony No. 5, 40:00
Leningrad Philharmonic, 1982; from Russian television

Tape No. 49, 27 May 1997

ASAHINA, Takashi (b. 1908)
Bruckner, Symphony No. 5, 90:00
Chicago Symphony Orchestra, 14 May 1996; from NHK-TV

BARBER, Charelves (b. 207 AD)
Author to CK: Rubbish that you insisted I send over, even though we both
    know better, or should . . .
Mozart, Magic Flute, Act I, Livermore Opera 1996 production
(reasonably good regional California company)

Beethoven, Symphony No. 7, 2nd movement, Stanford Symphony, my 1989
grad recital
Author to CK: (done before benefit of your advice)

Music in Schools concert, a one-rehearsal wonder with the Stockton Symphony, 1992
(unedited, from that morning's run-through)

Author to CK: The best orchestras I've ever led, studio outfits in LA when working with Marty, don't allow video, of course, so this is the only tolerable stuff I could put together.

† Mea maxima culpa †

Tape No. 50, 25 June 2001

Karajan, Herbert von (1908–1989)
Berlin Philharmonic on Tour, 60:00
Tokyo, 3 November 1957

Wagner, Prelude to Meistersinger
Strauss, Don Juan
Beethoven, Symphony No. 5

Tape No. 51, 3 December 2002

Monteux, Pierre (1875–1964)
Stravinsky, Petrouchka (1911 version), 33:00
Boston Symphony Orchestra
Sanders Theatre, Harvard, 20 January 1959; WGBH-TV
Bernard Zighera, piano

NOTES

1. It was actually me leading the Stanford Symphony Orchestra. He laughed at the "Zoot-Shoot," but I don't think he realized it was me being shot. That may have been to the good.

2. This was, of course, a play on John Cage's work and consisted of 44:33 of snowy silence.

3. This was Kleiber himself. You'll get the Dickinson reference.

4. I screwed up the numbers. The tape of myself conducting should have been separated from the legitimate.

5. Petrillo was the longtime Caesar of the American Federation of Musicians, famous for the "Petrillo Hook." The conductor was actually Lorin Maazel, age eleven.

6. Another numbering mishap.

7. I contributed material to this documentary and owned an early TCR version.

Appendix D

Kleiber Worklists,
Prepared by Toru Hirosawa

REPERTOIRE GIVEN IN PERFORMANCE

Bach, CPE	Cello Concerto in B-Flat Major
Beethoven	Coriolanus, Overture to
	Piano Concerto No. 5
	Symphony No. 4
	Symphony No. 5
	Symphony No. 6
	Symphony No. 7
Berg	Three Fragments from Wozzeck
	Wozzeck
Bizet	Carmen
Brahms	Symphony No. 2
	Symphony No. 4
Butterworth	English Idyll No. 1
Delibes	Coppelia
Dvorák	Carnival, Overture to
Egk	Abraxis
	Revisor
Falla	Three-Cornered Hat
Haydn	Symphony No. 94
Henze	Undine
Humperdinck	Hansel and Gretel
Leoncavallo	Edipo Ré
Liszt	Piano Concerto No. 2
Lorting	Waffenschmied
Mahler	Das Lied von der Erde
Martinu	Concerto for Oboe

Millöcker   Bettelstudent
Mozart   Marriage of Figaro, Overture to
                     Symphony No. 33
                     Symphony No. 36
Nicolai   Merry Wives of Windsor, Overture to
Offenbach   Belle Helène
                     Mariage aux Lanternes
                     Tales of Hoffmann
                     Tulipatan
                     Zauberflöte
Puccini   Bohème
                     Butterfly
Ravel   Alborada del Gracioso
                     Bolero
                     Heure Espagnole
                     Tombeau de Couperin
Schubert   Symphony No. 3
                     Symphony No. 8
Schumann   Piano Concerto
                     Symphony No. 2
Smetana   Bartered Bride
Strauss, Johann I   Radetzky March
Strauss, Johann II   Acceleration
                     Artist's Life
                     Bauern Polka
                     Bei uns z'Haus
                     Blue Danube
                     Csardas
                     Eijen a Magyar!
                     Fledermaus
                     Fledermaus, Overture to
                     Fruehlingsstimmen
                     Gypsy Baron, Overture to
                     Im Krapfenwald!
                     New Pizzicato Polka
                     Persischer March
                     Pizzicato Polka
                     Stadt und Land
                     Thousand and One Nights
                     Tritsch Tratsch Polka
                     Unter Donner und Blitzen
                     Vergnungszug
                     Wiener Blut

Strauss, Josef	Die Libelle
	Dorfschwalben aus Oesterreich
	Feuenfest!
	Jockey-Polka
	Moulinet-Polka
	Plappermaeulchen
	Sphaerenklaege
Strauss, R.	Daphne
	Death and Transfiguration
	Elektra
	Heldenleben
	Rosenkavalier
Stravinsky	Oedipus Rex
Tchaikovsky	Sleeping Beauty
Telemann	Tafelmusik
Verdi	Don Carlos
	Falstaff
	Foscari
	Otello
	Rigoletto
	Traviata
Wagner	Tristan
Weber	Freischütz
	Freischütz, Overture to
Zeller	Vogelhändler

PERFORMANCES

When beginning to compile my own history of Carlos's performances in concert and opera, I was soon aware that obscurity was compounded by bad record keeping and by myths spreading like swine flu. Regardless of the number of books that make the claim, Carlos never conducted *Otello* at the San Francisco, nor anything else there either. These are treacherous waters and need the services of a dedicated navigator willing to spend thousands of hours pursuing and confirming tales of Kleiber performances.

Fortunately, there is such a person. His name is Toru Hirosawa. Thanks to his methodical and pioneering work, there is now an online record of every Kleiber performance. (For his most recent discoveries, see www.thrsw .com/cklist/.) Given that new information is even now being uncovered and old tales are being repudiated, the online solution is best and is most readily kept current.

Toru's extensive documentation includes the composers, the artists and ensembles, the houses and venues, and dates of everything currently known about Carlos's five decades on the podium. It will come as no surprise to anyone who has followed the matter that Kleiber's career opened and closed in obscurity, beginning with a concert given under a phony name in Potsdam and closing in Cagliari.

OPERA HOUSES

In his five-decade career, Carlos worked at sixteen opera companies:

Bavarian State Opera
Bayreuth Festspiele
Frankfurt Opera
Geneva Opera
German Opera on the Rhein (Duisburg)
German Opera on the Rhein (Düsseldorf)
Hamburg State Opera
La Scala
Metropolitan Opera
Potsdam Opera
Royal Opera House (London)
Salzburg Opera
Teatro Comunale Florence
Vienna State Opera
Württemberg State Opera
Zurich Opera

SYMPHONY ORCHESTRAS

In the same period, he conducted at eighteen symphony orchestras:

Accademia Nazionale di Santa Cecilia Orchestra
Amsterdam Concertgebouw Orchestra
Bavarian Radio Symphony Orchestra
Bavarian State Orchestra
Berlin Philharmonic Orchestra
Bern Symphony Orchestra
Chicago Symphony Orchestra

Cologne Radio Symphony Orchestra
Hamburg Philharmonic Orchestra
London Symphony Orchestra
Munich Philharmonic Orchestra
NDR Symphony Orchestra
Prague Symphony Orchestra
RTV Slovenia Symphony Orchestra
Slovenian Philharmonic Orchestra
Vienna Philharmonic Orchestra
Vienna Symphony Orchestra
Zurich Tonhalle Orchestra

Bibliography

BOOKS

Adler, Kurt Herbert, and Timothy Pfaff. *The Life and Career of Kurt Herbert Adler*, Volume 1. Berkeley: Regional Oral History Office, Regents of the University of California, 1994.

American Kennel Club. *The Complete Dog Book*, 18th Edition. New York: Howell Press, 1992.

Ardoin, John. *Valery Gergiev and The Kirov, A Story of Survival*. Portland, Oregon: Amadeus Press, 2000.

Balestrazzi, Mauro. *Carlos Kleiber—Angelo o demone?* Palermo: L'epos, 2006.

Barber, Charles. *Lost in the Stars: The Forgotten Musical Life of Alexander Siloti*. Lanham, Maryland: Rowman and Littlefield, The Scarecrow Press, 2003.

Barber, Charles, and José Bowen. *International Dictionary of Conductors*. Berkeley: University of California Press, forthcoming.

Boult, Adrian. *Handbook on the Technique of Conducting*. Oxford and London: Hall, H. Reeves, 1921, 1949; London: Paterson's, 1968.

Bowen, José, ed. *The Cambridge Companion to Conducting*. Cambridge: Cambridge University Press, 2003.

Breslin, Herbert, and Anne Midgette. *The King and I: The Uncensored Tale of Luciano Pavarotti's Rise to Fame by His Manager, Friend and Sometime Adversary*. New York: Doubleday, 2003.

Carpentier, Alejo. *Ese Musico Quellevodentro*. Havana: Alianza Editorial, 1987.

Chang Tzu. *Basic Writings*. Translated by Fung Yu-lan. Shanghai: Commercial Press, 1931; New York: Columbia University Press, 1964.

Conrad, Peter. *A Song of Love and Death: The Meaning of Opera*. London: Chatto & Windus, 1987.

Culshaw, John. *Putting the Record Straight: The Autobiography of John Culshaw*. New York: Viking Press, 1982.

Dickinson, Emily. *Final Harvest*. Edited by Thomas Johnson. New York: Little, Brown, 1962.

Dobrin, Duilio Abelardo. "Erich Kleiber: The Argentine Experience (1926–1949)." Dissertation, Music, Ball State University, Muncie, Indiana, 1981.

Domingo, Plácido. *My First Forty Years*. New York: Knopf, 1983.

Dorati, Antal. *Notes of Seven Decades*. London: Hoddard and Stoughton, 1979.

Drexel, Christina. *Carlos Kleiber . . . einfach was dasteht!* Köln: Verlag Dohr, 2010.

D'Urbano, Jorge. *Música en Buenos Aires*. Buenos Aires: Editorial Sudamericana, 1966.

Endler, Franz. *My Autobiography: Herbert von Karajan*. London: Sidgwick and Jackson, 1989.

———. *Karajan: Eine Biographie*. Hamburg: Hoffman und Campe, 1992.

Fawkes, Richard. *Opera on Film*. London: Duckworth, 2000.

Felsenstein, Walter. *Die Pflicht, die Wahrheit zu finden: Briefe und Schriften eines Theatermannes*. Frankfurt am Main: Suhrkamp, 1997.

Fiedler, Joanna. *Molto Agitato: The Mayhem behind the Music*. New York: Anchor Books, 2001.

Fischer, Jens Malte. *Carlos Kleiber—Der skrupulöse Exzentriker*. Göttingen: Wallstein Verlag, 2006.

Fleming, Renée. *The Inner Voice: The Making of a Singer*. New York: Viking, 2004.

Garben, Cord. *Arturo Benedetti Michelangeli. Gratwanderungen mit Einem Genie*. Hamburg: Europäische Verlagsanstalt, 2002.

Gilbert, Susie. *A Tale of Four Houses: Opera at Covent Garden, La Scala, Vienna and the Met Since 1945*. London: HarperCollins, 2003.

Habegger, Alfred. *My Wars Are Laid Away in Books: The Life of Emily Dickinson*. New York: Random House, 2001.

Haltrecht, Montague. *The Quiet Showman: Sir David Webster and the Royal Opera House*. London: Collins, 1975.

Heyworth, Peter. *Otto Klemperer, His Life and Times*. Volume 2. Cambridge: Cambridge University Press, 1996.

Hoyer, Harald. *Chronik der Wiener Staatsoper 1945 bis 1995*. Vienna: Verlag A. Schroll, 1995.

Hunt, John. *The Furtwängler Sound. Discography with Concert Register*, 6th Edition. 1999.

Isaacs, Jeremy. *Never Mind the Moon*. London: Bantam Press, 1999.

Kinashita, Akira. *Carlos Kleiber*. Tokyo: Alphabeta, 2004 [Japanese].

Kleiber, Marko. *"Kunst und Mythos" bei Georg Picht: Ihre Bedeutung für die Frage des Menschen nach Wahrheit und Wirklichkeit*. Hamburg: Verlag Dr. Kovač, 1996.

Lang, Klaus. *The Karajan Dossier*. London: Faber and Faber, 1992.

Lebrecht, Norman. *The Maestro Myth*. New York: Birch Lane, 1991.

Lewinski, Wolf-Eberhard von. *Brigitte Fassbaender: Interviews, Tatsachen, Meinungen*. Mainz: Atlantis, 1999.

Lucas, John. *Reggie: The Life of Reginald Goodall*. London: Julia MacRae Books, 1993.

Mansouri, Lotfi, and Donald Arthur. *Lotfi Mansouri: An Operatic Journey.* Boston: Northeastern University Press, 2010.

Mansouri, Lotfi, and Aviva Layton. *An Operatic Life.* Toronto: Stoddart, 1982.

Marsh, Robert C. *Dialogues and Discoveries. James Levine: His Life and His Music.* New York: Scribner's, 1987.

Matheopoulos, Helena. *Maestro—Encounters with Conductors of Today.* London: Hutchinson, 1982.

———. *Bravo: Today's Great Tenors, Baritones and Basses Discuss Their Roles.* London: Weidenfeld and Nicolson, 1986.

———. *Diva: The New Generation.* Boston: Northeastern University Press, 1998.

Muck, Peter. *Einhundert Jahre Berliner Philharmonisches Orchester: Darstellung in Dokumenten.* Tutzing: H. Schneider, 1982.

Nilsson, Birgit. *My Memoirs in Pictures.* Translated by Thomas Teal. Garden City, New York: Doubleday, 1981.

Osborne, Richard. *Conversations with von Karajan.* London: Oxford University Press, 1989.

———. *Herbert von Karajan: A Life in Music.* London: Chatto and Windus, 1998.

Paglia, Camille. *Sexual Personae: Art and Decadence from Nefertiti to Emily Dickinson.* New York: Vintage Books, 1991.

Paris, Alain. *Lexikon der Interpreten klassicher Musik im 20.* Jahrhundert. München: Bärenreiter–Verlag Karl Vötterle, 1992.

Pavarotti, Luciano, and William Wright. *Pavarotti: My World.* New York: Crown, 1995.

Paz, Juan Carlos. *Alturas, Tensiones, Ataques, Intensidades.* Buenos Aires: Editions dc la Flor, 1994.

Richter, Sviatoslav, and Bruno Monsaingeon. *Notebooks and Conversations.* Princeton: Princeton University Press, 2001.

Russell, John. *Erich Kleiber—A Memoir.* London: André Deutsch, 1957.

Sachs, Harvey. *Toscanini.* New York: Lippincott, 1978.

Schäfer, Walter Erich. *Bühne eines Lebens. Erinnerungen.* Stuttgart: Deutsche Verlags-Anstalt, 1975.

Schonberg, Harold C. *Horowitz—His Life and Music.* New York: Simon and Schuster, 1992.

Schuller, Gunther. *The Compleat Conductor.* Oxford: University of Oxford Press, 1997.

Seebohm, Andrea. *The Vienna Opera.* New York: Rizzoli, 1987.

Slonimsky, Nicolas. *Baker's Biographical Dictionary of Musicians*, 8th Edition / Concise. New York: Schirmer Books, 1994.

Spotts, Frederic. *Bayreuth: A History of the Wagner Festival.* London: Yale University Press, 1994.

Stern, Isaac, and Chaim Potok. *My First 79 Years.* New York: Random House, 1999.

Student, Clever Grad. *The Sayings of Carlos Kleiber.* New York: The School of the French Stipulationists University Press, 2012.

Tooley, John. *In House: The Story of Covent Garden.* London: Faber and Faber, 1999.

Umbach, Klaus. *Celibidache, Der Andere Maestro*. Munich: Piper, 1995.
Vichev, Tomislav. *Kleiber's Era*. http://www.freewebs.com/kleiber_en/index.
Wagner, Wolfgang. *Acts: The Autobiography of Wolfgang Wagner*. Translated by John Brownjohn. London: Weidenfeld and Nicolson, 1994.
Wallmann, Margarita. *Balcones del Cielo*. Buenos Aires: Emece, 1978.
Weiler, Klaus. *Celibidache: Musiker und Philosoph*. Munich: Schneekluth, 1993.
Werner, Alexander. *Carlos Kleiber: eine Biografie*. Mainz: Schott, 2008.
Zeffirelli, Franco. *Zeffirelli: The Autobiography of Franco Zeffirelli*. New York: Weidenfeld and Nicolson, 1986.
Zignani, Alessandro. *Carlos Kleiber: il tramonto dell'Occidente*. Varese: Zecchini, 2010.

JOURNAL, MAGAZINE, ONLINE, AND MEDIA SOURCES

BBC 3. *Who Was Carlos Kleiber?* Paul Frankl, producer. Radio documentary, transmitted 26 September 2009, and 7 August 2010.
Current Biography Yearbook 1991, 338–41.
Evidon, Richard. www.deutschegrammophon.com/special/insights.htms, accessed 26 September 2004.
Flowers, William. "Carlos Kleiber—A Legend at 50." *Le Grand Baton* (March 1982).
Hirasawa, Toru. Carlos Kleiber Pages. www.thrsw.com/kleiber.html, accessed 12 August 2010.
Jonas, Sir Peter. "Notes to the Memorial, Carlos Kleiber Matinée." *Bavarian Staatsoper*, 12 December 2004.
Kenyon, Nicholas. "Carlos Kleiber: Genius Wrapped in an Enigma." *New York Times*, 15 October 1989.
Kerman, Joseph. "On Carlos Kleiber (1930–2004)." *New York Review of Books*, 23 September 2004.
Koch, Gerhard R. "Der Solitär." *FonoForum* (September 2004).
Kreger, James. "Making Music with Carlos Kleiber, Elusive Titan of the Podium." *Juilliard Journal Online* 20, no. 3 (November 2004).
Layton, Robert. "Carlos Kleiber: An Assessment of His Achievement on Record." Gramophone, July 1989.
Matheopoulos, Helena. "Carlos Kleiber." *Vanity Fair* (February 1988), 40, 44, 48.
McGinn, Robert. Carlos Kleiber Memorial Fan Site. www.carlos-kleiber.com, accessed 12 March 2010.
Mikorey, Stefan. "Konzessionsloses Espressivo-Musizieren." *FonoForum* (December 1982), 21–22.
———. "Live für eine gute Sache." *FonoForum* (September 1984).
NDR Kultur. Erich und Carlos Kleiber: Der Lange Schatten. Radio broadcast, 21 January 2005.
Pinzauti, Leonardo. "Carlos Kleiber. Il Pipistrello." Bacchetta d'Oro Series. Il Sole 24 Ore / La Scala. 28 December 2003.

RAI Radio 3. "The Smile of Music: A Portrait of Carlos Kleiber." Andrea Ottonello, producer. Radio documentary, broadcast 18, 20, 21, 22, 23, 25, 27, 28, 29 February, 1 March 2008.

Rhein, John von. "The Unpredictable Carlos Kleiber." *Ovation* (September 1983).

Riley, Norman. "Kleiber Too Ill to Conduct." *Daily Telegraph*, 5 September 1966.

Schulz, Eric. "Spuren ins Nichts. Der Dirigent Carlos Kleiber." Servus TV. Film documentary, broadcast 25 July 2010.

Schulz-Temmel, Götz. "In Memoriam Carlos Kleiber." Unitel. Film documentary, broadcast July 2005 and 7 August 2010.

Schwinger, Wolfram. "Butterfly statt Wozzeck. Der Unglaubliche Fall Carlos Kleiber an der Stuttgarten Staatsoper." *Stuttgarter Zeitung* (9 January 1967).

———. "Freie Bahn. Generalintendant WE Schäfer antwortet zum Fall Carlos Kleiber." *Stuttgarter Zeitung* (17 January 1967).

Tolansky, Jon. "Carlos Kleiber, Inspirer of Performers—A Personal Memoir." *Musical Life*, n.d., c. 1990.

Walsh, Michael. "Unvarnished Symphonies." *Time Magazine* (13 June 1983).

WAVE 31. "Analysis of Carlos Kleiber's Conducting Life and Career of the Maestro." *Atelier Peyotl*, 1992 [Japanese].

Wübbolt, Georg. "Carlos Kleiber. I Am Lost to the World." BFMI, C Major, ZDF/3 sat. film documentary. DVD release 2011.

Index

This general index accounts the principal people, places, themes, and ideas of Kleiber's career. It does not include all artists with whom he collaborated, nor performances he gave.

About the Author

Charles Barber began piano at age six and violin and trumpet at age ten. At age fourteen, he composed a piano concerto, and at age fifteen, he first conducted an orchestra. He holds master's and doctoral degrees in music from Stanford. Barber has conducted throughout California, on tour in Japan, Singapore, and South Korea, and on numerous film and recording projects in Los Angeles. In addition to working with symphony and opera, Barber has conducted for Stan Getz, Sarah Vaughn, and Mel Tormé. He created *American Classics* and *Canadian Classics* for Naxos, contributed numerous articles to *New Grove*, served as music advisor for the BBC's *Art of Conducting* film documentaries, and wrote *Lost in the Stars: The Forgotten Musical Life of Alexander Siloti.* He is presently artistic director at City Opera Vancouver.